Management and Leadership in Nursing and Health Care

Elaine La Monica Rigolosi, EdD, JD, FAAN, is the Program Coordinator of the Executive Program for Nurses and is a past Chair of the Department of Organization and Leadership at Teachers College, Columbia University. She holds a Juris Doctor degree from the Benjamin N. Cardozo School of Law, Yeshiva University, New York, New York; a Doctor of Education degree in human relations and counseling from the School of Education, University of Massachusetts, Amherst; a Master's degree in Medical and Surgical Nursing Administration from the College of Nursing, University of Florida, Gainesville; and a Bachelor of Science in nursing from Columbia Union College, Takoma Park, Maryland. She is a Fellow of the American Academy of Nursing.

In addition to her administrative and academic responsibilities at Teachers College, Columbia University, Dr. Rigolosi maintains a private consulting practice in management for health care organizations and other public and private industries throughout the United States and Canada. She has conducted training programs on organizational behavior and legal issues in health care both nationally and internationally. She is a member of the Board of Directors of Hooper Holmes, Inc., located in Basking Ridge, New Jersey, and listed on the American Stock Exchange. Dr. Rigolosi is a practicing attorney, admitted to the State of New York, State of New Jersey, and District of Columbia Bars.

The previously published academic book by Dr. Rigolosi is *Management and Leadership in Nursing and Health Care: An Experiential Approach* (2nd ed.), 2005, Springer Publishing Company, New York, New York. She also authored *Management in Health Care: A Theoretical and Experiential Approach*, 1994, Macmillan Press Limited, London, and *Management in Nursing: An Experiential Approach That Makes Theory Work for You*, 1990, Springer Publishing Company, New York, New York. This last book was translated into a Spanish edition in 1994. Dr. Rigolosi authored three books for Jones and Bartlett, Boston, Massachusetts: *Nursing Leadership and Management: An Experiential Approach*, 1986, *The Humanistic Nursing Process*, 1985; and *The Nursing Process: A Humanistic Approach*, 1979. In addition, Dr. Rigolosi published the *La Monica Empathy Profile*, 2009, and the *Empathy Construct Rating Scale*, 2009, both marketed by Human Resource Development Press, Amherst, Massachusetts. Two other instruments also have been published: the *La Monica Patient Satisfaction Scale*, 1986, and the *Pharmaceutical Care Questionnaire* (with Dick R. Gourley and Greta A. Gourley), 2001. Additional scholarly activities included serving as the Management Briefs' editor for *The Journal of Nursing Administration* and as a frequent author on management, empathy, research, and related topics.

Dr. Rigolosi also has recently published a self-help and self-improvement publication intended for a wide audience in the mass media. The emphasis is on empowerment and it is entitled *Unlock Your CAGE*, 2013.

Dr. Rigolosi maintains membership in the following professional organizations: American Bar Association, American Nurses Association, American Psychological Association, National Association of Corporate Directors, National League for Nursing, New York State Bar Association, New York State Nurses Association, Phi Alpha Delta Law Fraternity, and the American Association of Nurse Attorneys. She is an elected Associate-in-Law of the American College of Legal Medicine.

Management and Leadership in Nursing and Health Care

An Experiential Approach

THIRD EDITION

Elaine La Monica Rigolosi, EdD, JD, FAAN

SPRINGER PUBLISHING COMPANY

NEW YORK

Springer Publishing Company, LLC
11 West 42nd Street
New York, NY 10036
www.springerpub.com

Acquisitions Editor: Margaret Zuccarini
Production Editor: Joseph Stubenrauch
Composition: Absolute Service, Inc.

ISBN: 978-0-8261-0839-5
E-book ISBN: 978-0-8261-0840-1

12 13 14 15 / 5 4 3 2 1

The author and the publisher of this Work have made every effort to use sources believed to be reliable to provide information that is accurate and compatible with the standards generally accepted at the time of publication. Because medical science is continually advancing, our knowledge base continues to expand. Therefore, as new information becomes available, changes in procedures become necessary. We recommend that the reader always consult current research, specific institutional policies, and current drug references before performing any clinical procedure or administering any drug. The author and publisher shall not be liable for any special, consequential, or exemplary damages resulting, in whole or in part, from the readers' use of, or reliance on, the information contained in this book. The publisher has no responsibility for the persistence or accuracy of URLs for external or third-party Internet Web sites referred to in this publication and does not guarantee that any content on such Web sites is, or will remain, accurate or appropriate.

Library of Congress Cataloging-in-Publication Data

Rigolosi, Elaine La Monica, 1944–
  Management and leadership in nursing and health care : an experiential approach / Elaine La Monica Rigolosi. — 3rd ed.
    p. ; cm.
  Includes bibliographical references and indexes.
  ISBN 978-0-8261-0839-5 — ISBN 978-0-8261-0840-1 (e-ISBN)
  I. Title.
  [DNLM: 1. Nurse Administrators. 2. Administrative Personnel. 3. Leadership. 4. Nursing Care—organization & administration. WY 105]

  362.17'3068—dc23
                        2012020054

Special discounts on bulk quantities of our books are available to corporations, professional associations, pharmaceutical companies, health care organizations, and other qualifying groups.

If you are interested in a custom book, including chapters from more than one of our titles, we can provide that service as well.

For details, please contact:
Special Sales Department, Springer Publishing Company, LLC
11 West 42nd Street, 15th Floor, New York, NY 10036-8002s
Phone: 877-687-7476 or 212-431-4370; Fax: 212-941-7842
Email: sales@springerpub.com

Printed in the United States of America by Bang Printing.

My book is dedicated . . . today and always . . .

To my best friend
   My husband
      Robert S. Rigolosi. . . .

Always together
   Traveling life's journey
      Wherever
         Whenever
            In our own world . . .

And
   Loving our moments together. . . .

Elaine La Monica Rigolosi

Contents

Preface

The principle that never changes. . . . Nurses and health care professionals must become effective managers and leaders in order to fulfill their responsibilities—to themselves, to their clients, and to the professions. The goals of current health care delivery and health care reform mandate a nonpartisan and diverse approach to the education of nurses and all health care professionals and personnel. Professionals who practice in today's health care environments and shape tomorrow's reform must be collaborative interdisciplinarians, educated in an interdisciplinary environment and thinking within a diverse mind. These approaches are underscored by nursing and health care educational philosophies and practices—now and as projected into the future.

Trends in health care include (a) changing emphases imposed by federal and state cost-containment regulations, (b) changing and alternative methods for health care delivery, (c) increasing focus on health maintenance—primary care—in addition to the ever-present attention on secondary and tertiary care, and (d) greater quantities of data to support the mind/body relationship in health and disease, suggesting that not only is cure important, but altering behaviors is crucial so that the need to cure may become unnecessary or less frequent.

Wherever their placement in the health care arena, nurses and health care managers will be leaders of themselves; of colleagues and peers in interdisciplinary clinical teams of technicians and other health care providers; of colleagues in various management levels within formal health care organizations; of the public sector through media; of the individual clients in city, state, national, and international political entities, and so forth. In these positions, nurses and health care managers will be called upon for creative strategies, disciplines and cost-contained programs, and the abilities to research and analyze systems critically and chart growth—all on response to rapid and continuous health care changes. It is therefore mandatory that professionals perceive themselves in the roles of managers and leaders and increase their knowledge and application of theory and research in practice so that quality, comprehensive, and efficient care is provided to clients by the health care delivery team in any setting and throughout the world.

Leadership and management involve processes that are essential in making any health care role, in any environment, alive. Disciplines and professions such as organizational behavior, educational administration, and business administration and finance have developed theories that assist managers in increasing the probability of achieving specified goals. Managers and leaders must apply these theories into their specific roles and then extend applications into theory through research. Responsibility and authority granted by a state's Nurse Practice Act, an institution, an individual's unique experience and personality, and one's personal philosophy on the constituents of quality care and effective management, must be integrated with knowledge and an ability to apply existing theories of management into health care practice.

As a nurse's career develops, a nurse usually becomes the professional who embraces and interacts with every provider of health care services and every professional who works in direct and indirect health care services. These professionals include physicians, lawyers, nurses, social workers, physical therapists, occupational therapists, mental health professionals, psychologists, computer technologists, educational administrators, nurse practitioners, personnel managers, and so forth. Thus, the nurse must be a continually self-educating leader across professional domains, must understand organizational dynamics, and must be a leader and manager of organizational growth in the for-profit and nonprofit sectors.

This book covers the processes of management and leadership in health care practices. It evolves from my experience in teaching future managers of health care personnel. Content focuses on increasing organizational effectiveness in service and practice. Theories and concepts from the professions of business, organizational psychology, health care law, and educational administration are applied to topics in each chapter.

Sections of the book include simulations (e.g., case presentations and multimedia activities such as role plays, team assignments, and other creative learning activities) to provide experiences that illustrate the content of the chapters, as well as to expand the learner's range of experience. The simulations comprise the experiential approach; they provide learners with an opportunity to observe, experience, and carry out new behaviors in a safe, low-risk practice environment. Careful and detailed explanations are provided for each simulation. The textbook and exercises are designed for use both in self-learning and classroom environments, in both individual and group learning experiences. It is suggested that study be weighted between studying theory and working through simulations. More time should be devoted to the experiential elements, since enriched learning in management is derived more from actual and vicarious experiences rather than from reading and studying the printed word. The goal is "knowing" rather than simply "knowing about."

This book is written primarily for undergraduate students in nursing and health care management and leadership courses. It is also intended as a resource for graduate administration students, practitioners, learners in in-service and continuing education programs, and faculty. The intent is to present the basics of leadership and management for health care practice—what is essential in order to effectively motivate and educate people to achieve the set goals of a group, team, or organization. The web of managing and leading principles and applications expands thereafter . . . and as long as the awareness of learning stays in focus. . . .

Elaine La Monica Rigolosi

Acknowledgments

Even though the author first imagined and then created this book and what preceded it, the theory, exercises, and philosophy represented have been developed from many personal and professional resources. Some materials are original, and some are from established sources to whom credit is most gratefully given; others have evolved from an interchange with professionals and learners whose commitment has been to excellence.

I would like particularly to thank Professors Donald Carew, Kenneth Blanchard, and Paul Hersey, whose teachings and writings were the foundation of my doctoral education and remain the cornerstones of my current professional activities; Professor Frederic Finch for sharing his knowledge so freely; Professor Phil Graf for his reinforcement and assistance in my early years of public speaking—for believing that I had something to offer future managers; and my colleagues in education and practice for the constant interchange that has shaped my world as I know it . . . today.

Most importantly, I wish to express my love for my husband, Bob (also known as "HB"), for always understanding that when I get on the train to write, my mind is usually unavailable until I arrive at the station—wherever that stop may be planned, during any time of life's day.

Also, there are people I perceive everywhere who speak in a voice that I hear, who have said and done things that caused their energy to enlighten my brain, and who teach me wherever I journey. . . . I may or may not know your names—I simply wish to express my appreciation for sharing.

To all who have sculpted my beliefs, to all from whom I have received, I give my sincere gratitude.

Elaine La Monica Rigolosi

Introduction

Leadership and management theory has maintained its firm foundation moving from classical approaches to managing teams to situational and individual perspectives. Research that has been done supported the new approaches during the past several decades, while expanding the horizons in which the importance of managerial behavior has been evidenced in nonprofit and for-profit health care environments.

The web that flows out of the core of organizational behavior theory has increased, reflecting a global approach to practices as well as increasing diversity among the human resources. This has resulted in a need for leaders and managers who can work within and between cultures as well as employees. In nursing and in health care, this is extended to employees who must care for and educate a widespread array of people who come from different groups, both nationally and globally. These people in need of health care perceive different languages, both verbal and nonverbal, as well as open their hearing pathways through different channels of understanding.

Becoming more specific, management and leadership in health care involve an individual's efforts to influence the behavior of others in providing direct, individualized, professional care. The basic premise of management is that managers set goals that represent some level of growth for a particular group in a particular environment. Managers then develop strategies for reaching these goals. Results are evaluated and altered or new directions or adjustments are set. There is no value of good or bad in the actual state of the group, the group's goals, or the outcomes. Managers simply and constantly design strategies for moving groups of personnel to more efficient and higher qualitative levels of functioning—all to benefit the team and/or the organization. The most important point is the process of constantly developing strategies that result in identifiable, effective, and positive growth toward a previously set goal. In conducting these processes, managers plan, organize, motivate, and control the work of other allied health care personnel in the delivery of professional nursing care.

The processes of management and leadership are based on a scientific approach called the problem-solving method. The function of this scientific method is to increase the probability of success for a manager's actions, given the particulars of a unique environment. In a typical health care environment, there are staff members, clients, managers, situational variables such as policies and norms, and material resources; these are unique because it would be impossible to find this exact environment in another place and time. The goal of the manager is to identify the environment's resources and to put them to work as a whole system in accomplishing goals and facilitating growth—the intent is to unify the team and to direct energy toward goal accomplishment. Use of the scientific method in management simply assists the manager in assessing many needs of the system and in choosing the priorities, identifying the people and situational elements that are important in carrying out specified goals, critically assessing the strengths of those people, and developing strategies that put those strengths to work.

A manager can be functional and occasionally effective in a role without using the problem-solving method. This alternative, called "seat-of-the-pants" management, evolves from following only impulses and personal beliefs about self and others. Such management comes from involuntary behaviors that do not involve thinking about what a group specifically needs from the manager in order to accomplish its goals. It is possible for the seat-of-the-pants manager to be successful. That is, by some stroke of luck, the impulses, beliefs, and behaviors of this manager are exactly what the system requires. Though possible, however, such success is unlikely.

Use of the scientific approach does not determine outcomes exactly; there is no way to predict the behavior of others with complete accuracy. An effective manager analyzes an environment and chooses the best strategy for achieving a specified goal, given the particular strengths and weaknesses of the employees who will be working to carry out that goal. There is always some unknown that cannot be controlled—the risk factor. Because all managers desire success, their goal in choosing the best strategy should be to identify the strategy that balances the lowest risk factor with the highest rate of return. This automatically increases the probability for success. A manager who uses seat-of-the-pants thinking will have a higher risk factor in every undertaking than will the manager who applies a scientific approach. The scientific management method forces the nurse manager to plan, organize, motivate, and control logically and analytically. Further, it allows the manager to build contingency plans for all possible outcomes rather than to face problems unprepared. In a simple sense, use of the scientific management method increases a manager's batting average.

Why does use of the scientific method offer so much? It is derived from methodologically sound research within the disciplines and professions of business, educational administration, and psychology—the purists of management. Given the numerous investigations that allow the label *theory* to be attached to a process or belief, the results suggest that organizational theory, applied in a particular way, produces consistent and probable outcomes at least 95% of the time. A person who simply or randomly guesses in all decisions has a 50% chance of being right or wrong. Managers, however, should not be satisfied with such a 50/50 ratio—this is mediocrity. The use of intuition is appropriate and necessary only after the application of theory. Application of theory comes first and intuition is second. Intuition is the à la mode on the homemade apple pie, and both generally convey the "best dessert." In actuality, the previously stated process separates the sometimes acceptable manager from the superb manager. Remember, management requires a conscious, identifiable strategy that is built on theory, aimed toward an identifiable goal. This is all accomplished by working through people.

The book follows a human relations model, focusing on theory and experiential activities—knowing and obtaining knowledge, and then putting it all to work in a simulated setting. The intent is to know through experience rather than knowing through the printed words. There are ribbons that run throughout every part and chapter of this book. These ribbons include but are not limited to culture, diversity, and self-awareness. The goal of this book is to present the necessary beginnings of leadership and management theory and practice—what is absolutely necessary to make the scientific skeleton of management have life and what is absolutely essential to prepare a nurse or health care professional for a beginning role as a manager. Obviously, organization and leadership is vast and study can continue for a lifetime—both theoretically and experientially.

Five parts are presented in this book, each with pertinent chapters. Part I presents the process steps of health care management and leadership. This involves the science and philosophy of management and leadership. Part II is the core of how managers work. It involves knowing self, diagnosing others and the task, and applying the best leader behavior style given the beginning of a particular journey toward goal accomplishment. Revolving around the core of management and leadership, there are basic managerial skills that are perceived as the "how to" satellites. These make up Part III and include communication, power, assertiveness (also referred to as confident communication), conflict resolution, and time management. Part IV contains the "action" satellites—managerial roles such as change facilitator, teacher, team builder, interviewer, and performance appraiser. Part V reflects on the managerial mind, including philosophic essays on creativity, diversity, and ethics. The intent of Part V is to be both the end of this book . . . and the beginning . . . .

Again, the book is basic rather than expansive. The goal is to provide only enough theory to have a scientific foundation for actions. Chapters have their own conceptual and theoretical discussions with nursing and health care applications. Each chapter in Parts I through IV begins with a set of Expected Learning Outcomes. Also, at the conclusion of Parts I through IV, there are Experiential Learning Activities that put theory, concepts, and examples into action. These exercises are designed to set the book into motion for the learner. The simulations that are included in the Experiential Learning Activities present specific ways to learn the chapter's contents. These simulations are designed to provide experiences in applying theory in a low-risk setting. It is a known fact that as anxiety increases, perception decreases. When perception decreases, people most often do not think; they merely function intuitively. The higher the anxiety, the narrower is the intuitive field. These intuitive behaviors are derived from practices and experiences earlier in life—from behaviors that were previously learned and reinforced.

It is also known that in a real management environment, a person's anxiety is generally greater than it is in a classroom or a laboratory. This is due to tensions increasing when others are really looking to a person for guidance or are expecting something from that person. Because it takes time for learners to incorporate theory into practice, to think while doing instead of doing and then thinking, the use of simulations provides added experience so that the likelihood of a manager effectively applying theory increases while in any state of anxiety. This usually results in increasing the probability for more effective outcomes. The experiential model, the group dynamics laboratory, and the human relations model—all one in similarity—have been used widely in management training, and this author has adapted them into the health care simulations.

The Experiential Learning Activities at the conclusion of Part I of this book are ice-breaking, getting-acquainted activities. They are designed to help in the formation of effective groups and are most appropriately used at the beginning of study in a management and leadership course or program. The intent is to help in the formation of microcosms of a real work environment so that learners can have vicarious practice applying theories studied in hypothetical situations before using new practices in an actual professional environment where the stakes are high and really count.

The ultimate goal of this book is identical to the ultimate goal of health care: to assist the client to reach full health potential. In achieving this goal, an intermediate goal of assisting the manager to achieve optimal effectiveness is emphasized. The educational process attends to the unique individual learner. A satisfied manager has a high probability of having staff members who are also satisfied; satisfied staff members have a high probability of having satisfied clients; a satisfied client has a high probability of reaching full health potential.

Elaine La Monica Rigolosi

Understanding Management and Leadership: The Science and the Philosophy

Managing your way through change and coming out a winner are the philosophic foundations and goals of this book. A nurse manager's success in any situation is framed and grounded in expectations and goals, given a specific environment at a particular point in time. Part I provides a discussion of the theories and concepts on which the management processes for a realistic set of winning goals in a particular environment are based. These theories are derived from research in organizational psychology, business and finance administration, law, and educational leadership. The theories and concepts are applied to nursing and health care environments.

Chapter 1 defines leadership and management, differentiating the roles of managers and leaders from the processes of managing and leading. The management process and the scientific method are the foci of this chapter.

Chapter 2 involves a discussion of the conceptual roots on which contemporary management practices are built—nonclassical organization theory. General system theory forms the basis for leader behavior, and experiential learning is the mode used in this book for practicing leadership and management content as well as process. The theory of motivation is then explained as it relates to management and leadership responsibilities.

Management Processes

EXPECTED LEARNING OUTCOMES

- To define and discuss the theories and concepts of management and leadership
- To gain theoretical and practical knowledge of the management processes—roles and skills—in nursing and health care management
- To apply the managerial scientific method to nurse management practices

This chapter provides a definition of management and leadership and discusses the general processes of management. Management processes and roles basically frame all leadership activities. Broad areas of management skills are then presented. The chapter concludes with a discussion of the managerial scientific method. The content in this chapter forms the foundation for specific leadership and management responsibilities that are presented in Part II of this book.

MANAGEMENT AND LEADERSHIP

Many definitions of management and leadership can be identified when surveying the literature (Burns, 2003; Giuliani & Kurson, 2007; Koontz & Weihrich, 2010; Marriner-Tomey, 2009; Northouse, 2012). Themes, however, are evident. Hersey, Blanchard, and Johnson (2008) provided a comprehensive definition of management as " . . . working with and through individuals and groups and other resources (such as equipment, capital, and technology) to accomplish organizational goals" (p. 5). Leadership also involves working through individuals and groups to accomplish goals, but these goals may be different from organizational goals or they may involve one segment of the organizational goals. Leadership may also be shared (Pearce & Conger, 2003).

In a sense, the key difference between the concepts of management and leadership is the phrase "organizational goals." A manager works for an organization (e.g., a hospital administrator) and carries the responsibility of accomplishing the organization's goals through specific professional services. A manager's authority stems from an appointed or elected position in an organization.

Leadership is a much broader concept because all health care professionals are leaders. A person who is a recognized authority and has followers who count on this person's expertise to carry out their objectives is a leader. Furthermore, anyone who is responsible for giving assistance to others is a leader. The staff nurse is a leader to clients, the student nurse also is a leader to clients, the head nurse is a leader to all team followers, and parents are leaders to children.

It is necessary to define management and leadership to understand the differences between the roles of managers and leaders. To reiterate, the key difference is that managers are responsible for organizational goals, whereas leaders may only be responsible for one segment of the overall goals. Managers influence others with position authority and, it is hoped, personal power. Leaders influence others personally or by being delegated responsibilities. When management and leadership theory are applied to leader activities, however, the theory serves roles of both managers and leaders. What changes is the system that the leader influences.

Obviously, the system that the primary care nurse manages is much smaller in actual size than that of the nursing administrator. Also, there are both leader and manager roles in health care. The theory that people in these roles apply, however, is called management and leadership theory and should be the foundation upon which all influencing activities are based.

THE MANAGEMENT PROCESS

The process of management is relevant to all people who seek to influence the behavior of others. Many authors who discuss management and leadership believe that understanding the process is necessary, even though they often differ semantically when identifying the process components (Kelly-Heidenthal, 2003; Longest, 1990; Marriner-Tomey, 2009). Hersey et al. (2008) cited four precise managerial functions: planning, organizing, motivating, and controlling. Their definitions of these components are expanded here and combined with applications in health care. Remember, the managerial functions are presented as action verbs—these processes exemplify what a nurse manager does, broadly speaking.

Planning

Planning involves identifying problems, setting and specifying both long-term and short-term goals, developing objectives, and then mapping how these goals and objectives will be accomplished (Hersey et al., 2008). Longest (1990) asserted that planning involves a means to blend the actions of all participants in a system so that the group's members function together toward an identified goal. Planning greatly reduces the chance of being caught unprepared. Planning, according to Marriner-Tomey (2009), is the first and most important step of the management process.

Organizing

This part of the management process involves bringing all of the system's resources—people, capital, and equipment—into action toward goal accomplishment. Hersey et al. (2008) further discussed it as integrating resources. A leader's desire is to include all people and situational elements into the system that will be carrying out a particular goal and to organize them so that the group is working together toward goal accomplishment.

Motivating

Motivation is a large factor in determining the performance level of employees and the quality of goal accomplishment (Hersey et al., 2008). William James of Harvard (as cited in Hersey et al., 2008) conducted research on motivation and concluded that hourly employees could maintain their jobs by only working 20%–30% of their capacity. When properly motivated by their leader, however, they could work 80%–90% of their ability. James felt that approximately 60% of employee performance can be affected by motivation.

There is never a zero point or top level (100%) in employee performance because one should not say that people are at the maximum absolute level in their motivation to attain a goal. There are no limits on what human beings can accomplish, which is why Olympic records, for example, are exceeded. One must always strive to do a little bit better. Managers must always set goals that are higher than what employees had accomplished previously, based on the assessment that the set goals are within the stretched capabilities of the people trying to attain them. This process is a unidirectional and rewarding process of growth.

Controlling

This last component in the management process involves setting up mechanisms for ongoing evaluation. Hersey et al. (2008) stated that controlling is obtaining feedback of results and periodically following up to compare results with plans. Adjustments in plans can be made accordingly. Quality-control systems, client-care audits, and client census and acuity information are examples of this aspect of the process.

Controlling is one aspect of management that is subject to myths and misinterpretations. When students are asked to share the first adjective or emotion that comes to mind when the term *controlling* is presented, responses include "manipulating," "rigid," "tight," "autocratic," and "oppressed." Controlling need not be any of these things. It is an essential aspect of managerial functions because a manager is ultimately responsible for followers' actions, given that a manager energizes the resources of a group to accomplish a goal. An effective health care manager does not do everything. Rather, the manager leads the group to accomplish and keeps track of what is happening at given points in time. A manager, therefore, controls the situation to be sure that the camera stays in focus.

Misinterpretations of the concept *controlling* stem from the leader's verbal and nonverbal communications during the management process. It is possible to say, for example, that you as a manager would like to meet every week with your group to discuss progress and problems on a particular goal. This is the active process of controlling. However, a leader's verbal and nonverbal communication of these directions should neither be perceived as rigid, abrasive, nor punitive. Rather, directions can be given with warmth and portrayal of the respect of another's intelligence and self-esteem. This is an area that should be role played in a practice environment so that one's intent is perceived accurately and in the most effective manner possible.

Even though the four aspects of the management process are distinct, they are all interrelated (Hersey et al., 2008). When a leader plans, the plan also contains strategies for organizing, controlling, and motivating resources. Hence, all parts of the management process are connected. The case example in Chapter 7 illustrates this point further.

MANAGERIAL SKILLS

There are three general categories of skills that managers and leaders must possess: technical skills, human skills, and conceptual skills. Katz (1955/2009) first classified these skills, and Hersey et al. (2008) adapted them to the field of behavioral science.

- *Technical skill:* Ability to use knowledge, methods, techniques, and equipment necessary for the performance of specific tasks; acquired from experience, education, and training.
- *Human skill:* Ability and judgment in working with and through people that includes an understanding of motivation and an application of effective leadership.
- *Conceptual skill:* Ability to understand the complexities of the overall organization and where one's own operation fits in the organization. This knowledge permits one to act according to the objectives of the total organization rather than only on the basis of the goals and needs of one's own immediate group (Hersey et al., 2008, p. 9).

For example, suppose a nurse leader has the goal of increasing the quality of nursing care. Technical skill is the leader's ability to perform the comprehensive individualized nursing care that is expected from staff nurses and from nursing practice standards. Human skill involves ability to influence others by teaching, role modeling, and so forth to accomplish the goal. Conceptual skill involves seeing how the goal that is being accomplished fits into the overall organizational goals of client service in the agency—how it affects the entire health care facility.

Experience has shown that managers at different levels require varying amounts of technical and conceptual skills to carry out their responsibilities

FIGURE 1.1   Management Skills by Levels of Nurse Management

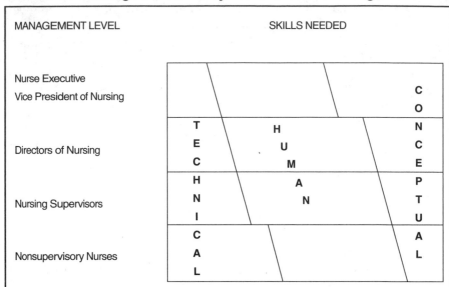

Note. These descriptions are nursing adaptations based on the classification done by Katz, R. L. (1955/2009). *Harvard Business Review Classics: Skills of an effective administrator.* Boston, MA: Harvard Business School Press. (Original work published 1955, *Harvard Business Review, 33,* 33–42, and later published in 1974, *Harvard Business Review, 52*(5), 90–102.) His work was later presented and adapted by Hersey, P., Blanchard, K., and Johnson, D. (2008). *Management of organizational behavior: Leading human resources* (9th ed.). Upper Saddle River, NJ: Prentice-Hall, p. 10.

effectively. Human skills are necessary and fairly constant in all levels and occupy the greatest portion of the manager's activities, as Figure 1.1 illustrates. It must also be noted that as a manager moves up the organizational chart, the need for technical skill decreases as the need for conceptual abilities increases.

THE MANAGERIAL METHOD*

Effective management and leadership are based on a conscious, identifiable strategy for accomplishing goals at a particular place and time and with identified individuals. It is not based on seat-of-the-pants thinking. Management

---

*This section is built on the author's learning during work on her doctorate in human relations and counseling at the University of Massachusetts, School of Education, Amherst, and particularly while taking classes from Professors Kenneth Blanchard, Paul Hersey, and Donald Carew.

roles mandate methodical problem solving that draws first from theory (what has been shown to be effective in a significant number of research investigations) and second from intuition (what has been shown to be effective in one's own experience, given application of research principles).

The priority goal of a manager is to accomplish goals (commonly referred to as growing, developing, or learning) by activating the system. Everything that a manager or leader does toward goal accomplishment should be based on an explicit strategy that has the highest probability for success. Again, there are no absolute points because human behavior cannot be predicted with complete accuracy. Rather, the manager seeks awareness of all in a system to mobilize forces toward goal accomplishment. Fortunately, a scientific method for doing this is available, just as one is available for giving nursing care. The latter is called the nursing process, and the former is called the managerial scientific method. Both are adapted from the pure scientific method, as is evident in Table 1.1.

TABLE 1.1   Comparison of the Management Method, the Scientific Method, and the Nursing Process

MANAGEMENT METHOD	SCIENTIFIC METHOD	NURSING PROCESS
Problem-Finding Steps		
Assess the problem Study the point of view	Gather information Examine information Interpret information	Collect data Process data
Identify the problem or goal	Identify problem(s) State the problem(s)	Diagnose problems
Analyze the problem and choose leader behavior		
Problem-Solving Steps		
Create alternative solutions	Develop alternatives Make a decision	Develop care plans
Recommend an action plan	Decide on plan of action	
Implement action plan	Execute the plan of action	Implement care plan
Evaluate results	Evaluate the results Redefine the problem and change as necessary	Evaluation results

Note. The nursing process is derived from this author's previous publication: La Monica, E. L. (1985). *The humanistic nursing process.* Boston MA: Jones and Bartlett.

FIGURE 1.2   Identifying the Problem or Goal

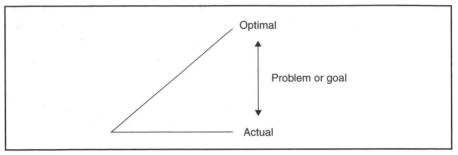

The management method is presented theoretically in this chapter. It is the framework upon which all management practices are built. Part II of this book is devoted to the process of carrying out this method. Examples are provided for making the process alive.

Assess the Information

Assessing the information is the first step in the management method. A problem or goal is identified by the difference between what is actually happening (the actual) in a situation and what one wishes to occur (the optimal). Figure 1.2 illustrates this point. To determine a problem area, it is necessary to gather, examine, and interpret information from all sources available—primary and secondary—and to decide whether the problem area warrants attention. Primary sources are your followers, and secondary sources are all other people from whom information can be collected—clients, doctors, associates, superiors, and others. Data can be gathered from these sources on one-to-one or group bases. The nurse manager's own point of view should be studied by being conscious of individual self-perceptions and beliefs. These data may be shared with members of a team or colleagues to validate perceptions.

Identify the Problem or Goal

After a situation has been assessed to determine a priority need area, to identify where a group is in relation to this need (the actual), and to identify where one wishes to go relative to this need (the optimal), then a problem or goal can be stated as shown in Figure 1.2. The problem or goal represents the difference between real and optimal and should be specific.

Managers who identify problems may be comforted by the knowledge that problems are indicative of growth. A manager should always be identifying problems—specifying where a group is and delineating where it can go. This is the process of growth. Once the optimal is attained, it becomes the actual or the real situation and the whole process of identifying problems and future goals should begin again.

Problems and goals should be explicit and tractable. For example, if performance is the focal point, it is necessary to determine the aspects of performance that one wishes to change. Is it that care plans are not routinely written? Or do employees spend too much time with administrative tasks? A clearly stated problem structures the whole management process because what has to be done to solve the problem or attain the goal, as well as to evaluate outcomes, becomes apparent only when the problem statement is clear and specific. Further, Goode and Fowler (1949) demonstrated early that a clear statement of problems contributed to follower support in solving the problem because followers were aware of the focus of their efforts. Locke, Shaw, Saari, and Latham (1981) asserted that designating problems and setting goals "affect performance by directing attention, mobilizing effort, increasing persistence, and motivating strategy development" (p. 125).

A goal is simply a restated problem. Hence, goals flow from the problem statement. If a problem is that nursing care plans are not written routinely, then the goal would be to have nursing care plans written for all clients. A problem statement can be thought of as a negative statement—that is, something one wishes to eradicate or get rid of, like a medical diagnosis. A goal is something one wishes to attain; it is a positive statement. Obviously, problems and goals comprise different ends of the same continuum. It is the individual choice whether a manager wishes to work with problems or goals, or both. This author's preference always is to accentuate positive thinking by working with goals rather than with problems. Think about reaching goals as an opportunity. Would you rather have something that you want to get rid of, like a problem or a diagnosis, or would you rather have something that you have the opportunity to attain or to work toward accomplishing? Always use the most effective language to enhance your goals and to under-score the point that you wish to make.

The specification of the optimal can be a long-term or a short-term goal. Even though it is essential that a manager identify both types of goals, one should be aware that research in motivation suggests that people are more highly motivated at the beginning of task accomplishment and when the goal is almost attained (Atkinson, 1957).

Because increased employee motivation usually results in an increase in productivity, with follower job satisfaction as a by-product, the manager should set goals with followers that can be accomplished within a reasonable amount of time. The success and rewards that follow goal achievement serve as both reinforcement and stimulus in further endeavors. Shorter-term goals may also be viewed by followers as more realistic and achievable. They should, however, be challenging enough to spark interest and to unleash motivational energy.

Livingston (1969/2009) aptly stated that subordinates must consider goals as realistic to be motivated to reach high levels of productivity.

For example, if care plans are never written for clients following a staff conference (the actual) and a leader desires that a staff discussion always precedes what is written for all clients (the optimal), an intermediate short-term goal (also the optimal) might be to have conferences and to write care plans on clients who have chronic health problems. There are many rungs in the ladder toward accomplishment of a long-term goal. Each should be accomplished in stepwise progression toward the highest level of desired attainment. At the achievement of each step, success should be celebrated and reinforced. This acts as a stimulus for the next climb.

Analyze the Problem or Goal and Choose Leader Behavior

After the problem or goal is identified, it must be analyzed. Analysis entails four steps: (a) determine why the problem exists, (b) identify the unique group who will participate in solving the problem or achieving the goal, (c) analyze the ability of a group to accomplish the goal (level of readiness), and (d) specify an appropriate leader behavior style, indicated by the group's level of readiness, that is required to meet the needs of a group as it accomplishes the goal. It is in this fourth phase that leader behavior theories are brought into focus. By applying theory in each of these four steps, one increases the probability that analysis will be comprehensive and that the decision on the appropriate leader behavior style will be based on what works according to research findings. When leader behavior is chosen, it becomes the way that a leader or manager begins the process of goal accomplishment. These steps will be discussed fully in Part II of this book.

The problem-generating process that was previously discussed can be compared with the health care and nursing process (La Monica, 1985), as portrayed in Figure 1.3. It is evident that vast information is boiled down in both methods to focus on a specific problem. Once the problem is specified, then analysis broadens to solve it. Assessing the problem and data collection and processing involve inductive thinking to make a conclusion about the problem or goal. All information in these processes is used to identify the problem or goal specifically. Problem analyses and care plans, however, are examples of deductive reasoning—a focal area exists and all that follows relates to solving the problem.

Create Alternative Solutions

Based on analysis, the next step is to brainstorm various alternative solutions or strategies that have the potential to solve the problem or to achieve the goal. Brainstorming, a step in the creative process (Henry, 2001), can be used to foster creativity and to develop alternatives that reflect the individuality

FIGURE 1.3 Comparison of the Problem-Finding Process With the Nursing Process

PROBLEM-FINDING PROCESS   NURSING PROCESS

Assess the   Collect
problem or goal   data

Inductive   Process
thinking   data

Identify the   Diagnose
problem or goal   problem or goal

Deductive
thinking

Analyze the   Develop
problem or goal   care plans
and choose   (treatments)
leader behavior

Note. The nursing process is derived from this author's previous publication: La Monica, E. L. (1985). *The humanistic nursing process.* Boston, MA: Jones and Bartlett.

of a unique system—people, environment, and time. This process is a way to expand possibilities by answering the question, "If I could achieve this goal with this identified system, ideally doing anything I wished, reflecting on my knowledge and experience, what would I want done and how should I get it done?" All ideas are important and during the process of brainstorming, no value judgments of good or bad operate.

After ideas are listed, each solution should be studied for anticipated positive results and anticipated negative results. In other words, it is necessary to play out behaviors and attempt to predict reactions of followers and superiors. These reactions should include both the negative and the positive possible outcomes.

Recommend an Action Plan

Following analysis of alternative solutions, one strategy must be chosen. Unfortunately, it is rare when a strategy played out has no possible negative consequences. The recommended action plan, therefore, usually has the highest probability for reducing the discrepancy between real and optimal and the lowest probability for resulting in negative consequences, given that there are most often some negative possibilities in all strategies. It should be noted that solution phases are too frequently hurried. A good analysis in these steps is important because strategic diligence most often results in the best recommended action plan becoming obvious—your best shot!

Implement Action Plan and Evaluate Results

Once the action plan has been decided, it must be implemented. Evaluation occurs on an ongoing basis and at goal accomplishment. Even though the management method seems to be linear, in fact, it is circular. Constant evaluation of daily outcomes or data begins the process again, and new information may result in a refocus of any step of the management method.

● SUMMARY

Management and leadership are different concepts when they are defined in terms of roles—managers are responsible for organizational goals, whereas leaders are such because people look to them for guidance. In leader/manager activities, however, management and leadership theory is applied in both roles.

The management process contains four interrelated elements: planning, organizing, motivating, and controlling. Technical, human, and conceptual skills are required to carry out this process. Different levels of management require lesser or greater amounts of technical and conceptual skills; human skills are consistently important in all levels of management.

The problem-solving process is the manager's scientific method. It is the foundation on which all manager activity should be based. A problem or goal must first be identified inductively, resulting in a specific problem or goal statement. Deductive processes are then employed to analyze the problem, choose beginning leader behavior, and create alternative solutions. A recommended action plan is the final outcome of the method prior to implementation and continuous evaluation.

● ● ● REVIEW CONCEPTS AND QUESTIONS

1. Describe the differences between management and leadership.
2. What are the managerial functions and how do they relate with each other?

3. Explain the skills of management and justify your position of whether or not one is more important than the other. Delineate how the skills vary according to an organization chart.
4. What are the steps of the Management Method? Compare them to the steps for the Scientific Method as well as the Nursing Process.

● ● ● SUGGESTED ASSIGNMENTS

1. Provide a clinical case. Ask learners to apply the steps of the Scientific Method or the Nursing Process to the case in working out a health care plan.
2. Provide a management case. Ask learners to apply the steps of the Management Method to the case in working out priority goals for the manager and a recommended action plan.
3. Learners can be requested to write their own individual or group clinical and/or management cases and follow the guidance in Suggested Assignments 1 and 2.
4. Ask learners to observe managers and executives in different roles in an organization and compare their position functions in the frames of management skills, that is, technical, human, and conceptual. Analyze what is actually found against what is theoretically recommended.

REFERENCES

Atkinson, J. (1957). Motivational determinants of risk-taking behavior. *Psychological Review, 64*(6), 359–372.

Burns, J. M. (2003). *Transforming leadership: The pursuit of happiness*. New York, NY: Atlantic Monthly Press.

Giuliani, R. W., & Kurson, K. (2007). *Leadership*. New York, NY: Miramax Books.

Goode, W., & Fowler, I. (1949). Incentive factors in a low morale plant. *American Sociological Review, 14*(5), 618–624.

Henry, J. (2001). *Creative management* (2nd ed.). London, United Kingdom: Sage.

Hersey, P., Blanchard, K., & Johnson, D. (2008). *Management of organizational behavior: Leading human resources* (9th ed.). Upper Saddle River, NJ: Pearson Prentice Hall.

Katz, R. L. (2009). *Harvard Business Review Classics: Skills of an effective administrator*. Boston, MA: Harvard Business School Press. (Original work published 1955, *Harvard Business Review, 33*, 33–42, and later published in 1974, *Harvard Business Review, 52*(5), 90–102.)

Kelly-Heidenthal, P. (2003). *Nursing leadership and management*. Clifton Park, NY: Thomson/Delmar Learning.

Koontz, H., & Weihrich, H. (2010). *Essentials of management: An international perspective* (8th ed.). New York, NY: McGraw-Hill.

La Monica, E. L. (1985). *The humanistic nursing process*. Boston, MA: Jones and Bartlett.

Livingston, J. S. (2009). *Harvard business review classics: Pygmalion in management*. Boston, MA: Harvard Business School Press. (Original work published 1969, *Harvard Business Review, 47,* 81–89, and later published in 1988, *Harvard Business Review, 81*(1), 97–106.)

Locke, E., Shaw, K., Saari, L., & Latham, G. (1981). Goal setting and task performance: 1969–1980. *Psychological Bulletin, 90*(1), 125–152.

Longest, B. (1990). *Management practices for the health professional* (4th ed.). Norwalk, CT: Appleton & Lange.

Marriner-Tomey, A. (2009). *Guide to nursing management and leadership* (8th ed.). St. Louis, MO: Mosby.

Northouse, P. G. (2012). *Introduction to leadership: Concepts and practice* (2nd ed.). Thousand Oaks, CA: Sage.

Pearce, C. L., & Conger, J. A. (2003). *Shared leadership: Reframing the hows and whys of leadership*. London, United Kingdom: Sage.

●●●● 2
Theories of Management and Leadership

EXPECTED LEARNING OUTCOMES

- To conceptualize individual organizational theories and concepts and use this knowledge in analyzing nursing and health care environments
- To gain understanding of the organizational structure of health care environments
- To discuss the differences between classical and nonclassical organization theory
- To apply general system theory into nursing and health care leadership and management environments
- To gain understanding about experiential learning as used in this book
- To define and apply motivation theory to management and leadership

The management process and the managerial method are the procedures for all management responsibilities. These procedures outline how managers should function. Chapter 2 contains the concepts and theories that seek to explain why managers function in particular ways. This chapter also provides the rationale for the educational design of the book, the intent of which is to enable learners to grow and therefore change. Change is synonymous with growing and learning.

The goal of this book parallels the goal of nursing and health care managers and leaders; that is, leaders facilitate change and growth in their personnel. The conceptual framework presented in this chapter applies to learning how to become a manager as well as to the role of actually being a manager. The conceptual and theoretic framework, therefore, holds together the education of future leaders and managers as well as the processes involved in managing and leading.

This chapter begins with the frame of core and satellite theories and concepts. Discussions follow on classical and nonclassical organization theory, general system theory, and the group dynamics laboratory using experiential learning as an educational mode. It concludes with the theory of motivation, which is an essential concept in understanding management and leadership processes.

THE CORE AND THE SATELLITES

As a way of framing the contents in this book, Part I focuses on the foundational principles and philosophy upon which leadership and management are based. Part II involves the core of leadership and management theories and behaviors. Being able to know and to apply the theories contained in the chapters in Part II is seen as minimal to base leadership and management actions on behaviors that have the highest probability for success. Parts III and IV contain the interrelated "how to" and "action" satellites that swirl around the core—what should be done in a variety of roles, based on identified goals. Part V refers back to philosophic dimensions.

Imagine that you are building a new house. The first step is to build the footprint of the house—the foundation. This can be aligned with Part I of this book. The second step is to build the frame of the house, including the roof—Part II or the "core." Step 3 of the building process is to decide how to use the inside space—what rooms should be built, and how should they be designed and decorated. Step 3 refers to Part III—the "how to" satellites. Carry out the picture a little further. In the rooms of your house, you can do many different things. You can entertain in the living room, prepare food in the kitchen, read stories to children in their bedrooms, and so forth—all of these are examples of the various roles that can be played out in each room. So, Part IV of this book is synonymous with how you may act in different roles. Your mind and your internal philosophic thoughts carry you throughout your new home. Hence, Part V is the parallel to Part IV.

All that is done to the previously described home is done on the foundation or the "core." Therefore, if there was a part of this book that trumps the others, it would be Part II. All parts, however, are included because they develop and frame the whole basic picture. The picture can be expanded by further studying research and the literature on the subject, but the basic frame and design must hold its presence. At this point, it is necessary to discuss several other foundational theories in order to have a footprint ready for further design.

CLASSICAL AND NONCLASSICAL ORGANIZATION THEORY

The literature reflects two categories of leadership: classical organization theory (COT) and nonclassical organization theory (NCOT). Prior to 1950, COT was the rule in organizations. NCOT, which has evolved from criticisms of COT, is the basis for contemporary management practices.

Classical Organization Theory

COT has a list of assumptions, delineated by McGregor (1960/2006), called Theory X assumptions about human nature. These are as follows:

1. Followers find work distasteful.
2. Followers are not ambitious and prefer direction.
3. Followers do not solve organizational problems creatively.
4. Followers are motivated only by physiological and safety factors.
5. Followers require close control and coercion in order to achieve goals.

Given the previous assumptions, organizations designed the leadership structure to counteract these traits of people so that organizational goals would be accomplished. The traditional organization, therefore, had centralized decision making and a pyramid form of superior–follower control. In essence, workers were told what to do and were neither expected nor required to think. The leadership style used with employees was autocratic (Hersey, Blanchard, & Johnson, 2008; Newstrom, 2011).

Nonclassical Organization Theory

Severely criticizing classical organizations, which were built on Theory X assumptions, McGregor (1960/2006) further proposed the following Theory Y assumptions about people:

1. Followers regard work to be natural, like play, when conditions are favorable.
2. Followers are self-directed in achieving organizational goals.
3. Followers are creative in solving problems.
4. Followers are motivated at all levels of Maslow's (1970) hierarchy of needs—physiological, safety, social, esteem, and self-actualization.
5. Followers are self-controlled if properly motivated.

Nonclassical organizations, which have Theory Y assumptions about people, design the organizational and leadership structures so that workers will be able to grow within the organization. The aim is to have people fulfill or work toward fulfilling the Theory Y assumptions.

Obviously, people are neither good nor bad, and it must be pointed out that there is no intent to portray them as good or bad when delineating Theory X and Theory Y. Rather, Theory X and Theory Y are intended only to understand what drives a person's behavior. The difference between Theory X and Theory Y, however, is that Theory Y assumptions allow managers in an organization to find out what motivates people and then to provide the appropriate leadership style that enables workers to grow within the organization. Some people may in fact need close control; then the autocratic style of leadership is appropriate. Others may need support from the leaders and a democratic leader behavior style may be indicated. There may be those who are completely self-motivated and are committed to the growth of the organization; they may also have the necessary skills and experience to be successful in their goals. These people are usually best if left alone—the laissez-faire leadership style. In contrast, Theory X assumptions fit everyone into one category that requires constant leader control to be sure that goals get accomplished.

Theory Y assumptions, therefore, permit the organization's leaders to respond to the needs of the people who make up the organization as these people work to achieve the organization's goals. It also has an avenue for people to grow and change within the organization. Leader behavior reflects the needs of a group given a particular problem or goal. If the group changes or the goal changes, the appropriate leader behavior style must be reassessed and designated again.

GENERAL SYSTEM THEORY

Contemporary management practices are based on NCOT. NCOT employs a situational and an environmental approach to leadership. It assumes that all people can be helped and educated to achieve organizational goals, that people vary as to what motivates them, and that the styles of leadership used in organizations must respond to the needs of the organization's constituency, including culture (Chemers, 2000). The situational approach to leadership is based on an understanding of general system theory, which provides a construct for studying people within their environment and as builders of their environment.

General system theory is a model developed by von Bertalanffy (1968/2003). It mandates analysis of all of the system's parts, the relationship between and among those parts, as well as the system's purposes, beliefs, and tasks.

Von Bertalanffy (1968/2003) designated two main types of systems, closed and open systems, as means of conceptualizing the world and the universe. Closed systems end when a quantity needed for fulfillment is obtained. Further, results are exactly predictable in closed systems. An example of a closed system is a chemical equation. If water (H_2O) is added to salt (NaCl), a chemist (or a manager) can predict and quantify exactly what will occur—water plus the breakup of sodium and chloride ions. Hence, the balanced equation:

$$NaCl + H_2O = H_2O + Na^+ + Cl^-$$

Open systems have no designated quantity and are not exactly predictable. In other words, open systems are not deterministic like closed systems. Human beings are open systems because even though one can spend great amounts of time finding out the properties, personality, wishes, and desires of people, there is and will always be the unknown. Open systems are the only concern, therefore, when general system theory is applied in management and leadership.

Von Bertalanffy (1968/2003) identified four assumptions of open systems.

1. *A system is more than a sum of its parts.* In other words, a system is composed of all people and things within it, but the composite system contains more than its constituents. This composite has a character of its own, is made up of the parts, but is different from those parts. The system or group becomes the "I" or first person, not the individuals and things within the system.

Another example of the first assumption involves taking 10 people in a group and giving each person an energy range that moves from 1 (lowest amount of energy) to 10 (highest amount of energy). If an assignment was given to one person in the group to use 10 units of energy and go out on a motorway and stop traffic in both directions from 8:00 a.m. to 8:30 a.m. one morning, would that person be successful? Maybe, but success is doubtful. Suppose the assignment was given to all 10 people to do the same in the same spot, but working independently. Then there would be a total of 100 units of energy working on a goal. The 10 people working separately would have more chances of being successful than the single person because there is more energy in the field. Now give the same assignment to 10 people, but instruct them jointly to plan a strategy for accomplishing the task, that is, to work together as a group on the goal by first planning a strategy and then implementing it. The chances of the group being successful would be far greater than the chances for success in either the single assignment or in the task in which 10 individuals worked alone.

Given a perfectly functioning group, the amount of energy contained within the group in the previous example is not simply 10 times 10 or 100 units. The amount of energy is 10 to the 10th power (10^{10}) or 100,000,000,000 units of energy, because the interactions between and among every combination of people in the group elicits energy toward goal accomplishment. So, a group of people working together toward a common goal is the manager's best bet, even though groups rarely, if ever, function perfectly. The greater the amount of energy a group has working toward a goal, the higher the probability for effective goal completion. This is the principle behind collective bargaining units and team building. This is a unified voice. The challenge for management, however, is to keep the groups working *for* the organization's goals rather than against the organization's goals.

2.   *A system is ever changing.* The absence of a member or part of a system or the inclusion of a new member or piece of equipment changes the system. On another scale, the passage of time changes a system. Because human beings are constantly learning from and therefore changing with the environment, people are different at every point in time. Even though a group may be composed of the same constituents, the group is always changing because the constituents are always changing. An effective leader must allow for the group's growth (or regression) to be reflected in the group's goals and the strategies that will best enable the goals to be attained. This process involves constant assessment of the group. It also means setting realistic goals that cause a group to put energy into attaining the goals. Goals, however, should not be out of reach because this may cause followers to give up or to not maintain interest.

3.   *A system has boundaries.* These are defined by the system's purpose. Community health care can be considered as one system. All of the human and the material resources in this unit are part of the system. In fact, the geographic community in which the unit is located can be conceptualized as the supra system. The universe is our absolute outer system, given the limits of human knowledge. All that occurs in the world falls into subsystems. One system is always related to or is part of a larger whole. Figure 2.1 provides one example of how this principle works.

The managerial method requires that boundaries be designated. In increasing the quality of health care as a goal, for example, the subsystem of the community is important but not as important as the health

FIGURE 2.1   The Nursing System Viewed from a Health Care Service
Perspective.

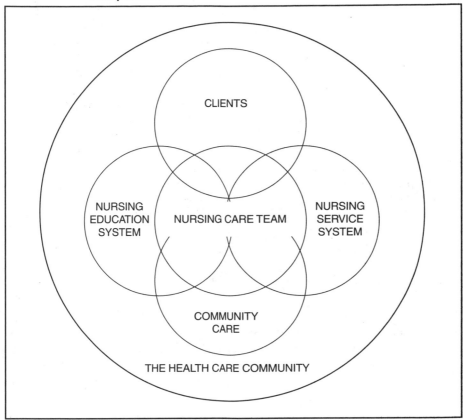

care team. Boundaries are circumscribed by responding to the question
"Who and what are the important components of the larger system
that will have the most direct and energetic effect on solving a given
problem, or on attaining a specified goal at a given point in time?" The
answer becomes the system for that problem, goal, or opportunity. It
follows that each system is unique for each problem, given the available
human and material resources in a specified time and place. The system that has a goal of increasing the quality of care in a given unit may
not be the same system in another unit or at another time in the same
unit. Part II contains discussion about designating systems in greater
detail than is presented here.

   4.   *Systems are goal directed.* This assumption flows directly from the
previous one. Once the problem or goal is specified, the boundaries of
a system can be specified. A system with no goal has no reason to exist,
no motivation to function, and no drive to succeed. A system with no

goals has nothing to evaluate because evaluation requires measurement points—a beginning point and an end point. Without goals, one can easily feel a lack of accomplishment and a feeling of "never getting anything done." Behaviorally, this can become a self-reinforcing negative cycle. Principles of time management, discussed in Chapter 12, are built on this goal-setting principle.

The previously presented four assumptions guide the manager to state problems or goals, to designate the system that will be primarily responsible for goal attainment, and to understand how the group working as a single, integrated unit of one becomes foremost in effective goal accomplishment. Does this sound like the nursing process or the managerial method? All are based on the pure scientific method. If general system theory had to be placed into a particular science, it would be physics. Nevertheless, the association of general system theory into what nurse leaders and managers do could neither be louder nor be more profound in its importance, as evidenced in the literature (Roussel, 2009).

GROUP DYNAMICS LABORATORY: AN EXPERIENTIAL APPROACH

A widely used method in management training is the human relations approach of experiential learning (Bass & Stogdill, 1990; Burke, 2002; Lieberman & Golant, 2002). Various group exercises form the experiential experience: case studies, films, role playing, business games, and other media that involve group problem-solving projects. Experiential exercises and simulations follow the topics in each part of this book.

In experiential activities, a microcosm of the real work world hypothetically is created. Hence, the experience takes place and is studied in a group dynamics laboratory, a group-created safe and trustworthy environment where risks can be taken with minimal fear. Participants have an opportunity to apply and to use the skills and behaviors that a manager must possess: how to lead, follow, draw out opinions, use power, resolve conflicts, be assertive, give and receive feedback, and so forth. Because the role of a manager always involves working with people in groups, experiential learning serves to enable both learning the required content in management and leadership as well as the actual process of being a manager.

Several underlying assumptions about the learning process distinguish experiential learning from other modes of instruction. According to Seashore (1970, pp. 15–16), these assumptions are

Learning Responsibility. Each participant is responsible for his [or her] own learning. What is learned depends upon . . . style, readiness, and the relationships . . . [developed] with other members of the group.

Staff Role. The staff person's role is to facilitate the examination and understanding of the experiences in the group. He [or she] helps participants to focus on the way the group is working, the style of an individual's participation, or the issues that are facing the group.

Experience and Conceptualization. Most learning is a combination of experience and conceptualization. A major aim is to provide a setting in which individuals are encouraged to examine their experiences together in enough detail so that valid generalizations can be drawn.

Authentic Relationships and Learning. A person is most free to learn when he [or she] establishes authentic relationships with other people, and thereby . . . increases his [or her] sense of self-esteem and decreases his [or her] defensiveness. In authentic relationships, persons can be open, honest, and direct with one another so that they are communicating what they are actually feeling rather than masking their feelings.

Skill Acquisition and Values. The development of new skills in working with people is maximized as a person examines the basic values underlying . . . behavior, as he [or she] acquires appropriate concepts and theory, and as he [or she] is able to practice new behavior and obtain feedback on the degree to which that behavior produces the intended impact.

The intent of experiential learning is to accomplish one or more of the following changes in attitudes or behaviors on the part of the leader trainees (Bass & Stogdill, 1990):

1. Increased sensitivity to the needs and desires of followers;
2. Increased openness;
3. Increased sharing of decision-making responsibilities with a team;
4. More intimate and friendly interpersonal relationships with followers; and
5. Increased team independence and interdependence in structure, leading to more productive output.

Blumberg (1977, pp. 15–16) asserted that in order for experiential training goals to be realized, certain conditions in the learning laboratory must be met. These conditions are the following.

Presentation of Self. Until an individual has an opportunity to reveal the way he [or she] sees things and does things, he [or she] has little basis for improvement and change.

Feedback. Individuals do not learn from their experiences. They learn from bringing out the essential patterns of purposes, motives, and behavior in a situation where they can receive clear and accurate information about the relevancy and effectiveness of their behavior. They need a feedback system that continuously operates so that they can change and correct what is inappropriate.

Atmosphere. An atmosphere of trust and non-defensiveness is necessary for people both to be willing to expose their behavior and purposes, and to accept feedback.

Cognitive Map. Knowledge from research, theory, and experience is important to enable the individual both to understand experiences and to generalize from them. However, information is usually most effective when it follows experience and feedback.

Experimentation. Unless there is opportunity to try out new patterns of thought and behavior, they never become a part of the individual. Without experimental efforts, relevant change is difficult to make.

Practice. Equally important is the need to practice new approaches so that the individual gains security in being different.

Application. Unless learning and change can be applied to back-home situations, they are not likely to be effective or lasting. Attention needs to be given to helping individuals plan application.

Relearning How to Learn. Because much of our academic experience has led us to believe that we learn from listening to authorities, there is frequently the need to learn from presentation-feedback-experimentation.

Regarding the group mode of experiential instruction, Carkhuff (1984) concluded that this model is goal- and action-directed in its work-oriented structure. Emphasis is on behavior that one wishes to effect, leaving the trainee with tangible and usable skills. Longer retention of learned skills results because learning is an outcome of actual experience. Further, the nature of the systematic training involves steps that lead to measurable outcomes, thereby making evaluation explicit. "In summary, what can be accomplished individually can be accomplished in groups—and more!" (p. 184).

MOTIVATION

The theory of motivation is the next to be discussed in the conceptual and theoretical framework of management and leadership. Motivation, as stated in Chapter 1, comprises the largest area of a manager's responsibilities and is under the umbrella of human skills. Its major importance in management activities remains constant regardless of one's management level.

In comparing motivated and unmotivated personnel generally, the more followers are motivated to accomplish a goal, the shorter time will be required to succeed. In addition, quality will increase, costs will decrease, and personnel will have a positive experience, which serves as a stimulus for motivating them to accomplish again. In short, as motivation increases, time and costs decrease, whereas quality and satisfaction increase.

Motivating personnel is the responsibility of managers. It involves a conscious, identifiable, behavioral strategy. Theories are available that guide the leader to find out what motivates individuals and then to apply the appropriate leader behavior style that will increase the probability of motivating people to get the task done while enabling them to grow in their positions. McClelland (1961) is well known for work studying the strong, positive relationships among needs and behaviors. Applications of motivation theories will be discussed and applied in Part II of this book. This section will present the theory of motivation, which is essential as a foundation to understanding the applied motivation theory that is explained later.

Motivation Factors

The following definitions provide keys to understand motivation (Hersey et al., 2008; Newstrom, 2011):

Motives are needs, wants, drives, or impulses within an individual that prompt behavior; motives may be conscious or unconscious.

Motive strength is a means for categorizing the strength or power of a motive or need. Because people normally have various motives, all competing for fulfillment, the highest-strength motive is satisfied through behavior first. Once a need is satisfied, it decreases in motive strength and the need next in priority receives attention.

Goals are "hoped for" rewards, incentives, and external desires. Goals are outside an individual; they are what one wishes to attain.

Attitudes are within an individual; they reflect what is felt inside. When attitudes are communicated, they are referred to as behavior. Attitudes, therefore, are silent to others unless an individual shares them behaviorally. Attitudes have no way to communicate except through behavior.

Behavior is what a person does and what others perceive. Behavior is observable, measurable action. It is both nonverbal and verbal.

FIGURE 2.2   Maslow's Hierarchy of Needs

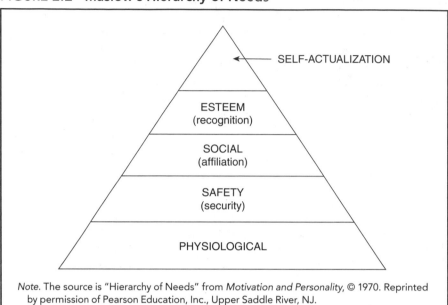

Note. The source is "Hierarchy of Needs" from *Motivation and Personality*, © 1970. Reprinted by permission of Pearson Education, Inc., Upper Saddle River, NJ.

If a need is present within an individual, the need (internal) is attached to a goal in the environment (external) and causes the individual to work toward attaining that goal, thereby satisfying the need. Newstrom (2011) discussed external goals as intrinsic and extrinsic factors. Intrinsic factors occur at the time work is performed, an example of which is positive reinforcement from a manager immediately following task completion. Extrinsic factors occur away from work, for example, fringe benefits and days off.

People work on satisfying needs in an orderly fashion. Those needs that have the highest motive strength receive attention first. Maslow (1970) presented a theory that designated categories of needs and their strength when unsatisfied. The theory is called Maslow's hierarchy of needs and is shown in Figure 2.2. According to Maslow's widely accepted theory of motivation, the physiological needs (shown at the bottom of the pyramid in Figure 2.2) are top priority in motive strength when unsatisfied.

Physiological needs have the highest priority until satisfied. Once physiological needs become less important or are in balance, safety needs take priority. This format follows as the pyramid climbs to self-actualization, which is a priority only when the other four needs are satisfied. It must be noted that all needs are present within an individual; the priority of the needs, however, shifts. A person may be functioning at a physiological level at 12:00 noon and then be at an esteem level after eating lunch.

Kreitner and Kinicki (2010) adapted more explanatory descriptions than were previously provided by Maslow (1970). Their more detailed definitions follow.

Physiological needs are most basic and involve having sufficient food, air, and water for survival.

Safety needs consist of being and feeling safe from physical and psychological harm.

Social needs include the desire to be loved and to love. Affiliation, interpersonal connections, affection, and belonging are included.

Esteem needs involve recognition, reputation, and prestige derived from others, as well as self-confidence and strength.

Self-Actualization involves the desire within self to be the best that one is capable of becoming; it is the desire for self-improvement.

Other theorists presented variations on motivation factors. Part II of this book contains a discussion of other dominant motivation theories.

To fully understand motivation, another concept requires discussion. This concept involves the difference between internal and external motivation. Internal motivation comes from within a person; external motivation is outside a person. The old saying, "You can lead a horse to water but you cannot make it drink," is true. A leader cannot make someone behave in a certain way. If someone has an internal need, the sight of an external goal increases the probability that behavior aimed at goal attainment will follow; no guarantee, however, exists. For example, if a person is hungry and food is in sight at a nearby restaurant, it is highly probable that the person will be motivated to travel to get the food, but one cannot be absolutely sure. Remember, management is not a closed system; it is not deterministic. Rather, it is an open system and an open system is probabilistic.

Applying Motivation Theory

A manager is responsible for motivating people to accomplish organizational goals. Using motivation theory toward this end, the leader must first assess the highest motive strength of the employee and then designate a goal having a reward that directly meets the need of the worker. The leader uses intrinsic and extrinsic factors in the goal. The route to obtaining the goal and thereby satisfying the need is through a journey that accomplishes the organizational goal—the action plan. Matching what people need with the goal managers need to have accomplished is a managerial challenge. This is a chief responsibility in the manager's position. Feel comfortable at this point, however, because accomplishing your responsibility is a conscious and identifiable strategy that can be learned. Keep reading, especially Part II of this book.

The process just described is theoretically how people are externally motivated. Because a manager can only attempt to motivate someone externally, it follows that the external motivational process may not work; it may fail to lead a person to act or behave. It is the manager's responsibility to try again by delineating another strategy to motivate the employee externally. Managers must be determined to accomplish (Northouse, 2012) if they believe in the accuracy of the identified needs of people as well as the specified goals that they have set.

It may be necessary to reassess or to rediagnose the needs of the follower. Obviously, if the first assessment was not on target, the chances increase that the external motivational strategy will not work. Also, different things work for different people. In a sense, being a manager or leader is a commitment and an opportunity to struggle—to constantly develop ways of motivating people to get the work done. This is your job! You have been hired to problem-solve and to manage others as all of you work toward the identified organizational goals. If a strategy for accomplishing an immediate organizational goal does not work, another strategy must be developed or the goal may be adjusted. Once the immediate goal is attained, another goal should be designated after success is celebrated and reinforced. New strategies must then be built on the needs of workers at that particular point in time.

The motivation process previously described was applied to motivating one person. Because a leader is most often trying to motivate a group to accomplish a task, motivation theory is applied to individual people in the group first. Individual needs are assessed and then the need that is the group mode, which is evident in the greatest number in the group, is used by the leader in planning a strategy for externally motivating the group to accomplish an organizational goal. It is logical to conclude that the strategy may not be best for all people in the group; however, it should be best for the majority of people in the group. A leader may not be all things to everyone. A leader should be on target for the majority (mode) of people in a group and then try to work on a person-to-person basis with those individuals who are not directly satisfied. Application of the theory of motivation is extended in Chapter 4.

SUMMARY

Two categories of leadership style are discussed in this chapter: COT and NCOT. NCOT forms the basis of contemporary leadership models and assumes that people must be motivated to fulfill themselves within the organization. Because people are different, leaders must diagnose what people need and then provide the appropriate leader behavior style that will enable a goal to be accomplished and enable workers to grow while in their positions. NCOT employs a situational approach to leadership and sees an organization as a system that is composed of human and material resources working as one unit toward goal accomplishment.

Von Bertalanffy's (1968/2003) general system theory is the framework that explains how systems work. Experiential learning is the educational mode that enables personal applications of management and leadership content. Experiential learning enables future leaders to experience the actual processes involved in being a manager. A manager's primary responsibility is externally motivating followers to achieve organizational goals. This is accomplished by diagnosing the highest internal need of a person at a particular time, specifying an external goal and reward, using intrinsic and extrinsic factors that fulfill the follower's need, and setting a path through which the follower can attain the goal and reward through behavior that accomplishes the particular goal of the organization at a given point in time.

● ● ● **REVIEW CONCEPTS AND QUESTIONS**

1. Discuss the differences among the management "core" and the different satellites that are presented in this book. Which one is the most important to learn first?
2. Differentiate the difference between classical and nonclassical organization theory. Who was the primary author responsible for classifying the previously stated two pillars of organizational theory? Which theory should frame current managerial practice and why?
3. What aspect of general system theory is applicable when working with people? Specify and describe the assumptions in systems when working with people.
4. Explain what is involved in a group dynamics laboratory. What is its purpose and why is it important in learning to become a manager and a leader? Specifically, what does it provide that is not evident in book learning?
5. Explain Maslow's theory of motivation. Specify and describe the motivational factors that are keys to understanding motivation and how to apply principles into management and leadership.

● ● ● **SUGGESTED ASSIGNMENTS**

1. Write a critique of McGregor's Theory X and Theory Y and use examples from experience in making your points alive.
2. Study a family environment and write how different people in various roles use motivation theory on each other to influence behavior.
3. Report on several multimedia advertisements and analyze how motivation factors are paired with what is being sold and to whom it is being sold.

REFERENCES

Bass, B., & Stogdill, R. (1990). *Bass and Stogdill's handbook of leadership: Theory, research, and managerial applications* (3rd ed.). New York, NY: Free Press.

Blumberg, A. (1977). Laboratory education and sensitivity training. In R. Golembiewski & A. Blumberg (Eds.), *Sensitivity training and the laboratory approach: Readings about concepts and applications* (3rd ed.). Itasca, IL: Peacock.

Burke, W. W. (2002). *Organization change: Theory and practice.* Thousand Oaks, CA: Sage.

Carkhuff, R. (1984). *Helping and human relations* (Vol. 2). Amherst, MA: Human Resource Press.

Chemers, M. M. (2000). Leadership research and theory: A functional integration. *Group Dynamics, 4*(1), 27–43.

Hersey, P., Blanchard, K., & Johnson, D. (2008). *Management of organizational behavior: Leading human resources* (9th ed.). Upper Saddle River, NJ: Pearson Prentice Hall.

Kreitner, R., & Kinicki, A. (2010). *Organizational behavior* (9th ed.). New York, NY: McGraw-Hill/Irwin.

Lieberman, M. A., & Golant, M. (2002). Leader behaviors as perceived by cancer patients in professionally directed support groups and outcomes. *Group Dynamics: Theory, Research, and Practice, 6*, 267–276.

Maslow, A. H. (1970). *Motivation and personality* (3rd ed.). New York, NY: Harper & Row.

McClelland, D. (1961). *The achieving society.* New York, NY: Free Press.

McGregor, D. (2006). *The human side of enterprise: Annotated Edition.* New York, NY: McGraw-Hill. (Original work published 1960)

Newstrom, J. W. (2011). *Organizational behavior: Human behavior at work* (13th ed.). New York, NY: McGraw-Hill/Irwin.

Northouse, P. G. (2012). *Introduction to leadership concepts and practice* (2nd ed.). Thousand Oaks, CA: Sage.

Roussel, L. (with Swansburg, R.). (2009). *Management and leadership for nurse administrators* (5th ed.). Sudbury, MA: Jones and Bartlett.

Seashore, C. (1970). What is sensitivity training? In R. Golembiewski & A. Blumberg (Eds.), *Sensitivity training and the laboratory approach: Readings about concepts and applications* (3rd ed.). Itasca, IL: Peacock.

von Bertalanffy, L. (2003). *General system theory: Foundations, development, application.* New York, NY: Braziller. (Original work published 1968)

Experiential Learning Activities:
Ice-Breaking and Getting Acquainted

ACTIVITY 1	GROUP FORMATION

Purposes

1. To divide the group into subgroups of six to eight members.

2. To increase group members' awareness of their self-perceptions concerning the roles assumed in group activities.

Facility

Large comfortable room in which participants can mill around.

Materials

Magic markers or crayons, 5-inch by 7-inch index cards, scotch tape, paper, and pencils.

Time Required

Thirty to 45 minutes.

Group Size

Unlimited.

Design

1. Participants should choose one word from each of the following four pairs of words. The word chosen should describe what they believe their behavior is when they are working on a group activity.

   A. Leader/follower
   B. Perfectionist/carefree
   C. Rigid/flexible
   D. Obsessive/loose

2. Have members use a magic marker or a crayon to write their four chosen words in large print on the index card.

3. Tape the index card to their clothes, back or front.

4. Instruct members to mill around the room, talk with each other, and form into groups of six to eight people. These small groups should stay the same throughout the course and should work as one unit on all small-group exercises. Explain that a group should be composed of all kinds of people—leaders, followers, perfectionists, carefree, rigid, flexible, obsessive, and loose—in order for the group to be balanced. Balance plays a large part in the effective outcomes of group activities (15–30 minutes).

ACTIVITY 1	GROUP FORMATION *(continued)*

5.   When groups have been formed, ask that each group record the names, addresses, and telephone numbers of the members. These records should be duplicated and given to every member of the subgroup.

Discussion

The formation of groups early in a class is necessary to encourage a group identity to begin. The groups will further develop throughout the course as they do the experiential exercises that require small groups. If possible, do not add any members to the groups once they have been formed. These subgroups are intended to become microcosms of the real work world.

Variation

The four pairs of words can be expanded to include other areas that might be important. Examples are smoker/nonsmoker, likes to write/ hates to write, enjoys presenting to a large group/hates presenting to a large group, and needs to talk/needs to listen. The longer the list of word pairs, the longer time is required to decide on group membership. Having more than seven word pairs should be avoided because arriving at a balance in the group is too complicated and time-consuming.

ACTIVITY 2	MEMBER INTRODUCTIONS

Purposes

1. To introduce members of the small group to each other.
2. To begin formation of the team.
3. To establish an atmosphere that is conducive to experiential learning.

Facility

Large room with tables so that the members of the small group can sit facing one another.

Materials

None.

Time Required

Thirty minutes.

Group Size

Six to eight.

Design

1. Have small group members form into pairs or triads (if there is an odd number in the group).
2. Request that each pair (triad) share information about themselves—thoughts, experiences, backgrounds, goals, hobbies, likes, dislikes, and so forth (15 minutes). Discussion should avoid labels such as age, class year, and marital status. Labels do not tell others about the true self—what is inside.
3. Form into a group of the whole, which is composed of the six to eight members.
4. Ask each member of the pair (triad) to introduce the other(s) to the rest of the group.

Discussion

This exercise should be done after the small groups have been formed in Activity 1. It does not matter if members of the pairs or triads know one another. If they do, instruct them to introduce themselves by telling their partner(s) something that they know is unknown to the partner(s).

Variation

1. Have members wear name tags on which they have only drawn a picture. Then proceed with the design and have them relate to the picture in introducing themselves.
2. Use adjectives or animals in the above variation instead of a picture.

ACTIVITY 3	SELF—MY MANAGEMENT SHIELD

Purposes	1. To look at the thoughts, feelings, and experiences that develop one's desire to become a manager.
	2. To become aware of one's personal values or philosophy of management.
	3. To explore one's desire and beliefs about ideal management practice.
	4. To probe into the ways one actually practices while in a management position.
	5. To identify personal goals in management.
Facility	Large room with tables so that the members of the small group can sit facing one another.
Materials	Construction paper and felt-tipped pens or crayons.
Time Required	One hour.
Group Size	Six to eight.
Design	1. Working individually, have participants draw a large shield on construction paper and divide it into six parts as shown.
	2. Have participants place their names at the top of the shield. Explain that this is their personal management shield, symbolizing various aspects of themselves as managers.
	3. Request that the areas in the shield be lettered from A to F as shown.
	4. Ask that members draw in each designated area a picture or a symbol that answers the following six questions.

(continued)

This exercise is based on the PELLEM Pentagram, a model of "self" developed by Elaine La Monica Rigolosi and Eunice M. Parisi. It is an adaptation of an exercise published in La Monica, E. L. (1985).

ACTIVITY 3   **SELF—MY MANAGEMENT SHIELD** *(continued)*

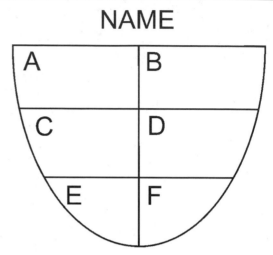

A. What or who has been significant to me in developing a desire to become a manager?
B. What describes the "best" manager I have known?
C. What do I believe the essence of management to be?
D. What signifies my personal practice in management?
E. How do I feel as a manager?
F. In 5 years, if all were ideal, how would I be as a manager?
5. After completing the shield, ask the small group members to discuss their shields with each other. Suggest that they explore the reasons, thoughts, and feelings that went into each picture or symbol.
6. Discuss the experience.

Discussion

It is necessary for a person to explore globally the various feelings and experiences that form the person today. From this point, the person can begin to conceptualize the ideal versus the reality. Goals can then be identified and strategies set up to meet them.

Variation

The questions to be answered and pictured in the shield can be changed according to the needs of the group. The questions stated in the activity can be made future oriented if the activity is used with students who have had no management experience.

ACTIVITY 4	BEGINNINGS

Purposes	1. To begin information and group interchange.
	2. To assist with group introductions.
	3. To assist participants to identify personal goals relative to the experience.
Facility	Large room with tables so that the members of the small groups can sit facing one another.
Materials	Worksheet 4-A (on page 40), pencils or pens, a chalkboard, and chalk.
Time Required	Thirty to 45 minutes.
Group Size	Six to eight.
Design	1. Each participant should sit alone and complete the questions on Worksheet 4-A. This should take approximately 15 minutes.
	2. After participants complete the questions on Worksheet 4-A independently, they should share their responses with each other in the small groups. Someone should record the list of major goals that the participants in the small group identified for the course/ experience/workshop.
	3. In the large group, the facilitator should list the major goals from all of the groups on the chalkboard and themes should be identified. These themes can be woven into the course content or can be achieved in course assignments or extra activities.
Discussion	Participants should have the opportunity to see that they can achieve their personal objectives by moving through an organized experience. By combining a participant's needs with the course objectives, motivation can be increased. Instructor expectations can also be compared with learner expectations. Similarity among expectations increases the probability for success.

(continued)

WORKSHEET 4-A

1. What is your name, where do you attend college/university/work, and what do you do?

2. What is your major goal while attending this course/workshop/experience?

3. What do you like most about your current educational program/position?

4. What is the most difficult aspect of your current program/position?

5. What is the easiest aspect of your current program/position?

6. Describe one of your recent achievements—one that made you feel proud.

7. Write some words that you would use to describe yourself.

Managerial Responsibilities: The Core

Part II contains a discussion of a manager's responsibilities and strategies in motivating followers to accomplish goals. Motivating followers is the most important aspect of management and leadership. As has already been discussed, properly motivated employees, in comparison with unmotivated employees, accomplish tasks more quickly, thereby costing the organization less money. In addition, quality of outcomes increases and employees have a greater chance of being satisfied. Employee satisfaction is a built-in positive reinforcement for accomplishing goals again and for continuing their part in creating a successful working cycle. Part II is the core of all managerial behavior.

Chapter 1 emphasizes that effective management and leadership begins with the identification of a problem, goal, or opportunity. The system must then be filled in with material and human resources that are important as well as essential in carrying out the goal or in solving the problem. All people and things that are essential or helpful to getting a specific task done should be included in a system. Every system, therefore, is unique, depending on the particular problem or goal. System boundaries should be methodically identified so that important parts are not omitted and nonessential parts are not included. One wishes to create a group that contains as much energy as possible working toward goal accomplishment. Nonessential parts of a system tend to detract from the group because energy can shift elsewhere. Remember that a group working together is affected by all parts of the group, so you want to build a system that has as much positive energy as is possible.

It is helpful to consider the followers' complete panorama of human and material resources when identifying a system for a particular problem.

Superiors are those above the leader in the organizational chart. If a problem is not delegated to the manager to solve in any way deemed appropriate, superiors maintain varying amounts of control in how a problem is solved. Therefore, they may have to be included in the planning process. Even if control and authority have been delegated, the manager may wish to include superiors in the problem-solving group because of various reasons, such as the superior has needed expertise or is a source of needed information.

Associates are those on the same level as the manager in the organizational chart. If associates have roles in the problem or goal, they must be a part of the system. If associates do not have roles in the problem but have had positive experiences in solving a similar problem, they should be included in the system if their expertise is desired and they are willing to participate.

Followers are those below the manager in the organizational chart. Followers usually comprise the largest part of the system.

Situational variables are time demands, budget allocations, and the nature of the task. These must be considered in the planning and action aspects of management. Situational variables form the frame of your goal-specific environment's reality.

Material resources include technical equipment and other things that are available for use in solving a problem. As with situational variables, these also must be taken into account as you build your frame of resources.

After the problem and the system for solving the problem have been designated, members of the system must be effectively motivated and educated to solve the problem and to accomplish the goal. The manager behaves with the goal of influencing and motivating others. Leader behavior thereby responds to the needs of the environment and can be expressed in the following equation:

Manager Behavior =
- Diagnosing the Organizational Environment
    - Self

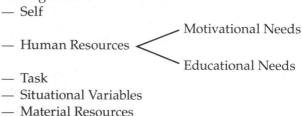

    - Human Resources
        - Motivational Needs
        - Educational Needs
    - Task
    - Situational Variables
    - Material Resources
- Plus Applying Leader Behavior Theory

The manager's behavior that results from following the previous equation becomes the pivot on which alternative solutions and the ultimate recommended action plan for solving a problem by working with and through the system are based. The appropriate manager's behavior can be thought of as an umbrella, guiding leaders in the strategy for goal accomplishment with ways that have the highest probability for success, given a unique problem and a unique system.

The previous equation forms the focus of Part II. Chapter 3 provides a discussion on how to know self. Diagnosing the system is explained in Chapter 4. Given the system diagnosis, an appropriate leader behavior style can be identified in Chapter 5. Chapter 6 contains discussion about how to diagnose the task, and Chapter 7 applies the theories and processes by presenting and discussing a case study. Chapter 7 puts the process of management into action. Experiential activities conclude Part II.

Knowing Self

EXPECTED LEARNING OUTCOMES

- To develop a personal perspective of the relationship between understanding self and understanding people and organizations
- To begin to focus on knowing one's own point of view regarding organizational problems, goals, and opportunities
- To consciously start or continue a lifestyle that involves self-study and evolving self-awareness as a lifelong process of growth
- To increase awareness of one's personal leadership style

Chapter 3 focuses on knowing self because the manager is a key and an important part of a unique system, and knowing self is the first step of the equation for diagnosing the organizational environment. This process of knowing (also recognized as increasing self-awareness) involves identifying the manager's view of the problem, goal, or opportunity. It also means recognizing that one's viewpoint and perspective of the unique environment will be influenced by the manager's personal values and perceptions. The manager must also discover the behavior style that is part of his or her leader personality—how the manager behaves involuntarily without cognitively thinking about actions. A discussion of the conceptual framework for knowing self begins this chapter. It must be stated that knowing self is a lifelong process of study that is never completed—it evolves constantly as one lives day by day. This chapter focuses on the aspects of self-awareness that are considered essential in putting the core of a manager's responsibilities into positive action—those that have the highest probability for generating successful outcomes.

CONCEPTUAL FRAMEWORK

The PELLEM Pentagram (named for its originators, Elaine La Monica Rigolosi and Eunice M. Parisi) is a model of self, composed of five interrelated yet separate parts (La Monica, 1985):

- Thoughts and feelings
- Philosophy and values
- Desires
- Behaviors
- Experiences

Figure 3.1 depicts the five-pointed star. While each point of the star represents one aspect of self, the aspects merge in the center to form the total self. The body, which contains the soul of self, is represented by a circular line running through each point. It is symbolized in this way because the physical and emotional body affects how and what one experiences, feels, and thinks, as well as how one behaves.

The points of the PELLEM Pentagram represent what theorists believe to be operating within a person's total experience. The body is the vehicle for self-expression—it is one's language—and therefore crosses all facets of the pentagram. Self, portrayed in the center of the model, is the blending of all.

The influence of psychic powers and mystical or unknown phenomena that may have a part in total experience is absent from the picture of this model. These energies, however, are neither denied nor claimed as fact even though their influence theoretically is undetermined and experiences often suggest that they exist.

The PELLEM Pentagram provides a way to study self holistically. The interplay of all parts produces the unique individual. It is all of the components

FIGURE 3.1   PELLEM Pentagram

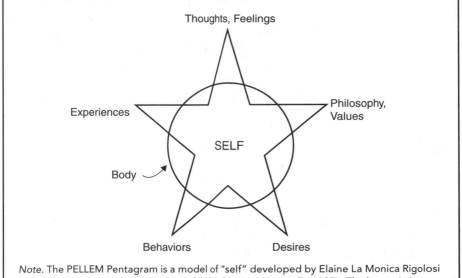

Thoughts, Feelings

Philosophy, Values

Experiences

SELF

Body

Behaviors   Desires

Note. The PELLEM Pentagram is a model of "self" developed by Elaine La Monica Rigolosi and Eunice M. Parisi in 1975. It is published in: La Monica, E. (1985). *The humanistic nursing process.* Boston, MA: Jones and Bartlett, © 2003 Elaine La Monica Rigolosi. May not be reproduced without permission.

acting in unison that determine experience at any given moment. Denying the significance of any one part denies an important aspect of being. This model provides one simple though comprehensive way to view the complexities of a person. It stems from personal and professional struggles to know and understand self—to direct self.

The areas of the PELLEM Pentagram should be explored in analyzing why problems and goals are considered important, why people are perceived in certain positions, and why self and others behave in certain ways. Self-exploration and self-awareness will provide the manager with insight, thereby raising self-awareness so that the environment being studied is looked at as objectively as is possible (Kinicki & Kreitner, 2009; Porter-O'Grady & Malloch, 2007). Finch, Jones, and Litterer (1976) asserted that "accurate self-perception increases the likelihood of accurate interpersonal perception, and realistic perceptions of others are key elements in our ability to communicate, engage in joint problem-solving, and otherwise work with others" (p. 167).

POINT OF VIEW

Identifying the leader's point of view means starting honestly with one's perceptions of the problem, goal, or opportunity, feelings about followers in the system, past experiences relating to the problem or goal, personal desires, and so forth. Day, Shleicher, Unckless, and Hiller (2002) and Kinicki and Kreitner (2009) referred to this process as self-monitoring. Frieze and Bar-Tal (1979) studied attribution theory, which is concerned with understanding perceptions of the causes of an event. They explained that people first form an idea about something or somebody and then collect data to support that idea.

Krech, Crutchfield, and Ballachey (1962) posited that the first step in responding to another is to form an impression. This impression influences the interpersonal behavior in the event; it steers reactions. Robbins (2002) suggested that distinctiveness, consensus, and consistency are the factors that can assist in determining behavior. De Cremer (2000) showed that the social value orientations of leaders had effects on perceptions of leadership behaviors by followers. Borkowski (2009) underscored that a person uses preconceived thoughts as a screen through which new data are filtered.

Based on the previously cited theories, therefore, leaders' and managers' points of view affect the outcomes of a problem-solving process, as broadly underscored by Burns (2003). Hersey, Blanchard, and Johnson (2008) and Livingston (1969/2009) discussed this concept in terms of an effective cycle and an ineffective cycle. In an effective cycle, people respond to a manager's high expectations with high performance. In an ineffective cycle, a manager's low expectations of employees generally results in low performance.

Even though it is human nature to form impressions, a manager can reduce the impact his or her own perceptions may have on others by being conscious of them and then controlling them. A manager cannot control impressions, however, if not aware of them. Cognitively thinking about personal perceptions increases the probability that the manager will not behave solely on the basis of those perceptions—at the very least not to the same degree that one would behave given no consciousness of the perceptions.

It is also important to note that even though high expectations generally result in high performance, set goals should be within the reach (with some stretching) of the people who are to be involved in accomplishing the goal. Setting expectations or goals that are unattainable result in high follower anxiety that becomes counterproductive (Livingston, 1969/2009). Further, this can often result in decreased motivation and maybe even "giving up" (Livingston, 1969/2009). Managers should always examine goals carefully and then set reasonable expectations that can incrementally move a group to a much better level of performance over a period of time. Major change can then be charted and visualized by looking backward to identify and add up all of the smaller accomplishments that were made. Figure 3.2 portrays this principle.

FIGURE 3.2   Progressive Setting of Attainable Goals

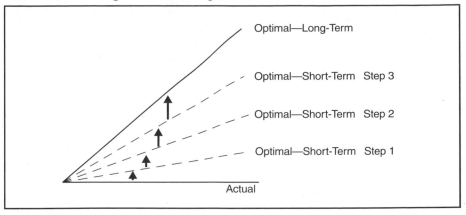

Finch et al. (1976) and Krech et al. (1962) were early in stating and documenting three persistent human tendencies that influence a manager's point of view: stereotyping, the halo-horn effect, and implicit personality theory. Today and tomorrow, cultural diversity increasingly must be addressed with subtle interpersonal skills ("A day in the life," 1989). Each aspect is discussed.

Stereotyping

Stereotyping occurs when an individual attributes characteristics to someone that are assumed, given the individual's past experience, to typify a particular group (Bargh, Chen, & Burrows, 1996; Finch et al., 1976). Racial, ethnic, and sexual stereotyping are most common, but stereotyping is seen in other areas as well. There are stereotypes about clinical instructors, doctors, nurses, and hospital administrators who have been in the same position for 40 years, and so forth. Leadership differences have been shown between men and women (Eagly & Karau, 2002; Lord & Maher, 2005). Nicholson (2001) suggested that masculine and feminine stereotypes exist in psychological theories. Further, there are stereotypes about rehabilitated people who have been on alcohol and drugs, those who have tattoos, or those who have been mentally institutionalized. These stereotypes can blind a manager to the unique characteristics of an individual filling any of these roles. Moreover, stereotypes can cause a manager to respond inappropriately to another person based on past values and assumptions about people in those previously identified roles.

It does not matter whether perceived stereotypes are negative or positive; behavior that is based on a stereotype has an extremely high chance of being inappropriate. A manager must become aware of his or her own snapshots that may be brought into the system's picture in view. Only when consciously aware can a manager attempt to put stereotypes aside and not function as if they were reality. In today's world, stereotyping is unacceptable not only in management practices but also in most aspects of life. Often, behavior based on a stereotype may be against the law.

Halo-Horn Effect

The halo-horn effect is another human tendency that must be checked. The halo effect refers to a favorable impression of one characteristic in an individual that the manager sees as important. This favorable impression becomes generalized to all of that individual's traits or characteristics. The horn effect is the same principle as noted above, but applied to an unfavorable impression of a characteristic the manager deems important.

Consider the following examples of the halo-horn effect in action. If an employee is efficient in organizing responsibilities, and the evaluating manager loves organized people, then the manager assumes the employee must be good in carrying out all of those responsibilities. Conversely, if an employee cannot organize work properly, the chances of being perceived as effective overall are slim. Such thinking is not discriminating; rather, it is biased and generally results in ineffective management practices. Borkowski (2009) underscored that an individual can easily view another through the halo-horn processes of social perception. Becoming increasingly self-aware and practicing self-consciousness raising thoughts become managerial essentials.

Implicit Personality Theory

Implicit personality theory refers to grouping personality traits together (Finch et al., 1976). It also involves the decisions that are made based on specified perceived characteristics and behaviors—also known as attributions (Hersey et al., 2008). If a person is observed to be inflexible, is that person also demanding, cold, and hostile? Maybe the person is and maybe not. Managers should always try to separate traits from one another to diagnose each unique individual objectively. Otherwise, misperceptions, misunderstandings, and inaccurate communication may result.

Informal group discussions with associates and superiors are effective means for uncovering biases such as those presented. Exploring why a problem or goal is considered personally important and why one reacts negatively or positively to certain people, cultures, or traits is an excellent consciousness-raising activity that reaps rewards in management and leadership, as well as in life. A trusting relationship among those discussing these often emotional issues is essential for positive outcomes to result in this process.

LEADER BEHAVIOR STYLE

A manager behaves first as a human being with unique personality characteristics and second in the role of manager. Some managers enjoy working
with people who are unskilled, training the unskilled worker every step of
the way. Other managers most enjoy working with skilled people who are
socially inclined—those who work together and also socialize together. Still
other managers are inclined to lead people who need little on-site direction
and reinforcement. All such inclinations are normal and expected given the
humanness of an individual.

If a manager's system for solving a problem requires the behavioral style
that is the leader's forte, leading that system toward accomplishing a goal
will be natural and will require only moderate cognitive thinking about
leader actions. A perfect match is not often the case, however, especially in
every situation. Because the system is always changing and the manager's
goal is to facilitate growth so that followers are both willing and able to
carry out their responsibilities, using only one leader behavior style is rarely
enough. A manager must be able to function appropriately using different
leader behavior styles, depending on the needs of the majority of people who
are working on a particular problem, goal, or opportunity.

Because all the styles of leadership are seldom the forte of the leader,
the manager must know one's inclinations (that which comes involuntarily)
and then cognitively think about how to behave to meet the requirements
of followers for other leader behavior styles. This requires diagnosing one's
personal leader behavior style. I recommend that the LEAD Self and LEAD
Other be used for diagnosing leader behavior styles.*

SUMMARY

Identifying the manager's view of a problem or goal, as well as the unique environment, are aspects of knowing self. The PELLEM Pentagram (La Monica,
1985), a model of self, is the conceptual basis for the process of diagnosing
self. A manager must be aware of personal beliefs such as stereotypes, halo-
horn effects, and implicit personality groupings. Only with such insight can
the manager reduce the impact of self-perceptions on others. This is necessary in management so that leader behavior responds to the unique characteristics of people and things in a system rather than to the effects of past
experience, which usually are not present reality.

---

*These instruments are authored by Paul Hersey and Kenneth H. Blanchard and can
be ordered from the Center for Leadership Studies, 230 West 3rd Avenue, Escondido,
California 92025.

A manager must also be aware of personal inclinations toward a specific leader behavior style. Because followers may require all styles of leadership at different points in time, the manager must know his or her own preference(s) for leading, and then consciously and carefully plan to meet the followers' needs for other leader behavior styles. A leader should follow the leader behavior style suggested by theory in order to provide followers with guidance. This is necessary in order to have the highest probability for being successful in goal accomplishment. Remember, Part II as a whole, is designed to make what you have just read both complete and alive.

● ● ● REVIEW CONCEPTS AND QUESTIONS

1. Differentiate the differences among the following: a problem, a goal, and an opportunity.
2. Identify the groups who can be included in designating a system to achieve a goal.
3. Describe the elements of the PELLEM Pentagram and how they interact with each other.
4. Discuss the rationale for why managers must become aware of what they cognitively and emotionally bring into a specific situation. Name and discuss several points of view that may influence a manager.
5. Present and discuss the information on which a manager's leader behavior should be grounded, as the process for goal accomplishment begins.

● ● ● SUGGESTED ASSIGNMENTS

1. Provide a managerial situation to the learner in which there are several team members and a unit problem has occurred. Have learners write a short paper describing their analysis of the situation, discussing the observed behaviors, and their perceptions of each of the team members in the situation.
2. Following their completion with the paper and allowing some time to pass, have each learner critique what they wrote, separating the facts from the fiction. What objective data from the situation supported their descriptions? What data came from within themselves?
3. Ask each learner to keep a personal diary in class, shared with no one but themselves. Every clinical day, ask that they enter one critical situation involving communication with a peer, superior, or follower followed by their responsive behavior in that situation. Looking back, on what belief was their responsive behavior based. Separate fact from fiction— or, what the actual situation presented from what was interpreted based on previous experience. Review and stay aware of the differences.

REFERENCES

A day in the life of tomorrow's manager: He or she faces a more diverse, quicker market (The Second Century). (1989, March 20). *The Wall Street Journal*, pp. B1, 3.

Bargh, J. A., Chen, M., & Burrows, L. (1996). Automaticity of social behavior: Direct effects of trait construct and stereotype-activation on action. *Journal of Personality and Social Psychology, 71*(2), 230–244.

Borkowski, N. (2009). *Organizational behavior in health care* (2nd ed.). Sudbury, MA: Jones and Bartlett.

Burns, J. M. (2003). *Transforming leadership.* New York, NY: Atlantic Monthly Press.

Day, D. V., Shleicher, D. J., Unckless, A. L., & Hiller, N. J. (2002). Self-monitoring personality at work: A meta-analytic investigation of construct validity. *Journal of Applied Psychology, 87*(2), 390–401.

De Cremer, D. (2000). Leadership selection in social dilemmas—Not all prefer it: The moderating effect of social value orientation. *Group Dynamics, 4*(4), 330–337.

Eagly, A. H., & Karau, S. J. (2002). Role congruity theory of prejudice toward female leaders. *Psychological Review, 109*(4), 573–598.

Finch, F., Jones, H., & Litterer, J. (1976). *Managing for organizational effectiveness: An experiential approach.* New York, NY: McGraw-Hill.

Frieze, I., & Bar-Tal, D. (1979). Attribution theory: Past and present. In I. Frieze, D. Bar-Tal, & J. Carroll (Eds.), *New approaches to social problems: Applications of attribution theory.* San Francisco, CA: Jossey-Bass.

Hersey, P., Blanchard, K., & Johnson, D. (2008). *Management of organizational behavior: Leading human resources* (9th ed.). Upper Saddle River, NJ: Pearson Prentice Hall.

Kinicki, A., & Kreitner, R. (2009). *Organizational behavior: Key concepts, skills & best practices* (4th ed.). New York, NY: McGraw-Hill/Irwin.

Krech, D., Crutchfield, R., & Ballachey, E. (1962). *The individual in society.* New York, NY: McGraw-Hill.

La Monica, E. (1985). *The humanistic nursing process.* Boston, MA: Jones and Bartlett.

Livingston, J. S. (2009). *Harvard business review classics: Pygmalion in management.* Boston, MA: Harvard Business Review Press. (Original work published 1969, *Harvard Business Review, 47,* 81–89, and later published in 1988, *Harvard Business Review, 81*(1), 97–106)

Lord, R. G., & Maher, K. J. (2005). *Leadership and information processing: Linking perceptions and performance.* Retrieved from http://www.eBookstore.tandf.co.uk (Original work published 1991)

Nicholson, I. A. M. (2001). Giving up maleness: Abraham Maslow, masculinity, and the boundaries of psychology. *History of Psychology, 4*(1), 79–91.

Porter-O'Grady, T., & Malloch, K. (2007). *Quantum leadership: A resource for health care innovation* (2nd ed.). Sudbury, MA: Jones and Bartlett.

Robbins, S. P. (2002). *Organizational behavior* (10th ed.). Upper Saddle River, NJ: Prentice Hall.

Diagnosing Others

EXPECTED LEARNING OUTCOMES

- To understand the importance of diagnosing the needs of human resources in a system
- To know about the theories that may be used to diagnose people in a system
- To increase awareness of the complexities involved in human motivation
- To apply theories for diagnosing the maturity and readiness of those people in a system who will be involved in accomplishing an identified goal

The introduction to Part II contained a discussion of the human and material resources that must be considered when designating the system that will carry out a goal or solve a problem. Once a system is identified, it must be diagnosed. This chapter presents the following system diagnosis that is part of the equation that was introduced in the introduction to Part II.

Manager Behavior =
- Diagnosing the Organizational Environment
  - Self
  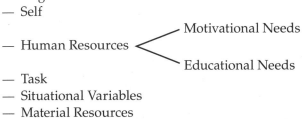
  - Human Resources
    - Motivational Needs
    - Educational Needs
  - Task
  - Situational Variables
  - Material Resources
- Plus Applying Leader Behavior Theory

Situational variables and material resources must be considered in the overall action plan because these resources have effects on goal attainment. A leader must be aware of all parts of the system. The last chapter looked at knowing self; this chapter focuses on the human resources that must be diagnosed by the leader in order to choose the best leader behavior style to begin the process of goal accomplishment. The theoretically best leader behavior style has the highest probability for motivating and educating followers to attain the organizational goals, given the situational variables and material resources.

Remember, motivated employees trump mere talent (Norman R. Augustine, as cited in Hersey, Blanchard, & Johnson, 2008). Mayo (1977) was early in conducting research on motivation. In his studies at a Hawthorne, Illinois' industrial plant (also commonly referred to as the Hawthorne Studies), he found that workers, when properly motivated, could increase their productivity significantly. Having personnel identify with management (Hersey et al., 2008) combined with manager's applying theory-based leader behavior that connected to the maturity and readiness of followers became the essential ingredients for having the highest probability for success in accomplishing specific goals with unique groups of human resources.

Six theories that can be used to diagnose a system are presented, discussed, and applied in this chapter. These theories are Maslow's (1954/1987) hierarchy of needs; Alderfer's (1969, 1972) ERG model; Hersey et al.'s (2008) levels of performance readiness; McGregor's (1960/2006) Theory X and Theory Y; Argyris's (1971) immaturity–maturity continuum; and Herzberg's

(1982) motivation–hygiene theory.* Maslow's theory can be best used to diagnose the internal and external motivational needs of the system, as introduced in Chapter 2, whereas the balance of theories are best used to diagnose the educational needs of the system. Building a strategy for goal accomplishment, therefore, involves a focus on (a) what the system needs to be motivated and willing to achieve and (b) what the system needs to be educated and able to achieve, thereby accomplishing the stated goal within an acceptable range of that identified as optimal. The strategy is implemented by the manager using the most appropriate leader behavior indicated (as will be presented and discussed in Chapter 5), taking into consideration the readiness or maturity level of the majority of people in the unique, goal-specific system.

The general purpose of diagnosing a system is to determine the readiness or maturity level of the system regarding the system's ability to carry out the goal or to solve the problem—this is commonly referred to as diagnosing the readiness or maturity of the system, or the performance readiness as suggested by Hersey et al. (2008). Maturity has nothing to do with chronologic years. Rather, its only concern is discriminating the system's ability to solve a problem or accomplish a goal; therefore, readiness or performance readiness may be the better terms to describe the process. You may see both terms, however, as different theories are in focus. Leader behavior rests predominantly on this aforementioned diagnosis.

Northouse (2012) described this diagnosis as a recognition reflecting needs of employees. The system's diagnosis, therefore, is the most important assessment made by managers. Accurate assessment results in the selection of the most appropriate leader behavior, which is theoretically based, and increases the probability for success in solving the problem. Unfortunately, the converse is also true—that inaccurate assessment usually results in inappropriate leader behavior and a decreased probability for success. The case called Urban City Hospital at the end of Part II is designed to enable learners to sharpen their diagnostic skills.

The theories presented in this chapter provide various clues to managers concerning different behaviors or concepts that may be studied in the system. Each theory offers a different perspective, and the assessor should choose a theory or a combination of theories that best fits the system and seems most appropriate in a particular situation. The method for diagnosing follows.

The leader first assesses the individuals of a system on each person's readiness or maturity to solve an identified problem, goal, or task. These data are then combined to determine the level of readiness of the system as a whole. Because leader behavior must respond to the greatest number of people in

---

*The integration of theories into maturity or readiness levels and their comparisons are adaptations of that presented by Hersey et al. (2008).

the group who share a particular level of performance readiness, the group's mode (or majority) of maturity or readiness is then used to determine the appropriate leader behavior style for beginning to solve a specific problem. People who are not part of the mode or majority can be lead individually as a leader's time permits. The majority of a leader's time and energy, nevertheless, must be given to the greatest number of people who are working on attaining the goal together. Beware of clinical inclinations to give the most to those who need the most or who are the sickest. Clinically, even though the sickest patient usually gets the most time from a care provider, being a manager mandates that one leads the greatest number of people first, and then as time permits, gives to those behind or in front of the dominant portion of the group.

If only one individual is in the system, then the manager can base leader behavior specifically on that individual's level of readiness. It is also essential to point out again that leader behavior varies according to the needs of the system in solving a particular problem. Even though the leader may be the same person for two systems and even though the systems may be the same for two problems or goals, the level of readiness of the system may be different as that system is diagnosed for its ability to solve different problems. Diagnosis is always done in response to a unique system's needs regarding a specified goal or problem.

MASLOW'S HIERARCHY OF NEEDS

The first theory to be discussed in diagnosing a system belongs to Maslow (1954/1987) who developed a hierarchy of human needs that contains five basic categories. In order of priority, these five needs are: physiological, safety, social, esteem, and self-actualization. All of these needs are vital parts of a person's system, but physiological needs are top priority when unsatisfied. When physiological needs are satisfied or in balance, then safety needs become top priority. This ladder effect follows to self-actualization, which is top priority only when all other needs are satisfied. All needs are present and operating within an individual, but the priority and dominant need shifts according to the time, the place, and the activity of an individual.

Maslow's (1954/1987) hierarchy of needs is diagrammed and discussed in Chapter 2 (see Figure 2.2). A manager can use Maslow's theory to diagnose the system's level of maturity, specifically its motivational needs, for accomplishing a particular problem. How the theory is applied for this purpose is discussed in the next section of this chapter, and how this assessment leads to the decision of the appropriate leader behavior style that should be used to begin to get the problem solved is the focus of Chapter 5.

Remember, to diagnose a system, diagnose the individuals in the system first and then decide on the group's (system's) modal level of maturity or performance readiness—that need level evident in the greatest number of the group. Being on target for the greatest number of people is usually your best shot at being the most effective because the group working together generates the greatest amount of energy. This process was introduced in Chapter 2 when von Bertalanffy's (1968/2003) general system theory was presented and applied.

Physiological Needs

Physiological needs are those that sustain life. They are biological and personal in nature and include air, water, food, clothing, and shelter (Maslow, 1954/1987). Assurance of income to meet physiological needs is an essential aspect in this area. Because most people can always use more money, assurance of income only becomes a priority need when basic needs are threatened or when a lower standard of living would occur due to decreased income, for example.

Adults are usually able to satisfy their own physiological needs when these are the priority. A wise manager, however, tries to make easy fulfillment of these needs possible. For example, if a leader plans a 9:00 a.m. meeting and the system contains coffee drinkers, somehow provide coffee for the group at the beginning of the meeting. Do not expect that people will be so dedicated to hearing about the agenda that they will forget about their physiological needs or that the people will bring their own coffee—taking these chances are risky decisions. Rather, most people during the meeting will start thinking about how nice it would be to have a cup of coffee. This means that participants will not be thinking about business.

Another example is that nurses and other health care personnel are often accused of spending much of their time in the staff room eating or socializing. If a leader knows that such behavior is prevalent in a group, to say that these nurses are remiss or not dedicated is foolish. It will only make the nurses resentful of authority and increase the need, which can and usually will in turn decrease the amount and the quality of time spent with clients—directly or indirectly. Rather, keep the coffeepot going, set up a system so that coffee is easily available, and tell the members of the system that even though they are on the unit to give nursing care, it is recognized that they need breaks—give people what they need. At the same time, tell followers that management's hopes are that necessary breaks will increase the quality of care provided because the providers will be more satisfied.

By giving system members what they need, thereby satisfying their need, a manager moves them to the next need level. Ideally, the manager wishes to move the system to esteem and self-actualization levels because motivation to solve a problem is highest at these levels. Physiological needs should be the easiest to satisfy unless a manager is in a crisis.

Safety Needs

Hersey et al. (2008) defined safety needs as those involved with self-preservation. Protection from physical injury in the environment is a safety need. Douglass (1996) further included stability and predictability in life, freedom from constant stressful situations, familiar surroundings, and provision for job security.

A leader can conclude that a member of a system is at a safety level of readiness when the physical environment is potentially harmful, when the member's position or status quo is threatened, when a performance appraisal is due, when someone is new in a position, or when the problem involves a noticeable change from normal service. These are several dominant examples, but they are not all inclusive. Suppose that new cardiac monitors were installed in the Intensive Care Unit (ICU). The goal is to orient the ICU staff to use these new monitors safely. Even though the ICU staff members were considered ready, mature, or experienced in ICU nursing care, they would be at a safety level regarding use of the new monitors until they become proficient in running the new equipment.

A newly graduate nurse or pharmacist beginning his or her first position is at a safety level of readiness; so is a 20-year veteran taking a position in a new unit or in a new hospital. Given the goal of orienting new staff, the new employee is most probably in a stressful state, not knowing the environment, the expectations others will have for the role, and whether the ability to fulfill the role is present. The 20-year professional veteran will most likely be concerned with the new environment and the expectations of others. Because the veteran has a library of previous experience, however, this person may move out of the safety level of readiness more quickly than the new graduate. Nevertheless, at the outset, both can be diagnosed as at a safety level of maturity or readiness.

Social Needs

Hersey et al. (2008) cogently expressed social needs as meaningful interpersonal relationships. Social needs involve a concern for others in the environment with focus of attention moving from self to others. Because the client should be the primary focus in health care agencies, health care personnel ideally should be at the social need level at the minimum whenever they are interacting with clients. If not, personnel will be more concerned with themselves—this is not the intent of any helping relationship. It would be the same as going to see a health care provider because you have a sore throat and the majority of your conversation shifts to discussing the provider's personal health concerns and issues. Even though ideal effective interpersonal communication is not always possible, the manager should work toward this goal by studying past behaviors.

Examples of people who are functioning at a social level are those who enjoy working together in groups or in teams, sharing warm relationships, viewing the work environment as a social situation (Douglass, 1996), encouraging people to feel a part of the work group, and generally expressing awareness of and concern for others in the environment. People who come to work primarily because they need the stimulation from and affiliation with others are at a social level of readiness. Social needs are a priority only when safety and physiological needs are in balance or are satisfied.

Esteem Needs

Maslow (1954/1987) identified two types of esteem needs: (a) the desire for achievement, competency, and mastery of one's personal and professional activities; and (b) the desire for prestige, status, importance, and recognition. People who have esteem needs seek fulfillment while achieving by overtly and covertly asking to be noticed. They may want to be told that they are super nurses or super practitioners, they always follow through on their responsibilities, they are accountable and reliable, and so forth.

Overt esteem needs of people are obvious because a person asks for what is wanted. In essence, they ask: "What is your reaction to my ability or my behavior?" Covert esteem needs may need to be diagnosed. For example, if a person comes back after having been asked to do something and shares that it was necessary to shorten lunch to get the task done, take this as a covert request for praise. Tell this person how much you appreciate what was done and how good it is to be so accountable and dependable. Maslow (1954/1987) cautioned against being superficial when giving praise and reinforcement because a person motivated at the esteem level wants respect, not phoniness. Therefore, be clear about discovering your own positive feelings about what was done and then share those positive feelings.

Self-Actualization Needs

This need structure is of the highest order, becoming prominent when all other needs are satisfied. It involves one's desire to reach fullest potential (Hersey et al., 2008; Maslow, 1954/1987). Furthermore, this potential is realistically based on awareness of one's own strengths and weaknesses. Hanley and Abell (2002) extended self-actualization to include positive views of relatedness to others.

Douglass (1996) characterized self-actualized employees as those finding meaning and personal growth in work—they actively seek new responsibilities, and work becomes play. Further, these people reinforce self (intrinsic reinforcement) rather than seeking reinforcement from others (extrinsic reinforcement). Extrinsic reinforcement characterizes people at the esteem level. Self-actualized people will accomplish, will tell the manager anything that is required, and then will go on with their responsibilities. They are dependent, interdependent, and independent according to their own direction and as the situation demands. An employee at this level strives to help self and others in the environment without being told to do so. Roussel (2009) referred to this level of Maslow's hierarchy as the emotional gold.

An Important Note

It must be pointed out that people move from one priority need level to another. A person may be operating at an esteem level in the morning, get very hungry at 11:30 a.m. because breakfast was skipped, and then move into a physiological level at 11:35 a.m. or a follower may be functioning at a social level and find out that someone in the group got laid off. At that point, the follower may move to a safety level fearing layoff personally. The diagnosis that one uses to select leader behavior, as discussed in Chapter 5, must be based on what is the norm for a person and the specific problem or goal.

ALDERFER'S ERG MODEL

Alderfer (1969, 1972) built on earlier models and suggested that there were three basic needs of individuals: existence needs, relatedness needs, and growth needs. These are in respective hierarchical order and, according to Gibson, Ivancevich, Donnelly, and Konopaske (2011), are similar and seem to be built on the model proposed by Maslow (1954/1987).

Existence needs are accounted for physiological and safety needs and included such things as pay, job security, and fringe benefits. Employees must first satisfy existence needs (Alderfer, 1969, 1972).

Relatedness needs, according to Alderfer (1969, 1972), refer to interpersonal relationships and being accepted by followers and superiors in the work environment. These needs parallel Maslow's (1954/1987) social need level and move into esteem needs.

Last, Alderfer (1969, 1972) proposed growth needs, similar to Maslow's esteem and self-actualization levels. These needs include the need to achieve, to develop esteem, and to be self-directed. Self-actualization needs dominate.

Alderfer's (1969, 1972) ERG model simplified Maslow's theory from five basic hierarchical steps to three. It also accounted for the fact that rarely are people totally self-actualized. Rather, people who are achievement motivated also may be self-actualized—in what could be called a dance back and forth.

HERSEY, BLANCHARD, AND JOHNSON'S LEVELS OF PERFORMANCE READINESS

The third theory that is considered to be appropriate in diagnosing health care environments is Hersey et al.'s (2008) levels of performance readiness, which has two major components: ability and willingness. The first component involves one's ability to solve a problem, including knowledge, skill, and experience. The second component refers to one's willingness to carry out a task with self-confidence, commitment to the task, and a motivation to achieve (Hersey et al., 2008).

Using the variables ability and willingness as just presented, Hersey et al. (2008, pp. 136–137) designated four benchmarks in performance readiness levels.

Performance Readiness level:	*Follower is:*
R1—Low performance readiness	Unable and insecure or unwilling
R2—Moderate performance readiness	Unable but willing or confident
R3—Moderate performance readiness	Able but unwilling or insecure
R4—High performance readiness	Able and willing or confident

As a hypothetical situation, suppose that the middle managers in an acute-care hospital decided to change from team nursing to primary care nursing as the nursing care delivery model. Further assume that one nursing unit was chosen as the pilot group for this goal. All of the nurses for all shifts on this unit, plus the director, nurse manager, and assistant director in charge of the unit, became the system. The assistant director was the manager for solving the problem. This director was involved as a middle manager in making the decision to change from team nursing to primary care nursing.

The system in the preceding hypothetical example would be at the R1 (unable and unwilling) level of performance readiness if the majority of its members neither knew about the primary nursing concept nor had experience with primary care nursing, and if the members verbally and non-verbally expressed no desire for change. If the members were excited about the change, wanting to gain the knowledge even though primary care nursing was new to them, the system would be diagnosed as R2 (unable but willing or confident). Using the same hypothetical example, the system would be at the R3 level of performance readiness (able but unwilling or confident) if the majority of the system's members had knowledge of primary care nursing and had previously experienced it but did not have a positive experience with the model and felt that team nursing was always going to be best. If the majority of members had knowledge about and experience with primary care nursing, liked it, and were eager to put it to work on their unit, this system would be at the R4 level of performance readiness (able and willing).

The above hypothetical example illustrated how to diagnose a system using all of the levels in the theory of performance readiness developed by Hersey et al. (2008). If the problem in the previous hypothetical example were real, a manager should probably choose the unit with the highest readiness level as the beginning target for the pilot project. This unit would provide the best chance for initial success, which is especially important when attempting a major change. The success of the pilot group would become a stimulus and positive reinforcement for the next group to grow or change. This is a stepwise ladder upward. Unfortunately, if the first pilot group is not successful, it may become a reinforcement downward because there is little stimulus to the next group to begin the project.

Another factor to remember when applying this theory is that a person is either willing or unwilling and able or unable. There are no gray areas. For example, if a person is willing to try something while doubting its usefulness, then for the purpose of applying the diagnostic theory, consider the person to be unwilling. People are able only when able to be left completely on their own—when they have the knowledge, the experience, and they understand the job requirements. People are willing or confident when they are willing to take responsibility, when they are secure in their abilities to perform effectively, and when they personally need to achieve. Therefore, if not totally able—a person is unable; if not totally willing—a person is unwilling. These decisions are only done to correctly select the leader behavior that has the highest probability for success in beginning to lead a person or a group toward goal accomplishment. This is information is only for the manager's analysis and should not be shared with personnel. Chapter 5 should clarify this process by adding leader behavior theory.

MCGREGOR'S THEORY X AND THEORY Y

The fourth theory that can be used to diagnose a system is McGregor's (1960/2006) Theory X and Theory Y. It was introduced in Chapter 2 in a discussion of classical and nonclassical organization theory. Although McGregor's theory was intended for the purpose presented in Chapter 2, it can be used appropriately for diagnosing the system and is viewed as important in responding to motivation issues in management (Donnelly, Gibson, & Ivancevich, 1998). Table 4.1 lists the assumptions about human nature that underlie McGregor's theory.

Table 4.1 lists five traits and opposite statements for each trait. The statements are explicit descriptions of how the traits can be observed in followers who form the system. It should be noted, however, that your superiors may be included in a designated system. If you are the leader in accomplishing

TABLE 4.1   Assumptions About Human Nature Based on McGregor's (1960/1985) Theory X and Theory Y

THEORY X IMMATURE	TRAIT	THEORY Y MATURE
1. Followers find work distasteful.	Work Attitude	1. Followers regard work to be as natural as play when conditions are favorable.
2. Followers are not ambitious and prefer direction.	Ambition	2. Followers are self-directed in achieving organizational goals.
3. Followers do not solve organizational problems creatively.	Creativity	3. Followers are creative in solving problems.
4. Followers are motivated only by physiological and safety factors.	Motivation	4. Followers are motivated at all levels of Maslow's (1954/1987) hierarchy of needs: physiological, safety, social, esteem, and self-actualization.
5. Followers require close control and coercion to achieve goals.	Control	5. Followers are self-controlled if properly motivated.

Note. Theories X and Y are from McGregor, D. (1985). *The human side of enterprise: 25th anniversary printing.* New York, NY: McGraw-Hill. (Original work published 1960). Maslow's hierarchy of needs is from Maslow, A. (1987). *Motivation and personality* (3rd ed.). New York, NY: Harper & Row. (Original work published 1954, and later published 1970)

a goal, superiors are your followers—in that particular goal. They continue their role as superiors organizationally.

Because most people, however, may not fit totally into an either/or category when Theory X and Theory Y are applied, the manager should use McGregor's (1960/1985, 1960/2006) theory as a continuum for diagnosing a system. Table 4.2 is one example of how this continuum can be established.

The manager can indicate on Table 4.2 an assessment of where a system member is for each particular trait using a 4-point Likert-type scale. These individual assessments can then be tallied according to the number of people in each category of the trait. The category with the highest number of people (the modal category) should be used to determine the appropriate leader behavior style. The reader is cautioned not to average the assessments because the average (or mean) is affected by extremes and is not a purely representative figure of the majority of people. A manager should base leader behavior on the modal level of readiness.

TABLE 4.2   McGregor's (1960/1985) Theory X and Theory Y: A Continuum for Diagnosing a System

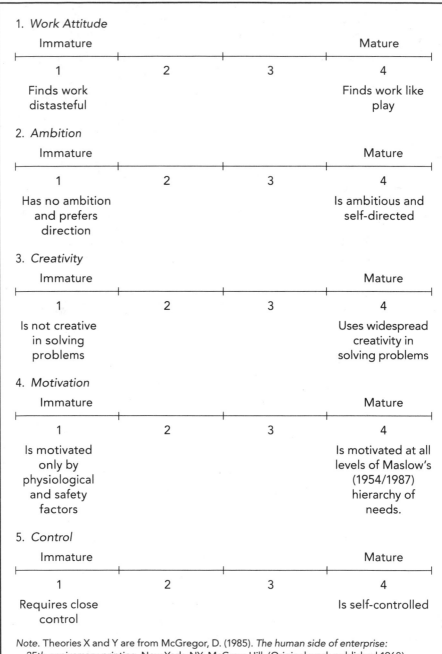

1. *Work Attitude*

Immature   Mature

⊢————+————+————+————⊣

1   2   3   4

Finds work   Finds work like
distasteful   play

2. *Ambition*

Immature   Mature

⊢————+————+————+————⊣

1   2   3   4

Has no ambition   Is ambitious and
and prefers   self-directed
direction

3. *Creativity*

Immature   Mature

⊢————+————+————+————⊣

1   2   3   4

Is not creative   Uses widespread
in solving   creativity in
problems   solving problems

4. *Motivation*

Immature   Mature

⊢————+————+————+————⊣

1   2   3   4

Is motivated   Is motivated at all
only by   levels of Maslow's
physiological   (1954/1987)
and safety   hierarchy of
factors   needs.

5. *Control*

Immature   Mature

⊢————+————+————+————⊣

1   2   3   4

Requires close   Is self-controlled
control

Note. Theories X and Y are from McGregor, D. (1985). *The human side of enterprise: 25th anniversary printing.* New York, NY: McGraw-Hill. (Original work published 1960). Maslow's hierarchy of needs is from Maslow, A. (1987). *Motivation and personality* (3rd ed.). New York, NY: Harper & Row. (Original work published 1954, and later published 1970)

ARGYRIS'S IMMATURITY–MATURITY CONTINUUM

The fifth theory that can be used to diagnose a system, developed by Argyris (1971), is called the immaturity–maturity continuum. Argyris depicted seven changes that take place in the personality of healthy people as they develop from immaturity to maturity. Argyris (1999) expanded on developing follower maturity in a later publication.

First, as people grow from immaturity to maturity according to Argyris (1971, 1999), people move from a passive state to a state of activity. Second, people are dependent on others when immature and grow to an independent state in maturity. Third, immature people possess few behaviors, but when mature they can behave in many ways. Fourth, immature people have erratic and shallow interests, whereas mature people have deep and intense interests. Fifth, people move from a concern only for the here and now (a short time perspective) to a concern for the past, present, and future (a long time perspective). Sixth, people move from a subordinate position to an equal or superordinate position. Seventh, a lack of self-awareness characterizes the immature, whereas awareness and control over oneself characterizes the mature. Even though Argyris used the concept of maturity level in his actual theory, the concept of readiness and performance readiness are considered to be parallel terms. Table 4.3 lists these developmental changes, according to Argyris.

Like McGregor's (1960/2006) Theory X and Theory Y, Argyris's (1971, 1999) immaturity–maturity continuum (Table 4.4) can be used to assess individual people in a system, again applying a 4-point scale.

TABLE 4.3   Argyris's (1971) Immaturity–Maturity Continuum

IMMATURE	TRAIT	MATURE
1. Passive	Work Attitude	1. Active
2. Dependent	Dependence	2. Independent
3. Behaves in a few ways	Behavior	3. Behaves in many ways
4. Erratic, shallow interests	Interests	4. Deep, strong interests
5. Short time perspective	Concern	5. Long time perspective (past, present, and future)
6. Subordinate position	Position	6. Equal or superordinate position
7. Lack of self-awareness	Self-Awareness	7. Awareness and self-control

Note. The Immaturity–Maturity Continuum is from Argyris, C. (1971). *Management and organizational development: The path from XA to YB*. New York, NY: McGraw-Hill. See also Argyris, C. (1999). *On organizational learning* (2nd ed.). New York, NY: Blackwell.

TABLE 4.4   Argyris's (1971) Immaturity–Maturity Continuum: A Continuum for Diagnosing a System

1. *Work Attitude*

Immature			Mature
1	2	3	4
Passive			Active

2. *Dependence*

Immature			Mature
1	2	3	4
Dependent			Independent

3. *Behavior*

Immature			Mature
1	2	3	4
Behaves in few ways			Behaves in many ways

4. *Interests*

Immature			Mature
1	2	3	4
Erratic, shallow interests			Deep, strong interests

5. *Concern*

Immature			Mature
1	2	3	4
Short time perspective			Long time perspective

6. *Position*

Immature			Mature
1	2	3	4
Subordinate position			Equal or superordinate position

TABLE 4.4   Argyris's (1971) Immaturity–Maturity Continuum:
A Continuum for Diagnosing a System *(continued)*

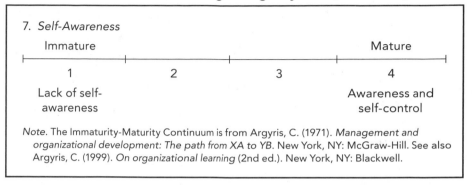

7. *Self-Awareness*

	Immature					Mature	
1		2		3		4	
Lack of self-awareness						Awareness and self-control	

Note. The Immaturity-Maturity Continuum is from Argyris, C. (1971). *Management and organizational development: The path from XA to YB.* New York, NY: McGraw-Hill. See also Argyris, C. (1999). *On organizational learning* (2nd ed.). New York, NY: Blackwell.

HERZBERG'S MOTIVATION–HYGIENE THEORY

The last theory to be discussed for diagnosing a system is Herzberg's (1982) motivation–hygiene theory, commonly referred to as his two-factor theory. Herzberg identified higher-order needs relating to job content that can raise performance and increase one's total work output—motivators, such as achievement, recognition, challenging work, responsibility, advancement, and growth. During his research, people who were satisfied with their work cited these aspects of their work as the reasons for their contentment. In contrast, Herzberg also delineated lower-order needs that referred to the job environment and context— hygiene factors, such as organizational policies, working conditions, interpersonal relations, money, status, security, and personal life. Herzberg found that employees who were dissatisfied with their work environment stated that these hygiene factors were the causes of their dissatisfaction. Dissatisfied employees had lower performance.

Herzberg's (1982) theory is useful for the manager in identifying insights to the goals and incentives that may satisfy needs according to Maslow's (1954/1987) hierarchy. For this purpose, Newstrom and Davis (2002) and Newstrom (2011) compared Maslow's need-priority model with Herzberg's (1982) motivation–hygiene model and Alderfer's (1969, 1972) model, showing that they work in parallel even though the descriptive terms are different (see Table 4.5). Herzberg's theory, therefore, can be used to amplify the diagnosis made using both Maslow's theory and Alderfer's model. This association provides greater insight into the reasons for the diagnosis, the strategies for motivating, and the validity of the theories.

Herzberg (1982) is often credited with the concept of job enrichment—the Herzberg Solution. According to Herzberg, the way to enrich a job is to enlarge the responsibility, scope, and the challenge in the position. In this way, the motivators of achievement, recognition, responsibility, and advancement

TABLE 4.5   A Comparison by Newstrom and Davis (2002) of Maslow's (1954/1987), Herzberg's (1982), and Alderfer's (1969, 1972) Models

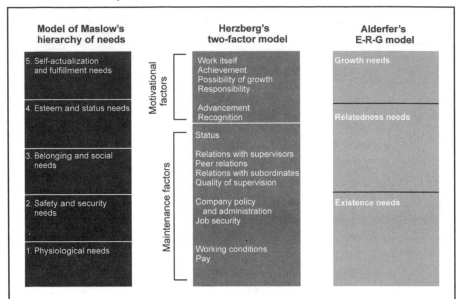

Model of Maslow's hierarchy of needs	Herzberg's two-factor model	Alderfer's E-R-G model
5. Self-actualization and fulfillment needs	Motivational factors: Work itself, Achievement, Possibility of growth, Responsibility	Growth needs
4. Esteem and status needs	Advancement, Recognition	Relatedness needs
3. Belonging and social needs	Maintenance factors: Status, Relations with supervisors, Peer relations, Relations with subordinates, Quality of supervision	
2. Safety and security needs	Company policy and administration, Job security	Existence needs
1. Physiological needs	Working conditions, Pay	

Note. The model was compared by Newstrom, J. W., & Davis, K. (2002). *Human behavior at work: Organizational behavior* (11th ed.). New York, NY: McGraw-Hill/Irwin. Reproduced with permission of the McGraw-Hill Companies. See also Newstrom, J. W. (2011). *Organizational behavior: Human behavior at work* (13th ed.). New York, NY: McGraw-Hill/Irwin. The original theories are from the following sources: Alderfer, C. P. (1969). An empirical test of a new theory of human needs. *Organizational behavior and human performance*, 4(2), 142–175; Alderfer, C. P. (1972). *Existence, relatedness, and growth: Human needs in organizational settings.* New York, NY: Free Press; Herzberg, F. (1982). *The managerial choice: To be efficient or to be human* (2nd ed.). Salt Lake City, UT: Olympus; Maslow, A. (1987). *Motivation and personality* (3rd ed.). New York, NY: Harper & Row. (Original work published in 1954, and later published 1970)

would be amplified, thereby giving employees what they value in the position. Be clear, however; enlarging a scope of practice does not mean giving a follower ten patients to care for instead of eight patients. Rather, it means amplifying the responsibilities that a follower might have in caring for the eight patients or in providing a person with a unit project that might be new and of interest to that particular individual.

SUMMARY

Diagnosing the maturity, readiness, or performance readiness level of a system in terms of the system's ability to solve a problem is the most important aspect of the environmental diagnosis. Leader behavior is based on the system's diagnosis of human resources. A manager diagnoses the individuals in a system first and then uses the modal level of maturity or readiness to determine leader behavior. This leader behavior is then used to begin implementation of the strategy for goal accomplishment.

Six theories for diagnosing a system were presented and discussed in this chapter. The manager may use one or more theories to diagnose a system, depending on what seems to be appropriate in a given context. Table 4.6

TABLE 4.6   Comparison of Six Theories for Diagnosing a System

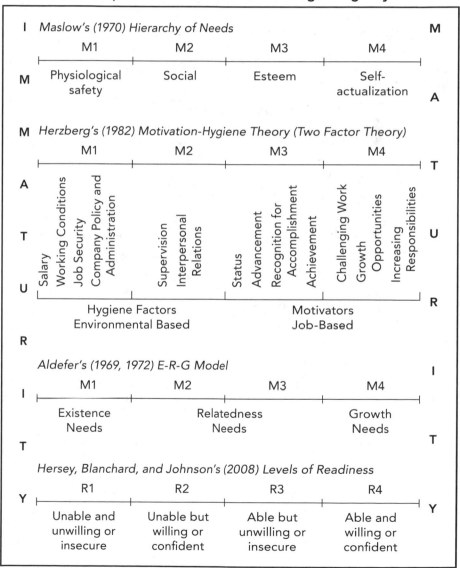

I *Maslow's (1970) Hierarchy of Needs*   M

M1	M2	M3	M4
Physiological safety	Social	Esteem	Self-actualization

M *Herzberg's (1982) Motivation-Hygiene Theory (Two Factor Theory)*

M1	M2	M3	M4
Salary, Working Conditions, Job Security, Company Policy and Administration	Supervision, Interpersonal Relations	Status, Advancement, Recognition for Accomplishment, Achievement	Challenging Work, Growth Opportunities, Increasing Responsibilities
Hygiene Factors Environmental Based		Motivators Job-Based	

Aldefer's (1969, 1972) E-R-G Model

M1	M2	M3	M4
Existence Needs	Relatedness Needs		Growth Needs

Hersey, Blanchard, and Johnson's (2008) Levels of Readiness

R1	R2	R3	R4
Unable and unwilling or insecure	Unable but willing or confident	Able but unwilling or insecure	Able and willing or confident

(continued)

TABLE 4.6   Comparison of Six Theories for Diagnosing a System *(continued)*

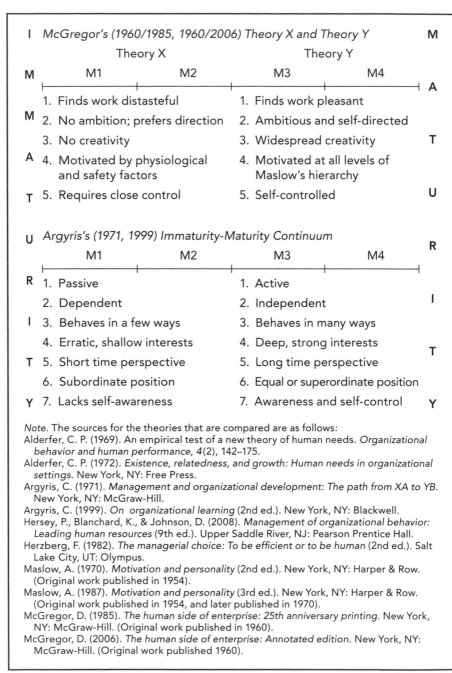

I *McGregor's (1960/1985, 1960/2006) Theory X and Theory Y*

Theory X   Theory Y

M1   M2   M3   M4

1. Finds work distasteful   1. Finds work pleasant
2. No ambition; prefers direction 2. Ambitious and self-directed
3. No creativity   3. Widespread creativity
4. Motivated by physiological   4. Motivated at all levels of
   and safety factors   Maslow's hierarchy
5. Requires close control   5. Self-controlled

Argyris's (1971, 1999) Immaturity-Maturity Continuum

M1   M2   M3   M4

1. Passive   1. Active
2. Dependent   2. Independent
3. Behaves in a few ways 3. Behaves in many ways
4. Erratic, shallow interests 4. Deep, strong interests
5. Short time perspective   5. Long time perspective
6. Subordinate position   6. Equal or superordinate position
7. Lacks self-awareness   7. Awareness and self-control

Note. The sources for the theories that are compared are as follows:

Alderfer, C. P. (1969). An empirical test of a new theory of human needs. *Organizational behavior and human performance, 4*(2), 142–175.

Alderfer, C. P. (1972). *Existence, relatedness, and growth: Human needs in organizational settings.* New York, NY: Free Press.

Argyris, C. (1971). *Management and organizational development: The path from XA to YB.* New York, NY: McGraw-Hill.

Argyris, C. (1999). *On organizational learning* (2nd ed.). New York, NY: Blackwell.

Hersey, P., Blanchard, K., & Johnson, D. (2008). *Management of organizational behavior: Leading human resources* (9th ed.). Upper Saddle River, NJ: Pearson Prentice Hall.

Herzberg, F. (1982). *The managerial choice: To be efficient or to be human* (2nd ed.). Salt Lake City, UT: Olympus.

Maslow, A. (1970). *Motivation and personality* (2nd ed.). New York, NY: Harper & Row. (Original work published in 1954).

Maslow, A. (1987). *Motivation and personality* (3rd ed.). New York, NY: Harper & Row. (Original work published in 1954, and later published in 1970).

McGregor, D. (1985). *The human side of enterprise: 25th anniversary printing.* New York, NY: McGraw-Hill. (Original work published in 1960).

McGregor, D. (2006). *The human side of enterprise: Annotated edition.* New York, NY: McGraw-Hill. (Original work published 1960).

provides a concise summary and comparison of the theories presented. It is developed to document how all theories relate to the same dynamics in diagnosing followers. All theories are shown using a 4-point scale for diagnosing readiness or maturity.

● ● ● REVIEW CONCEPTS AND QUESTIONS

1. Six theories have been presented in this chapter. All were explained as ways in which followers in a specific system or group can be diagnosed individually to find the group's modal level of readiness in order to move on to Chapter 5 and theoretically select the best leader behavior to begin the process of goal accomplishment. On which of the six theories in this chapter are all of the others based? Explain your decision.
2. Compare and contrast the six theories that can be used for diagnosing a person's performance readiness. Examine their similarities as well as their differences.
3. Select the one theory that is your preference and explain why you made that decision.

● ● ● SUGGESTED ASSIGNMENTS

1. Provide a hypothetical management case for study that simply describes the players in a group as well as their environment in which they are employed. Ask learners to write a hypothetical goal for the group and then to diagnose the group's players on their ability and willingness to work as a group toward attaining the goal. The importance of this suggested assignment simply is to have learners apply the theory to whatever they have created in the management case. It follows that everyone asked to do this assignment may have different descriptions of the players as well as different diagnoses. The purpose of this assignment is application of the theory.
2. Ask learners to think of a group in their home environment. Identify a group project like planning a party, cooking for a dinner party, making costumes, and so forth. Then use one of the theories in this chapter and analyze the individual behavior of the group's participants. Follow individual diagnoses for identifying the group model level of performance readiness. Request that learners express what they would or could do, if time permits, with the those people outside of the modal level of performance readiness.

REFERENCES

Alderfer, C. P. (1969). An empirical test of a new theory of human needs. *Organizational behavior and human performance, 4*(2), 142–175.

Alderfer, C. P. (1972). *Existence, relatedness, and growth: Human needs in organizational settings.* New York, NY: Free Press.

Argyris, C. (1971). *Management and organizational development: The path from XA to YB.* New York, NY: McGraw-Hill.

Argyris, C. (1999). *On organizational learning* (2nd ed.). New York, NY: Blackwell.

Donnelly, J. H., Gibson, J. L., & Ivancevich, J. M. (1998). *Fundamentals of management* (10th ed.). New York, NY: Irwin/McGraw-Hill.

Douglass, L. M. (1996). *The effective nurse: Leader and manager* (5th ed.). St. Louis, MO: Mosby.

Gibson, J. L., Ivancevich, J. M., Donnelly, J. H., & Konopaske, R. (Eds.). (2011). *Organizations: Behavior, structure, processes* (14th ed.). New York, NY: McGraw-Hill.

Hanley, S. J., & Abell, S. C. (2002). Maslow and relatedness: Creating an interpersonal model of self-actualization. *Journal of Humanistic Psychology, 42*(4), 37–56.

Hersey, P., Blanchard, K., & Johnson, D. (2008). *Management of organizational behavior: Leading human resources* (9th ed.). Upper Saddle River, NJ: Pearson Prentice Hall.

Herzberg, F. (1982). *The managerial choice: To be efficient or to be human* (2nd ed.). Salt Lake City, UT: Olympus.

Maslow, A. H. (1970). *Motivation and personality* (2nd ed.). New York, NY: Harper & Row. (Original work published 1954)

Maslow, A. H. (1987). *Motivation and personality* (3rd ed.). New York, NY: Harper & Row. (Original work published 1954, and later published 1970)

Mayo, E. (1977). *The human problems of an industrial civilization.* Salem, NH: Ayer.

McGregor, D. (1985). *The human side of enterprise: 25th anniversary printing.* New York, NY: McGraw-Hill. (Original work published 1960)

McGregor, D. (2006). *The human side of enterprise: Annotated edition.* New York, NY: McGraw-Hill. (Original work published 1960)

Newstrom, J. W. (2011). *Organizational behavior: Human behavior at work* (13th ed.). New York, NY: McGraw-Hill/Irwin.

Newstrom, J. W., & Davis. K. (2002). *Human behavior at work: Organizational behavior* (11th ed.). New York, NY: McGraw-Hill/Irwin.

Northouse, P. G. (2012). *Introduction to leadership concepts and practice* (2nd ed.). Thousand Oaks, CA: Sage.

Roussel, L. (with Swansburg, R.). (2009). *Management and leadership for nurse administrators* (5th ed.). Sudbury, MA: Jones and Bartlett.

von Bertalanffy, L. (2003). *General system theory: Foundation, development, applications.* New York, NY: Braziller. (Original work published 1968)

Leader Behavior

EXPECTED LEARNING OUTCOMES

- To understand the magnitude of leadership
- To gain knowledge of the theories of leader behavior

- To apply system diagnoses of readiness and maturity in the selection of leader behavior styles to use in beginning goal accomplishment
- To understand the process and content—the how and what—of effective leadership
- To evaluate leader and organizational effectiveness through conceptual applications

This chapter contains a discussion of leader behavior theory with an application of theory to a system diagnosis to determine the appropriate leader behavior for a unique system that is beginning a journey to accomplish a specific goal.

Leader behavior will be defined, followed by a discussion of well-known leader behavior theories. Components of leader behavior and leadership styles will then be discussed. A leader behavior model will be applied in determining the appropriate leader behavior style for beginning goal accomplishment, given a system's diagnosis. The process and content of leader behavior styles will be further delineated with a discussion of transactional and transformational leadership. An examination of the components for evaluating leader and organizational effectiveness concludes this chapter.

DEFINITION OF LEADERSHIP

Bass (2008), Bass and Stogdill (1990), and Northouse (2012) aptly noted that there are various definitions of leadership, just as there are numbers of people who have provided definitions of the concept. Leadership has evolved in definitions and in professions (Moiden, 2002). Bass and Stogdill provided a rough scheme of classification and a thorough review of the literature in this area.

Historically, leadership was considered to be a personality trait; leaders were born, not made. The act of influencing others, persuasion, goal-oriented people, and people who focused on group processes later became traits that could be based within a personality and also could be taught socially. Giuliani and Kurson (2007) noted that leaders do not simply happen—they are taught, they learn, and they develop. Hesselbein and Cohen (1999) shared that leaders must be healers and unifiers; they must build bridges and succeed through the efforts of followers. Further, they stated that "leadership is a matter of how to be, not how to do" (p. xii). Obviously, definitions of leadership take on many characteristics (Welford, 2002).

The definitions of leadership developed by Fleishman (1973) and Hersey, Blanchard, and Johnson (2008) will be combined. For the purpose of this book, the definition of leadership is using communication processes to influence the activities of an individual or of a group toward the attainment of a goal or goals in a unique and given situation. Leader behavior is *how* a manager acts toward members of the system; it is the process of leading. *What* a leader says puts the process to work; it is the content of leader behavior and is how a leader operationalizes or gives life to the process. Fleishman pointed out that leadership always involves attempts to influence. Further, he stated that all interpersonal relationships can involve elements of leadership. This latter remark affirms the statement, which was made in Chapter 1, that all people in the health care system who influence others are leaders.

COMMON LEADER BEHAVIOR STYLES

There are three common labels for leader behavior: autocratic, democratic, and laissez-faire. *Autocratic leaders* are often described as authoritarian, firm leaders who make unilateral decisions, whereas *democratic leaders* are seen as involving the group in decision making and giving responsibilities to followers. *Laissez-faire leaders* are generally viewed as maintaining minimal control over their followers.

An informal survey of leaders' and followers' opinions of the best leader behavior style usually results in the democratic style obtaining the most votes—by a great margin. But, imagine the following scenario:

> You are in a car with two of your associates driving home on a country road after work. The car in front of you is sideswiped; you and your associates are the only people at the scene. The driver in the accident has a severely lacerated head wound and is semiconscious. You must do something. The bleeding must be stopped, and an ambulance must be called.

If you wanted to be a democratic leader in response to the previous scenario, you might say to your associates, "Listen, the bleeding must be stopped, and someone has to call 911 immediately or find someone who can call. It does not matter who does what . . . both of you jointly decide and let me know your decision."

The beauty of the democratic style is that participants have a choice, but is choice appropriate in the situation just described? No! An autocratic statement is quickly needed to tell your associates what each must do. It is important to point out that autocratic statements are frequently perceived as hostile, mean, and unfriendly. Autocratic leaders, however, can be perceived as benevolent (Nowicki & Summers, 2003). Remember that any statement can be hostile or warm, mean or friendly, depending on the verbal and nonverbal communication patterns that are used by the speaker.

Changing the scenario slightly, suppose that you and your associates were emergency room nurses and had worked together for 5 years. Would it be necessary for anyone to say what should be done? No! In this example, laissez-faire leader behavior would be appropriate. Everyone should know what was needed and begin doing whatever was not being done at the moment.

Each leader behavior style can be appropriate, depending on the situation. Determining the appropriate leader behavior style often is more complex than in the previously cited example. For this reason, theorists have broken leader behavior into components and then used models to determine scientifically the appropriate behavior for a specific situation. This approach is viewed as replacing traditional leadership approaches with models that respond to all followers and the unique environment. Porter-O'Grady and Malloch (2007) referred to this process as perceiving a new framework in leadership. Leader behavior, therefore, is selected as a strategy for getting followers to attain a goal or eliminate a problem, given their environment.

COMPONENTS OF LEADER BEHAVIOR

Management theorists designated two basic components of leader behavior, even though the theorists named the components differently. One component deals with getting the job done, and the other is concerned with interpersonal behavior—one is about the task and one is about the people who are responsible for doing the task. Hersey et al. (2008) referred to *task behavior* and *relationships behavior* in Situational Leadership. The Ohio State Leadership Studies staff called the components *initiating structure* and *consideration* (Fleishman, 1973). Tannenbaum and Schmidt (1958/1973, 1958/2009) labeled the components as *use of authority by the leader* and *area of freedom for subordinates,* and Blake and Mouton (1985) said that the aspects are *concern for production* and *concern for people.*

A leader's behavior style is never one component or the other. Rather, one's leader behavior is a composite of both components with the weight of each varying, given the whole. Figure 5.1 portrays this balance.

In Figure 5.1, all of leader behavior is conceptualized as filling the rectangle. As task behavior decreases, relationship behavior increases. There is always an element of job-related behavior and relationship behavior in any style because people or leaders always have both aspects of their personality operating—all people need to give both aspects and to receive both aspects in a communication exchange.

LEADERSHIP MODELS

There are several theories that delineate leadership styles. Authors differ on the style labels, as with the components of leader behavior, even though the framework and meaning of the models remain the same. Three prominent leader

FIGURE 5.1   The Balance of Leader Behavior Components

AUTHORITARIAN   DEMOCRATIC

Source of Authority

Task Behavior
Initiating Structure
Use of Authority by the
    Leader
Concern for Production

Relationship Behavior
Consideration
Area of Freedom for
    Followers
Concern for People

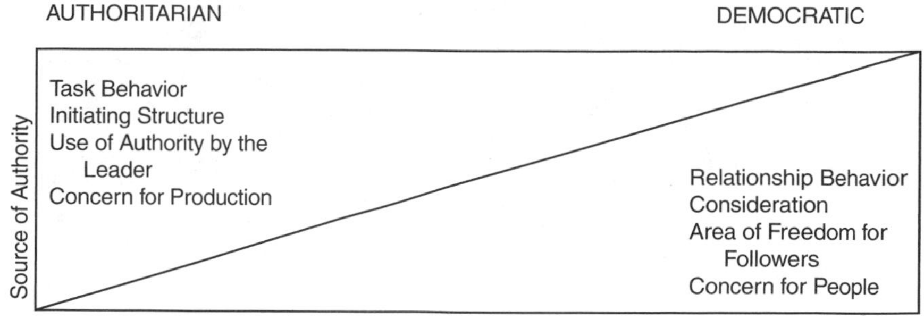

Note. Reprinted by permission of the Harvard Management Update—The balance of leader
behavior components. From "How to choose a leadership pattern," by Robert Tannenbaum
and Warren H. Schmidt, March/April, 1958; May/June, 1973. Copyright © 1958 and 1973 by
the Harvard Business School Publishing Corporation; all rights reserved.

behavior models will be discussed and compared. The Ohio State Model (Bass, 2008; Bass & Stogdill, 1990; Fleishman, 1973) will be used predominantly in later sections of this chapter and in Chapter 7. It can be observed, however, that learning how to apply one leader behavior theory is almost the same as learning how to apply many others. The words and descriptions of the theories may change but the principles are the same, thereby providing increased validity to the various theories of leadership. The theories converge on one another.

Ohio State Model of Leader Behavior

The Ohio State Model (Bass, 2008; Bass & Stogdill, 1990; Fleishman, 1973) for identifying leadership styles contains the following two components of leader behavior, as further discussed by Kreitner and Kinicki (2010) and Hersey et al. (2008):

Initiating Structure refers to a leader's attempt to organize and define the roles and activities of group members. It is stating a goal and delineating what is to be done, how it will be done, when it will be done, where it will be done, and who is responsible for specific tasks. Structure involves one-way communication; the leader tells followers what to do to accomplish a goal.

Consideration involves two-way communication, responding to the group's needs by requesting opinions, beliefs, desires, and so forth. Group activities and discussions are consideration interventions. Further, consideration refers to establishing mutual trust between and among group members, as well as showing respect and warmth. Establishing effective interpersonal relationships are part of consideration.

FIGURE 5.2   Ohio State Model of Leadership

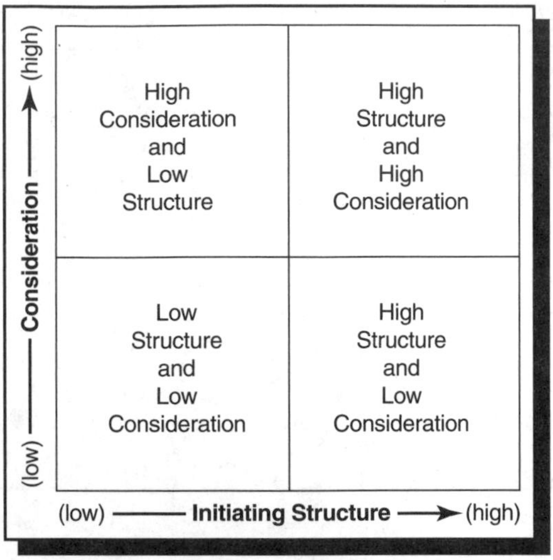

Note. The source for the figure is Hersey, P., Blanchard, K., & Johnson, D. (2008). *Management of organizational behavior: Leading human resources* (9th ed., p. 81). Upper Saddle River, NJ: Prentice-Hall. Reprinted with permission of Prentice-Hall, Inc.

The source of the Ohio State Model of Leadership is from the following:

Bass, B. M. (2008). *The Bass handbook of leadership: Theory, research, & managerial applications* (4th ed.). New York, NY: Free Press.
Bass, B. M, & Stogdill, R. M. (1990). *Bass & Stogdill's handbook of leadership: Theory, research, and managerial applications* (3rd ed.). New York, NY: Free Press.
Fleishman, E. (1973). Twenty years of consideration and structure. In E. Fleishman & J. G. Hunt (Eds.), *Current developments in the study of leadership: A centennial event symposium held at Southern Illinois University at Carbondale*. Carbondale, IL: Southern Illinois University Press.

The Ohio State Model (Bass, 2008; Bass & Stogdill, 1990; Fleishman, 1973) as portrayed by Hersey et al. (2008) can be seen in Figure 5.2. When the two components of leadership are placed on separate axes and the window boxes are filled in, four leader behavior styles result.

Situational Leadership

Situational Leadership (Hersey et al., 2008) grew out of the Ohio State Model and can be seen in Figure 5.3. Situational Leadership has a window-pane design just like the Ohio State Model except that the names of the leader behavior components are different. Task/directive behavior parallels initiating structure, and relationship/support behavior parallels consideration.

FIGURE 5.3   Situational Leadership Theory

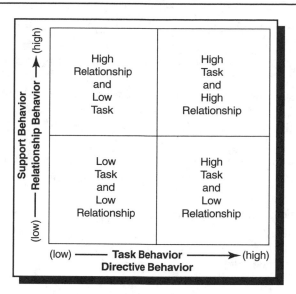

Note. The source of the figure is Hersey, P., Blanchard, K., & Johnson, D. (2008). Management of organizational behavior: Leading human resources (9th ed., p. 104). Upper Saddle River, NJ: Prentice-Hall,. Reprinted by permission of Prentice-Hall, Inc.

The four quadrants in the Ohio State Model and in Situational Leadership can be explained as follows (Bass, 2008; Bass & Stogdill, 1990; Hersey et al., 2008; Kreitner & Kinicki, 2010).

Quadrant 1. High Structure/High Task and Low Consideration/ Low Relationships

A leader primarily defines the task, explains to the group each person's responsibility, and states when tasks should be done. One-way communication characterizes the leader's behavior even though the low relationship's behavior should be observable. The low relationship's behavior is simply respect and warmth toward another person and positive reinforcement after a goal is completed. No group decision making is included in this style—the leader is in full control of the followers in directing how the task is to be accomplished.

Quadrant 2. High Structure/High Task and High Consideration/ High Relationships

A leader balances concern for the intricacies of getting a task accomplished with a concern about the beliefs, desires, and needs of the group. The leader might define a goal, designate what needs to be done and who has specific responsibilities, and invite questions or reactions. The leader's original plan may or may not be altered given the followers' reactions. In this style of leadership, the leader is still in control of task accomplishment, but group interaction and preferences begin to enter into the communications.

Quadrant 3. High Consideration/High Relationships and Low Structure/Low Task

In this style, the leader's primary concern is not the task and its various intricacies. Rather, concern is for the process, for getting the group to work together effectively to accomplish the task. The leader still has some control over how the group accomplishes the task. In this style, for example, a leader might define the problem and ask the group members to make further decisions about how they will work together to accomplish the task.

Quadrant 4. Low Structure/Low Task and Low Consideration/ Low Relationships

The leader maintains a low profile in this style, permitting followers to function within previously defined limits. At times, the leader may be available for consultation, to give direction, or for positive reinforcement. Such interaction is not planned on a regular basis, but rather occurs as the need arises. Information concerning progress in goal accomplishment may be requested by the leader at any time. Followers may also ask the leader for assistance or an opinion whenever necessary. This leader behavior style is delegation because control of task accomplishment is predominantly shifted from the leader to the follower(s).

The Leadership Grid®

Blake and Mouton (1985) developed the original Managerial Grid (see Figure 5.4) and applied it to nursing leadership (Blake, Mouton, & Tapper, 1981). The Managerial Grid was later renamed The Leadership Grid by Blake and McCanse (1991). The Leadership Grid has five styles of leadership based on a combination of concern for production and concern for people. The scale for each component moves from 1 (*low*) to 9 (*high*) and is shown in Figure 5.4. The five leadership styles are described as follows:

> *Authority-Obedience* (9,1). The leader assumes a position of power by arranging work conditions efficiently and in such a way that human elements interfere minimally.

> *Team Management* (9,9).* People are committed to accomplishing a task, group members are interdependent, and everyone holds a "common stake." Relationships of trust, respect, and equality characterize the work climate.

---

*Research by Blake and Mouton (1985) determined that managers prefer the team (9,9) style.

FIGURE 5.4   The Leadership Grid®

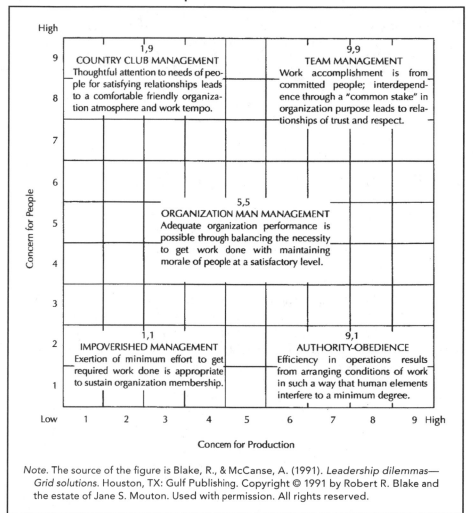

Note. The source of the figure is Blake, R., & McCanse, A. (1991). *Leadership dilemmas—Grid solutions.* Houston, TX: Gulf Publishing. Copyright © 1991 by Robert R. Blake and the estate of Jane S. Mouton. Used with permission. All rights reserved.

Country Club Management (1,9). The leader pays thoughtful attention to the needs of group members and fosters a comfortable, friendly atmosphere and work tempo.

Impoverished Management (1,1). The leader exerts minimal effort in accomplishing the required work.

Organization Management (Middle-of-the-Road) (5,5). The leader balances the behavior that is task-related while maintaining the morale of group members at a satisfactory level.

Comparison of Theories of Leadership

The three models of leadership discussed earlier are conceptually similar. Figure 5.5 merges the Ohio State Model (Bass, 2008; Bass & Stogdill, 1990; Fleishman, 1973), Situational Leadership (Hersey et al., 2008), The Leadership Grid (Blake & McCanse, 1991), and the three common styles of leadership. It is evident that the various theories presented in this chapter converge on one another. As previously stated but worthy of repeating, this observance enhances the validity of all of the presented theories.

DETERMINING APPROPRIATE LEADER BEHAVIOR STYLE*

Leader behavior responds to the environmental diagnosis of self, the system, and the task plus applied leader behavior theory. Leadership and followership are strongly related. As Tanoff and Barlow (2002) noted, they are the "same animal, [with] different spots" (p. 157). Diagnosis of the task will be discussed in Chapter 6. In this current chapter, a bridge will join the diagnosis of the system and the selection of the appropriate leader behavior style. This bridge becomes the most important element in determining leader behavior at the beginning of goal accomplishment. Self-diagnosis, which was discussed in Chapter 3, is information for the leader concerning what needs to be done or thought about so that one can actually behave according to the theory-specified leader behavior style that is theoretically the best place to begin goal accomplishment in a particular situation.

The leader behavior that will be used as the example in applying a system diagnosis in this section is the Ohio State Model, shown in Figure 5.2. It should also be evident from Figure 5.5 that other leader behavior styles may be preferential to the reader and totally appropriate to use. Once someone understands how to choose the best leader behavior style after applying the system diagnosis, it is possible to use the leader behavior theory of choice with ease. Therefore, one leader behavior theory will be used at this time. Chapter 4 contained a discussion of six theories that can be used to diagnose a system (see Table 4.6). The Ohio State Model of leader behavior and six diagnostic theories are combined in Figure 5.6.

---

*This section grew from association with and teachings from Paul Hersey and Kenneth Blanchard at the University of Massachusetts, School of Education while I was their formal student—1972 to 1975—and remained an informal learner thereafter. It also stems from their books on management and leadership, the most recent one being Hersey et al. (2008).

FIGURE 5.5   Theories of Leadership: Ohio State Model (Bass, 2008; Bass
& Stogdill, 1990; Fleischman, 1973), Situational Leadership
(Hersey, Blanchard, & Johnson, 2008), The Leadership Grid®
(Blake & McCanse (1991), and Common Leader Behavior
Styles

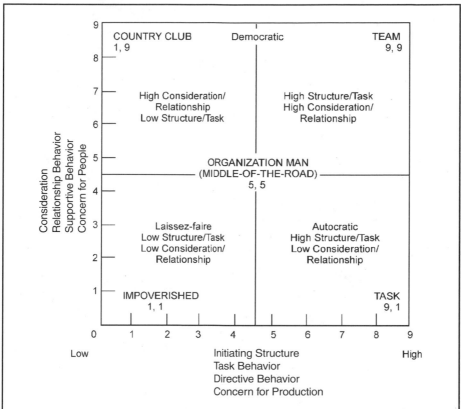

Note. The sources for the theories are as follows.

Bass, B. M. (2008). *The Bass handbook of leadership: Theory, research, & managerial applications* (4th ed.). New York, NY: Free Press.

Bass, B., & Stogdill, R. (1990). *Bass and Stogdill's handbook of leadership: Theory, research, and managerial applications* (3rd ed.). New York, NY: Free Press.

Blake, R., & McCanse, A. (1991). *Leadership dilemmas—Grid solutions.* Houston, TX: Gulf Publishing.

Fleischman, E. (1973). Twenty years of consideration and structure. In E. Fleischman & J. G. Hunt (Eds.), *Current developments in the study of leadership: A centennial event symposium held at Southern Illinois University at Carbondale.* Carbondale, IL: Southern Illinois University Press.

Hersey, P., Blanchard, K., & Johnson, D. (2001). *Management of organizational behavior: Leading human resources* (8th ed.). Upper Saddle River, NJ: Prentice-Hall.

Hersey, P., Blanchard, K., & Johnson, D. (2008). *Management of organizational behavior: Leading human resources* (9th ed.). Upper Saddle River, NJ: Prentice-Hall.

The figure was adapted from Hersey, Blanchard, and Johnson, (2001).

FIGURE 5.6   Theories for Diagnosing a System and Determining Appropriate Leader Behavior

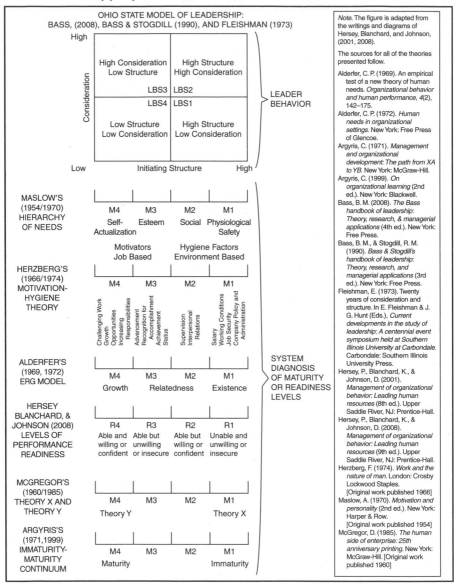

The theories used to diagnose the system read in progression from right to left in Figure 5.6. In other words, the lowest level of development is on the right side and the highest level of development is on the left side. Also, leader behavior style numbers (LBS1, LBS2, LBS3, and LBS4) are placed in the four leader behavior quadrants, moving counter-clockwise.

To determine the appropriate leader behavior style given a system's diagnosis, the bottom part of Figure 5.6 (system diagnosis) must be bridged to the top part of the figure (leader behavior). Suppose that the task is to change from a team approach to a primary care model with 24-hour responsibility as the model of nursing care delivery on one nursing unit. The leader may apply the theory of Hersey et al. (2008) for diagnosing the performance readiness level of the people in a system regarding their ability, willingness, and confidence in accomplishing a goal.

Following the previous example further, suppose the modal performance readiness level of the system is designated as performance readiness level 1 (R1). The group, therefore, is predominantly unable and unwilling or insecure to carry out the task. The numbers in the theories to diagnose the system and the numbers in the leadership behavior model should be paired. Therefore, R1 level of performance readiness corresponds directly to LBS1. To accomplish the task, therefore, the leader's best bet is to begin the process of goal accomplishment by behaving according to LBS1, high structure and low consideration. This leader behavior style is the pivot on which alternate solutions and the ultimate recommended actions are based *in the beginning of the journey toward task accomplishment*—in the movement from actual to optimal.

In the example given, task behavior from the leader becomes paramount at this point in time. The leader must develop a strategy that gives people knowledge about the 24-hour primary care model and lets people know their responsibilities. In other words, the leader must take full responsibility for getting this task accomplished at this point in time.

The diagnosis and designation of a leader behavior style gives the leader a place to start—a place that, according to research, has the highest probability for success. Once a start has been made, the changing maturity or readiness of the system should be reflected in the leader's behavior, either moving forward one quadrant (growth) or backward one quadrant (regression).

Recalling the previously described example, if a leader started in LBS1 and found that the group was becoming more receptive to 24-hour primary care, the leader should gradually change from LBS1 to LBS2, high structure and high consideration. In LBS2, group interaction is started, but the leader still maintains control of task accomplishment. If a leader is in LBS2 and finds that the group is regressing in performance readiness, that is, becoming less willing to carry responsibility for the task, then a leader would have to move back to LBS1.

The stepwise move from LBS1 to LBS4 represents a gradual decrease in leader control concerning how the group accomplishes the goal and a gradual increase in follower control concerning the process of goal accomplishment. The opposite stepwise move, LBS4 to LBS1, represents increased leader control and decreased follower control. A leader must move forward or backward gradually—one small step at a time, giving people guidance that is needed in order to get a job done according to an action plan.

Determination of the appropriate leader behavior style is necessary before the leader develops solutions to a problem or goal. Once in the leader behavior model, the leader moves forward one quadrant or backward one quadrant in response to the growth or the regression of the system in relation to accomplishing the task. The speed with which leader behavior movement occurs is variable, depending solely on the system.

The goal of the leader is to move the system so that they require LBS4— low structure and low consideration—from right to left using Figure 5.6. Remember, the right side of Figure 5.6 represents immaturity or lack of readiness, and the left side represents maturity or readiness. When a system is mature, it can monitor itself and accomplish the task. The leader can then delegate to the system and be free to work toward getting another task accomplished. Delegation occurs only in LBS4.

One simple example has been used to show how to bridge the system diagnosis with the leader behavior that should be used as the pivot for solutions to a problem. The steps in the example were

1. *Determine the system diagnosis* using one or more theories, depending on preference and ease in application;
2. *Pair the maturity or readiness number with the same leader behavior style number* to determine where leader behavior should begin; and then
3. *Move one leader behavior style forward or one leader behavior style backward,* depending on the growth or regression of the system in relation to task accomplishment. The leader's goal is ultimately to have the system require LBS4.

Now that the basics for determining the appropriate leader behavior style have been presented, examples from each theory or combination of theories will be discussed. A case example in Chapter 7 will amplify this discussion, and Urban City Hospital, an experiential learning activity at the end of Part II, can be used for practice in applying the content that has been presented.

It is most unlikely that a person or a group can be diagnosed as mature using one theory and immature using another theory, given the same task. A leader makes a decision based on an individual's predominant need. If a follower is predominantly motivated to achieve at an esteem level according to Maslow (1954/1970, 1954/1987), then it is most unlikely that he or she would be able but unwilling or insecure when the theory by Hersey et al. (2008) is applied, or primarily concerned with working conditions when using Herzberg's (1966/1974, 1982) theory, or passive and dependent according to Argyris's (1971, 1999) theory.

The variety of theories that can be used to diagnose a follower or a system offers different aspects or descriptions of the same process—the development of a person from immaturity to maturity in solving a particular problem or accomplishing a specific goal. For this reason they can all be applied toward the same purpose. Each theory should offer information through a different lens that can be helpful in building a specific strategy for goal accomplishment that *motivates* and *educates* people to accomplish an identified goal. Examples are provided in the diagnostic theories that follow.

Maslow's Hierarchy of Needs

Suppose that a new nurse with the title "nurse manager" joins a community care unit. After 6 months, the nurse manager wishes to streamline the charting system, eradicating any routine nurses' notes. This need is based on feedback from the staff. The system is composed of the entire staff—ten registered nurses. After individually diagnosing each nurse on ability to accomplish the task, the modal level of maturity is at the esteem level on Maslow's (1954/1970, 1954/1987) hierarchy. Performance appraisals and observed data suggest that the nurses are diligent, independent, motivated to achieve, and like to be noticed for the quality and quantity of work that is accomplished.

Using Figure 5.6, esteem is M3; the corresponding leader behavior style is high consideration and low structure—LBS3. Strategies for accomplishing the task, therefore, should focus on getting the group working together on the problem. The leader, for example, could convene the group, broadly state the issue based on comments received from the group, and facilitate the group's work in further specifying the problem and developing solutions.

Maslow's (1954/1970, 1954/1987) theory is predominantly used to diagnose motivational needs. It is best used in combination with another diagnostic theory to diagnose educational needs.

Herzberg's Motivation–Hygiene Theory

An acute-care hospital unit admits approximately three newly diagnosed clients with diabetes per week. No computerized diabetic teaching program has been formalized. The manager has been on the unit one year. The unit has registered nurses, licensed practical nurses, nurse's aides, and orderlies on staff. The goal, therefore, is to develop a formal, computerized diabetic teaching program. The system involves only the registered nurses at the point of drafting the program.

The manager assesses the system's ability to carry out the task and finds that members are often talking enthusiastically together about the idea and have knowledge about diabetic teaching; all want to be leaders in the process. They are pushing to plan the program over dinners and after working hours. Developing a computerized program, however, is new.

The system described in the previous paragraph can be diagnosed as M2, because its modal focus is on interpersonal relations and supervision, according to Herzberg's (1966/1974, 1982) motivation–hygiene theory. The leader should start behaving in LBS2, high structure and high consideration, and be alert for the ability of the group to become able to control how the goal is further accomplished. If the leader believes that the group is able, then a gradual move into LBS3 is appropriate, thereby providing reinforcement for the group's work and some structure as needed. The manager would then function simply as a group member, letting the group establish its own informal leader and structure itself. The manager, however, would still be involved. In LBS3, the manager predominantly provides support, reinforcement, and guidance.

Alderfer's ERG Model

A group of nurses want to set up a party for all personnel on their unit, including all shifts of personnel. They decide to have it on July 4th in the hospital cafeteria and garden. The party line is that everyone would love the celebration because they could bring spouses, partners, and children—sharing the holiday with their colleagues and families. Who will set up the party and food, however, is not known, and no one seems to be taking charge.

Using Alderfer's (1969, 1972) ERG Model, the group of people is functioning with relatedness needs in priority—M2 or M3. Because the application of theories in Figure 5.6 suggests either LBS2 or LBS3 would be appropriate, the leader should begin with LBS2. This style allows the leader to keep more control than does LBS3, and the leader can move out of it quickly when the group becomes able and confident. It is always better to hold on to control and let go of the control gradually rather than start out with less control and take control back. The former movement from one leader behavior style forward to another usually is viewed as a positive behavior from the leader, whereas the latter movement backward often can be seen as a negative, punitive behavior from the leader.

Hersey, Blanchard, and Johnson's Levels of Performance Readiness

Nursing care plans are not being done fully on all clients and an audit from an accrediting organization is six months away. Care plans are supposed to be written, computerized, and updated by the nurses in charge on all shifts. The charge nurse on the evening shift should make the initial nursing assessment following admission of the client.

The manager decides to start the process of goal accomplishment with the three evening charge nurses. Using the theory developed by Hersey et al. (2008), the system is diagnosed as able but unwilling—R3. Rationale for this decision is that the charge nurses have each worked on the unit a minimum of three years, they all have had formal education that taught the nursing process, they have previously written excellent care plans, they are all computer savvy, and they know that full care plans should be written on all clients in a timely, appropriate sequence.

High consideration and low structure, LBS3, is the appropriate style to use for an R3 system diagnosis. Since the charge nurses in this example know what they are supposed to do, telling them in a highly structured style initially would probably only make them defensive, possibly making them hold more tightly on the reins that kept them from doing the care plans as always required. It is necessary first to find out why they are unwilling to do the nursing care plans and then work from there. This involves two-way communication, which is high consideration. Once a manager knows why the charge nurses are unwilling, solutions to these causes must be sought. Once the unwillingness is relieved, then the nurses should be both able and willing. It must be noted, nevertheless, that if LBS3 does not work, then the leader must move back into LBS2, using more structure to be sure that the care plans are written according to expectations.

McGregor's Theory X and Theory Y

Suppose a director of an inservice education for nursing must set up an orientation program for six new baccalaureate nurses who have just graduated and will take their board examinations within four weeks to become licensed registered nurses. They were hired as graduate staff nurses. The director must plan the program without having met the new nurses.

What would be safe to assume about the maturity level of the graduates in this example using cues from McGregor's (1960/1985, 1960/2006) Theory X and Theory Y? It would be helpful for the director to think back to how he or she felt in the situation. One's first position after graduation is likely to be a high-stress state, promoting unsafe feelings and a need for direction—definitely on the Theory X side at an M1 level. The director should therefore be high in structure and low in consideration—LBS1. A detailed plan of activities should provide knowledge of the environment, practical experience with supervision, and clear expectations of the graduates. The director should be warm and caring but be the guide and leader in satisfying the graduates' needs for structure. At the same time, the director must be acutely alert for signs of growth and confidence from the new graduates. When growth is evident, a gradual move by the leader to LBS2 is indicated.

Argyris's Immaturity–Maturity Continuum

The director of nursing services needs three nurses from the intensive care unit as well as the physician intensivist to review and update the emergency resuscitation plan for the hospital. The nurse manager of the unit posts a notice on the desk asking each shift to nominate a full-time nurse who would be willing to serve.

In this example, the nurse manager's behavior should be low structure and low consideration—LBS4. This choice was based on the following data about the nurses and the physician intensivist, applying Argyris's (1971, 1999) theory: the nurses (a) are all equal in ability, (b) have worked on the unit a minimum of three years, (c) are flexible and effectively meet the demands of a situation, (d) are all able to assume the role of charge nurse, and (e) are all insightful. Further, the physician intensivist is an expert. Given these data, the director can assume that the group is at a mature point on Argyris's continuum—M4.

DISCUSSION OF APPLIED LEADER BEHAVIOR THEORIES

The initial determination for the appropriate leader behavior style is the leader's best bet at the start of goal accomplishment (Fiedler, 1987; Vecchio, 1997). It has the highest probability for motivating people to accomplish the task. How one operates within the style, considering that it can be interpreted broadly, depends on the particular needs of the group that were identified during the diagnosis. Vaughn (2003) referred to needs as motivators. These particulars are then used in the alternative solutions and recommended action. The umbrella leader behavior style remains constant until the system matures or regresses. Then movement is only one quadrant forward or backward—in a systematic, gradual, stepwise progression or regression. In reality, movement through a leader behavior quadrant should be a gradual, step-wise journey either giving more control to followers or diminishing follower control, depending on what is needed to be sure that the goal is accomplished.

A leader never jumps from LBS1 to LBS3, for example. Why? Because the leader behavior model is designed from learning theory, which says that reinforcing behavior increases the probability that the behavior will continue. Because the task is the most important concern for the leader, it is primary in LBS1. It is reinforced in LBS2, but consideration for the individual employee or group becomes equal in importance. If the task is not getting accomplished, the manager must move back to LBS1. Should LBS1 be successful, reinforcement of the task behavior would not occur if one jumped to LBS3.

Another example would be an employee to whom you have always delegated responsibilities (LBS4). Noticing that quality in outcome is slipping, the manager should move to LBS3 and use high consideration to discover why quality is slipping. Jumping back to any other style initially would be inappropriate at this time because the leader is aware that the employee knows what to do. High structure therefore would not be the leader's best behavior unless LBS3 failed to work and minimum quality standards were in jeopardy. Then the leader would need to become firmer and more structured, gradually moving back to LBS2 and then to LBS1, if indicated.

The leader is advised that if any serious doubt exists concerning the system's readiness or maturity, then it is better to hold on to control until data are observed suggesting that followers are mature enough to carry effectively the responsibility that comes with control. A manager's move from LBS2 to LBS3, for example, is usually interpreted as a positive, rewarding change. Should a manager relinquish control too quickly and then have to take it back, such as a quick move from LBS3 to LBS2, is often interpreted as punishment or leader dishonesty. Both interpretations are negative forces that may make goal accomplishment difficult because of the defensiveness that they engender in participants. Sometimes, however, a move from LBS3 to LBS2 is necessary.

Another issue that is often raised concerns feelings that leader behavior must be consistent. Consistency must be clarified by saying that leader behavior consistently responds to the context and system of resources. Leader behavior, therefore, changes as indicated from diagnoses relative to a particular problem or goal. Experience has shown that employees respond negatively to changes in a leader's affect and tone but not to caring and respectful changes in how one carries out leader responsibilities. By using a situational approach, a manager essentially is giving employees what they need. Moodiness, however, is not what employees need—so diagnose and know yourself and your own motives before you act; be consistent in selecting the appropriate leader behavior to begin goal accomplishment; and always be consistent in treating followers with respect, warmth, and genuineness.

THEORY Z LEADERSHIP

A leader behavior application that is worthy of understanding is Ouchi's (1981/1993) Theory Z, considering current culturally diverse environments in health care. Theory Z is a concept that represents management behavior in successful Japanese organizations. Smith, Reinow, and Reid (1984) contrasted typical Theory Z Japanese management practices with those routinely used in the United States. Japanese concepts involve the culture in Japan where work environments are described as having permanent employment, few evaluations and promotions, non-specialized career options, implicit managerial control, collective decision making (quality circles), work group responsibilities, and holistic concern for employees. Management practices in the United States do not seem to match exactly. For example, the emphasis in the United States is on specialization, accelerated evaluation and promotion, explicit or implicit organizational control, individual accountability, financially driven employment, and delegation of authority to individuals when indicated.

Although much has been written on applying Theory Z practices in the United States, it is not considered to be the answer in all managerial problems, even though some adaptations may be beneficial (Smith et al., 1984). Theory Z practices predominantly incorporate democratic approaches to leadership—LBS2, high relationships or consideration and high task or structure; or LBS3, high relationships or consideration and low task or structure. Use of only these two styles assumes that followers are all at moderate levels of maturity, readiness, or performance readiness and should be kept at those levels. The authors cited in this paragraph did not believe that those assumptions about followers hold in Western societies; however, they may be appropriate for some Eastern-type corporate cultures. This author agrees. Techniques that are used from Theory Z should therefore be carefully evaluated so that leader behavior matches the needs of the majority of followers.

TRANSACTIONAL AND TRANSFORMATIONAL LEADERSHIP

The leader behavior theories previously presented in this chapter mainly focus on the process of leading—*how* managers motivate followers to accomplish goals or solve problems. This is considered *transactional leadership* (Kreitner & Kinicki, 2010). It involves behaviors between managers and followers; it involves interpersonal communications between or among people. In short, it involves transactions.

Transformational leadership (Burns, 2004) is a philosophic extension of the process of leader behavior. It describes the leader who creates a vision for followers and then promotes the energetic movement toward making that vision a reality. Bilchik (2001) referred to transformational leaders as inspiring followers. According to Kreitner and Kinicki (2010), transformational leaders create charisma, share inspirational messages, support their visions nonverbally with deep feeling, display confidence in themselves and followers, and extend themselves beyond usual responsibilities. These leaders are often referred to as *charismatic leaders*. They produce change in an organization because they transform employees from self-focus into accomplishing for the organization and bonding together with fellow employees.

It must be noted that transformational leadership, according to Burns, (2004) is related to an individual's personality—it is more subjective than other leadership theories presented in this chapter. For example, Eagly, Johannesen-Schmidt, and Engen (2003) suggested that there were small differences in transformational leadership behaviors between men and women. Charismatic or transformational leaders produce electricity in an organization and between and among members of the people that they lead. They are dedicated to their work and are energizing to others—their electricity is more catching than a common cold and certainly is better for the organization and the people who work in the system. Transformational leadership has been shown to be more effective than transactional leadership (Gellis, 2001).

Transformational leadership embellishes all of the leader behavior theories presented in this chapter. In a sense, it is like frosting on a four- or five-layer cake. The frosting touches and covers all of the layers. The process for selecting the best style of leadership to begin goal accomplishment remains as presented earlier in this chapter. However, the energy of transformational leadership can be added to any leader behavior style, thereby enriching any behavioral style that is theoretically appropriate for a group working toward goal accomplishment.

LEADER EFFECTIVENESS

A leader's behavior or influence over an individual or group can be either successful or unsuccessful, as is evident in Figure 5.7. The specific leader behavior used by the manager can be called successful if the desired goal is reached (approximately or exactly). Conversely, if the desired goal is not

FIGURE 5.7   Bass's (1960) Successful and Effective Leadership Outcome Evaluation

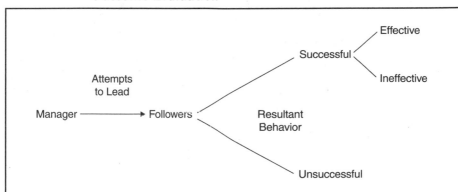

Note. This figure is based on the writings of Bass, B. M. (1960). *Leadership, psychology, and organizational behavior* (pp. 90, 448). New York, NY: Harper & Brothers. It is in the Public Domain.

This figure is adapted from Hersey, P., Blanchard, K., & Johnson, D. (2008). *Management of organizational behavior: Leading human resources* (9th ed., p. 115). Upper Saddle River, NJ: Prentice-Hall,

See also Bass, B. M. (2008). *The Bass handbook of leadership: Theory, research & managerial applications* (4th ed.). New York, NY: Free Press; and Bass, B. M. & Stogdill, R. M. (1990). *Bass and Stogdill's handbook of leadership: Theory, research, and managerial applications* (3rd ed.). New York, NY: Free Press.

reached within an acceptable range, then the leader behavior can be called unsuccessful (Hersey et al., 2008). When leader behavior fails to influence an individual or a group to achieve a specified goal, then the manager must evaluate what occurred using the steps of the management process and redesign the strategy for goal accomplishment.

When leader behavior is successful, success can range from very ineffective to very effective, depending on how followers feel about the leader's behavior (Hersey et al., 2008). For example, if the leader used personal power to influence followers, thereby making goal accomplishment a personally rewarding experience for the followers, then the leader's behavior is both successful (the goal was accomplished) and very effective (the followers feel terrific about their accomplishments).

On the other hand, followers can be coerced to accomplish by a manager who uses position power, close supervision, and rewards and punishments. Even though the leader's behavior was successful, the leader's behavior is also very ineffective if the followers were unhappy and carrying negative feelings toward the leader. Generally, when leader behavior is successful and effective, the followers are self-motivated to accomplish the goal even when the manager is not present. When leader behavior is successful and ineffective, followers often relax the drive to accomplish when the manager is absent (Hersey et al., 2008).

ORGANIZATIONAL EFFECTIVENESS

The effectiveness of a leader's behavior should be determined on the basis of its relationship to the growth of an organization during a specified period of time (Hersey et al., 2008). Likert (1961) identified three sets of variables: causal variables, intervening variables, and end result or output variables. Hersey et al. (2008) added short-term and long-term goal accomplishment.

Organizational effectiveness should be a result of evaluating all four sets of variables to decrease the halo-horn effect, which was discussed in Chapter 3. Even though subjectivity is an element in any evaluation, looking at separate variables usually decreases the amount of subjectivity that can bias the evaluation. The following variables are used to evaluate the effectiveness of the organization over time.

Causal Variables

Causal variables have influence on the developments within an organization, including results or accomplishments (Hersey et al., 2008). These variables are under management's control; they can be changed or altered.

Causal variables refer to the following:

1. Appropriateness of leader behavior to the system's level of maturity or readiness;
2. Accuracy of the system's diagnosis;
3. Appropriate involvement of the system in decision making;
4. Effectiveness of the organization's philosophy and objectives in guiding its constituents; and
5. Use of available technology in a particular organization.

Intervening Variables

Intervening variables refer to the resources (people) within an organization. Likert (1961) asserted that they represent the internal state of the organization. Intervening variables refer to employees' commitment, motivation, morale, and skills in leadership, communication, and conflict resolution (Hersey et al., 2008).

End Result, or Output, Variables

End result variables, also known as output variables, represent the achievements of the organization. Output variables are quantifiable and include production (output or services), costs, earnings, turnover, management-union relations, and so forth (Hersey et al., 2008; Likert, 1961).

Short-Term and Long-Term Goals

This aspect involves short-term and long-term planning. A short-term perspective refers to immediate output. Long-term goals refer to the future development of the organization (Hersey et al., 2008). Managers tend to be evaluated on long-term goal achievement, which takes time to reach. Effective management, however, should be benchmarked at different steps along the journey of goal accomplishment. Both short-term and long-term goal accomplishment must be recognized and evaluated.

SUMMARY

Leadership has many definitions, all of which converge on several points. Leadership involves using communication processes to influence the activities of an individual or of a group toward the attainment of a goal in a unique situation. Democratic, autocratic, and laissez-faire are common labels for leader behavior styles. Even though the democratic style is often connoted as a best style, each style is appropriate, depending on the unique situation.

Management theorists have designated two major components of leader behavior: one refers to getting the task accomplished and the other is concerned with interpersonal behavior. Theorists have different labels for these components. The Ohio State Model of Leadership has initiating structure and consideration as its components. Structure refers to a leader's attempt to organize and define the roles and activities of group members. Consideration involves two-way communication—establishing trust, openness, respect, warmth, and effective interpersonal relationships between and among group members.

Several leadership models were presented, discussed, and compared. All of the models are appropriate to apply in health care and nursing systems. The Ohio State Model was applied in this chapter. The appropriate leader behavior style for a given system is determined by diagnosing the system's level of maturity or readiness and then pairing the maturity or readiness level with the parallel leader behavior style. This results in a place for the leader to start the journey toward goal accomplishment and represents the pivot upon which solutions for solving the problem are based.

A leader then changes from one style to another, depending upon the growth or regression of the system. The ultimate goal of the leader should be to facilitate in (a) getting the tasks accomplished and (b) moving the group members to the highest level of maturity or readiness and then delegating to them. Transformational leadership is an energetic and philosophic leader behavior—almost a type of leader personality—that can be applied to all leader behavior styles.

Leader behavior can move on a range from successful to unsuccessful. If successful, it can further range from very ineffective to very effective. The effectiveness of an organization over time should be evaluated by studying the stimuli (causal variables) that act upon a person or group (intervening variables) to create responses (output variables) (Hersey et al., 2008). Short- and long-term goals must also be considered.

● ● ● REVIEW CONCEPTS AND QUESTIONS

1. Define the difference between management and leadership.
2. Specify the common leader behavior styles and explain how they relate to the components of leader behavior.
3. Explain the differences and similarities among the three dominant leadership models.

4. Using one or more theories to diagnose follower readiness or maturity to accomplish a hypothetical goal, explain how to determine appropriate leader behavior using Situational Leadership Theory.
5. How does transformational leadership relate to the other leadership models presented in this chapter?
6. Explain leader effectiveness and the difference between being successful versus unsuccessful, and between being effective and ineffective.
7. How is a leader's effectiveness evaluated?

● ● ● SUGGESTED ASSIGNMENTS

1. Use the hypothetical management case for study developed in Chapter 4 as well as the diagnostic analysis done on the group's player's ability and willingness to work as a group toward attaining the goal. For the purpose of this chapter, take that diagnosis and apply it to a Leader Behavior Model of choice. Explain rationale for the decision and analyze your journey through goal accomplishment . . . specifically, what information or data you would need to observe to suggest that you should be moving from one quadrant of leadership to another.
2. Using the work begun in Chapter 4, specifically the analysis of the learner's home environment and a group project, refocus on the goal as well as on the follower's performance readiness levels. Using Situational Leadership, identify the best leader behavior style that you would use on friends and/or family to begin to motivate and educate them to accomplish the specified goal. Again, what follower behaviors would suggest that you should move forward one quadrant or backwards one quadrant? Write out behaviorally what you would do in the leader behavior quadrant that should begin your journey with followers toward goal accomplishment.

REFERENCES

Alderfer, C. P. (1969). An empirical test of a new theory of human needs. *Organizational behavior and human performance*, 4(2), 142–175.
Alderfer, C. P. (1972). *Human needs in organizational settings*. New York, NY: Free Press of Glencoe.
Argyris, C. (1971). *Management and organizational development: The path from XA to YB*. New York, NY: McGraw-Hill.
Argyris, C. (1999). *On organizational learning* (2nd ed.). New York, NY: Blackwell.
Bass, B. M. (1960). *Leadership, psychology, and organizational behavior*. New York, NY: Harper.
Bass. B. M. (2008). *The Bass handbook of leadership: Theory, research, & managerial applications* (4th ed.). New York, NY: Free Press.

Bass, B. M., & Stogdill, R. M. (1990). *Bass & Stogdill's handbook of leadership: Theory, research, and managerial applications* (3rd ed.). New York, NY: Free Press.

Bilchik, G. S. (2001). Leaders who inspire. *Health Forum Journal, 44*(2), 10–15.

Blake, R. R., & McCanse, A. A. (1991). *Leadership dilemmas—Grid solutions.* Houston, TX: Gulf Publishing.

Blake, R. R., & Mouton, J. S. (1985). *The Managerial Grid III: A new look at the classic that has boosted productivity and profits for thousands of corporations worldwide* (3rd ed.). Houston, TX: Gulf Publishing.

Blake, R. R., & Mouton, J. S, & Tapper, M. (1981). *Grid approaches for managerial leadership in nursing.* St. Louis, MO: Mosby.

Burns, J. M. (2004). *Transforming leadership: A new pursuit of happiness.* New York, NY: Atlantic Monthly Press.

Eagly, A. H., Johannesen-Schmidt, M. C., & Engen, M. L. (2003). Transformational, transactional, and laissez-faire leadership style: A meta-analysis comparing women and men. *Psychological Bulletin, 129*(4), 569–591.

Fiedler, F. (1987). When to lead, when to stand back. *Psychology Today, 21*(9), 26–27.

Fleishman, E. (1973). Twenty years of consideration and structure. In E. Fleishman & J. G. Hunt (Eds.), *Current developments in the study of leadership: A centennial event symposium held at Southern Illinois University at Carbondale.* Carbondale, IL: Southern Illinois University Press.

Gellis, Z. D. (2001). Social work perceptions of transformational and transactional leadership in health care. *Social Work Research, 25*(1), 17–25.

Giuliani, R. W., & Kurson, K. (2007). *Leadership.* New York, NY: Miramax Books.

Hersey, P., Blanchard, K., & Johnson, D. (2001). *Management of organizational behavior: Leading human resources* (8th ed.). Upper Saddle River, NJ: Prentice-Hall.

Hersey, P., Blanchard, K., & Johnson, D. (2008). *Management of organizational behavior: Leading human resources* (9th ed.). Upper Saddle River, NJ: Pearson Prentice Hall.

Herzberg, F. (1974). *Work and the nature of man.* London, England: Crosby Lockwood Staples. (Original work published 1966)

Herzberg, F. (1982). *The managerial choice: To be efficient or to be human* (Rev. ed.). Salt Lake City, UT: Olympus.

Hesselbein, F., & Cohen, P. M. (Eds.). (1999). *Leader to leader: Enduring insights on leadership from the Drucker Foundation's award winning journal.* San Francisco, CA: Jossey-Bass.

Kreitner, R., & Kinicki, A. (2010). *Organizational behavior* (9th ed.). New York, NY: McGraw-Hill/Irwin.

Likert, R. (1961). *New patterns of management.* New York, NY: McGraw-Hill.

Maslow, A. H. (1970). *Motivation and personality* (2nd ed.). New York, NY: Harper & Row. (Original work published 1954)

Maslow, A. H. (1987). *Motivation and personality* (3rd ed.). New York, NY: Harper & Row. (Original work published 1954, and later published 1970)

McGregor, D. (1985). *The human side of enterprise: 25th anniversary printing.* New York, NY: McGraw-Hill. (Original work published 1960)

McGregor, D. (2006). *The human side of enterprise: Annotated edition.* New York, NY: McGraw-Hill. (Original work published 1960)

Moiden, N. (2002). Evolution of leadership in nursing. *Nursing Management, 9*(7), 20–25.

Northouse, P. G. (2012). *Introduction to leadership concepts and practice* (2nd ed.). Thousand Oaks, CA: Sage.

Nowicki, M., & Summers, J. (2003). The benevolent autocrat: Is it the right fit for the times? *Healthcare Financial Management: Journal of the Healthcare Financial Management Association, 57*(10), 84.

Ouchi, W. G. (1993). *Theory Z: How American business can meet the Japanese challenge.* New York, NY: Avon. (Original work published 1981)

Porter-O'Grady, T., & Malloch, K. (2007). *Quantum leadership: A resource for healthcare innovation* (2nd ed.). Sudbury, MA: Jones and Bartlett.

Smith, H., Reinow, F., & Reid, R. (1984). Japanese management: Implications for nursing administration. *Journal of Nursing Administration, 14*(9), 33–39.

Tannenbaum, R., & Schmidt, W. H. (1973). How to choose a leadership pattern. *Harvard Business Review, 51*(3), 162–180. (Original work published 1958)

Tannenbaum, R., & Schmidt, W. H. (2009). *How to choose a leadership pattern (Harvard business beview classic).* Boston, MA: Harvard Business Review. (Original work published 1958, and later published 1973)

Tanoff, G. F., & Barlow, C. B. (2002). Leadership and followership: Same animal, different spots? *Consulting Psychology Journal: Practice and Research, 54*(3), 157–165.

Vaughn, R. M. G. (2003). Motivators get creative. *Nursing Management, 34*(4), 12–13.

Vecchio, R. (1997). Situational leadership theory: An examination of a prescriptive theory. In R. P. Vecchio (Ed.), *Leadership: Understanding the dynamics of power and influence in organizations* (pp. 334–350). Notre Dame, IN: University of Notre Dame Press.

Welford, C. (2002). Transformational leadership in nursing: Matching theory to practice. *Nursing Management, 9*(4), 7–11.

Diagnosing the Task

◯ EXPECTED LEARNING OUTCOMES

- To gain knowledge of a decision-making theory that can be used to
  diagnose the task
- To understand six major types of decision-making styles
- To blend the diagnosis of followers and selection of appropriate
  beginning leader behavior with diagnosis of the task

Part II of this book is devoted to identifying the appropriate leader behavior to use in beginning the process of motivating and educating people in a system to accomplish an identified goal. This process involves diagnosing the environment—self, system, and task—and then applying leader behavior theory, as presented in Chapter 5.

Diagnosing self, presented in Chapter 3, is necessary in identifying the leader's personal point of view on the problem or goal and on the environment. Further, diagnosing one's personal leader behavior style is helpful to fit behavioral intent with what is generally automatic behavior that stems from one's own personality. Diagnosing self is a consciousness-raising experience with an intent of reducing leader bias and matching needed leader behavior with what is actually given to and perceived by followers.

Chapter 4 contains a discussion of theories that can be used to diagnose a system. Once a diagnosis is made, leader behavior theory is applied to determine the leader behavior style that has the highest probability for motivating and educating people to accomplish a task. This leader behavior style is the umbrella or pivot upon which problem solutions and actions should be based.

Chapter 5 contains a discussion about matching a system's diagnosis to a leader behavior theory of choice to know the theoretically best leader behavior style that should be used to begin the process of goal accomplishment. The reader should be aware that leader behavior preferably should always be on target with what followers need. There is, however, another variable that adds to the overall diagnosis, as shown in the following equation, which was presented earlier and is worthy of reinforcement:

Manager Behavior =
- Diagnosing the Organizational Environment
    — Self

    — Human Resources  Motivational Needs

    Educational Needs
    — Task
    — Situational Variables
    — Material Resources
- Plus Applying Leader Behavior Theory

Diagnosis of the task is the last segment of leader responsibilities that will be discussed in Part II of this book. It completed the equation that forms the basis for the core of how managers work. Remember, as stated previously in Chapter 4, situational variables and material resources are considered in the overall developing action plan and are thought of as an awareness of what a leader has in an environment—they are what has been given and what must be worked with at a particular point in time. Situational variables and material resources do not require a diagnosis as do self, human resources, and the task.

The task is an addition to a leader's diagnosis. The nature of tasks may require different leader behavior styles to have the most effective outcomes. Ideally, the suggested best leader behavior style of a task should match the selected best beginning leader behavior style for the followers who will be doing the task. So, please place aside what Part II has presented so far and continue to hold it as your theoretically best suggestions for how managers work. Then study the contents in this chapter and blend everything when you understand what is presented. Diagnosing the task is another important piece of information that can be placed in the leader's picture of information—it purports to increase your batting average for success in leading others to accomplish goals.

THE VROOM, YETTON, AND JAGO MANAGERIAL DECISION-MAKING MODEL

The conceptual framework for diagnosing the task is the Vroom, Yetton, and Jago (VYJ) managerial decision-making model (Vroom, 1973; Vroom & Jago, 1978, 1988; Vroom & Yetton, 1973). This decision-making model is another theory destroying the myth that managers who use democratic styles are "good" and those who do not are "bad." The decision process used by a manager in a situation should depend on the nature of the unique situation— the diagnosis of the environment (Donnelly, Gibson, & Ivancevich, 1998; Gatewood, Taylor, & Ferrell, 1995; Kreitner & Kinicki, 2010).

The VYJ model provides a means to diagnose tasks in determining the most appropriate leader behavior style for the manager to use in getting something accomplished. Although diagnosing the nature of the task should be only one of three determinants of leader behavior, the VYJ decision-making model is a powerful one that reports validity for its purpose (Field, 1982; Jago & Vroom, 1978; Vroom & Jago, 1978) and has been widely evident in the literature (Hersey, Blanchard, & Johnson, 2008; Lord, Hanges, & Godfrey, 2003; Marquis & Huston, 2012; Newstrom, 2011; Vroom, 2000, 2001, 2002).

A general guide for diagnosing the task can be depicted by the following equation (La Monica & Finch, 1977):

Effective decisions = a function of (quality + acceptance + time)

Quality refers to whether there are a number of possible solutions to the problem and some alternatives could result in better outcomes than others— a qualitative judgment on the best solution must be made. *Acceptance* is concerned with whether staff members must accept the problem's solution to eliminate the problem or achieve the goal—must the staff do anything? *Time* relates to how much time is available to work on the problem or accomplish the goal. The VYJ managerial decision-making model integrates answers to these three variables and suggests a decision-making style that has the highest probability for effectiveness. These results will be combined with other diagnoses from previous chapters in determining leader behavior.

Table 6.1 contains six different managerial decision styles. Read each one and then study the case in Box 6.1. Select the decision-making style that you would use if you were the manager in the case. Write your response in the space provided after the case.

TABLE 6.1   Management Decision Styles

TYPE	DESCRIPTION
AI	You solve the problem or make the decision yourself, using information available to you at that time.
AII	You obtain the necessary information from your subordinate(s), then decide on the solution to the problem yourself. You may or may not tell your subordinates what the problem is in getting the information from them. The role played by your subordinates in making the decision is clearly one of providing the necessary information to you, rather than generating or evaluating the alternative solutions.
CI	You share the problem with relevant subordinates individually, getting their ideas and suggestions without bringing them together as a group. Then you make the decision that may or may not reflect your subordinates' influence.
CII	You share the problem with your subordinates as a group, collectively obtaining their ideas and suggestions. Then you make the decision that may or may not reflect your subordinates' influence.
GII	You share a problem with your subordinates as a group. Together you generate and evaluate alternatives and attempt to reach agreement (consensus) on a solution. Your role is much like that of chair . . . You do not try to influence the group to adopt "your" solution, and you are willing to accept and implement any solution that has the support of the entire group.
DI	You delegate the problem to your subordinate(s) providing. . . [him, her, or them] with any relevant information that you possess, but giving. . .[him, her, or them] responsibility for solving the problem . . . You may or may not request . . . [him, her, or them] to tell you what solution . . . [has been] reached.

Note. The source of AI through GII is: Reprinted from "A New Look at Managerial Decision Making," by Victor H. Vroom, *Organizational Dynamics*, Spring, 1973, ©1973. Reproduced with permission from Elsevier. All rights reserved.

The source of DI is an: Excerpt from Table 2.1, "Decision Methods for Group and Individual Problems," from *Leadership and Decision-Making*, by Victor H. Vroom and Philip W. Yetton, © 1973. Reprinted by permission of the University of Pittsburgh Press (print edition and e-book edition). Used by permission of the University of Pittsburgh Press (online edition).

BOX 6.1

Case Example

You are an assistant director of nursing in a large city hospital. The management has recently put into effect, at your request and consultation, the [newly organized and computerized] unit manager system on two floors. This was expected to relieve the nurses of administrative responsibility, increase their abilities to provide quality care to clients, ensure that health assessments and care plans could be accomplished for every client, and lower the nursing budget. Quality health care and nursing care plans reflected the suggestions made by the hospital accreditors. To the surprise of everyone, yourself included, little of the plan has been realized. In fact, nurses are sitting in the conference room more, quality has maintained a status quo, and employees and patients are complaining more than ever.

You do not believe that there is anything wrong with the new system. You have had reports from other hospitals using it and they confirm this opinion. You . . . [also have] had representatives from institutions using the system talk with your nursing personnel, and the representatives report that your nurses have full knowledge of the system and their altered responsibilities.

You suspect that a few people may be responsible for the situation, but this view is not widely shared among your two supervisors and four head nurses. The failure has been variously attributed to poor training of the unit managers, lack of financial incentives, and poor morale. Clearly, this is an issue about which there is considerable depth of feeling within individuals and potential disagreement among your subordinates.

This morning you received a phone call from the nursing director. She had just talked with the hospital administrator and was calling to express her deep concern. She indicated that the problem was yours to solve in any way you think best, but she would like to know within a week what steps you plan to take.

You share your director's concern and know that the personnel involved are equally concerned. The problem is to decide what steps to take to rectify the situation.

Decision style you would use: _____

Note. The source of the case is La Monica, E., & Finch, F. (1977). Managerial decision-making. *Journal of Nursing Administration, 7*(5), 21. Reproduced with permission. This case was originally adapted into nursing from a business example. The original material was presented by Vroom, V. (1973). A new look at managerial decision-making. *Organizational Dynamics, 1*(4), 66–80.

As you have probably noted, the six managerial decision styles can be considered as a continuum. AI and AII are autocratic styles, CI and CII are consultative styles, and GII is a group decision-making style. Delegation (DI) has been discussed by Vroom and Yetton (1973) and Vroom and Jago (1988) as a style for use in a two-person superior or follower relationship; delegation is at the opposite end of the continuum from AI. These decision

FIGURE 6.1   Vroom, Yetton, and Jago's Decision Styles Combined
with the Ohio State Model of Leadership

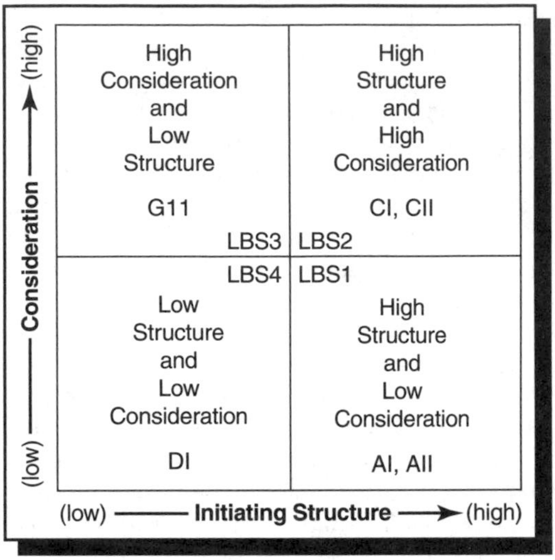

Note. The figure of the Ohio State Model of Leadership is adapted from: Hersey, P.,
Blanchard, K. H., & Johnson, D. (2008). *Management of organizational behavior: Leading
human resources* (9th ed., p. 81). Upper Saddle River, NJ: Pearson Prentice Hall. Reprinted
by permission of Pearson Prentice Hall.

The sources for the Ohio State Model of Leadership are as follows:

Bass, B. M. (2008). *The Bass handbook of leadership: Theory, research, & managerial
applications* (4th ed.). New York, NY: Free Press.
Bass, B. M., & Stogdill, R. M. (1990). *Bass and Stogdill's handbook of leadership: Theory,
research, and managerial applications* (3rd ed.). New York, NY: Free Press.
Fleishman, E. (1973). Twenty years of consideration and structure. In E. Fleishman &
J. G. Hunt (Eds.), *Current developments in the study of leadership: A centennial event
symposium held at Southern Illinois University of Carbondale.* Carbondale, IL: Southern
Illinois University Press.
The sources for the Vroom, Yetton, and Jago Decision Styles are as follows:
Vroom, V. (1973). A new look at managerial decision-making. *Organizational Dynamics,*
1(4), 66–80.
Vroom, V., & Jago, A. G. (1978). On the validity of the Vroom-Yetton model. *Journal of
Applied Psychology, 63*(2), 151–162.
Vroom, V., & Jago, A. G. (1988). *The new leadership: Managing participation in organiza-
tions.* Upper Saddle River, NJ: Prentice-Hall.
Vroom, V., & Yetton, P. (1973). *Leadership and decision-making.* Pittsburgh, PA: University
of Pittsburgh Press.

styles are paralleled with the Ohio State Model of Leadership, as shown in
Figure 6.1. Of course, they similarly would apply in the other leader behavior
models that are presented in Chapter 5. It must be noted that as a manager
moves from AI to GII, the amount of time involved in solving the problem or
in achieving the goal increases. This effect is because group interactions take
more time than autocratic behavior.

APPLICATION OF THE DECISION-MAKING MODEL

Now that your decision-making style has been selected for the case example from Box 6.1., the VYJ (Vroom, 1973; Vroom & Jago, 1978, 1988; Vroom & Yetton, 1973) model should be applied in diagnosing the task. Vroom (1973) and Vroom and Yetton (1973) developed the decision model using a tree format; it is commonly referred to as the *decision-making tree*, shown in Figure 6.2. This tree can be described as a series of questions that move through the situational parameters of the model (Chemers, 2000).

Notice that there are seven questions across the top of Figure 6.2. Questions A, B, and C refer to the variable of quality, and questions D through G refer to the variable of acceptance. Referring to the case in Box 6.1, it is necessary to start at the left of the model, Question A, and answer the question in a yes or no format. If the answer to Question A is "no," then follow the "no" line to the next node and answer the question on top of that node. Follow this format until the tree ends with a decision-making style. It should be noted that each successive question in the quality and acceptance sets of variables asks more specific information concerning the variable. This process is similar to programmed history taking when an answer of yes to "history of familial diabetes," for example, results in more specific questions concerning this matter being asked.

The decision model conceptually is communicating the following:

1.   If acceptance of decision by followers is crucial, then get the group involved in solving the problem.
2.   If quality is important, with expertise being a requirement, then find people who have the expertise and solve the problem with their input.
3.   When both quality and acceptance are required, then bring the experts and the group together for problem solving.

The purpose of the decision-making tree, however, is to integrate the variables of quality and acceptance and to suggest a decision-making style that will take the shortest amount of time, considering the requirements of the task. Time increases as one moves down is styles from AI to GII. Hence, if style CII is suggested at the end of the decision-making tree, quality and acceptance are important so one should not use styles AI, AII, or CI because the group would not be involved to the degree required in these styles. But one could use GII if the leader thought that the group was mature enough to solve the problem using that style *and* had the time available. The problem would be solved more quickly in style CII than in style GII.

Concluding simply, any decision-making style at or below the one indicated by the decision model in Table 6.1 is fine to use. More time, however, would be needed to solve the problem as the styles move downward.

FIGURE 6.2   Vroom's Decision Model (Tree)

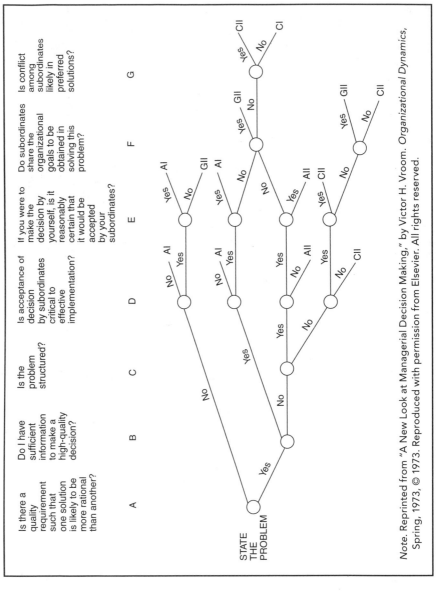

Decision-making styles above the one indicated by the decision model should not be used because the nature of the task requires more group interaction.

Let us walk through the case example from Box 6.1 using the decision-making tree from Figure 6.2. to see if Vroom (1973) and Vroom and Yetton (1973) agree with your choice for the best style to use given the nature of the task. Begin by starting at the left and answering Question A.

Question A: Quality—Yes

> There is quality requirement in this case. A number of possible solutions to the problem exist, and one could be better than another. There are several ways to solve this problem, and one way could result in more effective outcomes than another.
>
> Follow the "yes" line on the tree to the next node; look above it. Question B must be answered.

Question B: Manager's Information —No

> The assistant director obviously has neither the information nor the expertise to make a high-quality decision and to solve the problem.
>
> Follow the "no" line to the next node and answer the above further question on quality.

Question C: Structure—No

> This question requires explanation. A structured problem is one in which the decision is based on quantitative (objective) data, the location of those data is known, and the data can be obtained and retrieved. An unstructured problem has a subjective element. The decision is a qualitative assessment—a value judgment—and/or the location of the information is unknown or cannot be obtained. In the case example, information that is required for solving the problem is qualitative and its specific location is unknown.
>
> Follow the "no" line to the next node, look above the node, and answer Question D.

Question D: Acceptance—Yes

> Another way of asking Question D is: Do followers have to do anything in order for the problem to be solved? In this case, acceptance is critical. The followers must implement the new unit management system in order for the goal to be reached. One possible reason for why the system is failing may be that personnel were not involved in the initial planning.
>
> Follow the "yes" line to the next node and answer Question E.

Question E: Prior Probability of Acceptance—No

An autocratic decision in this case probably would not be tolerated.

Follow the "no" line to the next node and answer Question F located above the node.

Question F: Goal Congruence—Yes

Another way of asking this question is: If the problem is solved, will it benefit the people working in the environment? Obviously, the people will benefit in this case if the unit manager system works. The resulting style that is suggested by the model is GII. Bring the two supervisors together with the four head nurses and proceed in solving the problem as a group.

Did the style you chose match the style that you ended with on the decision-making tree? If so, your intuition was on target. Intuition, however, is as fluid as air—it comes and goes. Theory should be used first, and then intuition. Even if you were correct, diagnose every task and check on what your intuition tells you. You can raise your batting average continuously by using the theory. If your intuition does not match the decision-making tree (Vroom, 1973; Vroom & Yetton, 1973), it generally would be advisable to follow the suggestion from the decision-making tree over your own. Vroom and Jago (1978) reported on an experimental study suggesting that managers who apply the decision model have significantly more effective outcomes—more technical quality and more follower acceptance—than do managers who do not apply the model. Experiential Learning Activity, Exercise 7 at the conclusion of Part II of this book contains additional cases that can be used for practice.

DISCUSSION OF THE DECISION-MAKING MODEL

The decision model just discussed is used to diagnose the task; this is just one part of the environmental diagnosis. As noted earlier in this chapter, diagnosis of the system and self-diagnosis must be considered in determining leader behavior.

Suppose that you went back to the case example in Box 6.1 and applied the maturity or performance readiness theories from Chapter 4 and then the leader behavior theories from Chapter 5. You decided that the followers in the case example were at the M1 level of readiness, thereby requiring high structure and low consideration leader behavior. The diagnosis of the task in the case suggested that group decision making is indicated—that is, high consideration and low structure leader behavior style (see Figure 6.1). What should the manager do?

The best course for the leader to follow in the previous scenario is to bid for more time by presenting evidence to your superior, the nursing director. Advise your director that the nature of the task demands that the group become involved in solving this problem to have the best probability for an effective outcome. Further, the group is not mature or ready enough to handle a group problem-solving activity. More time is needed to help the group mature to the level required for solving the problem. The manager's best bet, therefore, is to try to get the task tabled until the group is mature enough to handle it—get more time. Then use other tasks that do not require group problem-solving experiences and have your followers practice and experience the group processes in a lower risk scenario so that they learn to communicate effectively while working together. Coach them in the learning process when the stakes are not too high.

The manager should try, to the degree possible, to match the decision-making style required by the task with the leader behavior suggested by the group maturity or readiness level—this is ideal. It is also a way to determine the problems or goals that should be the focus of group work at any given point. Tasks should be given to groups according to the group's ability to accomplish them effectively. Decision styles (AI through DI presented in Table 6.1) can be used by the manager to help followers progressively mature in group problem solving. Decision styles are a ladder to how a leader may bring followers to maturity in organizational group activities.

Going back to the case example, if the director of nursing says, "the task must be done even though the group is not ready to handle it," even though a case against this has been made repeatedly and with assertiveness, then the manager must act accordingly. Given that the situation is far from ideal, every effort must be taken to ensure the highest probability for success. The group must be involved even though the experts must maintain control of the group's process because quality and acceptance are both critical. The manager's best bet in this instance is to move into a leader behavior style that falls between what the system requires and what the task requires—high structure and high consideration—CI or CII. This would be the leader behavior style applied for beginning the process of goal accomplishment. This style would be a compromise between the group involvement indicated by the task diagnosis (LBS3—GII) and the leader control indicated by the modal performance readiness level diagnosis of the followers (LBS1).

It must be noted that group decision making in the case example, indicated as best by the decision tree, means that the manager presents the problem for the group members to solve. The problem or goal is to determine how to make the unit manager system work effectively, producing the anticipated outcomes. The problem or goal must be presented with clarity. Group members should not be given the opportunity to say that they do not want the new unit management system. The system exists, and now it must be made effective. This principle applies in all group decision-making processes. Group decision making should begin with the manager's statement of the problem or goal and the factors that have to be considered in the situation—those that must continue and those that may be changed.

Imagine that the task diagnosis required AI decision style and the follower diagnosis for performance readiness was M3. This is a reverse of the case example previously discussed and is for explanation purposes only. Just follow this thinking conceptually. According to VYJ's theory (Vroom, 1973; Vroom & Yetton, 1973), you can use any decision style under the one produced on the decision tree (refer to Table 6.1). Therefore, you can use GII (LBS3) and match the follower's performance readiness, and you can move quickly into DI to help your followers to continually grow in performance readiness. You can be reasonably sure that the diagnoses of followers and the task with the matching leader behavior style result in the best choice to begin the journey toward goal accomplishment. The Experiential Learning Activity, Exercise 7, contains one example of this example.

A FINAL NOTE

Foresight in management is always better than hindsight. The manager should always try to prevent the situation just discussed by a complete and accurate diagnosis of essential elements in the environment. However, when prevention has not worked (and prevention does not always work), then the manager must do what is best in the given situation, after considering the best leader behavior style based on diagnosis of followers and diagnosis of the task.

Self-diagnosis must also be studied because a manager who has a personality that matches the requirements of the system and task probably will have the smoothest journey through solving the problem. Should the leader's personal style not match, however, two alternatives are possible, given that the task must be accomplished by the system: (a) delegate leadership for solving the problem to an assistant whose personal leadership style matches the requirements or (b) provide the leader behavior style that is required by the system and task by being conscious that one's behavior must follow the style needed. If possible and comfortable, validate with someone if your intended behavior matches their perceptions. In the second alternative, the manager must be diligent in thinking about the leader behavior that must be provided for the system because one's personal inclination may be different from the desired behavior.

SUMMARY

The task is the third aspect of the environment that must be diagnosed to determine leader behavior. VYJ's (Vroom, 1973; Vroom & Jago, 1978, 1988; Vroom & Yetton, 1973) managerial decision-making model was discussed for this purpose. The variables of quality, acceptance, and time are considered important in specifying the task's requirements. A decision tree or model can be used to integrate elements of quality and acceptance for a given situation and to suggest a decision style that requires the least amount of time and has the highest probability for effective outcome as one begins the journey toward goal accomplishment.

One case was followed and discussed applying the decision model. An Experiential Learning Activity in Part II of this book contains three additional cases for practice using the model. The manager should try to match the decision-making style required by the task with the leader behavior suggested by the system's maturity or readiness level. The manager can use the model to decide on task priorities for a given group.

Chapter 7 contains a case application of the management process and problem-solving method. This chapter will put the content from Chapters 3, 4, 5, and 6 into action.

● ● ○ REVIEW CONCEPTS AND QUESTIONS

1. Describe and explain the variables of acceptance, quality, and time, according to the Vroom, Yetton, and Jago (VYJ) decision-making model.
2. Explain how to apply VYJ's decision-making model with the leader's behavior decision process that was explained in Chapter 5.
3. Discuss how the managerial decision styles can be applied to the leader's behavior pathway from LBS1 through LBS2, LBS3, and LBS4.

● ● ○ SUGGESTED ASSIGNMENTS

1. Use the hypothetical managerial case that was developed for the suggested assignment in Chapter 4. Diagnose the task using VYJ's decision tree (Figure 6.2.) from this chapter. Blend the diagnostic analyses to select the best leader behavior to begin the journey toward goal accomplishment. Specifically, blend the follower maturity of performance readiness (Chapter 4) and the leader behavior style suggested in Chapter 5, with the task diagnosis in this chapter. Provide discussion about your decision.
2. Again, follow the analysis done with the learner's home environment in the suggested assignment in Chapter 4. Follow the same analysis of the task in the home environment as suggested in the first assignment above, Suggested Assignment No. 1.

REFERENCES

Bass, B. M. (2008). *The Bass handbook of leadership: Theory, research, & managerial applications* (4th ed.). New York, NY: Free Press.

Bass, B. M., & Stogdill, R. M. (1990). *Bass and Stogdill's handbook of leadership: Theory, research, and managerial applications* (3rd ed.). New York, NY: Free Press.

Chemers, M. M. (2000). Leadership research and theory: A functional integration. *Group Dynamics, 4*(1), 27–43.

Donnelly, J. H., Gibson, J. L., & Ivancevich, J. M. (1998). *Fundamentals of management* (10th ed.). New York, NY: Irwin/McGraw-Hill.

Field, R. H. G. (1982). A test of the Vroom-Yetton normative model of leadership. *Journal of Applied Psychology, 67*(5), 523–532.

Fleishman, E. (1973). Twenty years of consideration and structure. In E. Fleishman & J. G. Hunt (Eds.), *Current developments in the study of leadership: A centennial event symposium held at Southern Illinois University of Carbondale.* Carbondale, IL: Southern Illinois University Press.

Gatewood, R. D., Taylor, R. R., & Ferrell, O. C. (1995). *Management: Comprehension, analysis, and application.* Chicago, IL: Irwin.

Hersey, P., Blanchard, K. H., & Johnson, D. E. (2008). *Management of organizational behavior: Leading human resources* (9th ed.). Upper Saddle River, NJ: Pearson Prentice Hall.

Jago, A. G., & Vroom, V. (1978). Predicting leader behavior from a measure of behavioral intent. *Academy of Management Journal, 21*(4), 715–721.

Kreitner, R., & Kinicki, A. (2010). *Organizational behavior* (9th ed.). New York, NY: McGraw-Hill/Irwin.

La Monica, E., & Finch, F. (1977). Managerial decision-making. *Journal of Nursing Administration, 7*(5), 20–28.

Lord, R. G., Hanges, P. J., & Godfrey, E. G. (2003). Integrating neural networks into decision-making and motivational theory. *Canadian Psychology, 44*(1), 21–38.

Marquis, B. L., & Huston, C. J. (2012). *Leadership roles and management functions in nursing: Theory and application* (7th ed.). Philadelphia, PA: Wolters Kluwer/ Lippincott Williams & Wilkins.

Newstrom, J. W. (2011). *Organizational behavior: Human behavior at work* (13th ed.). New York, NY: McGraw-Hill/Irwin.

Vroom, V. (1973). A new look at managerial decision-making. *Organizational Dynamics, 1*(4), 66–80.

Vroom, V. (2000). Leadership and the decision making process. *Organizational Dynamics, 28*(4), 82–94.

Vroom, V. (2001). Leadership style: Managing the decision making process. In S. Rimar (Ed.), *The Yale management guide for physicians.* New York, NY: Wiley.

Vroom, V. (2002). The person versus the situation in leadership. *Leadership Quarterly, 13*(3), 301–323.

Vroom, V., & Jago, A. G. (1978). On the validity of the Vroom-Yetton model. *Journal of Applied Psychology, 63*(2), 151–162.

Vroom, V., & Jago, A. G. (1988). *The new leadership: Managing participation in organizations.* Englewood Cliffs, NJ: Prentice-Hall.

Vroom, V., & Yetton, P. (1973). *Leadership and decision-making.* Pittsburgh, PA: University of Pittsburgh Press.

●●● 7

Management in Action

EXPECTED LEARNING OUTCOMES

- To gain knowledge of the application of organizational behavior theories in a health care situation
- To understand how theories of leadership are applied in a hypothetical example
- To recognize how the management process and managerial method is placed into action
- To increase awareness of the operations involved in problem-solving and goal attainment

This chapter provides an application of the theories that have been presented in Chapters 1 through 6. A case example is studied by following the steps of the problem-solving/managerial method, all of which has been discussed previously. As a review, this problem-solving/managerial method involves the following:

1. Assessing the information
2. Stating the problem or goal
3. Analyzing the problem or goal
4. Creating alternative solutions
5. Recommending an action plan
6. Implementing the action plan and evaluating the results

The management process, as concisely stated by Hersey, Blanchard, and Johnson (2008), comprises planning, organizing, motivating, and controlling. These processes will be interrelated with the manager's activities in the case example at the end of this chapter. The premise in contemporary leadership theory is that there is no style that fits all situations. Leadership style must be adapted to the needs of the followers and the situation (Hersey et al., 2008; McNichol, 2000; Moiden, 2003; Reynolds & Rogers, 2003).

Box 7.1 contains a description of the case that forms the basis for this chapter. Assume the role of the leader or manager in the described environment, reviewing the data presented in Box 7.1 to carry out the managerial method.

ASSESS THE INFORMATION

A problem or goal is identified by the difference between what is actually happening in a situation (the actual) and what one would like to have occur (the optimal).* The manager should first write down the problem areas. These are then narrowed down to one or two areas and defined succinctly, as shown in Table 7.1.

After thinking about these problem areas, it is necessary to focus on a particular problem or goal. Several questions must be answered: (a) Are the problem areas related to one another? (b) Are any of the problem areas caused by another problem? (c) Which problem is tractable and can be solved directly? (d) Which problem has the highest priority?

In looking at the three problem areas delineated in Table 7.1, it is possible that as nursing care is systematized, it becomes repetitive, boring, and monotonous. Staff members may not have the opportunity to develop

---

*Note. Remember, a problem is a statement of what you want to move away from, whereas a goal is what you want to attain. They are opposite terms for the same issue. The terms, therefore, will be used interchangeably throughout this book.

BOX 7.1

Case Example

You are the head nurse of a 54-bed orthopedic unit in a 400-bed general hospital located in a northern city. You have held the position for 5 years and work during the day shift. During the ski season, December to April, the unit maintains a full capacity and often overflows with clients who are set up in the halls and in the solarium.

Clients are generally healthy, robust people who are forced into dependency by various incapacitating fractures, most frequently the broken tibia and/or fibula. Clients fall into two categories: those who require a short hospital stay (1 to 2 days) and those who need a long stay (1 week to 10 days) due to the severity of the injuries.

The organization is old and traditional, sporting an excellent reputation for the quality of its services. There is a bureaucratic hierarchy of control in nursing, with power and authority belonging to the position—there is a right way of doing things and a wrong way of doing things. The director of nursing generally makes the decisions regarding policy and passes the information down the organizational ladder.

A team approach to nursing care delivery is the model that is practiced. Nurses have developed their perspective on team nursing into a packaged procedure, dividing the labors of the team, using flow charts, setting up informal routines for getting the work done, and compartmentalizing all team responsibilities. Nursing histories and care plans have been made up so that they can be used for all clients; nurses simply check what applies to the particular client. Giving medications to all clients on the unit is the responsibility of one registered nurse on each shift. Because the task is perceived as boring, it is rotated on a weekly schedule.

The quality of nursing care is considered good at the present time. Each team has 18 clients, and there is usually one registered nurse, one licensed practical nurse or nurse's aide, and one orderly assigned to each team during the day shift. The staff has been fairly stable over the past year.

You meet with the staff every morning and afternoon for report and again for team conference when time permits. Allied health care personnel also join the conferences as necessary. These caregivers can include inhalation therapists, dieticians, social workers, physical therapists, occupational therapists, and others. If there are problems, the team leaders come to you for assistance and vice versa. Otherwise you generally leave them alone. You try to make rounds every day, but that is not always possible because managerial responsibilities have been increasing since the nursing organization was decentralized.

For the past several weeks, you have noticed increasing tardiness at morning report. Also, staff seemed to be more concerned with the individual functions of their position rather than with the gestalt. You believe that nursing care is not as individualized as it could be. Staff members are spending more and more time talking and complaining with each other in the conference room, reporting that their "work is finished." You check on this and they are right—the work they set out to do is done, charts are completed, and the clients seem happy and comfortable.

Note. The sources of selected aspects of this case were originally prepared by Anita R. Madea, Doctoral Candidate, Teachers College, Columbia University, Department of Nursing Education, 1981. It has been edited by Elaine La Monica Rigolosi, author of this book.

TABLE 7.1   Stating the Problem

ACTUAL	PROBLEM	OPTIMAL
1. Tardiness is increasing	Tardiness	1. No tardiness
2. Nursing care is becoming increasingly routine	Routine nursing care	2. Nursing care is becoming increasingly individualized
3. Nursing time spent with clients is decreasing	Decreased time spent with clients	3. Nursing time spent with clients is increasing

new skills and capacities, and work is getting done too quickly. Innovation and creativity are suppressed as nursing care becomes procedure bound. The three problem areas are seen as interrelated. Because nursing care is becoming a set routine, it gets done fast, leaving the staff with excess time. This may contribute to a lack of enthusiasm, accentuated by the lack of creativity that is present in nursing care planning. The head nurse must now use the knowledge available and make a decision on the priority problem, goal, or opportunity, which basically are synonymous.

STATE THE PROBLEM OR GOAL

The priority problem area of those stated in Table 7.1 is that nursing care was increasingly becoming routine. The goal should be for nursing care to become more individualized. This problem area includes many aspects of nursing care. Because problem statements should be specific, what aspect of nursing care requires the first emphasis? Suppose the head nurse decides that the client should become involved in developing the care plan, using the established core care plans as baseline information and cues to nursing responsibilities in caring for clients with orthopedic needs. The problem and goal might sound like the following:

Actual   The client has no input into the nursing care plan, which is routine for all clients with orthopedic problems.

Optimal   The client and the team leader develop an individualized nursing care plan using the routine care plan as minimal expectations.

Problem   Routine nursing care plans are not individualized; clients do not plan with the team leaders.

Goal   To individualize nursing care plans by having the team leader and the client build on the routine care plan.

ANALYZE THE PROBLEM OR GOAL

In problem analysis, the environment must be diagnosed to choose a leader behavior style that has the highest probability for success in beginning to motivate the system to accomplish the task. It is the pivot upon which all solutions are based. In order to diagnose the environment, the system must first be specified.

In the case example in Box 7.1, the head nurse decides to work with the three team leaders on the day shift because they are mainly responsible for taking nursing histories and personalizing the routine care plan. In addition, the main physical therapist who comes to work with clients on the unit will be considered part of the group. The two regular staff nurses who cover the team leaders on days off are also considered part of the system. Nothing will be added to the normal material resources in solving the problem. In essence, the system consists of three team leaders, one physical therapist, two staff nurses who act as team leaders when necessary, and the head nurse who is the manager. The system for solving the problem and accomplishing the goal can be diagnosed as follows.

Knowing Self

The manager sits back alone and considers why this problem has surfaced. After thoughtful self-study, the manager becomes aware that routine nursing care has always been considered boring and dull. As a client several years ago, the manager had found routine care dehumanizing and ritualistic—in other words, uncaring and impersonal. This is the antithesis of humanistic nursing practice.

Thinking more, the manager realizes that the staff has generally been left alone concerning their task responsibilities. Support was offered often, and the presence of a manager was constant. This style of leadership seemed easy and was most enjoyable and rewarding. The goal was to keep everyone happy.

Diagnose Others

The manager decides to use the following two theories to diagnose the system: (a) Maslow's (1954/1970, 1954/1987) hierarchy of needs to diagnose motivational needs and (b) the levels of performance readiness by Hersey et al. (2008) to diagnose educational needs. Staff members are diagnosed individually regarding their ability and willingness to fulfill the goal and/or to solve the problem. Remember that the theory by Hersey et al. (2008) requires a "yes" or "no" response—if not totally "yes," then the answer is "no." Individual diagnosis by the head nurse of every person in the system follows.

Team Leader 1 is a bright, energetic registered nurse with four years of experience on the unit. The team leader has learned the position's responsibilities quickly but lacks ability to solve problems scientifically. There are procedures and a short list of acceptable behaviors for everything.

Diagnosis   Maturity level 2 (M2)—Social
Performance Readiness level 2 (R2)—Unable but willing or confident

Team Leader 2 is a Bachelor of Science in Nursing (BSN) graduate who has been on the unit in this position for seven years. Responsibility for establishing a routine history form rested predominantly with this team leader, who always enjoyed starting new things once a cue had been given. Planning nursing care with the client, however, has never been part of nursing practice since she attended school. This nurse spends the most time sharing information about clients with associates.

Diagnosis   M2—Social
R2—Unable but willing or confident

Team Leader 3 is a registered nurse and adores team nursing. The nurse is flexible and goes along with all new ideas, giving much of self to accomplishing new projects, especially if working with friends. This nurse has had little experience since graduation.

Diagnosis   M2—Social
R2—Unable but willing or confident

The physical therapist seems to love his profession, enjoys working with clients with orthopedic issues, and has excellent rapport with staff on the unit. Advice is offered when pertinent and also is given freely when requested.

Diagnosis   M4—Self-actualized
R4—Able and willing

Staff Nurse 1 has a wide knowledge base but seems bitter. The nurse always carries out and individualizes responsibilities with pride and makes thoughtful comments in reports about clients, yet often resists group efforts toward change.

Diagnosis   M3—Self-esteem
R3—Able but unwilling or insecure

Staff Nurse 2 is a new nursing graduate. This nurse's chief complaint on the unit is insufficient time to sit and talk with clients. This nurse is used to having the time to collaborate with the client in developing the care plan, being a graduate of a school of nursing that used Orem's (Orem, Taylor, & Renpenning, 2001) theory of nursing as a conceptual framework. However, this nurse always seems frustrated and rarely feels satisfied with the completed work.

Diagnosis   M1—Safety
          R2—Unable but willing or confident

The manager must identify the modal level of maturity and performance readiness. The majority of people in the system are at R2 and M2—unable but willing or confident and motivated at the social level. The leader behavior style that is indicated for an M2 and R2 level of maturity and performance readiness is leader behavior style 2 (LBS2), high structure and high consideration. This style becomes the beginning pivot upon which alternative actions and the recommended action are based.

The level of maturity and performance readiness of the system in the previous example suggests that the leader must give direction to the group concerning the task—what is to be done—and also involve them in problem-solving activities. The leader should meet with the group on a regular basis, suggesting solutions to issues as they arise and offering directions after receiving the group's advice. When talking with the two staff nurses and the physical therapist individually, the manager can behave according to the leader behavior style that is indicated by their individual levels of maturity and performance readiness. However, when communicating with the group, LBS2 is indicated as the best beginning leader behavior style on the journey toward goal accomplishment.

Diagnose the Task

The last diagnosis to be made by the leader is of the nature of the task. Using Vroom and Yetton's managerial decision model (Vroom, 1973, 2000, 2001, 2002; Vroom & Jago, 1978, 1988; Vroom & Yetton, 1973), the questions shown in Figure 6.2, found in the previous chapter, must be answered, starting with Question A.

Question A: Quality—Yes
    Clearly, there are a number of possible solutions, and one could be more effective than another.

    Follow the "yes" line to the next node on the tree; look above it. Question B must be answered.

Question B: Manager's information —No
    The manager would certainly have ideas on how this can best be accomplished. Given that there are various client problems and that

the system has been directly involved in planning care, the staff would obviously have information and expertise that is not possessed by the leader.

Follow the "no" line to the next node and answer Question C, a further question on quality.

Question C: Structure—No

The manager has to make a subjective decision on how this problem will be solved. The decision will not be based on objective (quantitative) data. Further, the exact location of the data that will be used to solve the problem is unknown.

Follow the "no" line to the next node, look above the node and answer Question D.

Question D: Acceptance—Yes

The team leaders must accept the decision in order for the goal to be accomplished.

Follow the "yes" line and proceed to answer Question E.

Question E: Prior Probability of Acceptance—No

This is a sticky question in this case. There are neither data to suggest that the manager's decision would be followed nor data to suggest that the manager's decision would be rejected. The "no" response is based on the team leaders' deep involvement in developing and implementing the current procedure. Moreover, when in doubt on this question, always favor group discussion. This course of action covers the possibility of group rejection, and the only loss is a little time. The gain of team building can trump time.

Follow the "no" line to the next node and answer Question F, which is located above the node.

Question F: Goal Congruence—Yes

The staff will certainly gain from the experience of collaborating with clients and from the feeling of helping another in this personalized way. The resulting style that is suggested by the model is GII. Bring the system together and solve the problem as a group. As shown in Figure 6.1, GII is LBS3, high consideration and low structure.

Synthesize the Diagnoses and Choose Leader Behavior

As the manager, you diagnose yourself as committed to solving the problem because of personal and managerial reasons. You enjoy LBS3, and that seems to be the one in which you function most often with the team leaders.

Upon diagnosing the system, however, you find that the modal level of maturity and performance readiness is M2/R2 (socially motivated and unable but willing or confident), requiring LBS2, high structure and high consideration. This is moving one quadrant back from your preferred style of LBS3. The nature of the task requires LBS3, group decision-making with high consideration and low structure. The group should be involved in how the problem will be solved.

The manager must first follow the leader behavior style suggested by the system's maturity and readiness levels, that is, LBS2. It must be recognized that the problem cannot be totally solved until the system understands "why" and "how" to collaborate with clients in developing nursing care plans. Once this is accomplished, then the majority of the group should have become both able and willing. The manager can then move into LBS3, which is required by the task. Even though the group is seen as able and willing, do not move to LBS4 at this time. Remember that once a leadership style quadrant is in use, you gradually move one quadrant forward for a progressing group or one quadrant backward for a regressing group. This provides reinforcement for learning or change, which is also known as education.

Going back to the case example and diagnosis, the manager must also be aware that a conscious effort must be made to give the initial high task behavior to the group—given the personal preferences or inclination of the manager. Such a style may be neither involuntary nor most pleasing for the manager even though it is necessary.

In introducing the problem or goal to the staff, the manager should share the cues that led to the problem definitions, including one's own feelings, if comfortable sharing them. This is included in high relationship behavior. Also, a social flavor to the meetings should be staged.

CREATE ALTERNATIVE SOLUTIONS

Create alternative solutions by putting aside the rules and regulations. Rather, ask yourself, "If I could solve this problem or accomplish this goal in any way that I could imagine, what would I do?" After alternative solutions are listed, then evaluate them in reality for possible negative and positive effects as well as their match to the leader behavior style indicated by the diagnoses.

The alternative solutions should be ways of solving the problem or accomplishing the goal that use the indicated and best leader behavior style—LBS2—high structure and high consideration. Expected positive and negative results should be delineated for each alternative solution (see Table 7.2).

TABLE 7.2 Alternative Solutions and Evaluations

ALTERNATIVE ACTIONS	POSSIBLE RESULTS
Alternative Action One	
Set up an informal potluck dinner at the leader's house, inviting the system members. Introduce the problem after dinner. Explain everything that has led up to the problem as you see it—tardiness, lack of creativity, and so forth. Positively reinforce the excellent care plans that are being done and suggest that collaboratively planned individualized care seems like the next step in growth.	+ Staff Nurse 2 offers to develop a protocol and try it with several clients. The nurse will report on the strengths and weaknesses of the protocol and revise it with all of the team leaders before going any further.
	− This result may dampen group involvement in learning about the problem.
Explain your perception of the problem solution and stress that this is just one way to solve the problem. What you would like is to spend time discussing concerns and getting and sharing information about the problem. The team leaders would develop a plan for designing the new care plan protocol and implementing it. Prior to leaving, a series of information sessions is planned.	+ It may be a good idea at a later point in time.
	− All of the system does not come to the informal dinner.
	+ The group decides to meet once a week in order to get more information about what they are going to do, prior to designing or implementing anything.
	+ The three regular team leaders expressed insecurity in their ability to do this; they request help from someone who has done this before.
In Alternative Action One, the manager is being high task in delineating the problem and its rationale. Knowledge is the first priority, and then the manager states that group problem-solving is expected. The manager provides reinforcement in a discussion. This all characterizes starting at LBS2, high structure and high consideration, with a planned shift to LBS3, high consideration and low structure, as soon as possible when the group appears ready.	− Staff Nurse 1 expounds that it will not work because clients expect to be told what to do.
	+ The group openly discusses the problem, asking questions of the manager and of each other.
	+ The physical therapist participates and offers guidance freely. Suggestions are often new, creative, and warmly received.

TABLE 7.2   Alternative Solutions and Evaluations *(continued)*

ALTERNATIVE ACTIONS	POSSIBLE RESULTS
Alternative Action Two	
Announce a meeting for team leaders during the conference time slot on the regular shift. Then introduce the goal and follow the same agenda as in the first alternative action. Provide coffee and snacks.	− Those nurses not scheduled to work that day will not attend. + All positive possible results as stated in the first alternative action. − The negative result stated in the first alternative action from Staff Nurse 1 could occur.
Alternative Action Three	
Invite the unit supervisor to the first meeting that has been set up during a team conference time slot. The problem and goal is introduced in the same way as Alternative Actions One and Two. In addition, the supervisor emphasizes that the goal is favorable with administration.	+ In addition to the results stated in Alternative Action Two, the staff members may be encouraged by support from higher administration. − The staff members may be resentful that an authority figure, who is not a regular part of the group, was aware of the problem or goal before they became aware.

Note. A possible positive outcome is signified by +.
A possible negative outcome is signified by −.

RECOMMEND AN ACTION PLAN

After evaluating the created alternative solutions, the manager decides on the action plan. Referring back to the case example, that second alternative action in Table 7.2 is considered the most favorable at this time. This decision is based on the awareness that team leaders are not accustomed to meeting together just for social reasons. Further, they never meet outside of the work environment, even for work-related issues.

Putting the solution in operation, the meeting would be scheduled, if possible, on a day that all members of the system are working. If not possible, then select a day when the greatest number in the system would be on duty. The person(s) not scheduled to work would be asked to come in for this meeting. Compensation time would be offered, if at all possible. The manager should attempt to neutralize negative outcomes of this alternative action.

Following delineation of the recommended action, it must be implemented and then evaluated. Discussion on these areas follows.

IMPLEMENTATION AND EVALUATION

To implement simply means "to do" or "to put into action." It follows that after one has specified a recommended action, it must be implemented. Prior to implementation, evaluation emerges as a responsibility and continues to be important until after the action is completed—the problem is erased or the goal is attained, depending on the eyeglasses that you wish to put on.

Evaluation is most effective when it includes all three aspects. These were discussed by Newman (1975) as types of control, a broader concept that includes evaluation.

   1.   *Steering controls*. In this form of evaluation, results are predicted prior to implementation. If things are not going along as desired, corrective action is taken prior to or during the implementation process.

   Referring back to the example, if at the team conference the nurses were not responding in general accordance with the expected positive results, the manager might change the recommended action strategy immediately.

   2.   *Yes–no controls*. This is a checkpoint where action does not proceed to another step until quality and effectiveness with the previous step are confirmed.

   Again going to the case example, all members should generally be satisfied with the first meeting's outcomes and be clear and agreed on the agenda for the next meeting prior to adjourning.

   3.   *Post-action controls*. This form of evaluation is after the fact. Action has been completed, the problem is solved, and the goal is reached. Accomplishments and what is being done regarding care plan development and implementation are compared with the manager's original intent.

THE MANAGEMENT PROCESS

Chapter 1 contains a discussion of the four interrelated components of the management process as concisely presented by Hersey et al. (2008): planning, organizing, motivating, and controlling. These relationships are discussed regarding the case example. Notice how they are woven together in the following paragraphs that describe what was done by the leader in the case example that was presented in Box 7.1.

In order to plan to solve the problem or attain the goal, the leader had to be organized logically and follow a problem-solving method. It had to be decided what was to be done first and why. The system was then organized to contain only the people who were primary in solving the problem. The next step in the organized process was to diagnose self, the system, and the task to identify personal preferences and to figure out how to motivate and educate the system at the beginning of goal accomplishment.

Moving further, the determination of a leader behavior style that responded to the modal level of maturity and performance readiness of the system was a planned intervention intended to motivate the system to accomplish by giving the nurses what they needed. The manager had to (a) plan for behaviors that filled the indicated leader behavior style requirements and (b) organize alternative actions and choose a recommended action that responded to the group's needs and the leader's goal of getting the task accomplished.

In each of the four components of the management process—planning, organizing, motivating, and controlling—the manager is also comparing accomplishments with intent using the information collected; this process is evaluative. Information is collected verbally and nonverbally, through primary and secondary sources. Are all necessary nurses and health care personnel and caregivers included in the system? Should anyone be added? Is my diagnosis accurate or do I need more data? Did my recommended action provide a structured taking-off place for the system? Did it kindle interest in the problem? Will high structure be required for the second session? Was the entire group involved? Following implementation of the action plan, evaluation will be an ongoing process.

SUMMARY

This chapter uses a case study to apply all of the material in Chapters 1 through 6. Theory is applied in the problem-solving method. The chapter concludes with a discussion of the interrelatedness of the management process in the described case example. The Experiential Learning Activities at the conclusion of Part II contain guidelines for applying the managerial method to a case from a learner's real-world scenario.

● ● ○ REVIEW CONCEPTS AND QUESTIONS

1. Differentiate the management/problem-solving method from the management processes. How do the steps of each one relate to each other?
2. State and explain the control steps in ongoing evaluation of action plans. Differentiate the timing of each step.

● ● ● **SUGGESTED ASSIGNMENTS**

1. Develop a case analysis from a real clinical work environment. Write a paper using the managerial method presented in this chapter.
2. Put the previous plan into action, discuss the process, and evaluate the results. Be sure to present, discuss, and critique the results—what you would do the same way and what you would do differently.
3. The previous two assignments can be done over an entire semester or learning period. Activity 8 in the Experiential Learning Activity section of Part II of this book contains further guidance for this formal assignment.

REFERENCES

Hersey, P., Blanchard, K., & Johnson, D. (2008). *Management of organizational behavior: Leading human resources* (9th ed.). Upper Saddle River, NJ: Pearson Prentice Hall.

Maslow, A. H. (1970). *Motivation and personality* (2nd ed.). New York, NY: Harper & Row. (Original work published 1954)

Maslow, A. H. (1987). *Motivation and personality* (3rd ed.). New York, NY: Harper & Row. (Original work published 1954, and later published 1970)

McNichol, E. (2000). How to be a model leader. *Nursing Standard, 14*(45), 24.

Moiden, N. (2003). A framework for leadership. *Nursing Management, 9*(10), 19–23.

Newman, W. H. (1975). *Constructive control: Design and use of control systems.* Englewood Cliffs, NJ: Prentice Hall.

Orem, D. E., Taylor, S. G., & Renpenning, K. M. (2001). *Nursing: Concepts of practice* (6th ed.). St. Louis, MO: Mosby.

Reynolds, J., & Rogers, A. (2003). Leadership styles and situations. *Nursing Management, 9*(10), 27–30.

Vroom, V. (1973). A new look at managerial decision-making. *Organizational Dynamics, 1*(4), 66–80.

Vroom, V. (2000). Leadership and the decision-making process. *Organizational Dynamics, 28*(4), 82–94.

Vroom, V. (2001). Leadership style: Managing the decision-making process. In S. Rimar (Ed.), *The Yale management guide for physicians.* New York, NY: Wiley.

Vroom, V. (2002). The person versus the situation in leadership. *Leadership Quarterly, 13*(3), 301–323.

Vroom, V., & Jago, A. G. (1978). On the validity of the Vroom-Yetton model. *Journal of Applied Psychology, 63*(2), 151–162.

Vroom, V., & Jago, A. G. (1988). *The new leadership: Managing participation in organizations.* Englewood Cliffs, NJ: Prentice Hall.

Vroom, V., & Yetton, P. (1973). *Leadership and decision making.* Pittsburgh, PA: University of Pittsburgh Press.

Experiential Learning Activities: Managerial Responsibilities— The Core

| ACTIVITY 5 | DIAGNOSING PERSONAL LEADER BEHAVIOR STYLE |

Purposes

1. To diagnose one's personal leader behavior style.
2. To identify one's expectations of leader behavior.
3. To explore the implications of one's personal leadership style.
4. To explore the similarity or disparity between one's personal style and one's expectations of leader behavior.

Facility

Classroom.

Materials

LEAD Self: Leadership Style/Perception of Self and

LEAD Directions: Directions for Self-Scoring and Analysis.

The authors are Paul Hersey and Kenneth Blanchard.* These instruments can be purchased from:

Center for Leadership Studies
230 West Third Avenue
Escondido, California 92025
Telephone: 760-741-6595
Facsimile: 760-747-9384
www.situational.com

Pencil or pen.

Time Required

Forty-five minutes to 1 hour.

Group Size

Unlimited.

Design

1. Instruct members to respond individually and to follow the directions contained in the instrument. Detailed instructions are provided.

---

*The LEAD instruments are discussed in the following book: Hersey, P., Blanchard, K. H., & Johnson, D. (2008). *Management of organizational behavior: Leading human resources* (9th ed.). Upper Saddle River, NJ: Pearson Prentice Hall.

ACTIVITY 5

DIAGNOSING PERSONAL LEADER BEHAVIOR STYLE *(continued)*

Variation

Other leadership instruments are available and may be used. Also, you may want to give the LEAD-Other to coworkers, followers, and superiors and ask then to rate you on how they perceive you would respond to the situations. This instrument can also be obtained from the aforementioned address.

If LEAD-Other instruments are done, average the responses and you will have a more valid picture of your leadership style. The greater the number of people who say the same thing, the more likely it is to be closer to the truth. Also, remember that leader behavior is as perceived by others. Therefore, what others perceive is closer to your actual leader behavior style. If you are not currently in a leadership role, then complete the instrument noting how you think that you would act in a hypothetical management role.

ACTIVITY 6	DIAGNOSING OTHERS

Purposes	1. To gain experience in specifying the priority problem in a case.
	2. To practice identifying particular leader behavior styles.
	3. To determine leader effectiveness.
	4. To develop a problem solution.
Facility	Large room to accommodate learners working around tables of six to eight.
Materials	Worksheet 6-A: Case Study—Urban City Hospital.
	Worksheet 6-B: Diagnostic Skills Worksheet.
	Worksheet 6-C: Discussion Based on Experts' Diagnosis and Rationale. Pencils or pens.
	Blackboard and chalk.
Time Required	Two and one-half hours.
Group Size	Unlimited groups of six to eight.
Design	1. Using the Case Study (Worksheet 6-A) and the Diagnostic Skills Worksheet (Worksheet 6-B), each individual working independently and viewing self as an outside consultant is to
	a. Specify the priority problem or goal in Urban City Hospital.
	b. Identify the dominant leader behavior styles used by George Jones and May Conte.
	c. Determine the organizational effectiveness of Urban City Hospital under the management of George Jones and May Conte.
	d. Develop a recommended action for the problem or goal.
	e. Write down detailed rationale for A through D. The rationale will serve as a basis for discussion in reaching group consensus (see Step 2 that follows). Record individual decisions on the Diagnostic Skills Worksheet (30 minutes).

Note. The exercise was adapted by permission from La Monica, Elaine L., *The Nursing Process: A Humanistic Approach* (pp. 385–394). Copyright © 1979. Reprinted by permission of Pearson Education, Inc., Upper Saddle River, NJ.

| ACTIVITY 6 | DIAGNOSING OTHERS *(continued)* |

2. Following the individual diagnosis and continuing use of Worksheet 6-B, each work group of six to eight should then reach consensus as to the problem or goal, action, leader behavior styles of the characters, and their organizational effectiveness. The group should discuss rationales even if they are in agreement and should make every attempt to reach consensus. A group recorder must be chosen to record the group decisions (45 minutes to 1 hour).

3. Form into a total group and have each recorder share the work group's decisions and discuss rationales. Record decisions on a blackboard using the following suggested format:

PROBLEM/GOAL	LEADERSHIP STYLE		EFFECTIVENESS		ACTION
	Jones	Conte	Jones	Conte	
Group 1					
Group 2					
Group 3					

4. Refer to Worksheet 6-C: Discussion Based on Experts' Diagnosis and Rationale and share and discuss the interpretations that are provided.

5. Discuss the experience.

Variation

1. The individual diagnosis can be given as a homework assignment.

2. The activity can be used only to identify leader behavior styles and leader effectiveness, deleting the aspects of specifying a problem or goal and developing an action. This is recommended if the exercise is used after studying Chapters 4 and 5 and prior to completing Chapters 6 and 7.

(continued)

WORKSHEET 6-A: CASE STUDY—URBAN CITY HOSPITAL*

Janis Monroe, chief financial officer (CFO) of Urban City Hospital, was concerned by reports of absenteeism among some of the staff. From reliable sources, she had learned that some of the staff were punching the time cards of fellow workers who were arriving late or leaving early. Monroe had only recently been appointed to head Urban City Hospital. She judged from conversations with the previous director and other administrators that people were, in general, pleased with the overall performance of the hospital.

Urban City Hospital has a reputation for quality medical care with a particularly good reputation in the areas of coronary care, intensive care, and emergency care. Located in the center of Urban City, the hospital draws many lower socioeconomic families from that area but also services many clients from the suburban areas. The staff, who had various educational backgrounds and training, were generally from the small state in which Urban City is located. In fact, a number of nurses are graduates of the hospital's nursing program that currently continues as an excellent hospital-based nursing program.

It is thought that clients usually enter Urban Hospital for one of the following reasons:

- High quality of care
- Somewhat lower costs than other nearby facilities
- A variety of available medical care
- Fiscal solvency in a tough health care environment

George Jones, a longtime employee in the hospital, was administrator of Urban City Hospital. He generally left the staff alone, spending most of his time scheduling administrative personnel, procuring funds and supplies, overseeing budget matters, fund-raising, and tending to related issues. Jones had an assistant, Rudy Lucas. When he needed to communicate with people in a particular area, George would just call them together or talk to an individual in the area and ask him to "pass the word." The latter was his usual approach.

Work situations at the hospital were quite varied. Some departments, such as the laboratory, were cramped and less than adequate by some standards for the job required, whereas others more than met minimum criteria. Work efficiency did not seem to be related to these circumstances.

It should be noted that as far as hospitals are concerned, Urban City Hospital was one of the finest in the area. Clients generally liked their care and spoke highly of the facility.

The pay scale for the staff was low compared with other similar facilities. The age of the building made working conditions generally more difficult than might be desirable. Employees, however, never made issues of either wages or working conditions. No one in the hospital was a union employee and it was never brought to any group of employees for consideration.

Judy Mulry, a first-year administrative assistant to the director, provided the data that follows in this case study. After she had been working at the hospital for

---

*The author of the contents of this case is unknown. This author, Elaine La Monica Rigolosi, received it at the School of Education, University of Massachusetts, 1974, and has adapted it.

WORKSHEET 6-A: CASE STUDY—URBAN CITY HOSPITAL (continued)

a month or so, Mulry noted that certain members of the staff tended to seek each other out during free time and after hours. She then observed that these informal associations were enduring, built upon common activities and shared ideas about what was and what was not legitimate behavior in the hospital. Her estimate of these associations is diagrammed in Exhibit 6.1. The hospital responsibility for each person also is shown in the exhibit.

The Conte group, so named because May Conte was its most respected member and the one who seemed to take responsibility for maintaining good relations within the group, was the largest. The group invariably tried to eat lunch together and operated as a team, regardless of the differences in individual assignments. Off the job, Conte's group members often joined parties or got together for weekend trips. Conte's summer camp was a frequent rendezvous point.

Conte's group was also the most cohesive one in the hospital in terms of its organized punch-in, punch-out systems. The time clock system for the staff had been started three years before by the Board of Trustees, which had been taken over by a conservative element. There might be times, however, when an individual staff member would have completed any specific responsibilities from one half to three quarters of an hour prior to the scheduled time to leave. If there were errands or other things to do in that extra free time, another member of the group would punch out for the one who left early. The "right" to leave early was informally balanced among the members of the group. In addition, the group members would punch a staff member "in" if he or she were unavoidably late.

Conte explained the logic behind the system to Mulry. "You know we don't get paid as well here as in other hospitals," she said and then continued.

What makes this the best hospital to work in is that we are not continually bothered by administrators. When things are under control, as they are now, and the clients are satisfied, the top brass seems to be happy. It seems silly to have to stay to punch out on those few occasions when a little extra free time would be of help to you. Of course, some people abuse this sort of thing . . . like Marsha . . . but the members of our group get the job done and it all averages out.

Conte went on:

When there is extra work, naturally I stay as late as necessary. So do a lot of others. I believe that if I stay until the work is done and everything is in order, that's all the administration expects of us. They leave us alone and expect the job to get done . . . and we do it—all of it.

When Mulry asked Conte if she would not rather work at a newer hospital at a higher salary, she just laughed and said, "Never."

The members of Conte's group were explicit about what constituted a good job. Customarily, they cited Marsha Jones, who happened to be the administrator's

(continued)

WORKSHEET 6-A: CASE STUDY—URBAN CITY HOSPITAL *(continued)*

EXHIBIT 6.1 Urban City Hospital Staff—Informal Groupings

McBride
  Executive
  Housekeeper

Harris
  Assistant
  Housekeeper

Mulry
  Administrative
  Assistant

Smith
  Accountant

Lucas
  Administrator

G. Jones
  Administrator

Blanche
  Manager,
  Food Service

Kane
  Dietician

Roberto
  Assistant
  Laboratory
  Manager

Conte
  Laboratory
  Manager

Pellegrini
  Pharmacist

Luciano
  Inservice|
  Educator

Venko
  Pharmacist

Impolitto
  Physical
  Therapist

Nappa
  X-ray
  Technologist

Roberts
  Controller

Leighton
  Credit
  Manager

Parant
  Manager,
  Business Office

Manfred
  Director, Plant
  Operations

Patti
  Supervisor,
  Admitting

Proctor, RN
  Supervisor,
  Operating Room

Roman
  Supervisor,
  Records
  Department

Johnson, RN
  Supervisor,
  Nursing

Pope, RN
  Assistant
  Supervisor,
  Nursing

Jones, RN
  Supervisor,
  Nursing

Spaulding, RN
  Discharge Planner

WORKSHEET 6-A: CASE STUDY—URBAN CITY HOSPITAL *(continued)*

sister, as a woman who continually let others down. Mulry received an informal orientation from Marsha during her first few days at the hospital. As Marsha put it:

> I've worked at this hospital for years, and I expect to stay here a good many more. You're just starting out, and you don't know the lay of the land yet. Working in a hospital is tough enough without breaking your neck. You can wear yourself out fast if you're not smart. Look at Manfred, the director of plant operations. There's a guy who's just going to burn himself out, and for what? He makes it tough on everybody and on himself, too.

Mulry reported further on her observations of the group activities:

> May and her group couldn't understand Marsha. While Marsha arrived late a good deal of the time, May was usually early. If a series of emergency situations had created a backlog of work, almost everyone but Marsha would spend extra time to help catch up. May and members of her group would always stay later. While most of the staff seemed to find a rather full life in their work, Marsha never got really involved. No wonder they couldn't understand each other.

Mulry continued discussing her observations.

> There was quite a different feeling about Bob Manfred, the director of plant operations. Not only did he work his full shift but he often scheduled meetings with maintenance and other plant personnel on other shifts to consider better ways of getting their jobs done. He was also taking courses in the evening to complete the requirements for a degree. He often worked many Saturdays and Sundays . . . and all for 'peanuts.' He hardly got paid a cent extra. Because of the tremendous variance in responsibilities, it was hard to make comparisons, but I'm sure I wouldn't be wrong in saying that Bob worked twice as hard as Marsha and 50% more than almost anyone else in the hospital. No one but Marsha and a few old-timers criticized him for his efforts. May and her group seemed to feel a distant affection for Bob, but the only contact they or anyone else had with him consisted of brief greetings.

Mulry's comments continued.

> To the members of May's group, the most severe penalty that could be inflicted was exclusion. This they did to both Manfred and Marsha. Manfred, however, was tolerated; Marsha was not. Evidently, Marsha felt her exclusion keenly, and she answered it with derision and aggression. Marsha kept up a steady stream of stories concerning her attempt to gain acceptance outside working hours. She wrote popular music, which was

(continued)

WORKSHEET 6-A: CASE STUDY—URBAN CITY HOSPITAL *(continued)*

always rejected by publishers. She attempted to join several social and literary clubs, mostly without success. Her favorite pastime was attending concerts. She told me that 'music lovers' were friendly, and she enjoyed meeting new people whenever she went to a concert. But, she was particularly quick to explain that she preferred to keep her distance from the other people on the staff at the hospital.

Having more to say, Mulry provided additional information.

May's group emphasized more than just effort in judging a person's work. Among them had grown a confidence that they could develop and improve on the efficiency of any responsibility. May herself symbolized this. Before her, May's father had been an effective laboratory manager and helped May a great deal. When problems arose, the directors and other staff would frequently consult with May, and she would give counsel willingly. She had a special feeling for her job. For example, when a young lab technician couldn't seem to get off the ground, May was the only one who successfully stepped in and probably saved a promising young technician. To a lesser degree, the other members of the group were also imaginative about solving problems that arose in their own areas.

Mulry shared,

Marsha, for her part, talked incessantly about her accomplishments. As far as I could tell during the year I worked in the hospital, there was little evidence to support these stories. In fact, many of the other staff members laughed at her. What's more, I never saw anyone seek Marsha's help.

Discussing others, Mulry said,

Willingness to be of help was a trait the staff associated with Conte and was prized. The most valued help of all was of a personal kind, though the jobs were also important. The members of Conte's group were constantly lending and borrowing money, cars, and equipment among themselves and, less frequently, with other members of the hospital staff.

In contrast to Conte's group, Mulry stated,

Marsha refused to help others in any way. She never tried to aid those around her who were in the midst of a rush of work, though this was customary throughout most of the hospital. I can distinctly recall the picture of the day supervisor trying to handle an emergency situation at about 3 p.m. one day while Marsha continued a casual telephone conversation. She acted as if she didn't even notice the supervisor. She, of course, expected me to act this same way, and it was this attitude in her I found virtually intolerable. . . . More than this, Marsha took little responsibility

WORKSHEET 6-A: Case Study—Urban City Hospital *(continued)*

for breaking in new nurses, leaving this entirely to the assistant supervisor. There had been four new nurses on her shift in the space of a year. Each had asked for a transfer to another shift, publicly citing personal reasons associated with the 7:00–3:00 shift but privately blaming Marsha. May was the one who taught me the ropes when I first joined the staff.

Moving to other members of the staff, Mulry said,

The staff members who congregated around Pat Johnson were primarily nursing supervisors, but as a group tended to behave similarly to the Conte group, though they did not quite approach the creativity or the amount of helping activities that May's group possessed. They were, however, all considered 'good' in their jobs. Sometimes the Johnson group sought outside social contact with the Conte group. Even though they worked in different areas, both groups seemed to respect each other, and several times a year, the two groups went out on the town together.

Speaking about members of different groups, Mulry shared,

The remainder of the people in the hospital stayed pretty much to themselves or associated in pairs or triplets. None of these people were as inventive, as helpful, or as productive as Conte's or Johnson's groups, but most of them gave verbal support to the same values as those groups held.

Mulry then discussed group contrasts by saying:

The distinction between the two organized groups and the rest of the hospital was clearest in the punching-out routine. McBride and Harris; Blanche and Kane; and Roberts, Parant, and Leighton arranged within their small groups for any early punch-outs. George Jones was frequently out of the building during any punch-outs, and he didn't seem to pay attention to such things like the time clock anyway. His assistant, Lucas, although always in the hospital, wasn't seen by many people. He seemed to 'hide' in his office. Jones and Patti had no early punch-out organization to rely upon. Marsha was reported to have established an arrangement with Patti whereby the latter would punch Marsha out for a fee. Such a practice was unthinkable from the point of view of Conte's group. Marsha constantly complained about the dishonesty of other members of the staff in the hospital.

"Just before I left Urban City to take another position," stated Mulry, "I casually met Ms. Monroe (the CFO) on the street. She asked me how I had enjoyed my experience at Urban City Hospital. During the conversation, I learned that she knew of the punch-out system. What's more, she told me she was wondering if she ought to 'blow the lid off the whole mess.'"

(continued)

WORKSHEET 6-B: DIAGNOSTIC SKILLS WORKSHEET

Problem/Goal/Opportunity (Individual Diagnosis) _____

_____

_____

_____

_____

_____

Problem/Goal/Opportunity (Group Diagnosis) _____

_____

_____

_____

_____

_____

LEADER BEHAVIOR STYLE (LBS)—Check the dominant (LBS) for each character.

LEADERSHIP STYLE	INDIVIDUAL DIAGNOSIS			GROUP DIAGNOSIS	
	George Jones	May Conte		George Jones	May Conte
High Structure and Low Consideration					
High Structure and High Consideration					
High Consideration and Low Structure					
Low Structure and Low Consideration					

WORKSHEET 6-B: DIAGNOSTIC SKILLS WORKSHEET (continued)

EFFECTIVENESS DIMENSION—Indicate by a checkmark your decision on the degree of effectiveness or ineffectiveness for each character identified below. Consider causal variables, intervening variables, and end-result/output variables.

	Ineffective					Effective			
	−4	−3	−2	−1		+1	+2	+3	+4
INDIVIDUAL DIAGNOSIS									
George Jones									
May Conte									
GROUP DIAGNOSIS									
George Jones									
May Conte									

Recommended Action (Individual) _____

_____

_____

_____

_____

_____

Recommended Action (Group) _____

_____

_____

_____

_____

_____

(continued)

WORKSHEET 6-C: DISCUSSION BASED ON EXPERTS' DIAGNOSIS AND RATIONALE*

Problem or Goal

The problem is that the time clock policy is being applied inconsistently. There may be other potential problems in the case, but managers should identify the simplest, most tractable present problem and attack it. The time clock problem has the potential for erupting in such a way that people may be labeled dishonest or commanded to attend to a policy under threat; such would undoubtedly decrease productivity. If stated as a goal, one would not want to have a time clock policy that is not followed.

Leadership Styles

Leader behavior is as perceived by others. George Jones exhibited low structure and low consideration behavior—he was not constantly telling followers what needed to be done, how to do it, when to do it, and so forth. Neither was he observed involving staff members in two-way communication or in establishing interpersonal rapport.

Given the data provided, May Conte was considered to be high consideration and low structure because she was observed relating with the group, giving support and reinforcement, and establishing a team. One did not observe Conte defining facets of task accomplishment. Even though the case did not portray Conte as high task, it could be assumed safely that such a manager also directed the task. It can be said, therefore, that Conte's basic style was high consideration and low structure, whereas her supporting style was high structure and high consideration.

Effectiveness

Organizational effectiveness under the management of May Conte and George Jones should be evaluated on the causal, intervening, and end result/output variables discussed in Chapter 5. It is easy to create a halo-horn effect and judge a manager's overall effectiveness on the basis of one or two traits that are important to the evaluator. If the manager has the trait, then the manager is good in everything, and vice versa. This effect is tempered significantly by rating a manager on each variable, summing the ratings, and dividing by the number of variables to get an average effectiveness rating.

Because the scale of −4 to +4 is arbitrary, it is simplest to say that Jones and Conte were +4 unless a negative point in the area is noted. Remember that manager effectiveness should be judged on the basis of the majority of people concerned and what is being evaluated. There will always be the unreachable point or the possibility that a fact occurred spuriously.

---

* The experts are Kenneth Blanchard and Paul Hersey. Oral presentation, School of Education, University of Massachusetts, 1974. The activity and rationale have been slightly adapted by this author, Elaine La Monica Rigolosi.

WORKSHEET 6-C: DISCUSSION BASED ON EXPERTS' DIAGNOSIS AND RATIONALE *(continued)*

In Urban City Hospital, both managers were considered excellent. Jones, however, was slightly more effective than Conte. The case is designed to bring out the halo-horn effect because most groups see Conte as the more effective manager. Conte is certainly more likeable because one gets a feel for her personality and one knows more about her. Also, it is easy to say that Jones should not be credited with success because he does not seem to do anything. Such a conclusion relates only to the evaluator's past experience with a low structure and low consideration manager who behaved that way because she or he did not care. LBS4, however, is a legitimate strategy, and one should assume that Jones is behaving this way because that is what his followers require. To think otherwise would be aiming to perpetuate a previous negative experience. What would have happened to Conte's group if Jones had started to tell Conte what to do and had sought invitations to the group's social events? This author sees beginning disaster.

Experts' Diagnosis of Organizational Effectiveness

Variable	Jones	Conte	Discussion
1. Causal Variables • Leadership strategies • Management's decisions • Organizational philosophy, policies, and objectives.	+3		One point was deducted because Jones had a policy in the hospital that was not being followed. His management style was appropriate given the level of maturity or performance readiness of his immediate followers.
		+3	One point was deducted because Conte did not attend to the time clock policy. While a policy is in effect, it should be supported. If the policy seems inappropriate, do something to change it—it should not be ignored. Conte's management style was appropriate given the follower's level of maturity or performance readiness.
2. Intervening Variables • Employee's personal commitment to objectives and growth • Motivation and morale	+4	+4	The majority of people being led by Jones and Conte were happy, committed, and growing within the organization.

(continued)

WORKSHEET 6-C: DISCUSSION BASED ON EXPERTS'
DIAGNOSIS AND RATIONALE (continued)

Experts' Diagnosis of Organizational Effectiveness (continued)

Variable	Jones	Conte	Discussion
3. End Result/Output Variables • Production • Costs • Earnings • Turnover	+4	+4	From the perspective of both managers, output was excellent. The hospital was not in the red, clients were satisfied, quality of care was very good, and people would rather work there than any place else. Conte's group also always got their work done.
Totals:	+11	+11	
Divided by 3 =	+ 3.67	+ 3.67	

Generally speaking, Urban City Hospital was an effectively running organization and both Conte and Jones were excellent leaders. There is every reason to believe that this time clock issue would be handled effectively and that both managers would continue to improve.

It should, however, be noted that when evaluating long-term and short-term goals, Jones would be a little more effective than would Conte. This is due to the fact that Jones's followers functioned effectively when he was in LBS4—low structure and low consideration. Conte's group, on the other hand, probably would not be able to function effectively without steady input from her. This was evident since Conte was appropriately in LBS2 or LBS3—high structure and consideration or high consideration and low structure. The long-term goal is always to enable followers to be able and willing to continue accomplishing when the leader is not present—when the leader should effectively delegate.

Action

The action to the problem is to get rid of the time clock or to appoint a committee to make recommendations on this problem. Policies are put into place because of a need by the majority of the group. Once passed, policies tend to live forever, even though this should not occur. Policies need to be reevaluated to see if they best serve the majority of people in the organization. Is the policy what is needed given their level of maturity or performance readiness? A time clock is a high-task intervention and obviously is not required given the majority at Urban City Hospital. The hospital is running beautifully, and the work is getting done. There will always be a couple of freedom abusers as well as obsessive workers. *Policies, however, must reflect the needs of the majority.*

ACTIVITY 7	DIAGNOSING THE TASK

Purpose	To practice applying the Vroom, Yetton, and Jago managerial decision-making model.
Facility	Large room to accommodate learners working in groups of six to eight.
Materials	Table 6.1. (Chapter 6): Management Decision Styles.
	Worksheet 7-A: Cases 1, 2, and 3.
	Figure 6.2. (Chapter 6): Vroom's Decision Model (Tree).
	Chalkboard and chalk.
Time Required	One and one-half hours.
Group Size	Unlimited groups of six to eight.
Design	1. Individuals working alone are to read each case on Worksheet 7.A and choose the decision style that they (as individuals) would use if they were the manager in each situation. The decision styles are found in Chapter 6, Table 6.1. Record responses and rationale for decisions in spaces provided after each case. (Provide 15 minutes for this step.)
	2. After completing Step 1, individuals in each work group of six to eight should then discuss their choices for decision styles with each other, citing reasons for each selection. A recorder for each group should write down the group consensus by majority vote. (Provide 30 to 45 minutes for this step.)

(continued)

Note. The sources for the Vroom, Yetton, and Jago Decision-Making Model and Decision Styles follows: Vroom, V. (1973). A new look at managerial decision-making. *Organizational Dynamics, 1*(4), 66–80; Vroom, V. (2000). Leadership and the decision making process. *Organizational Dynamics, 28*(4), 82–94; Vroom, V. H., & Jago, A. G. (1974). Decision making as a social process. *Decision Sciences, 5*(4), 750; Vroom, V., & Jago, A. G. (1978). On the validity of the Vroom-Yetton model. *Journal of Applied Psychology, 63*(2), 151–162; Vroom, V., & Jago, A. G. (1988). *The new leadership: Managing participation in organizations.* Englewood Cliffs, NJ: Prentice Hall; Vroom, V., & Yetton, P. (1973). *Leadership and decision-making.* Pittsburgh, PA: University of Pittsburgh Press.

ACTIVITY 7   DIAGNOSING THE TASK *(continued)*

3. Following discussion in small groups, form into a total group and have the recorders share the group's decisions and rationale. Record decisions on a chalkboard using the following suggested format:

	Case 1	Case 2	Case 3
Group 1			
Group 2			
Group 3			

4. In the total group, use the decision model found in Chapter 6, Figure 6.2, to determine the diagnosis of each task. Refer to the discussion section and hold an open discussion case by case for each of the three examples. Compare decision styles arrived at by consensus (displayed on the blackboard) with those determined by application of the decision model.

Discussion

Case 1

Question A.	Quality	Yes
Question B.	Manager's information	Yes
Question D.	Acceptance	No

Minimum-time decision style: AI

There is a quality requirement, and because the supervisor has been in that position for 10 years, it is reasonably certain that he or she would possess the information to make a high-quality decision. The nurses are only concerned that supplies are available; therefore, they have to accept nothing. Once supplies are ordered and stocked, the problem is alleviated; people must live with the results. Since AI can be used given the task, all styles could be used depending on how much time is available. A supervisor who wanted to develop problem-solving skills in followers could use this task to accomplish it.

ACTIVITY 7   **DIAGNOSING THE TASK** *(continued)*

Case 2

Question A.	Quality	No
Question D.	Acceptance	Yes
Question E.	Prior probability of acceptance	No

Minimum-time decision style: GII

There is no quality requirement because who attends the conference does not affect staffing. The decision must be accepted by the staff, and it is doubtful whether a supervisor's choice would be accepted. The wise supervisor, therefore, would not use any style above GII and might even delegate the task (DI) by letting the nurses make a decision among themselves.

Case 3

Question A.	Quality	Yes
Question B.	Manager's information	No
Question C.	Structure	No
Question D.	Acceptance	Yes
Question E.	Prior probability of acceptance	Yes

Minimum-time decision style: CII

There is definitely a quality requirement; one location may be better than another. The manager needs to have the staff assess the community in order to make a wise choice. The problem is not structured, because there is a subjective element in making the decision—"what feels right"—and the executive director does not know exactly what information is needed to make the decision. The case says that the staff members are willing to accede to the director's judgment. CII is the decision style that would require the least amount of time, but GII might be used, especially if the manager wishes the group to mature so that there is less of a need for managerial reliance.

(continued)

ACTIVITY 7   DIAGNOSING THE TASK *(continued)*

Variations

1. Teaching designs for inservice education and for ongoing teams or units can be found in the original article: La Monica, E., & Finch, F. (1977). Managerial decision-making. *Journal of Nursing Administration, 7*(5), 20–28.

2. Further cases that have been adapted from business examples are in the following: Taylor, A. G. (1978). Decision making in nursing: An analytical approach. *Journal of Nursing Administration, 8*(11), 22–30.

3. Cases can be developed by individuals as a homework assignment and then discussed in small groups.

WORKSHEET 7-A: CASES

Case 1

You are the head nurse of a 50-bed orthopedic unit that is the first group to move to a new wing in 1 week. You must estimate the supplies and medications necessary to stock on the new floor so that nursing care can be maintained smoothly and without interruption.

Since you have been the head nurse for 10 years on this unit, you have the knowledge and experience necessary to evaluate approximately what you will need. It is important that nothing be forgotten because surgery will be uninterrupted and fresh postoperative patients will be arriving from surgery as well as preoperative patients needing preparation. Absent supplies may result in delayed surgery, confusion, frustrated personnel, and possible less than ideal nursing care. It is your practice to meet regularly with your managerial subordinates to discuss the problems of running the floor. These meetings have resulted in the creation and development of a very effective team.

Decision style you would use: _____
Rationale: _____

Case 2

You are the nursing coordinator of 12 registered nurses in an intensive care unit. Their formal education, responsibilities, and experience are very similar, providing for an extremely close-knit group who share responsibilities. Yesterday, your director of nurses informed you that she would supply funds for four of your nurses to attend the National Critical Care Nursing Association Convention for 5 days in San Francisco.

It is your perception that all of your nurses would very much like to attend, and from the standpoint of staffing there is no particular reason why anyone should attend over any other. The problem is somewhat complicated by the fact that all of the nurses are active officers and members of the local organization.

Decision style you would use: _____
Rationale: _____

(continued)

Note. The source of the cases with minor adaptations is La Monica, E., & Finch, F. (1977). Managerial decision-making. *Journal of Nursing Administration,* 7(5), 21–22. Reproduced by permission.
The first two nursing situations were adapted from business examples. The original material is represented in Vroom, V. H. (1973). A new look at managerial decision making. *Organization Dynamics,* 1(4), 72–73. The third adaptation is originally found in Vroom, V. H., & Jago, A. G. (1974). Decision making as a social process. *Decision Sciences,* 5(4), 750.

WORKSHEET 7-A: CASES *(continued)*

Case 3

You are the executive director of a small but growing Visiting Nurse's Association. The rural location and consumer needs are factors that contribute to the emphasis on expanded roles in nursing practice at all levels.

When you took the position 5 years ago, the nursing care was poor, and finances were slim. Under your leadership, much progress has been made. You obtained state and federal monies and personally educated your nursing resources. This progress has been achieved while the economy has moved into a mild recession, and, as a result, your prestige among your colleagues and staff is very high. Your success, which you are inclined to attribute principally to good luck and to a few timely decisions on your part, has, in your judgment, one unfortunate by-product. It has caused your staff to look to you for leadership and guidance in decision-making beyond what you consider necessary. You have no doubts about their capabilities, but wish they were not quite so willing to accede to your judgment.

You have recently acquired a grant to permit opening a satellite branch. Your problem is to decide on the best location. You believe that there is no formula in this selection process. It will be made by assessment of community needs, lack of available resources, and "what feels right." You have asked your staff to assess their districts since their knowledge about the community in which they practice should be extremely useful in making a wise choice.

The support from your staff members is essential because the success of the satellite will be highly dependent on their willingness to initially staff and then educate and assist new nurses during its early days. Currently, your staff is small enough for everyone to feel and function as a team; you want this to continue.

The success of the satellite will benefit everybody. Directly they will benefit from the expansion, and indirectly they will reap the personal and professional advantages of being involved in the building and expansion of nursing services.

Decision style you would use: _____

Rationale: _____

ACTIVITY 8	INDEPENDENT CASE ANALYSIS— A TERM PROJECT

Purposes	1. To carry out the steps of the problem-solving method.
	2. To apply theory and research findings in analyzing a health care or management situation.
	3. To report the results formally.
Facility	A clinical setting where learners work with a group of people (professional and nonprofessional) about the delivery of health care.
Materials	Worksheet 8-A: Evaluation of Written Assignment.
	Paper and a computer for word processing and printing.
Time Required	Variable, but generally a term project.
Group Size	Not applicable.
Design	1. Each learner is to develop a personal case experience as a leader, a follower, or a consultant/advisor, and analyze what is happening (or has happened) in the situation.
	2. The problem-solving method should be applied using individually selected theories to diagnose the system and to choose the appropriate leader behavior style.
	3. The paper is a formal project. It must be typed, double-spaced, and use an approved style and format. References must be included, and the paper's maximum length should be 30 pages.
	4. Worksheet 8-A, Evaluation of Written Assignment, will be the basis on which the paper will be graded. This worksheet can be used as an outline for the paper.
Variation	Grade determinations can be adjusted according to teacher preference.

(continued)

WORKSHEET 8-A: EVALUATION OF WRITTEN ASSIGNMENT

I.   Synthesis of Theoretic Framework Used in Analysis (10 points)

II.   Problem/Goal/Opportunity Identification and Definition (20 points)

III. Problem/Goal/Opportunity Analysis (30 points)

IV.   Alternative Actions with Anticipated Results for Each Action (20 points)

V.   Recommended Action and Rationale (10 points)

VI.   Style and Format (10 points)

Grading Scale

A+	100	B+	90 to 92	C+	80 to 82	F	72 and below
A	97 to 99	B	87 to 89	C	77 to 79		
A−	93 to 96	B−	83 to 86	C−	73 to 76		

Managerial Skills:
The "How-To" Satellites

The purpose of Part III of this book is to discuss the skills that managers require to carry out the steps of the management process and to bring life into the words. These steps were described in Part I, Chapter 1, of this book: planning, organizing, motivating, and controlling. The satellites circle the core of how managers work. They reflect what processes a manager must have in order for the core aspects of leadership theory to function in practice.

The satellites in Part III are some of the dominant and primary theories and concepts that put the management method—also first described in Part I, Chapter 1—into action. The steps of the managerial method are as follows: assess the information; identify and then analyze the problem, goal, or opportunity; choose leader behavior; create alternative solutions; recommend an action plan; implement the action plan; and evaluate the results.

The chapter topics in Part III are related fundamentally to management and leadership and are not meant to be considered all-inclusive. Rather, they are the basic satellites that should exist in a leader's knowledge foundation.

A conceptual framework is provided in each of the six satellite areas. Discussion of each focuses on basic skills that can be augmented and amplified by the manager through experience and continued education. The basic management skills are discussed in separate chapters even though all of the topics are interrelated, as are the steps of the management process and the management method. Areas that are covered in this part of the book are communication processes, power, confident communication or assertiveness, conflict resolution, time management, and creativity. Experiential Learning Activities for the satellites conclude Part III.

Communication

EXPECTED LEARNING OUTCOMES

- To gain greater experience in effective managerial communication techniques
- To recognize how communication processes work
- To validate messages received with messages sent
- To focus on verbal and nonverbal messages that may be given in interactions between and among managers and followers
- To conceptualize leadership theory as embraced totally with the communication processes

Communication is the most important skill in management and leadership. As a matter of fact, it is probably *the* most important concept in life. Communication occurs in every step of the management process; *everything* that a manager does involves communication—with followers, with superiors, and with associates. Communication is accepted as one of the most critical tasks that leaders must master (Chambers, 2003; Porter-O'Grady & Malloch, 2007; Reynolds, Bailey, Seden, & Dimmock, 2003; Smeltzer & Vlasses, 2004; Sullivan, 1998; Woodward, 2003). Kotter (2010, October), interviewed by Kehoe, found that leaders must communicate respectfully, concisely, and clearly. Further, responses must be filled with common sense.

This chapter begins with a definition of communication followed by a theoretic perspective on the actual communication process and the purposes of communication. Types of communications are then presented. How leaders communicate concludes the chapter.

DEFINITION OF COMMUNICATION

Humans are social beings who are dependent on, independent of, and interdependent on others in the environment. The only vehicle for reaching out to closely related others in an environment is communication through languages—both verbal (French, Italian, German, and so forth) and nonverbal (body language and gestures understood by particular cultures) (La Monica, 1985). Communication embraces the lives of all people and living creatures. The only way that it would not be important and necessary is if human beings existed in a vacuum, autonomously going through life in an impermeable cell; if they were born, lived, and died in isolation from others; or if individuals reached only within one's self to fulfill needs. Obviously, this type of descriptive situation is not a reality.

Shannon and Weaver (1948/1998) defined communication as all that occurs between two or more minds. Because behavior is what other people perceive, all behavior is communication, and all communication produces behavior. Newstrom (2011) referred to communication as an information transfer between people. It is the bridge between and among people. Johnson (2008) saw the concept as a means for one person to relay a message to another, expecting a response.

Communication, therefore, always involves a sender and a receiver. Even though Gibran (1923/2002) said that one can verbally speak with self, communication in organizations almost always includes at least two people and both roles of sender and receiver. Newstrom (2011) aptly pointed out that a manager sending a written message to a follower has communicated the message only when the follower receives, reads, and understands the message.

THE COMMUNICATION PROCESS

The communication process involves five basic steps, adapted from the works of Johnson (2008) and Newstrom (2011), and portrayed in Figure 8.1.

FIGURE 8.1   The Communication Process

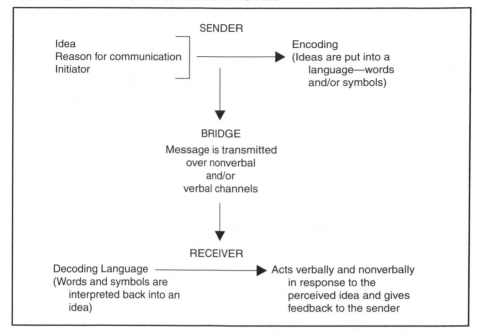

The sender has an idea and a wish to communicate that idea to another person. Newstrom (2011) cogently asserted that senders must think before sending a message; this step is critical. Once a sender has the idea clearly in mind, then the appropriate language(s) for communicating the idea must be selected. It is necessary to consider nonverbal body language as well as verbal language. Remember that management and leadership involve conscious, identifiable strategies for all behaviors. Choose the language that has the highest probability for sending the message accurately, for being received accurately, and for showing respect and clarity at the same time that one's point is evident. As Ramsey (2009) advised, communicate with adult followers by always keeping in mind that you are the professional. Make whatever you say be in harmony with your role.

After a message has been encoded, it is transmitted by the sender over selected nonverbal and/or verbal channels. The receiver, who must be tuned in to the sender's channels, receives the message and decodes it back from language to an idea. The receiver acts in response to the decoded message. The message may be stored or ignored. The receiver may communicate another idea back to the sender, or the receiver may simply perform a task in response to the message.

Whatever the receiver does in response to the sender's message is called "feedback," which is a message sent back to the sender. The receiver then becomes the sender and the communication process begins again. Such circularity continues until communication ceases.

Evaluating feedback is a way for the sender to validate that the message has been perceived according to intent. The goal of any communication, of course, is congruence between the sender's intended message and the receiver's perceived message. Validation is essential because people communicate and perceive in response to individual attitudes, knowledge, and experience (Berlo, 1960). Perception is selective. Hence, what is transmitted on "the bridge" (refer to Figure 8.1) may not be perceived as such. If necessary, further messages may be used by the sender to clarify the original intent . . . and the communication dance may continue.

PURPOSES OF COMMUNICATION

The overall purpose for managing and leading is to motivate systems to accomplish goals. Communication to and with others is "the bridge" by which the manager and the human resources in a system relate with one another. A manager must be able to communicate effectively in order to truly fulfill the role. Furthermore, it is the manager's responsibility to build and maintain the bridge even though other human resources participate in its design and structure. The manager is the leader, the pacesetter, and the educator.

Successful and effective teams must be developed in a system in order to carry out goals. Teams are developed by managers and leaders. This occurs through effective communications.

It is evident from von Bertalanffy's (1968/2003) general system theory that teamwork has a high probability for resulting in high quality, decreased costs, and high employee morale. Communication is the bridge on which teamwork connects.

Managerial use of communication processes is aimed at creating the will to work and the skill to work in team members. This can be related to Hersey, Blanchard, and Johnson's (2008) theory of performance readiness—willingness and ability. Recalling this theory presented in Part II of this book, the manager wishes to have human resources in a goal-directed system both willing and able. Then the system will accomplish the goal-oriented task because the people are intrinsically motivated and have the required knowledge and experience. The label *ability* can be paralleled with the word *skill*. Human resources who are not able to accomplish a task must be provided with the information necessary to make them skillful. The attitude of willingness with the team members must be developed because it fosters teamwork, motivation, and job satisfaction.

Hewitt (1981) delineated more specific purposes for which communication processes are used. It is pointed out that the following purposes are rarely, if ever, used in isolation of one another. These purposes are to:

1. Learn or teach something;
2. Influence someone's behavior;
3. Express feelings;
4. Explain one's own behavior or clarify another's behavior;
5. Relate with others;
6. Untangle a problem;
7. Accomplish a goal;
8. Reduce tension or to resolve conflict; and
9. Stimulate interest in self or in others.

TYPES OF COMMUNICATION

There are two basic types of communication: verbal and nonverbal. Each type can be further broken into one-way or two-way communication. Figure 8.2 illustrates these points.

Everything written or spoken is included in verbal communication. Verbal interactions, between or among superiors and followers, associates and associates, nurses and patients, nurses and other members of the health care team, and so forth, form the bases for verbal communication. Written memoranda, bulletin board notices and meeting announcements, newspaper items, written requests, written assignments, and other similar items are also verbal communications.

Nonverbal communication is body language—it is unspoken and unwritten but nevertheless powerfully communicated through the body's

FIGURE 8.2   Types of Communication

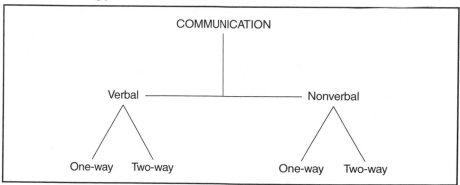

behavior. People nonverbally communicate through gestures, posture, eye contact, facial expressions, space variations, voice volume and tone, and so forth. Both the content and the intensity of interactions between or among individuals are greatly influenced by nonverbal communication. Differences between what a speaker is feeling and saying are often nonverbally communicated to the listener. Even though nonverbal communication amplifies, contradicts, and/or augments what is being communicated verbally, nonverbal communication, like silence, can stand alone.

Fast (2002) organized available information into a method for analyzing behavior. It was suggested that leaning the body forward communicated a positive attitude toward the addressee, whereas leaning the body backward communicated a negative attitude. Walters (1977) concisely specified research findings in various nonverbal attending skills with effective and ineffective uses of each. Table 8.1 lists Walters's findings.

One-way communication means that the message is sent from the sender to the receiver; it involves no feedback from the receiver back to the sender. Two-way communication uses feedback. Johnson (2008) continued this basic definition by saying that one-way communication occurs when the sender cannot perceive how the receiver is decoding the message. Two-way communication takes place when the sender receives feedback or validation. Referring back to the components of leader behavior discussed in Chapter 5 (Bass, 2008; Bass & Stogdill, 1990; Fleishman, 1973), structure predominantly involves one-way communication, and consideration involves almost always two-way communication. Both types of communication are used for verbal and nonverbal interactions in leadership and management. Some examples of each are provided.

  1. Sender gives verbal message and does not provide an avenue or time for feedback (one-way).
  Example: Manager announces a luncheon staff meeting by posting notices on bulletin boards.
  2. Sender gives verbal message and provides an avenue for feedback but receiver does not comply with the request (one-way).
  Example: Inservice educator sends out a memorandum requesting all care-providers to specify one of three areas that they would prefer to be the topic of the next staff development meeting. A space is provided on the memorandum to respond. No responses, however, are received.
  3. Sender gives verbal messages and waits for a response; receiver replies (two-way).
  Example:
  Director to supervisor: "You have been using the primary nursing care model on your unit for six months. Have you had any reactions from the clients?"

TABLE 8.1   Attending Skills

INEFFECTIVE USE	NONVERBAL MODES OF COMMUNICATION	EFFECTIVE USE
Doing any of these things will probably close off or slow the conversation		These behaviors encourage talk because they show acceptance and respect for the other person
Distant; very close	Space	Approximate arms-length
Spread among activities	Attention	Given fully to talker
Away	Movement	Toward
Slouching; rigid; seated leaning away	Posture	Relaxed but attentive; seated leaning slightly toward
Absent; defiant; jittery	Eye contact	Regular
You continue with what you are doing before responding; in a hurry	Time	Respond at first opportunity; share time with them
Used to keep distance between the persons	Feet and legs (when sitting)	Unobtrusive
Used as a barrier	Furniture	Used to draw persons together
Sloppy; garish; provocative	Dress; grooming	Tasteful
Does not match feelings, scowl; blank look	Facial expression	Matches your own or other's feelings; smile
Compete for attention with your words	Gestures	Highlight your words; unobtrusive; smooth
Obvious, distracting	Mannerisms	None, or unobtrusive
Very loud or very soft	Voice: volume	Clearly audible
Impatient or staccato; very slow or hesitant	Voice: rate	Average, or a bit slower
Apathetic; sleepy; jumpy; pushy	Energy level	Alert; stays alert throughout a long conversation

Note. The source of the attending skills is from Walters, R. (1977). The amity book: Exercises in friendship and helping skills. In G. Gazda, F. Asbury, F. Balzer, W. Childers, & R. Walters (Eds.), *Human relations development: A manual for educators* (2nd ed.). Boston: Allyn and Bacon. Copyright 1977 by R. Walters. Reprinted with permission of the author.

Supervisor to director: "Not specifically to primary nursing care, but our recent survey of patient satisfaction showed that our clients are generally more satisfied now than they were when surveyed last year at this time."

The literature is replete with discussions of types of communications. Basics have been discussed in this chapter. It is important to understand, however, that various cultures have different interpretations of verbal and nonverbal communication. The next section of this chapter looks at how managers communicate. Chapter 10 broadens communication theory with the concept of "confident" communication, which is often referred to as assertiveness, and Chapter 19 focuses on diversity. It must be underscored that communication is involved in every aspect of leadership and management. Therefore, it embraces every chapter in this book.

HOW MANAGERS COMMUNICATE

Managers communicate in the following several ways: Hersey et al. (2008) stated that managers use the active verbs of telling, selling, participating, and delegating. Newstrom (2011) noted that managers also use listening and giving and receiving feedback. Figure 8.3 portrays the relationship between how managers communicate and the Ohio State Leadership Model (Bass, 2008; Bass & Stogdill, 1990; Fleishman, 1973) that was discussed in Chapter 5. The leadership model represents how leaders behave toward followers; leaders behave by communicating to (one-way communication) and with (two-way communication) followers.

Telling, Selling, Participating, and Delegating

Hersey et al. (2008) used Situational Leadership theory (task and relationships behavior) to specify and explain the active verbs for each leader behavior style (LBS). It should be noted, however, that the Ohio State Model of Leadership theory (initiating structure and consideration) (Bass, 2008; Bass & Stogdill, 1990; Fleishman, 1973) parallels the model by Hersey et al. in application of these active verbs.

High Structure and Low Consideration or High Task and Low Relationships (LBS1) is referred to as "telling" because this style is characterized predominantly by one-way communication in which the manager defines the roles of followers by telling them what, how, when, and where to do the identified tasks. The manager guides and structures activities for followers.

FIGURE 8.3   How Leaders Communicate in the Ohio State Model of Leader Behavior

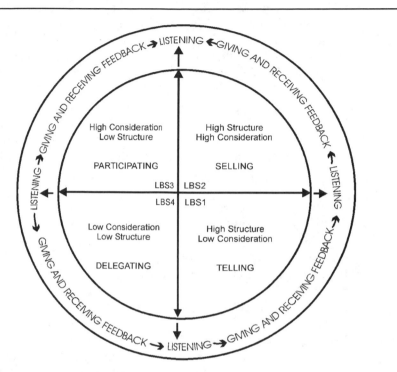

Note. The figure was created by this author, Elaine La Monica Rigolosi. The sources of the Ohio State Model of Leader Behavior are Bass, B. M. (2008). *The Bass handbook of leadership: Theory, research, & managerial applications* (4th ed.). New York, NY: Free Press. Bass, B. M., & Stogdill, R. M. (1990). *Bass & Stogdill's handbook of leadership: Theory, research, and managerial applications* (3rd ed.). New York, NY: Free Press. Fleishman, E. (1973). Twenty years of consideration and structure. In E. Fleishman & J. G. Hunt (Eds.), *Current developments in the study of leadership: A centennial event symposium held at Southern Illinois University at Carbondale.* Carbondale, IL: Southern Illinois University Press.

The source for the action verbs telling, selling, participating, and delegating is Hersey, P., Blanchard, K. H., & Johnson, D. E. (2008). *Management of organizational behavior: Leading human resources* (9th ed.). Upper Saddle River, NJ: Pearson Prentice Hall.

The source for giving and receiving feedback and listening is Newstrom, J. W. (2011). *Organizational behavior: Human behavior at work* (13th ed.). New York, NY: McGraw-Hill/Irwin.

High Structure and High Consideration or High Task and High Relationships (*LBS2*) is referred to as "selling" because most of the direction is provided by the manager, even though dialogue and clarification are encouraged. Through two-way communication and socioemotional support, the manager tries to get the follower(s) psychologically to buy into decisions that have to be made. It can also be seen as persuasive leadership.

High Consideration and Low Structure or High Relationships and Low Task (*LBS3*) is called "participating" because the manager and follower(s) jointly share in decision making through two-way communication, discussion, use of the group process, and problem solving. The manager reinforces, encourages, and calms.

Low Consideration and Low Structure or Low Task and Low Relationships (*LBS4*) is labeled "delegating" because the style involves letting follower(s) develop and implement their own goal-accomplishing strategies. General supervision is minimal because the follower(s) are high in ability, willingness, and security.

Listening and giving or receiving feedback are represented in Figure 8.3 as a circle that runs around all of the leader behavior styles. A manager behaves by communicating to and with followers in the leader behavior style that has the highest probability for motivating them to accomplish the task. The manager should then listen to the feedback that is verbally and nonverbally provided by followers in response to the message given by the leader through one of the leader behavior styles. Then the manager decodes the feedback and sends another message to the followers. This process occurs until communication ceases; hence, no further message is required at that time.

Listening

Listening involves the ability to tune into people, the environment, and the meanings of messages that are spoken and unspoken (La Monica, 1985). Newstrom (2011) asserted that one hears with one's ears, but listening occurs in the mind. Listening is the ability to perceive the exact message that the sender intended, to the degree that is humanly possible. When messages are perceived accurately, better decisions result because the information inputs are on target—perception matches intent. Time is also saved when people listen because more—both in quality and in quantity—can be learned in a given period of time. Newstrom further pointed out that good listening skills represent good manners and are forms of behavior modeling that may enable others to listen more effectively in return. Table 8.2 provides guides for effective listening.

TABLE 8.2   Ten Guides for Effective Listening

1. *Stop talking!*
   You cannot listen if you are talking.
   Polonius (*Hamlet*): "Give every man thine ear, but few thy voice."

2. *Put the talker at ease.*
   Welcome the person, and express your availability.
   Help the person feel free to talk by making him or her comfortable.
   Create a permissive atmosphere by establishing rapport.

3. *Show the talker that you want to listen.*
   Look interested. Establish eye contact and give nonverbal responses.
   Act interested. Do not read your mail while someone talks.
   Listen to understand rather than to oppose.

4. *Remove distractions.*
   Don't doodle, tap, or shuffle papers.
   Offer to shut the door.

5. *Empathize with a talker.*
   Try to see the other person's point of view.
   Connect with the person by sharing a similar experience.

6. *Be patient.*
   Allow plenty of time. Do not interrupt a talker. Wait out the short pauses.
   Don't start for the door or walk away.

7. *Hold your temper.*
   Pause before you speak or respond.
   An angry person takes the wrong meaning from words.

8. *Go easy on argument and criticism.*
   These approaches put a talker on the defensive, and she or he may clam up or become angry.
   Do not argue. Even if you win, you lose.

9. *Ask relevant questions.*
   Asking questions encourages a talker and shows that you are listening.
   It helps develop points further and discloses relevant emotions.

10. *Stop talking!*
    This guideline is both first and last, because all others depend on it.
    You cannot be an effective listener while you are talking.
    • Nature gave people two ears but only one tongue, which is a gentle hint that they should listen more than they talk.
    • Listening requires two ears, one for meaning and one for feeling.
    • Decision makers who do not listen have less information for making sound decisions.

Note. The source for the guides for effective listening is Newstrom, J. W, & Davis, K. (2002). *Organizational behavior: Human behavior at work* (11th ed., p.64). Boston: McGraw-Hill/Irwin. Reproduced with permission.

Giving and Receiving Feedback

Effective communication involves two-way communication, also referred to as feedback. The purposes of feedback are to increase shared understanding about behavior, feelings, and motivations; to facilitate development of trusting and open relationships between and among people; and to give information concerning the effects of individual behavior on others (La Monica, 1985). Feedback is also "the process of adjusting future actions based upon information about past performance" (Haynes, Massie, & Wallace, 1975, p. 260). It refers to the return of generated behavior (Luft, 1984). Feedback can be verbal or nonverbal and, according to Donnelly, Gibson, and Ivancevich (1998), it can come in many forms.

Feedback can be given and received in a variety of formal and informal ways. Time can be set aside at the conclusion of meetings for the group to discuss how it functioned. The Experiential Learning Activities at the conclusion of Part III provide some paper and pencil instruments for encouraging this form of feedback. People can ask for feedback in formal or informal interactions. Performance appraisals at six-month intervals involve feedback; a simple comment like "you have really worked hard today" is also feedback. A casual, understanding nod (nonverbally) is feedback, too.

Feedback, therefore, occurs whenever the receiver of a message sends a message back to the sender regarding the message received. In a casual sense, feedback is given constantly. In a more designed sense, however, feedback should be elicited and given by managers so that information on which decisions are based is as accurate as possible. Feedback should also be used to reinforce behavior that the leader wishes a follower to continue.

Napier and Gershenfeld (2003) believed that feedback involves upward communication, thereby making it a high-risk activity for followers. Giving and receiving feedback can do more damage than good by increasing risk and defensiveness if certain criteria are not followed. Managers can dampen this risk factor by minimizing defenses and maximizing acceptance. This is accomplished if feedback is useful; giving and receiving feedback is a skill.

The National Training Laboratory (NTL) Institute for Applied Behavioral Science was early in suggesting characteristics of useful feedback that remain alive and vibrant today (*Laboratories in Human Relations Training*, 1971, pp. 27–28).* These characteristics follow.

Note. The characteristics of feedback were from NTL Institute, "Feedback: The Art of Giving and Receiving Help," by C. R. Mill, *Reading Book for Laboratories in Human Relations Training* (pp. 18–19), edited by C. R. Mill and L. C. Porter, 1972, Washington, DC: National Training Laboratory Learning resources Corporation. Copyright 1972. Adapted with permission.

1.   *It is descriptive rather than evaluative.* By describing one's own reaction, it leaves the individual free to use it or not to use it as he or she sees fit. By avoiding evaluative language, it reduces the need for the individual to react defensively.

2.   *It is specific rather than general.* To be told that one is "dominating" will probably not be as useful as to be told that "just now when we were deciding the issue, you did not listen to what others said, and I felt forced to accept your arguments or face attack from you."

3.   *It takes into account the needs of both the receiver and the giver of the feedback.* Feedback can be destructive when it serves only our own needs and fails to consider the needs of the person on the receiving end.

4.   *It is directed toward behavior that the receiver can do something about.* Frustration is only increased when a person is reminded of some shortcoming over which he or she has no control.

5.   *It is solicited, rather than imposed.* Feedback is most useful when the receiver . . . has formulated the kind of question which those observing can . . . answer.

6.   *It is well timed.* In general, feedback is most useful at the earliest opportunity after the given behavior (depending of course on the person's readiness to hear it, support available from others, etc.).

7.   *It is checked to ensure clear communication.* One way of doing this is to have the receiver try to rephrase the feedback received to see if it corresponds to what the sender had in mind.

SUMMARY

Communication is the most important skill in management and leadership; everything that a manager does involves relating to others. It is defined as a process of passing information (messages) between or among people. Therefore, it involves a sender, a message, and a receiver who may give feedback to the sender on the message that was received. Because the purpose of managing is to motivate systems of people to accomplish goals, communication is necessary (a) to provide the system with the skills to work and (b) to facilitate the system's will to work as a team in goal accomplishment.

Two types of communication exist: verbal and nonverbal. In each type, communication can be one-way or two-way. Verbal communication involves the written or spoken word. Nonverbal communication involves body language. One-way communication means that a message is sent from a sender to a receiver, and it involves no feedback. Two-way communication also involves a sent message, but it also includes responses and feedback.

Managers communicate by telling, selling, participating, delegating, listening, and giving and receiving feedback.

● ● ○ REVIEW CONCEPTS AND QUESTIONS

1. Define communication and describe the communication process.
2. Describe the types of communication and how each can be used effectively and ineffectively.
3. Discuss the purposes of communication and different aspects of communication that conceptually relate to leader behavior theories.
4. List basic rules for giving and receiving feedback. Provide an example for each one.

● ● ○ SUGGESTED ASSIGNMENTS

1. Ask that learners each have dinner with family and friends and write a paper analyzing the communication patterns noted during the dinner among the individuals who were present. Reflect on both verbal and nonverbal behaviors.
2. Using the same situation as the preceding situation (Item 1), have learners each extend their analyses by critiquing the effectiveness and ineffectiveness of the verbal and nonverbal behaviors observed.
3. Request that learners write a short paper on a "listening" experience that they choose. This experience can occur personally or professionally. The purpose is to listen and report what was perceived—verbally and nonverbally. During this experience, learners should just be observers.

REFERENCES

Bass, B. M. (2008). *The Bass handbook of leadership: Theory, research, & managerial applications* (4th ed.). New York, NY: Free Press.
Bass, B. M., & Stogdill, R. M. (1990). *Bass & Stogdill's handbook of leadership: Theory, research, and managerial applications* (3rd ed.). New York, NY: Free Press.
Berlo, D. (1960). *The process of communication: An introduction to theory and practice.* New York, NY: Holt, Rinehart, and Winston.
Chambers, S. (2003). Use of non-verbal communication skills to improve nursing care. *British Journal of Nursing, 12*(14), 874–878.
Donnelly, J. H., Gibson, J. L., & Ivancevich, J. M. (1998). *Fundamentals of management* (10th ed.). New York, NY: Irwin/McGraw-Hill.
Fast, J. (2002). *Body language.* New York, NY: M. Evans.
Fleishman, E. (1973). Twenty years of consideration and structure. In E. Fleishman & J. G. Hunt (Eds.), *Current developments in the study of leadership: A centennial*

event symposium held at Southern Illinois University at Carbondale. Carbondale, IL: Southern Illinois University Press.

Gibran, K. (2002). *The prophet.* London, United Kingdom: Penguin. (Original work published 1923)

Haynes, W. W., Massie, J. L., & Wallace, M. J. (1975). *Management: Analysis, concepts, and cases* (3rd ed.). Englewood Cliffs, NJ: Prentice Hall.

Hersey, P., Blanchard, K. H., & Johnson, D. E. (2008). *Management of organizational behavior: Leading human resources* (9th ed.). Upper Saddle River, NJ: Pearson Prentice Hall.

Hewitt, F. S. (1981). The nurse and the patient communication skills: Questions and listening. *Nursing Times, 77*(26), 21–24.

Johnson, D. W. (2008). *Reaching out: Interpersonal effectiveness and self-actualization* (10th ed.). Boston, MA: Allyn and Bacon.

Kotter, J. P. (2010, October). Managing yourself: How to save good ideas. *Harvard Business Review, 88*(10), 129–132.

Laboratories in human relationship training: Book of readings. (1971). Washington, DC: National Training Laboratory Learning Resources Corporation.

La Monica, E. (1985). *The humanistic nursing process.* Boston, MA: Jones and Bartlett.

Luft, J. (1984). *Group processes: An introduction to group dynamics* (3rd ed.). Palo Alto, CA: Mayfield.

Mill, C. (1972). Feedback: The art of giving and receiving help. In C. R. Mill & L. C. Porter (Eds.), *Reading book for laboratories in human relations training.* Washington, DC: National Training Laboratory Learning Resources Corporation.

Napier, R. W., & Gershenfeld, M. K. (2003). *Groups: Theory and experience* (7th ed.). Boston, MA: Houghton Mifflin.

Newstrom, J. W. (2002). *Organizational behavior: Human behavior at work* (11th ed.). New York, NY: McGraw-Hill/Irwin.

Newstrom, J. W. (2011). *Organizational behavior: Human behavior at work* (13th ed.). New York, NY: McGraw-Hill/Irwin.

Porter-O'Grady, T., & Malloch, K. (2007). *Quantum leadership: A resource for health care innovation* (2nd ed.). Sudbury, MA: Jones and Bartlett.

Ramsey, R. D. (2009). *How to say the right thing every time: Communicating well with students, staff, parents, and the public* (2nd ed.). Thousand Oaks, CA: Corwin Press.

Reynolds, J., Bailey, S., Seden, J., & Dimmock, B. (2003). Understanding people. *Nursing Management, 10*(7), 32–35.

Shannon, C. E., & Weaver, W. (1998). *The mathematical theory of communication.* Urbana, IL: University of Illinois Press. (Original work published 1948 by Shannon)

Smeltzer, C. H., & Vlasses, F. (2004). Storytelling: A tool for leadership to shape culture . . . listen to nurses' stories. *Journal of Nursing Care Quality, 19*(1), 74–75.

Sullivan, T. J. (1998). *Collaboration: A health care imperative.* New York, NY: McGraw-Hill.

von Bertalanffy, L. (2003). *General system theory: Foundations, development, applications.* New York, NY: Braziller. (Original work published 1968)

Walters, R. (1977). The amity book: Exercises in friendship and helping skills. In G. Gazda, F. Asbury, F. Balzer, W. Childers, & R. Walters (Eds.), *Human relations development: A manual for educators* (2nd ed.). Boston, MA: Allyn and Bacon.

Woodward, W. (2003). Preparing a new workforce. *Nursing Administration Quarterly, 27*(3), 215–222.

• • • • 9

Power

● EXPECTED LEARNING OUTCOMES

- To understand the concept of power and the energy that power generates
- To gain knowledge of the types of power
- To develop awareness of the sources of power
- To gain knowledge of how power can be used effectively in practice

Managers and leaders must have knowledge about the phenomenon of power and be astutely able and willing to put its forces to work effectively in accomplishing specified goals. A manager without such ability and willingness is relatively impotent. A useful example of this statement involves a car. A car functions because of its driver, its parts, and the fuel or gasoline that is used to make it run. Without fuel, the car does not function.

With bad fuel, it functions poorly. Gasoline is the car's energy, similarly to power being the energy that puts a manager's education, experience, and position into action. A car cannot run without gasoline, a human body cannot work without food and water, and a manager cannot be effective without power. The purpose of this chapter is to discuss power by first looking at various definitions of the concept. The types and sources of power followed by uses of power are then presented.

POWER DEFINED

Power is simply the exercise of control or influence over another person or over a group. Given the spirit of inquiry, however, researchers have been diligent in specifying more discriminating theories of social power.

Adler (1998/2009) defined power as intentional force or control. Others believed that power is inferred from observing the effects of interactions on those engaged. Still another school of thought described power as a social exchange (Blau, 1964/2009). Contemporary theorists conceptualized power as one's potential for influencing another person (Hersey, Blanchard, & Johnson, 2008; Kreitner & Kinicki, 2010). Bennis (2009) described power as a combination of collaboration and reason.

TYPES OF POWER

Etzioni (1975) delineated two types of power: *position power* and *personal power*. He viewed power as one's ability to induce or influence the behavior of another person.

Position Power

Position power is derived from within an organization. A manager who can influence a group to accomplish a goal because of his or her position in an organization is said to use position power (Etzioni, 1975). Hersey et al. (2008) asserted that position power flows down in an organization—superiors delegate authority and responsibility to followers, who repeat the process again. In a sense, one's position power may be related to the amount of authority and responsibility that is given to and/or taken from one's superior. Borkowski (2009) underscored this point. Simply having a position of management, therefore, does not always mean that one has position power. Further, if one does have power, it may or may not continue.

An essential aspect of position power is the concept of authority. Bennis (1959) saw authority as "the process by which an agent induces a subordinate to behave in a desired manner" (p. 295). In a sense, authority is thereby granted to a leader; in actuality, it is a legitimate right that may or may not be given by superiors in an organization. Authority is also granted by right of office—parent, manager, bishop—and by right of knowledge—lawyer, doctor, nurse (Francis, 1982). Power is the intrinsic ability to influence or to control others; authority is a possession of granted or delegated power; leader behavior or any behavior is required in order to use or to bring power to life. Power can only be communicated through behavior.

Personal Power

According to Etzioni (1975), personal power is derived from followers. It flows upward to a manager and is the extent to which followers respect and are committed to their leader (Hersey et al., 2008). Personal power is informal power and position power is formal power. Informal power is seen as a day-to-day phenomenon because it can be earned from followers and also can be taken away (Hersey et al., 2008). Informal leaders in groups are examples of people who have been given or have taken personal power.

Reference has been made in the preceding paragraphs to power being given or taken. Each person has control over his or her own power—not complete control because of the social interacting system, but control nevertheless. Superiors give position power by delegating authority and responsibility to a manager. A manager earns the trust of superiors by behaving in a confident, able, willing, and trustful manner. Followers give personal power to a manager—they allow themselves to be led. A manager earns personal power by treating people with respect, by being fair, and by having and using the knowledge and experience necessary to lead others in accomplishing goals.

Power is a tension between or among people—it is a dance. To say that one is given power puts power in the control of the giver, not the receiver. To say that power is taken implies that the giver has less than the receiver, has little power, or has given it all away. Power can and usually does exist implicitly in all parts of a system. Behavioral evidence of its existence, however, is observable in different people at different times in various contexts. All people cannot exert control at the same time—not without a massive, dysfunctional power struggle.

Etzioni (1975) and Machiavelli (1950) believed that it is best to have both position power and personal power—to be both feared and loved at the same time. (Descriptors are stated according to their philosophy.) What happens if such a combination is not feasible? Hersey et al. (2008) said that if one cannot have both position and personal power, then personal power alone is better than position power alone. This author tends to agree—a manager soon becomes impotent if followers collectively choose not to follow. Both types of power, however, are best.

Niccolo Machiavelli (1950) described Machiavelli's sixteenth-century treatise entitled *The Prince and the Discourses*. He believed that a relationship based on fear of retaliation (position power) tends to endure longer than one based on love because the latter relationship can be terminated quickly with no sanction or price. Terminating the former relationship may carry a price. Even though contemporary managers do not follow Machiavellian guidelines as principles for their behavior, Machiavelli made statements that all managers should understand.

Collins (1999) cogently asserted, ". . . executives must accept the fact that the exercise of true leadership is inversely proportional to the exercise of power" (p. 25). Collins furthered his point by saying that one is ". . . a leader if and only if people follow. . .when they have the freedom not to [follow]" (p. 25). As a manager works to develop positions of effective power with followers, it would be wise to recall the teachings of Giuliani and Kurson (2007). To paraphrase, they stressed that a leader must always be a person of his or her word. This builds trust in followers. The opposite is also true; followers must be people of their words in order for leaders to trust them. Tying Collins's with Giuliani's and Kurson's teachings, trust builds power and the dance can carry on with greater amounts of energy, proportionate to the levels of trust between or among the dancers.

SOURCES OF POWER

Power is derived from a variety of sources. These sources are also called *power bases* and are described by Hersey et al. (2008) and Newstrom (2011). Each source is discussed separately, according to these authors. A manager may possess and use several sources at any given time.

Coercive Power—This power source may be based on fear. Compliance is induced because failure to comply will result in punishment or penalties.

Connection Power—A manager with connection power is believed to have bonds with influential and important people within and outside of an organization. By complying with the manager, followers believe that favor will be gained with the important people connected with their leader.

Reward Power—This is grounded on the belief of followers that the manager can provide rewards for them. Compliance with the manager's strategies results in gains such as increased pay, recognition, and so forth.

Legitimate Power—Based on a manager's position, title, or role, followers believe that the manager has the right to influence them; their compliance follows. The higher one's position, the more legitimate power one possesses.

Referent Power—This source is based on the manager's personality trait; it is a part of one's personal power. A manager who is admired, liked, and identified with can induce compliance from followers.

Information Power—Information power is based on possession of or access to information. This can influence people because of the belief that compliance will result in sharing of information—followers often have the need to be "in on things."

Expert Power—Competence, knowledge, expertise, and skill comprise expert power. Followers are influenced because their manager is seen as possessing the ability to facilitate accomplishment of their work assignments.

Even though these power sources are discussed distinctly, they are related to one another. Coercive power and reward power are two ends of the same continuum; a manager can give rewards to those who comply and can punish those who fail to comply. Such authority may be granted by the nature of a position, that is, legitimate power. Referent power and expert power are contained within a person and therefore can be labeled as personal power. Connection power can involve position or can refer to those connected to the manager regardless of the position held. Connection power, therefore, can be both position power and personal power. Information power also can be both personal and position power because a manager can have access to information given the nature of one's position or because of personal reasons. Table 9.1 provides a list of the sources and types of power.

TABLE 9.1   Sources and Types of Power

SOURCES OF POWER	TYPES OF POWER
Coercive	Position
Connection	Position and/or Personal
Reward	Position
Legitimate	Position
Referent	Personal
Information	Position and/or Personal
Expert	Personal

USES OF POWER

Management literature is replete with suggestions that power should be an essential aspect of managers' personalities (Beech, 2002; Collins, 1999; Giuliani & Kurson, 2007; Lashley & Kenny, 1998; Newstrom, 2011; Rahim, 2000; Vugt & De Cremer, 1999; Zohar, 2002). Managers must therefore know about and exercise power (Upenieks, 2003). It is through the use of power that managers can be an advocate for followers (Cantor & Bernay, 1992).

In addition to the sources from which power is gained, the manager can employ power strategies to accomplish goals.

1. *Rules and regulations* can be used to thwart attempted change by followers that is not in line with specified goals (Claus & Bailey, 1977).
2. *Direct confrontation* in facts and figures is a maneuver that can be used to push toward a desired end (Peterson, 1979).
3. *Attractive personal attributes* can be amplified when selling a position because research has suggested that the more personable and attractive an individual is, the more influence that person has over others (Claus & Bailey, 1977).
4. *Coalitions* or group alliances, formed so that varied resources are pooled and a united front exists, can be used to overcome opposition (Claus & Bailey, 1977, Peterson, 1979).
5. *Social space* is a phenomenon Korda (1991) studied. The position and arrangement of desks and chairs can be a strategy to gain power. Sitting spaciously behind a desk while positioning a visitor or follower in a cramped area decreases the visitor's psychological comfort. Being situated in the "middle of things" also results in power because of access to information.
6. *Assertiveness* is a method of confident communication that powerful people know about and use in daily interactions. It is vitally important in management and is discussed in Chapter 10 of this book.
7. *Reciprocal open consultation* is used when managers and followers are open to be influenced by another. Equality and reciprocity are essential features of this strategy (Mulder, de Jong, Koppelaar, & Verhage, 1986).

SUMMARY

Power is the ability to exercise control or influence over another person or a group. Two types of power exist: (a) position power, which is formally derived, and (b) personal power, which is informally derived. Authority is part of position power. It is important to have both types of power.

Seven sources of power are noted in the literature—coercive power, connection power, reward power, legitimate power, referent power, information power, and expert power. Various strategies for using power were discussed. These include confronting directly, falling back on existing rules and regulations, amplifying attractive personal attributes, forming coalitions, and using space powerfully.

● ● ● REVIEW CONCEPTS AND QUESTIONS

1. Define the concept of power and name the early theorists.
2. Differentiate between the two types of power and defend the importance of each, separately and together.
3. Name and describe the predominant sources of power and describe each of their placements in position and/or personal power.
4. Provide examples and descriptors for the uses of power.

● ● ● SUGGESTED ASSIGNMENTS

1. Examine the formal classroom in which the management and leadership class or course is taught. Write an analysis of power in a class or course by presenting the people involved, their positions, their use of power types, and their power sources.
2. Do the same analyses as above, only use a personal situation such as roommates, families, and so forth.
3. The previous analyses can be applied into any group setting, professionally or personally, and can be done in writing or simply in a verbal presentation.
4. Ask that learners roll the script backwards into the most recent experience each one had trying to win his or her point(s) during a disagreement with personal or professional friends. The experience may also be one professionally in which they were trying to convince someone about an issue or sell their point(s). Ask that each learner write a paper analyzing their "power" personality. Include an analysis of the types of power used, sources of power, and uses of power. Tie the analyses to their own actual behaviors. Ask that the paper concludes with what they learned that can be carried forward for further effectiveness in similar situations.

REFERENCES

Adler, A. (2009). *Social interest: Adler's key to the meaning of life*. Oxford, England: Oneworld. (Original work published 1998)

Beech, M. (2002). Leaders or managers: The drive for effective leadership. *Nursing Standard, 16*(30), 35–36.

Bennis, W. G. (1959). Leadership theory and administrative behavior: The problem of authority. *Administrative Science Quarterly, 4*(3), 259–301.

Bennis, W. G. (2009). Changing organizations. In W. W. Burke, D. G. Lake, & J. W. Paine (Eds.), *Organization change: A comprehensive reader* (pp. 21–34). San Francisco, CA: Jossey-Bass.

Blau, P. M. (2009). *Exchange and power in social life.* New Brunswick, NJ: Transaction Books. (Original work published 1964)

Borkowski, N. (2009). *Organizational behavior in health care* (2nd ed). Sudbury, MA: Jones and Bartlett.

Cantor, D. W., & Bernay, T. (1992). *Women in power: The secrets of leadership.* Boston, MA: Houghton Mifflin.

Claus, K. E., & Bailey, J. T. (1977). *Power and influence in health care: A new approach to leadership.* St. Louis, MO: Mosby.

Collins, J. (1999). And the walls came tumbling down. In F. Hesselbein, M. Goldsmith, & I. Somerville (Eds.), *Leading beyond the walls.* San Francisco, CA: Jossey-Bass.

Etzioni, A. (1975). *A comparative analysis of complex organization: On power, involvement, and their correlates* (Rev. ed.). New York, NY: Free Press.

Francis, E. (1982). Using your power. *Health Services Manager, 15*(5), 7–9.

Giuliani, R. W., & Kurson, K. (2007). *Leadership.* New York, NY: Mirimax Books.

Hersey, P., Blanchard, K. H., & Johnson, D. E. (2008). *Management of organizational behavior: Leading human resources* (9th ed.). Upper Saddle River, NJ: Pearson Prentice Hall.

Korda, M. (1991). *Power: How to get it, how to use it.* New York, NY: Grand Central Books.

Kreitner, R., & Kinicki, A. (2010). *Organizational behavior* (9th ed.). New York, NY: McGraw-Hill/Irwin.

Lashley, B. R., & Kenny, D. A. (1998). Power estimation in social relations analyses. *Psychological Methods, 3*(3), 328–338.

Machiavelli, N. (1950). Of cruelty and clemency, and whether it is better to be loved or feared. *The prince and the discourses* (Chapter 17). New York, NY: Random House.

Mulder, M., de Jong, R. D., Koppelaar, L., & Verhage, J. (1986). Power, situation, and leaders' effectiveness: An organizational field study. *Journal of Applied Psychology, 71*(4), 566–570.

Newstrom, J. W. (2011). *Organizational behavior: Human behavior at work* (13th ed.). New York, NY: McGraw-Hill/Irwin.

Peterson, G. (1979). Power: A perspective for the nurse administrator. *Journal of Nursing Administration, 9*(7), 7–10.

Rahim, M. A. (2000). Power, conflict, and effectiveness: A cross-cultural study in the United States and Bulgaria. *European Psychologist, 5*(1), 28–33.

Upenieks, V. (2003). Nurse leaders' perceptions of what compromises successful leadership in today's acute inpatient environment. *Nursing Administration Quarterly, 27*(2), 140–152.

Vugt, M. V., & De Cremer, D. (1999). Leadership in social dilemmas: The effects of group identification on collective actions to provide public goods. *Journal of Personality and Social Psychology, 76*(4), 587–599.

Zohar, D. (2002). Modifying supervisory practices to improve subunit safety: A leadership-based intervention model. *Journal of Applied Psychology, 87*(1), 156–163.

Confident Communication

*Patricia M. Raskin**

* Patricia M. Raskin, PhD, is an Associate Professor Emerita of Psychology and Education in the Department of Organization and Leadership, Teachers College, Columbia University, New York. She is on the faculty of the Columbia Coach Certification Program and has a private practice in psychotherapy and executive coaching. As a psychologist, she consults nationally with industry, health care systems, and educational institutions. Dr. Raskin's scholarly interests include career development of women, identity, and work and family issues. She is a former coordinator of the Women's Task Force of the American College Personnel Association.

CONCLUSIONS
SUMMARY
REVIEW CONCEPTS AND QUESTIONS
SUGGESTED ASSIGNMENTS
REFERENCES

EXPECTED LEARNING OUTCOMES

- To understand the concepts that involve being able to communicate with confidence
- To be aware of the importance and difficulty of listening to others
- To continue the process of self-education concerning assertiveness
- To conceptualize the voice of authority

Although power and communication can be examined in groups and organizations, the ability to communicate with confidence is a highly individual skill. Although some people seem to be able to do that naturally, many others may benefit from learning how to engage in the behaviors that comprise confident communication. This involves a relationship between power and communication; this relationship is quite direct. People in the business and leadership world must develop the communications skills that are required to accomplish organizational goals with success.

In this chapter, the focus of communication is what occurs in a work environment, even though communication sweeps through everything that human beings do. At work an individual may occupy one or all of three roles: supervisor, peer, and subordinate. Although the ability to communicate easily and assertively cuts across all three roles, the elements of that communication may differ, depending not only on the role that is occupied at the moment but also on the purpose and timing of the communication desired.

This book concerns the nurse or health care provider in a management role—that is, as peer and supervisor, rather than in more subordinate roles (although it is clear that all people assume subordinate roles from time to time, no matter what title is held). There is a wide history about the different characteristics between men and women in the area of communication styles. Without getting into this area, it is essential simply to state that effective and confident communication is required in executive positions and must be developed continually—throughout life.

This chapter is designed to provide the theory and concepts that a future nurse executive should learn and practice during individual journeys that involve continuing education and self-development. Specifically, the chapter contains the following components of confident communication: preparation, listening skills, assertiveness—verbal and nonverbal, language usage, and, finally, authority.

PREPARATION

If one is communicating about facts or tasks, nothing makes one more confident than preparation. Knowing what one is going to talk about, having relevant facts and information, and organizing that information beforehand provides an anchor for the communication process. Although that is especially true for formal presentations, preparation is also important for regularly scheduled, less public events, such as staff meetings, classes, or occasional scheduled events with supervisors and subordinates.

Formal Presentations

How an audience perceives a formal speaker is not random. Gender, power, external and internal status—all influence how someone is viewed even before the presentation begins. Butler and Geis (1990) suggested that likability in women has been shown to be more important to male audiences than likability in men, and women's leadership is seen as different from male leadership. Nevertheless, being prepared can mitigate some of those effects, especially when the audience consists of people familiar with the speaker.

Not being prepared for a formal presentation can do considerable damage. For example, if a manager is in a position of power, credibility may be lost with the audience because peers make judgments about the competence of colleagues. Moreover, if trying to increase status within the organization, being perceived as not having done the necessary homework does not support the goal. The author recently attended a conference where the speaker lost her notes. The effect on her credibility was immediate and devastating, even though the high-powered audience had been initially prepared to see her as competent and powerful.

Speaking extemporaneously is almost never a good idea, even if one feels more relaxed and personable when speech is casual and unplanned. Not every word has to be rehearsed; rather, every point one plans to communicate should be prepared in advance. Although there are many models of preparation that can be used to think about formal presentations, all of them involve similar elements, some of which follow:

- Who is the audience?
- How many of the people will you know?
- What is your relationship to the audience?
- How many people will be there?
- What is(are) the purpose(s) of the presentation?

    ✧ Giving information?
    ✧ Persuading people to take a particular point of view?
    ✧ Teaching?

- How much time will you have to make the presentation?
- Will the audience participate?

    ✧ If so, what will the ratio be between your remarks and the audience participation?

- What is the nature of the presentation—is it a rare event or a regular report?
- Will you have access to visual aids?

    ✧ How familiar are you with the technology that you will be using?
    ✧ Can you make sure it works before the presentation?

- How much detail are you going to impart?

    ✧ Can the most detailed parts of the presentation be made available on handouts?

- Can you make sure that the audience is listening and participating rather than passively taking notes?

The more familiar you are with your presentation, the more relaxed you will be, the more confident you will feel, and the more respect you will show for your listeners.

Informal Presentations

Informal presentations are the kinds of presentations that you are likely to make more often. They can be brief committee reports, reports on the status of an ongoing project, reporting on a staff meeting, and/or expressing the concerns of constituents.

The guidelines suggested previously hold for informal presentations as well, but the presentations may be shorter. There may not be an "audience" per se, and one may have less time to prepare. If these presentations occur fairly regularly, try to organize the template of the content so that people will know what to expect and when to expect it; include old business and new business. Use bullet points to help organize thinking. Notes do not have to be detailed but enough to jog one's memory so that talk can be conversational.

Meetings

Even if not presenting, a manager may be spending a lot of time in meetings with subordinates and peers, as well as with supervisors. The key to being a confident communicator during meetings is not different from being confident at other times. The skills used to either run a meeting or be a participant are related to interpersonal communication that occurs every day. Behaviors that should be included at every meeting are as follows:

- Being prompt;
- Being attentive;
- Taking notes;
- Knowing the objective of the meeting;
- Speaking when what you have to say is on point; and
- Observing the interpersonal dynamics.

In contrast, behaviors that should be avoided at meetings include the following:

- Being distracted;
- Doodling;
- Speaking when you feel like speaking even if what you have to say is not relevant;
- Competing for "air time;"
- Leaving early; and
- Derailing the agenda.

LISTENING SKILLS

Listening is not as natural as it seems. Because of human physiology and because the brain can listen faster than a person can speak, "listening gaps" occur in average people, causing the mind to wander (Hersey, Blanchard, & Johnson, 2008). It is important to realize that listening and talking do not coexist simultaneously, but they both should exist in any interaction.

If managers are not listening, then distractions occur. This can be consciously controlled, albeit not completely controlled. Nevertheless, good managers listen more often and are more aware of their need to listen than less effective managers. Highly successful executives often say that their most important asset is their ability to listen to people who know more than they do on a particular topic. This section on listening is more detailed and informative than is the introduction to listening presented in Chapter 8.

People who listen are more likely to be genuinely engaged in discussion and more confident about their own participation in the conversation or dialogue. However, people often make the assumption that they are good listeners simply because listening is such a commonplace event. In fact, most people do not listen, or at least they do not hear much of what another person is communicating.

Many factors impede listening, including having a preconception about (a) what others will *say*, (b) what others are *thinking*, or (c) how others are going to feel about what is said. Some barriers to good listening are deep seated, such as race or gender bias, whereas others are more superficial and temporary. Boyle (1999) suggested that the effects of good listening deepen the sense of connection to others and foster mutual respect and collegiality. Working in an environment where these affective connections are strong creates confidence and mutual respect among those involved. Exhibit 10.1 contains a list of assumptions underlying effective listening, as well as the

EXHIBIT 10.1   Beliefs and Benefits of Effective Listening

Beliefs of Effective Listening

Listening is an effective intervention in and of itself.

The person who is talking to me is as smart as me.

It is not my job to solve a problem—only to listen.

The person talking has already thought of the solutions that I might develop.

Benefits of Effective Listening

Learning	Broadening understanding
Hearing another person's ideas and feelings	Developing confidence and empowerment in subordinates
Reducing misunderstanding	Developing insight
Reducing friction	Resolving problems
Winning trust	Creating an audience—the more you listen, the more others will listen to you

EXHIBIT 10.2   Characteristics of Effective and Ineffective Listening

Characteristics of Effective Listening

Readiness to learn

Preparing to listen and stopping other activities

Being physically relaxed

Being attentive

Being aware of both the process and content of what is being said

Understanding—clarifying what is not quite understood or not heard

Asking open-ended questions

Getting feedback to make sure that what was heard was intended

Using appropriate verbal and nonverbal cues

Acknowledging what has been heard

Requesting clarification and/or more information, if necessary

Characteristics of Ineffective Listening

Filling silences

Talking

Rehearsing what is to be said next

Not being interested—it usually shows nonverbally

Being distractible

Being passive

Being judgmental or critical

Moving the focus to one's self—self-involvement

benefits. Exhibit 10.2 presents the characteristics of effective and ineffective listening.

Burley-Allen (2001) suggested that listening quality can be divided into three levels, explaining each level.

A *Level I* listener's focus is to listen with understanding and respect. Only about 20% of the work population listens at Level I. Level I listeners:

- Are aware of personal biases and attitudes;
- Are able to avoid making automatic judgments about the speaker;
- Are able to avoid being influenced by emotionally charged words;
- Are empathic about the talker's feelings;
- Look for an area of interest in the talker's message;
- Are able to take the speaker's perspective; and
- Do not advocate.

A *Level II* listener is mainly listening to words and content. The meaning and understanding of the words and content may get lost in translation. Level II listeners often miss the intent by not reading:

- Nonverbal cues;
- Vocal intonation; and
- Facial expressions, among other things.

Little effort is made to understand the intent. This can lead to misunderstanding, incorrect actions, loss of time, and negative feelings.

Level III listeners are not really listening at all. Instead, they may be:

- Tuning out the speaker;
- Daydreaming;
- Forming rebuttals or advice internally;
- Faking attention while thinking about unrelated matters;
- More interested in talking than in listening; or
- Responding before the speaker has finished talking, usually because they "think" that they know what will be said.

ASSERTIVENESS

Although the concepts underlying assertiveness training initially gained public attention in the 1970s (Jakubowski-Spector, 1973), the usefulness of the training model to the helping professions was first noted in 1949. Originally conceived as a limited form of behavior therapy (Wolpe, 1958), assertiveness training has been found to have so many applications that it can no longer be considered as a single technique, but rather as an array of techniques designed to be effective with a large, varied number of target populations (Shoemaker & Satterfield, 1977). Most of the strategies and techniques, however, rest on three basic assumptions about human nature (Percell, 1977):

- That feelings and attitudes relate closely to behavior;
- That behavior is learned; and
- That behavior can be changed.

What Is Assertiveness?

It is not unusual for people to make the assumption that the words *assertive* and *aggressive* have the same meaning. According to many dictionary definitions, they are synonyms or close in meanings. Professionals who teach

FIGURE 10.1   Assertiveness Continuum

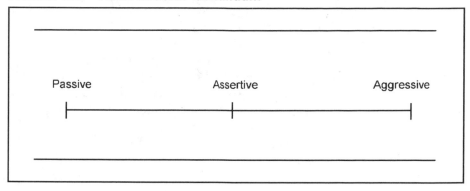

people how to be more assertive, however, make a distinction between those words. A continuum along which assertive behavior can be rated is presented in Figure 10.1.

A *passive* communication is one in which an individual's needs, wishes, desires, or concerns are not expressed explicitly, usually because the sender believes the receiver of the message wants something different, or the sender consciously or unconsciously feels the receiver is responsible for caretaking or mind-reading. An *aggressive* communication involves pushing or railroading one's needs, wishes, desires, and concerns onto another.

In *assertive* communication, it is clear that in any given dyad there are two actors. Two people may express their needs, wishes, desires, or concerns, and the opportunity exists for both to listen and respond to one another without defensiveness. An assertive message is an open one that facilitates or enhances effective communication, understanding, and/or closure.

People are rarely completely passive, assertive, or aggressive; rather, messages are usually context bound. It is entirely possible, for instance, that a staff nurse who is tongue-tied with a supervisor at work can be clear, direct, and confident with family members, children's teachers, and a mechanic at the local garage. The same supervisor, who is an effective, assertive administrator, may have difficulty returning clothing to a store, changing an order in a restaurant, or asking a family member for a favor.

Why Is Assertive Behavior Desirable?

Both passive and aggressive messages are costly, sometimes only to the conversation in which they occur, but often to relationships as well. A *passive* communication leaves the sender or responder with thoughts or feelings that still need expression. This often leads to resentment or a belief that one is misunderstood or that what is said is of no consequence to the other. Even with resentment evident, its source may be unclear.

A passive message is deficient in information, so it does not help the other person to understand the needs, wishes, desires, concerns, or limits of the sender as fully as may be possible. The hidden agenda in a passive message is often an unwillingness to take responsibility for the matter at hand, a wish to be taken care of, a set of unrealistic expectations ("If she really cared about me, she'd figure out what I need"), or an unwillingness to accept the consequences for one's own actions.

Aggressive communications have more directly observable costs to their recipients and therefore may not be brought to the attention of the aggressor for some time. Aggressive behaviors tend to elicit "fight or flight" reactions; people either respond with equal or greater aggression or else they withdraw. In both cases, the aggressor ought to be sensitive to the fact that she or he is at least partly responsible for the reaction that occurs. That sensitivity, however, is exactly the trait that is in shortest supply at the moment of aggression.

Extended periods of passivity often lead to an explosion of aggression given the "right" stimulus—the straw that breaks the camel's back. In this instance, the time is long past for discussion and mediation. The statement, "I've had it up to here, and I quit," may reflect a buildup of resentment that resulted from passivity. It is clear that there is not much left to negotiate when an individual making those statements ends the discussion abruptly.

The need for assertive behaviors in managers and executives in general has been well-documented (Buback, 2004; Grohar-Murray, DiCroce, & Langan, 2011; Trofino, 1997; Walczak & Absolon, 2001). There also is evidence to suggest that helping individuals to develop those skills has reduced perceptions about gender differences among leaders (Diekman & Eagly, 2000). Assertive behavior is desirable because (a) it represents an open, mature, and direct way of communicating that allows the other to learn about one's feelings and identity while enhancing self-esteem (Percell, 1977), and (b) it is more likely to preserve effective interpersonal relationships than are either passive or aggressive behaviors.

COMPONENTS OF ASSERTIVENESS

Assertive behaviors can be broadly separated into two components: verbal and nonverbal. In order for a communication to be categorized as assertive, both components must be present. It is entirely possible that an individual says all the right words, for example, "I'd like the sweater back that you borrowed," but does so in either such an aggressive way (hands on hips, eyes glaring, edge to the voice) or in such a passive way (small voice, downcast eyes, pleading tone) that the receiver of the message is either offended or uncomfortable.

In order for a message to be truly assertive, the words and the music behind the words have to go together. People have learned, for instance, that tenderness is not expressed in a loud tone of voice, that intimate conversations do not take place between people who are 15 feet apart, and that anger is not expressed with a smile. As a matter of fact, when the words and the music do not go together, it is difficult to know what to believe. Confusion results, and the natural response of the listener to this mixed message is avoidance, withdrawal, anger, or some other form of interpersonal distance.

Nonverbal Components

Serber (1977) suggested that the nonverbal components of behavior are:

- Loudness of voice;
- Fluency of spoken words;
- Eye contact;
- Facial expression;
- Body expression; and
- Distance from person with whom one is interacting (p. 69).

Loudness of Voice

Neither screaming nor whispering is assertive. Tone of voice does not depend on the content of the message sent. An assertive tone should be loud and firm enough so that it is heard clearly; it should not, however, be so loud that it is assaultive to the ear of the receiver.

Fluency

Fluency of spoken words also does not depend on the content of the message. People who use too many pauses or "filler" words such as "uh," "er," "huh," "you know," "like," and so forth are likely to be perceived as hesitant, whereas people who speak too quickly are often experienced as overwhelming. A moderate, unbroken rate of speech is assertive.

Eye Contact

It is impossible to be assertive when not looking at the intended receiver of one's message. Without eye contact, there is no way of gauging a response, and the receiver of a message is forced to intrude on the sender in order to give feedback about the communication. Staring or glowering, of course, is intrusive by its very nature. Assertive eye contact means that one is able to look at the receiver's face more or less continuously without such intensity that the receiver's gaze is challenged.

Facial Expression

People who giggle when angry or frown when saying loving, affectionate words sabotage the content of their messages. When people are angry, they do not smile; when expressing appreciation, they do. Although facial expression is hard to measure or describe, most people have been socialized to be capable of choosing congruent facial expressions for the meaning of their words. It is often a signal of discomfort or anxiety when one is unable to get the words and music together. Although congruence and anxiety are mutually exclusive reactions, being congruent may help to reduce the anxiety.

Body Expression

Like facial expression, how one stands, sits, or moves conveys a complex series of attitudes. A person who is slouching can be perceived as hostile, uninterested, or frightened. Crossed arms may give the impression that one is guarded, armed, or unreceptive. Hands on hips may indicate a combative, patronizing attitude, whereas a rigid, wooden posture can indicate fear. People who are assertive in their body expression seem relaxed but do not slouch, stand straight without being rigid, and use their hands and shoulders to embellish their conversation without being too forceful or abrupt.

Distance

How far away one stands from the person while interacting varies from culture to culture and individual to individual. The term *bubble* has been applied to the invisible boundary that people use to protect themselves from intrusion (Sommer, 1959). In southern Europe, for example, one may become uncomfortably aware of how close people stand when engaging in a conversation. It is natural for Americans to back away in order to feel more comfortable—to protect their bubble. Although the example just given is of a cultural difference rather than interpersonal style, it is possible to experience new European friends as aggressive or intrusive partly because of their differences in understanding an American's concept of social space during communications.

Another extreme involves too much distance. A meaningful interpersonal dialogue usually does not occur at a distance of five feet. People who are assertive in their distance from others stand close enough so that not much can pass between them and their receiver (like another person, for instance) but not so close they break the receiver's bubble.

Verbal Components

What is said is just as important as how one says it. It is unlikely, for instance, that someone who makes an unclear statement or request will get an appropriate response. It may not be that the listener is unresponsive, but rather that the message is too ambiguous for a lucid answer. Cooley and Hollandsworth (1977) suggested three verbal components of assertive statements:

- Saying "No" or taking a stand;
- Asking favors or asserting rights; and
- Expressing feelings, including anger.

Saying "No"

Assertive statements can be either initiations or reactions. There are ways to say no assertively in response to another's request or demand. Many people feel backed into a corner when asked to do something that they do not want to do. "I just couldn't say no" is a common complaint. The reasons people cannot or will not say no vary. Some are afraid of the other's anger or disapproval, some are afraid of hurting others' feelings, some are afraid of rejection, and some feel that to say no would violate their self-concept as "nice." Nevertheless, everyone wants to or needs to refuse a favor or a request from time to time. If saying no is uncomfortable, one may unintentionally become aggressive or overjustify a refusal.

A crucial aspect of saying no assertively is that the refusal be understood and believed. Saying too much makes one less convincing, whereas saying too little may seem rejecting. The object is to say no firmly and uncompromisingly while acknowledging the other's right to ask. Saying no assertively means that one can refuse a request and give a reason for refusing the request while indicating that the other person has been heard: "I appreciate your need to change shifts with me, but I can't on Thursday because I already have plans."

Taking a Stand

This component of assertion may be either an initiation or a response to a situation. The key elements in this area are the clarity of one's position, the self-respect with which such a position is stated, and an understanding of the other's position: "I know that you believe that Mrs. Lloyd is recovering.

I'm not convinced, however, that she's ready for discharge, and I will not support her release."

Asking Favors

Many people believe that they do not have the right to ask for a favor. This is not true. People do not have the right to get everything they request, but permission to ask is unnecessary. If one has trouble asking for favors, it sometimes means that more meaning may be attached to a refusal than is appropriate in the circumstance: "If he says no to this, it means he doesn't love me." Or it may mean that one will feel guilty and obligated for asking: "If she lends me her car, I'll have to do whatever she wants whenever she wants it done."

When asking for favors, being assertive means stating the problem clearly and making a specific request. How long to persist with the request is a matter of judgment; the request should end with either it being granted or with the understanding of why it cannot or will not be granted. One should not end a request before this point has been reached.

Asserting Rights

In today's society, no human being has the right to take advantage of another; every human being has the right to speak. Differences in power between two individuals do not alter those fundamental rights, although sometimes the less powerful person in the pair may feel the need to remind the more powerful member that this is the case. Of course, the consequences of power inequities between or among people need to be considered.

The key components of asserting one's rights are similar to those in asking favors: stating the problem, making a specific request for resolution or change, and persisting until one has effectively communicated a point. For example, "I understand that you sometimes need me to work later than usual. I don't like it when you simply expect that and don't check with me. If you give me some advance notice, I'm sure I'll be able to accommodate you most of the time."

Expressing Feelings, Including Anger

Although feelings often appear to be obvious from nonverbal behavior, people may have no idea of another's feelings unless they are expressed in words. A colleague may not be aware of making a peer angry, and a friend may be blind to the pain that laughing at a neighbor's handwriting caused that person. Part of being assertive is expressing emotions such as anger and affection. "I appreciate your saying that" is a more assertive way of responding to an expression of gratitude than "it's nothing" or "it's just my job," which belittles both the sender and the receiver of the message of thanks.

Also, anger is a normal emotion (Hareli, Rafaeli, & Parkinson, 2008; Parkinson, 1996). Most often, anger is a result of interactions between or among people. It is usually present in organizations where groups interact with each other (Glomb, 2002; Grandey, Dickter, & Sin, 2004; Inness, LeBlanc, & Barling, 2008;). Anger sometimes has been shown to make people work harder in select situations, but anger is said to dampen creativity (Miron-Spektor, Efrat-Treister, Rafaeli, & Schwartz-Cohen, 2011). They suggested that being emotionally neutral seemed to be the best behavior. This conclusion was further underscored by Sinaceur, Van Kleef, Neale, Adam and Haag (2011) who suggested that a calm communication of a threat during negotiations is more effective than showing anger, which they considered to be unnecessary.*

APPROPRIATE USE OF ASSERTIVENESS TECHNIQUES

As discussed earlier, few people are completely nonassertive (passive) or aggressive. Most people vary in assertiveness from situation to situation, and the degree of intimacy shared with others accounts for some of this variation as well. It is possible to be appropriately assertive with one's spouse and to become quite passive with one's mother-in-law. Alternately, being assertive with strangers may be easy, and canceling a date with a friend because of a whim to stay home may seem out of the question. Even at work, people may have a range of responses like being direct with a supervisor and being unable to give followers explicit directions on assignments.

One of the more common differences in assertiveness within rather than between individuals has to do with "managing up" versus "managing down." In the workplace, this is often compounded when authority figures are male and subordinates are female. When the component of unequal training or education is added, one can see how being assertive can be potentially confusing and difficult.

Being Assertive With Authority Figures

Many people have been raised to respect their elders and obey their parents. Although unchallenged in childhood when dependent on parents and teachers, those attitudes are not appropriate dicta for self-directed adults who bear sole responsibility for their lives. It is unlikely that parents, for instance, can rescue a subordinate from a tyrannical superior. Further, it is unlikely that the authority figure's attitudes will change simply because a subordinate wants them to change. Subordinates, also known as followers, need to help the supervisor to understand that they are not doormats or children or passive troops, ready to blindly follow orders without thinking. Although most supervisors know this, some are not as adept as others in interpersonal skills.

---

* This paragraph on anger was added by Elaine La Monica Rigolosi, author of this book.

Being assertive with supervisors may be the only way that subordinates express the right to be treated as adults, even though supervisors have position power—more responsibility and more authority. Of course, tact and understanding of the supervisor's role responsibilities are essential in asserting oneself. Diplomacy must be evident and genuine.

Being Assertive With Subordinates

People learn how to be managers and parents by watching role models. If fate looked kindly and provided such modeling by assertive leaders, managers, parents, and helping professionals, effective interpersonal skills would be perpetuated. Fate is not always so benevolent, however, and in moments of stress, it is easy to pass on the aggressive or manipulative behaviors that were learned in the past. If people can be assertive with superiors, there is less angry residue that can spill on to contacts with subordinates, patients, and children. Moreover, there also is less likelihood of forgetting that others less powerful have a right to determine their own responses. An illustration of this "domino theory" of aggression can be seen in the following example:

> Mrs. Roy is perceived by some as a whining, complaining patient. She has been calling with various complaints and requests every 10 minutes since the shift began. Responding to her for the fourth time, you feel annoyed that other responsibilities are not being carried out. Your supervisor, meeting you on your way out of Mrs. Roy's room, snaps at you because a second-year resident snapped at her because another patient was neglected. You remain silent with your supervisor, secretly cursing Mrs. Roy and the resident. The next time Mrs. Roy calls for attention, it takes you 20 minutes to respond, and when in her room, you seem gruff, uncaring, and irritated.

The irony in the preceding situation is that everyone (except perhaps Mrs. Roy) perceives a problem and wants it solved. Assertion in this circumstance is breaking the cycle of smoldering anger and serial accusation. On the fourth response to Mrs. Roy, an assertive statement might be "I understand that you are uncomfortable and unhappy, but I have other patients to care for, and I will not be back for a while. What is the most important thing that I can do for you right now?" The supervisor might be responded to by saying "It seems like the staff shortage is getting to all of us. It doesn't help when you snap at me because I am trying to do my best." By being assertive, considerably more control over both the situation and personal feelings can be exercised without resentment of the supervisor or of the patient. Each of them is also given a chance to respond further.

MONITORING ONE'S OWN ASSERTIVENESS

Two mechanisms give feedback about assertiveness: internal and external feedback mechanisms. Each mechanism is discussed separately.

Internal Feedback Mechanisms

Not being assertive can be felt in the body and is usually expressed as a tension in the stomach, chest, throat, shoulders, or neck. There may also be a sense of shame attached, often felt physically as a flush. There may be a wish to strike back, with an equal sense that to do so is risky. Aggressive anger is often felt as internal rage with a wish to overpower the target of aggression.

External Feedback Mechanisms

The receiver of nonassertive or aggressive messages provides feedback to the sender. Senders who act like victims are likely to be either attacked or ignored. Victims of aggression, however, probably respond by withdrawal and passive resistance; occasionally the response is a counter-assault. No one is assertive all of the time. If one has the feeling of losing contact with another through aggression, that person might say something like, "I think I just ignored your feelings—I'm sorry. Can we talk about what just happened?" Alternatively, if hindsight makes one aware of no assertion in an encounter, one can respond assertively later. For example, "I was really upset yesterday when you yelled at me. I understand that you were frustrated, but I'd rather talk out our difficulties than be shouted at."

Assessing and Applying Assertiveness Techniques

Because assertiveness training has been so popular for so long, there are many assessment devices to help determine whether or in what domains benefits could be derived from assertion training. Good general sources for that purpose can be found in *The Assertive Woman* (Phelps & Austin, 2002) and *Your Perfect Right* (Alberti & Emmons, 2008). The information presented in these two books continue to be applicable and pertinent today.

One of the best ways to improve skills is to practice through role playing in groups. Practice situations abound, of course, and some particularly useful exercises are included in the Experiential Learning Activities in Part III of this book. Practicing these with colleagues is a useful and educative way to get feedback about personal strengths and weaknesses in assertive communication.

A FINAL NOTE ON ASSERTIVENESS

Although assertiveness can be taught and can be seen as simply another skill to be learned, the ramifications of not being assertive go much deeper than simply choosing not to use a new technique. Nursing and other health care professions involve responsibilities that are often demanding; other people such as patients, physicians, administrators, and families often assume that they have the right to define the professional identities. Not only are patients and their families likely to misunderstand the nurse's role, for example, but patients also are likely to be in their most anxious and least levelheaded states when faced with a serious illness or even a not-so-serious illness.

Effective interpersonal relationships are an important aspect of a leader's responsibility and individual career satisfaction (Kaplan & Kaiser, 2003). Although no one can control the responses of others, and it is impossible to educate all of those who misperceive your role, one can exert control over one's own behavior. Despite difficult and trying working conditions, frustration can at least be reduced if one expresses feelings and thoughts directly, adequately, responsibly, and with accountability.

LANGUAGE USAGE

Language per se is an important component of all communication and deserves its own section, even though much of language usage is embedded in the other sections in this chapter. In the series of books that begin with the title "How to say it . . . " (Griffin, 1998; Mindell, 2001), the authors asserted that how one speaks is so important that life on the job can depend on the language used. Language is perceived as power in a workplace environment (Penelope, as cited in Mindell, 2001).

The words used in life connote much more than the verbal message sent— the words are reflections of the sender's internal and external reality. It should be noted that most people are unconsciously adept at reading these reflections. When a person listens to a speaker's state of mind, then emotion, anxiety, anger, comfort, and passion can be accurately perceived. Although many of these cues are nonverbal, and some are even physiological, many of them are verbal. To make the point, imagine someone expressing a passionate point of view using words like "maybe" or "I think so." Exhibit 10.3 provides language that expresses confidence as well as language forms that should be avoided.

Speaking With Authority

Chapter 9 presented the fact that authority is an essential aspect of position power. Authority is a legitimate right in a position that is delegated to

EXHIBIT 10.3   Confident Language and Language Forms to Avoid

Confident Language

- Use action verbs.
- Be positive. Even if you are talking about something that has a negative component, frame it in the positive. For example, rather than saying, "I don't want you to do x.," say, "I would rather that you do y than x."
- Be constructive.
- Use jargon when it identifies you as an expert.

Language Forms to Avoid

- Emotion-laden words.
- "Filler" words; for example, "er," "uh," "um." Speak fluently.
- "Hedge" words such as "sort of," "kind of," "maybe."
- Modifiers—avoid adjectives.

the holder of that position. The purpose of this section, however, is to place another lens on authority and to give it operational life by saying that the voice of authority comes from inner confidence.

Speaking with authority requires the internal belief that one has the requisite skills and abilities to do the work and to both manage and be managed. This sense of confidence hinges on a person's ability to be aware of one's own limits—to know what is known as well as what is not known. The following list provides some guidelines on speaking with authority.

- Say what you mean—be direct.
- Express your opinions as opinions, not facts.
- Indicate how you come to know what you know—be prepared.
- Avoid extreme words such as "always" or "never."
- Gather information, test assumptions.
- Take informed intelligent risks.
- Do not undermine authority.
- Do not ask others to guess at what you want. This puts both of you in an uncomfortable position.

CONCLUSIONS

Communicating confidently does not mean using the same tactics across all situations and with all the people. In some cases, it means having the security to simply listen, and to know that the act of listening well to the other person has meaning. In other cases, communicating confidently means knowing that one has the authority to make the requests being made, and that peers and subordinates will take those requests seriously, even if what is requested is not always received.

Remember that time matters. Some kinds of communication take longer than others. In an emergency, the ability to use expertise strategically matters more than being assertive. If managing an ongoing project, there is more freedom to use more collaborative communication styles.

Interpersonal relationships matter more than any other set of skills. Emotional intelligence, social skill, a sense of humor, and fairness undergird every communication.

Finally, confident communication hinges on the ability to create relationships that are not completely based on logic. Sometimes the need to influence another person or to communicate visions is emotional. In other words, a person may need to inspire others from time to time and may also need to be personally inspired.

SUMMARY

This chapter has built on basic understanding of communication theory. The elements of confident communication were discussed and included preparing for formal and informal meetings as well as listening skills. Assertiveness was presented next, covering both verbal and nonverbal discussions as well as examples. The use of assertiveness techniques with authority figures and with followers was given; self-examination followed. Language usage and the operation of authority concluded this chapter.

● ● ● REVIEW CONCEPTS AND QUESTIONS

1. Describe the relationship between power and communication.
2. Differentiate the key differences between confident communication in formal presentations and confident communication in informal presentations.
3. Describe the characteristics of effective listening.
4. Define assertiveness and discuss the differences among passive, assertive, and aggressive communications. Include both verbal and nonverbal behaviors.
5. Present guidance on being assertive with authority figures in contrast to being assertive with subordinates.
6. Discuss how confident language sounds—verbally and nonverbally, paying particular attention to speaking with authority figures.

● ● ● SUGGESTED ASSIGNMENTS

1. Write a paper describing a recent lecture or program that was attended. Critique the communications of all of the speakers as well as the person who introduced the main speaker(s) and closed the program. Following the critique, present the feedback that you would give to the speakers, if you were asked to do so.
2. Analyze a recent interaction you had with someone during which you felt that you were passive. What did you say and what would you say differently applying the concepts of confident communication? Also, what could you do or say at this time as a follow-up to the interaction?
3. Do the same as described in Suggested Assignment Number 2, only analyze an interaction in which you believed that you were aggressive.
4. Make a diary of 10 interactions that you observed in others that were considered to be excellent examples of confident communication. Describe what you learned in each interaction.

REFERENCES

Alberti, R. E., & Emmons, M. L. (2008). *Your perfect right: Assertiveness and equality in your life and relationships* (9th ed.). Atascadero, CA: Impact.

Boyle, R. C. (1999). A manager's guide to effective listening. *Manage, 51*(1), 6–7.

Buback, D. (2004). Assertiveness training to prevent verbal abuse in the OR. *AORN Journal, 79*(1), 148–164.

Burley-Allen, M. (2001). Listen up. *HR Magazine, 46*(11), 115–120.

Butler, D., & Geis, F. L. (1990). Nonverbal affect responses to male and female leaders: Implications for leadership evaluations. *Journal of Personality and Social Psychology, 58*(1), 48–59.

Cooley, M., & Hollandsworth, J. (1977). A strategy for teaching verbal content of assertive responses. In R. E. Alberti (Ed.), *Assertiveness: Innovations, applications, issues*. San Luis Obispo, CA: Impact.

Diekman, A. B., & Eagly, A. H. (2000). Stereotypes as dynamic constructs: Women and men of the past, present, and future. *Personality & Social Psychology Bulletin, 26*(10), 1171–1188.

Glomb, T. M. (2002). Workplace anger and aggression: Informing conceptual models with data from specific outcomes. *Journal of Occupational Health Psychology, 7*(1), 20–36.

Grandey, A. A., Dickter, D. N., & Sin, H. (2004). The customer is not always right: Customer aggression and emotion regulation of service employees. *Journal of Organizational Behavior, 25*(3), 397–418.

Griffin, J. (1998). *How to say it at work: Putting yourself across with power words, phrases, body language, and communication secrets*. Paramus, NJ: Prentice Hall.

Grohar-Murray, M. E., DiCroce, H. R., & Langan, J. C. (2011). *Leadership and management in nursing* (4th ed.). Upper Saddle River, NJ: Prentice Hall.

Hareli, S., Rafaeli, A., & Parkinson, B. (2008). Emotions as social entities: Interpersonal functions and effects of emotion in organizations. In N. M. Ashkanasy & C. L.

Cooper (Eds.), *Research companion to emotion in organizations* (pp. 349–359). Northampton, MA: Edward Elgar.

Hersey, P., Blanchard, K. H., & Johnson, D. E. (2008). *Management of organizational behavior: Leading human resources* (9th ed.). Upper Saddle River, NJ: Pearson Prentice Hall.

Inness, M., LeBlanc, M. M., & Barling, J. (2008). Psychosocial predictors of supervisor-, peer-, subordinate-, and service-provider-targeted aggression. *Journal of Applied Psychology, 93*(6), 1401–1411.

Jakubowski-Spector, P. (1973). Facilitating the growth of women through assertive training. *The Counseling Psychologist, 4*(1), 75–86.

Kaplan, R. E., & Kaiser, R. B. (2003). Rethinking a classic distinction in leadership: Implications for the assessment and development of executives. *Consulting Psychology Journal: Practice and Research, 55*(1), 15–25.

Mindell, P. (2001). *How to say it for women: Communicating with confidence and power using the language of success.* Paramus, NJ: Prentice Hall.

Miron-Spektor, E., Efrat-Treister, D., Rafaeli, A., & Schwarz-Cohen, O. (2011). Others' anger makes people work harder not smarter: The effect of observing anger and sarcasm on creative and analytic thinking. *Journal of Applied Psychology, 96*(5), 1065–1075.

Parkinson, B. (1996). Emotions are social. *British Journal of Psychology, 87*(Pt. 4), 663–683.

Percell, L. (1977). Assertive behavior training and the enhancement of self-esteem. In R. E. Alberti (Ed.), *Assertiveness: Innovations, applications, issues.* San Luis Obispo, CA: Impact.

Phelps, S., & Austin, N. (2002). *The assertive woman* (4th ed.). Atascadero, CA: Impact.

Serber, M. (1977). Teaching the nonverbal components of assertiveness training. In R. E. Alberti (Ed.), *Assertiveness: Innovations, applications, issues.* San Luis Obispo, CA: Impact.

Shoemaker, M., & Satterfield, D. (1977). Assertion training: An identity crisis that's coming on strong. In R. E. Alberti (Ed.), *Assertiveness: Innovations, applications, issues.* San Luis Obispo, CA: Impact.

Sinaceur, M., Van Kleef, G. A., Neale, M. A., Adam, H., & Haag C. (2011). Hot or cold: Is communicating anger or threats more effective in negotiation? *Journal of Applied Psychology, 96*(5), 1018–1032.

Sommer, R. (1959). Studies in personal space. *Sociometry, 22*(3), 247–260.

Trofino, J. (1997). The courage to change: Reshaping health care delivery. *Nursing Management, 28*(11), 50–53.

Walczak, M. B., & Absolon, P. L. (2001). Essentials for effective communication in oncology nursing: Assertiveness, conflict management, delegation, and motivation. *Journal for Nurses in Staff Development, 17*(3), 159–162.

Wolpe, J. E. (1958). *Psychotherapy by reciprocal inhibition.* Stanford, CA: Stanford University Press.

Conflict Resolution

EXPECTED LEARNING OUTCOMES

- To define and discuss the types and causes of conflict in a nursing and health care environment
- To understand the conflict resolution process
- To understand the basic conflict resolution styles
- To discuss the major types of conflict resolution strategies
- To describe successful negotiation techniques

Every human being has a unique set of drives, goals, and needs that are constantly seeking satisfaction. Earth contains all of these individuals who move in various directions across time and space on their journeys. If these journeys could be thought of as self-contained capsules that floated around other capsules, then each would be autonomous, and humans would not need to be considered sociologically; general system theory would not be viable.

In a sense, people are capsules, but needs are met by being dependent and interdependent on other capsules and independent of other capsules. If all people and their capsules desired complementary things, that is, what one wanted to obtain the other wished to give, and what one wanted to keep the other did not want, then systems could exist with total integration. Such harmony, however, does not exist in reality. Conflict exists in the absence of harmonious total integration. Conflict always exists, therefore, even though it may be suppressed. People simply do not think, believe, and desire the same things. In reality and under normal circumstances, therefore, it is wise to believe that life and conflict coexist.

Conflict is absolute; a manager must learn to facilitate effectively the resolution of conflict among people in order to accomplish goals, which is the content of this chapter. The chapter begins with definitions of conflict, followed by discussion of the types and causes of conflict. These content areas set the stage for the conflict process and strategies for resolving conflict. Productive and destructive outcomes of conflict are the final topics.

DEFINITIONS OF CONFLICT

Deutsch (1973) defined conflict as a clash or a struggle that occurs when one's balance among feelings, thoughts, desires, and behavior is threatened. This disturbance results in incompatible behavior that interferes with goals. Conflict is a struggle between or among interdependent, independent, or dependent forces. Struggles can be within an individual (intrapersonal conflict), within a group (intragroup conflict) (Nielsen, 1977), or between or among individuals (interpersonal conflict) (Newstrom, 2011). Porter-O'Grady (2003) described two conflict sources in organizations: manager to staff interactions, and interactions between or among staff members.

Because conflicts exist, a manager has the power to move the conflict to a constructive or to a destructive resolution. Remember, conflict is normal (Porter-O'Grady & Malloch, 2007). In the constructive conflict resolution approach, the outcomes of an encounter result in individual and/or group growth, heightened awareness and understanding of self and others, and positive feelings toward the outcomes of the interaction. Destructive resolutions result in an expansion of the conflict and negative feelings toward self and/or others. Conflict, therefore, can result in positive or negative outcomes (Borkowski, 2009; Kotter, 2008).

TYPES OF CONFLICT

Conflict arises within, between, and among people out of differences in facts, definitions, views, authority, boundaries, competition, goals, values, and controls (Kreitner & Kinicki, 2010). Conflict in an organization can be structurally categorized as vertical or horizontal (Marriner, 1979a). Vertical conflict involves differences between or among superiors or managers and followers. It often results from poor communication and a lack of shared perceptions regarding expectations of appropriate behavior for one's own role or that of others. Horizontal conflict is line-staff conflict and has to do with domains of practice, expertise, authority, and so forth. It is often inter-departmental strife.

Conflict can be further broken down into types as shown in Table 11.1. Examples are provided for each type of conflict.

CAUSES OF CONFLICT

Health care literature was early with discussions of the predisposing factors of conflict (Coombs & Avrunin, 1988; Nielsen, 1977). Edmunds (1979) cited the following nine general factors that seem to account for all possible causes.

1. *Specialization*—A group that assumes responsibility for a particular set of tasks or area of service sets itself apart from other groups. Intergroup conflict often results.
2. *Multitask Roles*—The nursing role requires that one be a manager, a skilled caregiver, a human relations expert, a negotiator, an advocate, and so forth. Each role with its different tasks requires different orientations that may cause conflict.
3. *Role Interdependence*—A role of nurse practitioner in private practice would not be as complicated as one being a part of a multidisciplinary health care team. In the latter, the individual domains of practice have to be discussed with others who may compete for certain areas of practice in the delivery of administrative functions and care.
4. *Task Blurring*—This results from role ambiguity and failure to designate responsibility and accountability for a task to one individual or one group.

TABLE 11.1   Types of Conflict

CONFLICT AND DESCRIPTION	EXAMPLE
Intrasender Same sender, conflicting messages	The same manager demands high-quality care, refuses to hire incompetent staff members, and refuses to argue for additional staff.
Intersender Conflicting messages from two or more senders	Top nursing management stresses the need to adopt primary nursing as the nursing care model; followers believe that they can achieve individualized, quality nursing care using the old and faithful team method.
Interrole Same person belonging to conflicting groups	The Vice President of Patient Services belongs to a community-based consumer group seeking to consolidate obstetrical and pediatric services in a geographic locality by having all obstetrics shared between two of four hospitals and all pediatrics shared between the other two hospitals. The same executive is also an employee of one hospital that is fighting to keep both services.
Person-role Same person, conflicting values (cognitive dissonance)	A nurse manager believes that patients should receive individual attention in a clinic by one nurse who follows them from visit to visit. Requirements of the position and the system for delivering care make achieving such a goal infrequent if not impossible.
Interperson Two or more people acting as protagonists for different groups	Hospital executives compete with others for permission to hire for new budgeted positions.
Intragroup New values from outside are imposed on an existing group	Continuing education is mandated by the state for continuing nursing licensure. The rural health care agency has no funds to send staff nurses to continuing education programs. Staff nurses, who are underpaid but satisfied, cannot afford to support their own continuing education.

TABLE 11.1 Types of Conflict *(continued)*

CONFLICT AND DESCRIPTION	EXAMPLE
Intergroup Two or more groups with conflicting goals	The nursing department demands that the operating and recovery room nurses organizationally come under nursing. The surgery department, controlled by physicians, believes that they should control nurses in these specialized areas.
Role Ambiguity A person is not aware of the expectations others have for a particular role	A newly hired nurse manager has no position description and has no previous experience as a manager.
Role Overload A person cannot meet the expectations of others for a role	A recently qualified registered nurse is expected by a nursing director to be in charge of a 40-bed acute medical unit on the night shift.

Note. The source of the "Conflict and Description" part of Table 11.1 is Marriner, A. (1979a). Conflict theory, *Supervisor Nurse, 10*(4), 12–16. Copyright 1979 by S-N Publications. Reprinted with permission of the author. Examples were developed by this author, Elaine La Monica Rigolosi.

5. *Differentiation*—A group of people may occupy the same role, but the attitudinal, emotional, and cognitive behaviors of these people toward their role differ. This engenders conflict, especially in problem-solving and decision-making activities.

6. *Scarcity of Resources*—Competition for money, patients, and positions is an absolute source of interperson and intergroup conflict.

7. *Change*—Whenever change occurs, conflict is not far behind. As change becomes more apparent or threatening, the probability and depth of conflict increases proportionately.

8. *Unequal Rewards*—When people are rewarded differently, conflict is often a result unless they were involved in developing the reward system.

9. *Communication Problems*—Ambiguities, perceptual distortions, language failures, cultural misunderstandings, and incorrectly used communication channels all may cause conflict.

Newstrom (2011) added to or amplified the causes listed above by Edmunds (1979). He stated that conflict occurs when people (a) have different sets of values, (b) have threats to status, (c) have contrasting perceptions, (d) lack trust, and (e) have personality clashes.

In conclusion, it is assumed that conflict exists within people and within groups; the causes of conflict, although stated generally, are unique to a situation. The next portion of the chapter contains a discussion of the conflict process.

THE CONFLICT PROCESS

Filley (1975), building on earlier works, depicted the following six steps to the conflict process, shown in Figure 11.1.

1. *Antecedent conditions* are causes of conflict and were discussed in the previous section of this chapter.
2. *Perceived conflict* is the recognition of conditions that exist between parties or within self that can cause conflict. Perceived conflict is logical, impersonal, and objective.

FIGURE 11.1 The Conflict Process

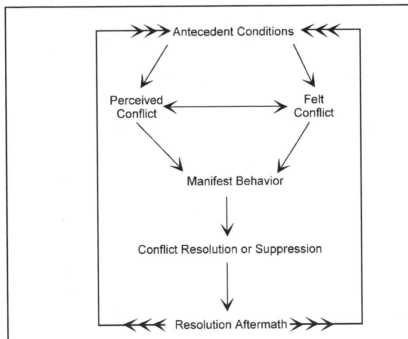

Note. The source for this figure was *Interpersonal Conflict Resolution* by Alan C. Filley. Copyright © 1975, Scott, Foresman and Company. Reprinted with permission.

3. *Felt conflict* is subjective because people feel the conflict relationship. These feelings are often described as a threat, hostility, fear, and/ or mistrust.

4. *Manifest behavior* can take the forms of aggression, non-assertion, assertion, competition, debate, or problem solving. Perceived and/or felt conflict generally result in action—actual overt behavior.

5. *Conflict resolution or suppression,* the next step in the conflict process, brings the conflict to an end either by agreement among those involved or through the defeat of one party. In competitive conflict, rules specify the outcome.

6. *Resolution aftermath* is the legacy left at the end of this cycle—feelings, beliefs, awards, and so forth. Sometimes these leftovers are called "consequences." Because conflict is experienced, learning takes place within an individual, and both negative and positive learning can become antecedent conditions for conflict in another time and place.

RESOLVING CONFLICT

Now that one has an understanding of how conflict works, what can a manager do to facilitate positive conflict resolution? Authors within and outside of the management profession offer a myriad of ideas for helping groups to resolve conflicts. There probably is not one or two best ways to resolve or to de-escalate conflict. An array of suggestions from the literature and experience are offered so that learners can choose what they believe to be best in a unique situation. All strategies are useful to have accessible in one's repertoire, available for use given a diagnosis of the system, including the environment. Basic strategies for resolving conflict are presented first, followed by negotiation techniques. A formal approach for resolving potential areas of conflict by planning ahead is then presented— Management by Objectives. This section concludes with additional points on resolving conflict.

Basic Strategies for Resolving Conflict

Blake, Shepard, and Mouton (1964) discussed five possible strategies for resolving conflict. There is no best style; rather, each has its own uses, strengths, and limitations. The rationale for making a choice of one over the other by a manager should be conscious and identifiable. In a sense, these styles should be decided as a chess player chooses to move pieces on a chessboard. The goal is to win or to be successful; many different moves can be made toward that purpose.

1. *Problem Solving (Confronting)*—Conflict is directly faced and worked through until a mutually satisfactory solution is reached. This tactic may be time consuming because the goal is to be sure that both parties and groups involved feel like winners.

2. *Compromising*—A compromise is a middle-of-the-road approach between or among parties involved. It reflects concern for everyone, but everyone gives up something in order to reach a solution.

3. *Smoothing (Accommodating)*—Smoothing means that the other person's interest has greater or is given greater emphasis than one's own. In other words, one party gives in to the other's needs, wants, or desires.

4. *Forcing (Dominating)*—Forcing is an aggressive approach and involves using power tactics to achieve personal goals. As learned in Chapter 10, aggressive behavior means winning at another person's expense.

5. *Avoiding*—When a person uses this approach in conflict, it involves withdrawal from the problem. It is either passively ignoring the issue or being sure that the issue is suppressed, which is active.

It is important to remember that all of the preceding strategies have a place in reaching the best solution to a problem or a conflict at a particular point in time. Sometimes it is important to avoid an issue. A person may not have necessary information or the issue may be too big to address at a certain time. Under other circumstances, such as in more competitive problems like budgeting, other approaches may be used. Smoothing is appropriate when people's emotions are involved and you want to be sure that the resolution aftermath is positive. However, if the problem is extremely important, smoothing may worsen the situation. Problem solving works best when time is not of the essence.

Negotiation Techniques

Negotiation is about the problem-solving behaviors that a manager uses when resolving conflicts. It always involves verbal and nonverbal communications, as well as intense listening skills. Negotiation has been developed as a concept, and Newstrom (2011) offered 10 points that should be considered during the negotiation process. Table 11.2 contains these recommendations.

TABLE 11.2   Guidelines for Conflict Resolution Through Negotiation

1. Agree on the common goal: to solve the problem.
2. Commit yourself to fluid, not fixed, positions.
3. Clarify the strength and weakness of both party's positions.
4. Recognize the other person's, and your own, possible need for face-saving.
5. Be candid and up-front; don't hold back key information.
6. Avoid arguing or using "yes-but" responses; maintain control over your emotions.
7. Strive to understand the other person's viewpoint, needs, and bottom line.
8. Ask questions to elicit needed information; probe for deeper meanings and support.
9. Make sure that both parties have a vested interest in making the outcome succeed.
10. Give the other party substantial credit when the conflict is over.

Note. The source of these guidelines is Newstrom, J. W. (2011). *Organizational behavior: Human behavior at work* (13th ed., p. 283). New York, NY: McGraw-Hill/Irwin. Reproduced with permission of McGraw-Hill .

Planning Ahead: Contracting

Planning ahead involves contracting with followers and superiors in order to identify expectations that people have for each other before the operations begin. This approach can be extremely positive because the various expectations and goals that people have are specified and decided before goal accomplishment begins. The method of contracting that has been studied extensively is called *Management by Objectives*.

Management by Objectives (MBO) is a participative approach for developing and sharing performance expectations among staff members at all levels in an organization. The concept was originally developed in 1954 by Drucker (1967/2009) and also advanced by Odiorne (1979). The concept has received a wealth of attention in the literature, both in the disciplines of business and in health care, including nursing (Cain & Luchsinger, 1978; Marquis & Huston, 2011; Tappen, 2001).

MBO is defined by Odiorne (1979) as a process whereby superiors and their followers jointly identify and set goals, define individual areas of responsibility, plan strategies and designate tasks for achieving goals, and measure and evaluate success. The MBO approach, when effectively implemented, enables expectations with followers and superiors to be public. Potential conflict is thereby reduced because goals are negotiated between or among involved parties, and then a contract is set; mutual commitment is, therefore, gained. MBO can provide a useful framework for achieving organizational goals with employee satisfaction and reinforcement as a result.

Even though the attention MBO has received in the literature might lead someone to suggest that MBO is a managerial epiphany, the concept has received criticism and may not be appropriate in all situations (Ford, 1979; Hersey, Blanchard, & Johnson, 2008). Nevertheless, MBO is worthy of study, assessment, and critique concerning whether it is an appropriate strategy in an environment and with a goal, both of which are unique.

MBO is participatory in nature—equal control by superiors and followers. Not all followers are mature enough in their position to be able to set realistic objectives for themselves. Hersey et al. (2008) pointed out that the role a superior will play in helping the follower to accomplish the set objectives is not clearly defined in MBO. Further, if a leader behavior style is in the contract, it can tie a manager to one way of behaving, which may not be appropriate for all tasks. Ford (1979) asserted, among other important issues, that companies using MBO may overlook opportunities that develop after objectives were set.

Be wise in the use of MBO. It has many positive points and it has many negative points. MBO should be employed by the leader if appropriate given the needs of the system or the individual follower. It can be an excellent means for clarifying the expectations that managers and followers have. MBO can also be as specific or as generalized as desired by the manager. It may or may not include the specification of leader behavior style, or it may note leader behavior style as a beginning point in goal accomplishment.

Apply MBO creatively; use only the part of the theory that is thought to work best for a particular problem, in a unique situation, and at a specified time. Remember, every approach for resolving conflict effectively should be available for use as a manager creates strategies to accomplish goals that are successfully achieved and have a constructive resolution.

Other Ways to Resolve Conflict

Nielsen (1977) suggested an approach called *creative conflict resolution* that is composed of six phases, similar to the problem-solving method, which follows:

1. Problem recognition with desire to solve it;
2. Concentrated effort to solve the problem through routine behavior;
3. A period of frustration due to failure of customary actions, resulting in withdrawal;
4. An incubation period to reformulate the problem into a new perspective-redefinition;

5. A tentative solution to the newly defined problem; and
6. A final solution.

One of the benefits of the previously delineated creative approach is that conflict is given time to breathe and change. Forcing conflict resolution often has the effect of heightening the energy in the direction of greater conflict.

Marriner (1979b) suggested three ways of dealing with conflict. *Win-lose* methods include use of position power, mental or physical power, silence, majority rule, and railroading. *Lose-lose* strategies include compromise, bribes for accomplishing unpleasant tasks, arbitration, and use of general rules instead of looking at issues qualitatively. *Win-win* strategies focus on goals, emphasizing consensus and integrative approaches to decision making. The steps to win-win strategies follow the problem-solving method. Hackley (2011) underscored using a win-win negotiating strategy that is problem-focused and involves joint problem solving and effective feedback.

Edmunds (1979) underscored what Marriner (1979b) suggested and added that the most constructive way to handle conflict involves verbal rather than nonverbal communication—talking out rather than acting out. The author of this book, Elaine La Monica Rigolosi, believes that both behaviors are important. Verbal communication is often best when it precedes and matches nonverbal communication—talk it out and then act on the basis of what has been discussed.

Assertive communication, as presented in the previous chapter, is a way to resolve conflict. Express opinions, feelings, and ideas directly and honestly in a way that does not insult, degrade, or humiliate others. Group-processing activities and giving and receiving feedback are other useful ways for resolving potential and present conflict. Newstrom (2011) suggested employee counseling as another way to resolve conflict, especially individual conflict. Kilmann and Thomas (1977) identified five conflict resolution modes: accommodating, avoiding, competing, compromising, and collaborating. These are similar in content to those previously presented in this chapter.

OUTCOMES OF CONFLICT

Conflicts result in outcomes that can be productive to the growth of an individual or an organization. Conversely, conflict can be extremely destructive (Briles, 2008; D'Souza, 2003; Dunn, 2003; Lehane & Carver, 2003; Willers, 2004). Newstrom (2011) delineated four distinct outcomes that conflict produces among the people who are involved. These will be presented first, followed by the four primary factors that determine the outcomes of conflict in situations, according to Deutsch (1973). These factors are the issue, power, responsiveness to needs, and communication. The discussion of the four factors encompasses that provided by Kramer and Schmalenberg (1976).

The People

There are four distinct outcomes, according to Newstrom (2011), that can occur among people in a conflicting situation. In a *win–win* situation, both parties perceive that they are in a better position after a conflict is resolved. In contrast, in a *lose–lose* situation, the conflict has resulted in a deterioration of a relationship and the resolution aftermath probably will be negative— parties are worse off than before resolution began. The last two outcomes are a *win–lose* or *lose-win* situation where one party feels positive about the outcome and the other feels negative or vice versa. Simply, one party loses and the other wins. Managers, of course, should strive for a *win–win* scenario.

The Issue

In constructive conflict, according to Deutsch (1973), the issue is focused and kept to a manageable size. Only peripheral issues that relate to the main point are discussed, and the process of choice is action rather than reaction. In destructive conflict, the issue is amplified, broadly defined with the addition of tangential and emotionally charged items.

Power

Constructive power involves finding an acceptable solution that may be a compromise or a new one (Deutsch, 1973). Personal needs and views are not imposed on others. In destructive power, situations are maintained or changed through threats and coercion. Competition is the climate with a resultant winner and loser.

Responsiveness to Needs

Constructive conflict resolution is characterized by solutions that respond to the needs of all participants in the conflict as further described by Deutsch (1973). Only one's own needs are considered in destructive conflict. Further, as time goes on, one can become stronger on the feelings that one's beliefs and behaviors are right.

Communication

Last, Deutsch (1973) discussed constructive resolution as involving open and honest dialogue, sharing individual concerns, and listening with the desire to understand others. The intent is to get the problem out in the open so that it can be dealt with effectively. Mutual distrust, misperception, and escalated emotional charges make up a destructive conflict course.

Conflict is beneficial in an organization, providing that the leader is skilled in facilitating constructive conflict resolution. When different opinions on an issue are voiced and when problems are aired, it shows that people are involved and care. People are able to talk about normal conflicting feelings and beliefs.

The opposite of love is not hate; it is indifference. With both love and hate there is energy—those about whom one cares have the power to engender hate. Indifference is empty. Energy derived through effective conflict resolution can be used positively toward goal accomplishment. Nielsen (1977) said that conflict is "the root of personal and social change" (p. 153). It stimulates problem solving and the resultant creative solutions, it can be enjoyable, and it permits the development of a personal identity.

SUMMARY

Conflict is a clash or a struggle that occurs when one's balance among feelings, thoughts, desires, and behavior is threatened. The struggle can be within an individual or within a group. Leaders can move the conflict to destructive or constructive outcomes.

Structurally, conflict can be vertical, involving differences between superiors and followers, or it can be horizontal as in line-staff relationships. Nine types of conflict are noted in the literature: intrasender, intersender, interrole, person-role, interperson, intragroup, intergroup, role ambiguity, and role overload.

Causes of conflict are unique and compounded. General causes, however, are cited and discussed. These refer to areas such as specialization, multitask roles, role interdependence, task blurring, differentiation, scarcity of resources, change, rewards, and communication. The process of conflict starts with antecedent conditions that move to perceived and/or felt conflict. Behavior follows with the conflict either being resolved or suppressed.

Constructive conflict resolution is an important aspect of managerial responsibility. An array of approaches, including Management by Objectives, was discussed. Outcomes of conflict resolution were presented. There is no best method for facilitating conflict resolution. A manager must have knowledge of all possible strategies together with knowledge of the processes of managing and leading people; the best strategy given the unique environment must then be chosen and implemented.

● ● ● REVIEW CONCEPTS AND QUESTIONS

1. Define conflict and discuss the differences between the early and current beliefs regarding the acceptance of conflict in the workplace.
2. Discuss the types of conflict as well as the antecedent conditions of conflict.
3. Explain the conflict process and, particularly, separate perceived conflict from felt conflict, defining each one.
4. Present and explain the basic strategies for resolving conflict.
5. Analyze the differences between constructive conflict resolution and destructive conflict resolution. Apply the discussion to people as well to the parts of the system.

● ● ● SUGGESTED ASSIGNMENTS

1. Select a social group in which you have just experienced a group inter-action in which conflict was expressed, verbally or nonverbally. Step outside of the situation, as if you were an observer. Analyze the conflicts that occurred in that situation, paying particular attention to the types of conflict, the causes of conflict, and the modes in which the conflicts were handled. Follow the conflict process and discuss the presumed resolution aftermath.
2. Extend the previously outlined paper and present what you would have suggested as more effective strategies for resolving the conflicts. Discuss your rationale.
3. Analyze a professional situation in which you were involved in a conflict with an organizational peer. Write a paper presenting each step of the conflict process. Carry the paper further. If you were to interact in that same scenario presently, what would you do differently or the same in order to escalate the outcome of a constructive resolution aftermath?
4. Follow the same analysis as in the third suggested assignment. But instead, analyze a professional situation involving conflict with a superior in the organizational chart.

● REFERENCES

Blake, R. R., Shepard, H., & Mouton, J. S. (1964). *Managing intergroup conflict in industry.* Houston, TX: Gulf Publishing.

Borkowski, N. (2009). *Organizational behavior in health care* (2nd ed.). Sudbury, MA: Jones and Bartlett.

Briles, J. (2008). *Zapping conflict in the health care workplace.* Aurora, CO: Mile High Press.

Cain, C., & Luchsinger, V. (1978). Management by objectives: Applications to nursing. *Journal of Nursing Administration, 8*(1), 35–38.

Coombs, C. H., & Avrunin, G. S. (1988). *The structure of conflict.* Hillsdale, NJ: Lawrence Erlbaum Associates.

Deutsch, M. (1973). *The resolution of conflict: Constructive and destructive processes.* New Haven, CT: Yale University Press.

Drucker, P. F. (2009). *The effective executive.* New York, NY: HarperCollins. (Original work published 1967)

D'Souza, F. (2003). Promoting democracy—avoiding conflict. *Community Practitioner, 76*(12), 474–475.

Dunn, H. (2003). Horizontal violence among nurses in the operating room. *AORN Journal, 78*(6), 977–988.

Edmunds, M. (1979). Conflict. *Nurse Practitioner, 4*(6), 42, 47–48.

Filley, A. C. (1975). *Interpersonal conflict resolution.* Glenview, IL: Scott, Foresman.

Ford, C. (1979). MBO: An idea whose time has gone? *Business Horizons, 22*(6), 48–55.

Hackley, S. (2011). Intervening in workplace conflict. *Executive Leadership, 26,* 7.

Hersey, P., Blanchard, K. H., & Johnson, D. E. (2008). *Management of organizational behavior: Leading human resources* (9th ed.). Upper Saddle River, NJ: Pearson Prentice Hall.

Kilmann, R. H., & Thomas, K. W. (1977). Developing a forced-choice measure of conflict-handling behavior: The "MODE" instrument. *Education and Psychological Measurement, 37*(2), 309–325.

Kotter, J. P. (2008). *A sense of urgency.* Boston, MA: Harvard Business Review Press.

Kramer, M., & Schmalenberg, C. (1976). Conflict: The cutting edge of growth. *Journal of Nursing Administration, 6*(8), 19–25.

Kreitner, R., & Kinicki, A. (2010). *Organizational behavior* (9th ed.). New York, NY: McGraw-Hill/Irwin

Lehane, M., & Carver, L. (2003). Hurt feelings. *Nursing Standard, 18*(10), 18.

Marquis, B. L., & Huston, C. J. (2011). *Leadership roles and management functions in nursing: Theory and application* (7th ed.). Philadelphia, PA: Lippincott Williams and Wilkins.

Marriner, A. (1979a). Conflict theory. *Supervisor Nurse, 10*(4), 12–16.

Marriner, A. (1979b). Conflict resolution. *Supervisor Nurse, 10*(5), 46, 49, 52–54.

Newstrom, J. W. (2011). *Organizational behavior: Human behavior at work* (13th ed.). New York, NY: McGraw-Hill.

Nielsen, H. (1977). Resolving conflict. In K. E. Claus & J. T. Bailey (Eds.), *Power and influence in health care: A new approach to leadership.* St. Louis, MO: Mosby.

Odiorne, G. S. (1979). *MBO II: A system of managerial leadership for the 80s.* Belmont, CA: Fearon Pitman.

Porter-O'Grady, T. (2003). When push comes to shove: Managers as mediators. *Nursing Management, 34*(10), 34–40.

Porter-O'Grady, T., & Malloch, K. (2007). *Quantum leadership: A resource for health care innovation* (2nd ed.). Sudbury, MA: Jones and Bartlett.

Tappen, R. M. (2001). *Nursing leadership and management: Concepts and practice* (4th ed.). Philadelphia, PA: F. A. Davis.

Willers, L. (2004). Global nursing management: Avoiding conflicts of interest. *Nursing Administration Quarterly, 28*(1), 44–50.

●●● **12**

Time Management

EXPECTED LEARNING OUTCOMES

- To understand the philosophy of time management
- To be more empowered in controlling one's use of time
- To facilitate identification of time wasters
- To analyze time wasters
- To become aware of strategies for using time more effectively

People plan within a boundary of time, look on the past over a span of time, and set goals for the future that are to be met within a period of time. Time can facilitate goal accomplishment, and it can be an oppressive force in finishing tasks. It can make people nervous in one context and can relax those same people in another context. Life is run on a time schedule—in some instances the schedule is philosophical, and in other instances it is concrete. For example, one has six months to live or one has a whole lifetime. Is there any philosophical difference in these statements? Clocks, calendars, watches, seasons, holidays, birthdays, and so forth, all point to time—the unidirectional process of growth.

Managers should attend particularly to time because it costs money to an organization—efficiency as well as inefficiency always carries price tags. Life without wasted time is impossible. A manager, however, can increase the probability that time will be used efficiently by following some general guidelines that have been primarily developed by Drucker (1967/2009), Lakein (1973/1989), Mackenzie (1972), Mackenzie and Nickerson (2009), McCay (1959/1995), and Oncken and Wass (1974/1999, 1974/2008). Applications of the time management concept also have been observed in literature from the helping professions (Berwick, Godfrey, & Roessner, 2002; Ferri, 1987; Getting things done, 2004; Marquis & Huston, 2011; Marriner, 1979; Tappen, 2000).

Every person has all the time there is, yet few people have enough time (Mackenzie, 1970, 1972, 1990, 1997; Mackenzie & Nickerson, 2009; Porter-O'Grady & Malloch, 2007). Because no manager is going to get more time, the time one has must be used more efficiently. Believe it or not, this is possible. The philosophy of time will be discussed first in this chapter, followed by the time management process. Time management techniques are discussed in the concluding part of the chapter. The intent is to help managers to learn how to get "a little more" out of the time given. In a sense, a goal is to empower your realization that you can exert control of your time.

PHILOSOPHY OF TIME

Time has been defined by Arnold (cited in Volk-Tebbitt, 1978) as a system of references for understanding and describing the occurrence and sequence of events. It is also a resource (Mackenzie, 1972, 1990, 1997; Mackenzie & Nickerson, 2009) that can neither be stockpiled nor accumulated—it cannot be turned on or off. According to Drucker (1967/2009), time is so important that unless it is managed, nothing else can be managed.

Classifying Activities

Activities are either time wasters or time consumers. The Health Care Management Team of the Minnesota Hospital Association (Volk-Tebbitt, 1978) said that a time waster is an activity that has a lower payoff than an alternate activity that could be done during a particular time period. Drop-in casual or social visitors, unproductive meetings, e-mail chat systems, telephone interruptions, and so forth, often are examples of time wasters.

Lakein (1973/1989) viewed a time-consumer activity as complex or difficult with high payoffs. He classified activities as As, Bs, and Cs. Cs are activities that no one asks about; they are trivial and have little or no payoff. If a memo is received, then the activity is a B—moderately important with moderate payoff. Activities receiving an A are important—calls get received on them, and people come to visit and inquire about them. As have a high payoff. Lakein (1973/1989) claimed that people spend 80% of their time doing C activities and only 20% doing A activities. Yet, A priorities make the difference. This factual philosophy led into the Pareto Principle.

The Pareto Principle

The Pareto Principle, named after the 19th century Italian economist and sociologist Vilfredo Pareto, stated that a relatively small number of items, tasks, or behaviors in a group are significant ones (Mackenzie, 1972, 1990, 1997; Mackenzie & Nickerson, 2009). Juran (1995) labeled these items as the "vital few" and the balance of items as the "trivial many." The Pareto Principle is a way of explaining that normally the "trivial many" situational activities use 80% of the group's time in producing 20% of the positive results. In contrast, the "vital few" situations or activities use 20% of the expended time to produce 80% of the positive results.

Applying the Pareto Principle to health care and nursing management, suppose the goal of increasing patient satisfaction with nursing care was sought. The nursing system, above average in performance readiness on this task, required Leader Behavior Style 3—high consideration and low structure, according to Situational Leadership (Hersey, Blanchard, & Johnson, 2008). Suppose the nursing staff identified 20 interventions that could be made to increase patient satisfaction. When the Pareto Principle is applied in principle, four of the 20 would generally account for 80% of the change in patients when the interventions were implemented and evaluated. The rest of the interventions would reap little payoff in terms of cost-effectiveness. The time used in low-payoff activities—that is, time wasters—could be channeled into higher-payoff interventions connected to solving another problem, which is also of high priority but on a different level. Figure 12.1 portrays this priority process.

The primary goal of time management is to make activities count, to the degree that is possible. This goal is achieved by controlling time so that the least amount of effort produces the greatest positive outcomes—making the 1:4 (effort:payoff) ratio shown in Figure 12.1 even better with less effort and better results.

FIGURE 12.1   Priority Process Using the Pareto Principle

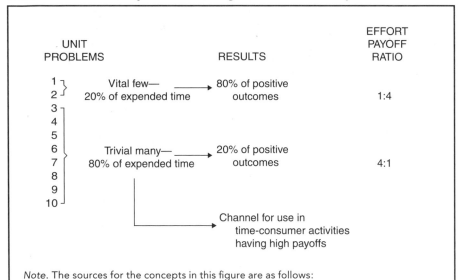

Note. The sources for the concepts in this figure are as follows:

Mackenzie, R. A. (1972). *The time trap: Managing your way out.* New York, NY: AMACOM (A Division of the American Management Association).

Mackenzie, R. A. (1997). *The time trap.* New York, NY: AMACOM.(Original work published 1972).

Juran, J. (1995). *Managerial breakthrough: The classic book on improving management performance* (Rev. ed.). New York, NY: McGraw-Hill.

Kinds of Time

A manager has two categories of time: specialty time and managerial time (Graf, 1979; Mackenzie, 1972, 1997; Mackenzie & Nickerson, 2009). Specialty time involves those responsibilities that are accomplished alone. This does not exclude the need of input from others, as required by the task. It simply means that when the activity is to be done, it is usually done by the manager. A health care manager might see staffing, mapping out long-term goals, and preparing the agenda for the next grand rounds as specialty items. Keep in mind that the inclusion of activities into either category is relative to the unique system and its particular needs.

Managerial time is time that is shared with or given to others in a system—it involves some level of interaction between or among people. Managerial time can be subdivided into response time and discretionary time. Response time generally involves such activities as speaking on the telephone to a caller or returning a call, having office visits, attending meetings, answering e-mails, and making rounds. Discretionary time has to do with activities that suggest or ask for a response, but the leader has the option of deciding whether or not to actually behave in accordance with the request. Time may be better used in another activity.

Specialty and managerial time contain activities that can be prioritized according to Lakein's (1973/1989) ABC system, described earlier in this chapter. There is no formula for the ratio of managerial time to specialty time in a manager's position. This is purely according to the environment that includes the unique manager, system, and tasks. One general rule of thumb, however, is that the more generally mature or performance ready a system is, the greater opportunity the manager has to corner specialty time. Obviously, the opposite is also true—the more generally immature or unwilling and unable a system is, the fewer options the manager has to corner specialty time. Nevertheless, manager time invested in developing followers is beneficial when the long-term perspective is considered.

THE TIME MANAGEMENT PROCESS

The time management process is another extension of the managerial method, as shown in Table 12.1. Perusing Table 12.1 and thinking about the focus of this chapter can lead to the conclusion that the managerial method pertains to managing others with the ultimate aim of increasing cost-effectiveness. In contrast, one may conclude that the time management process focuses on managing self so that the ratio of effort to payoff is high. The goals of both processes are parallel; however, the content and subjects differ. Both processes have the common aim of cost-effectiveness. Remember, time

TABLE 12.1   The Time Management Process and The
Managerial Method

TIME MANAGEMENT PROCESS	THE MANAGERIAL METHOD
Analyze the present situation (Where am I now?)	Assess the information
Develop relevant assumptions (What conditions will most likely exist within the time span of the plan?)	Study point of view
Establish objectives (What do I want to achieve?)	Identify the problem, goal, or opportunity
	Analyze the problem, goal, or opportunity
Develop alternatives (What ways might I attain objectives?)	Create alternative solutions
Make a decision	Recommend an action plan
Implement the decision	Implement action plan
Establish review and control procedures	Evaluate results

Note. The source for the Time Management Process is Mackenzie, R. A. (1972). *The time trap: Managing your way out.* New York, NY: AMACOM (A Division of the American Management Association), pp. 44–45.

is expensive; therefore, time must be used with wisdom and precision. The benefits of using time must be balanced with the cost.

All the previously discussed principles of managing, goal setting, motivation, and so forth apply in this chapter also. A person must first look at his or her present situation (the actual) on personal and professional (specialty and managerial) grounds. One should pose and answer the question of where one is in important areas. Then, given reasonable projections of what environmental conditions will exist at different slices of time—one month, one year, five years, and whenever—ask where one would like to be in those same areas. What comes out of this thinking, as the reader of this book already knows, is the problem, goal, or opportunity. The objectives, which flow from the goal, describe the desired outcome. (Refer to Chapter 14 on teaching for further discussion of goals and objectives.)

Once objectives have been designated, they must be arranged on the basis of priorities. One useful way of doing this is according to Lakein's (1973/1989) ABCs. Or ponder each objective with the questions:

"How much effort will be involved in fulfilling this objective, and what is the expected payoff?"

Then assign priorities according to least effort–most payoff (high priority) down to most effort–least payoff (low priority). A scale of 1 to 5 (low to high) can be used if finer quantification in this process is sought. Then attack the top priorities—just the first two or three since priorities must be selected. A manager should not try to do everything all at once. Choose one, two, or, at the most, three priorities!

Develop alternative strategies for accomplishing your selected objectives. These strategies are concerned with how the objectives will be attained. The goals and objectives themselves are what are to be attained. Again, develop an effort/payoff ratio for each solution and pinpoint the best strategy for action. Implement that strategy and evaluate it by comparing intent with results.

The last step in the process is evaluation; this can range from completely subjective to extremely objective. At the simplest level, discuss what is described as an "effort" and compare it with observed results. At a more objective level, evaluation forms as well as other control systems may be used to quantify effort versus payoff. As a side note, formal evaluations are costly in terms of effort. They may, however, be worth it. Consult a book on evaluation procedures and evaluation research should formal evaluation methods be indicated or desired.

Now, do all of the previously discussed processes seem simple? Do not be fooled. Parasites eat and piranhas nip away at our time, and the concept called time management is most useful because readers on the topic can receive myriad helpful hints on controlling parasites and piranhas. The next portion of this chapter is devoted to discussing these techniques. The content is not inclusive—many more tips are available in time management literature and from personal experiences (Morgenstern, 2004). Read about available techniques and compare them with your own behaviors—professional and personal.

TIME MANAGEMENT TECHNIQUES

This section presents an array of techniques for attacking parasites and piranhas (Lakein, 1973/1989; Mackenzie, 1972, 1997; Mackenzie & Nickerson, 2009). Each topic is discussed separately.

Personal Commitment to Improving

How many psychiatrists does it take to change a light bulb? The answer—"only one, but the light bulb has to be willing"—is corny but true.

Brown (1980) termed personal commitment to time saving as the sine qua non. So, examine yourself. Those who care should finish the chapter. Those who discover unwillingness should try to discern why it exists and work on changing from unwillingness to willingness—then read on. McConnell (1983, 1991) underscored that in order to become an effective manager of others, a leader must first become an effective manager of self—through personal effort. Manage away habits perceived as unhelpful (Waldroop & Butler, 2000). This approach is why the author of this book, Elaine La Monica Rigolosi, placed Chapter 3, "Knowing Self," before all of the other chapters discussing how managers work—it is the center core of effective management. The reader is also referred to this author's latest book on empowering self-improvement entitled *Unlock Your CAGE* (Rigolosi, 2013).

Deciding What Not to Do

A requisite for success, according to Nunlist (cited in Mackenzie, 1997) is refusing to do the unimportant. People must do a fantastic job on the essentials. They must learn to step aside from the unnecessary and step over the irrelevant. If playing tennis, just think about getting the ball in the court where the opponent cannot run in time to return the shot. Forget about the perfection that drives a player to strive for the masterful shot that precisely hits the line. Whether or not the line is hit, if the ball is in the court, it is a winner if it cannot be returned. Learn to behave so that you act in ways that increase the probability of winning while saving energy to use in another important direction!

Learning to Say "No"

Read the book titled *When I Say No, I Feel Guilty* by Smith (1975/1985). Someone always has a priority that is classified as essential for someone else to do—immediately. In health care, the "someones" abound. The manager must sort out the important from the unimportant or high-payoff tasks from low-payoff tasks, and say "no" to the latter tasks and "yes" to the former ones. This ability should not be emotionally charged and should develop without generating guilt or some other self-defeating feeling.

Recording How Time Is Used

The "Time Analysis Worksheet" (Brown, 1980) that is found in the Experiential Learning Activities at the conclusion of Part III is one way to find out how time is used and where it goes. This raises consciousness of one's own behavior by making the abstract concrete. The "Time Log," also found in the same section, can be used for the same purpose.

Planning Use of Time

List responsibilities, choose priorities, and schedule for their accomplishment. Develop a daily, weekly, and/or monthly to-do list. Check off progress; this is self-reinforcement for further accomplishment. Do not let minutia intrude on the list, but also allow for some flexibility, especially in the longer-term lists. Swansburg (1996) suggested that managers and leaders have daily planning lists and activities.

Also, be aware that research suggested that performers invest more resources on tasks that receive high-quality feedback (Northcraft, Schmidt, & Ashford, 2011). Plan your priorities based on what your superiors see and reinforce. Further, provide feedback to your followers on what you want their foci to be.

Fire Fighting Versus Fire Prevention

Graf (1979) explained fire fighting as responding immediately to whatever comes up, like applying oil to the squeaky wheel. According to Bohn and Jaikumar (2000), it can consume the resources in an operation. Fire fighting is necessary when planning is poor. Fire prevention involves contingency planning—looking ahead and asking, "What can be done today to avoid problems in the future?" It is also known as risk management. Of course, preventing fires can become a parasite itself. It can become similar to over-insurance. Invest enough energy in the fire-prevention area to make the payoff worthwhile.

Also, be prepared to fight *necessary* fires. Notice that the word "necessary" is italicized in the previous sentence. Some people always seem to be in a rush to do something that needs to be done "right now." Analyze things carefully—learn how to diagnose real fires and fires that simply are important issues but imagined and self-created fires.

Prime Time

Most people have a certain portion of a day that they know is their "prime time." During this period, people are at their best, and work is usually easiest to accomplish. Find out what this block of time is and use it—hang a "Do Not Disturb" sign outside the door, refuse calls, do not schedule meetings, and so forth. This is probably the time when 80% of one's work gets accomplished in the least amount of time. Protect prime time—to the degree that is possible!

Programming Blocks of Time

Graf (1979) pointed out that "one of the best ways to complete big projects is to program large blocks of time for the effort" (p. 17). Otherwise, the task will be broken up into smaller pieces and much time will be wasted getting oriented to where one was at the end of the last work session. Try to program blocks of time into your prime time spaces.

Organizing the Workspace

Arrange the environment to make life easier. Make the office space fit your individual personality—from the color of the walls to the arrangement of furniture or the addition of plants to anything else that is pleasing. Keep the desk uncluttered; keep only the project in immediate focus on it. Any other material on the desk may become a distracter. Have tools such as pencil sharpeners, staplers, and so forth handy. Provide water, coffee, or whatever is needed on the workspace. Eliminate the need to get up and wander around—time gets wasted both from the short journey and from reentry.

Memoitis

Oh, the memoranda that infest offices! (Do not worry—this author will attack computers next!) Mackenzie (1997) reported an estimate that puts the paperwork cost of running the United States' economy at a sum equal to about one-seventh of the total yearly output of goods and services. Memos are part of this mountain.

Memos are to remind, to clarify, and to confirm (Mackenzie, 1972, 1997; Mackenzie & Nickerson, 2009). They involve one-way communication. Use them only when essential. In many instances, a phone call or e-mail is the better bet.

Learn to scan memos received for a quick assessment of their importance. If it passes the best of "reading worthiness," then read it fully. If not, throw it immediately in a conveniently placed wastebasket near the workspace. Take a speed-reading course if possible.

Handling Mail

Try to touch mail once. When you open it, read it and do whatever needs to be done—at that time. If it is not important, discard it immediately. If it is an invitation, study your calendar and answer it immediately. Then, file it either in your social calendar or in the waste basket. Try not to stack mail so that you have to go through it more than once unless it is a magazine or something similar.

Computeritis

Well, here it is—the best thing that has happened in life to help move us along more swiftly and to save time and paper in the process. Beware of the myth! Computers use up a tremendous amount of time, probably because people have easier access to sharing whatever they please in a convenient vehicle that is sometimes entertaining. Computer etiquette seems to enforce that an e-mail sent must be answered and people often have trouble being the person who stops saying "thank you," "good-bye," or "I will not answer this again."

Computers can be effective if they truly cut back on the paperwork; however, sometimes the paperwork is needed so time is used to send messages on the computer and to then send hard copies along the way to back up everything. Be careful of this pitfall. Also, computer lovers say that they do not have to answer telephone calls immediately; they can talk with people on their own clock. This is fine if it works like that but it is another task to accomplish several times a day if the system is not malfunctioning. This author knows people who sit at their desk trying to work but return to a computer as soon as a voice or bell communicates "You've got mail."

Do not allow your computer to run your life! Rather, use your computer as a device that you possess so that you can facilitate what you need to do and choose to accomplish—whenever you wish. Examine how your computer usage ranks on your effort/payoff ratio, given your task.

Blocking Interruptions

Common courtesy is always necessary but it should not be confused with a need to extend carte blanche to telephone calls, visits (Mackenzie, 1997; Mackenzie & Nickerson, 2009), or online buddy systems. A manager can extend the "open door policy" when it is decided that the door should be opened—definitely this should not be during one's prime time unless excruciatingly necessary.

Drop-in visitors should be discouraged. Simply and sincerely say once, "I would like to talk with you at a time when I am not involved in a project. We can schedule an appointment at. . . ." A drop-in-type person usually gets the message after the first or second such interchange. Confer with drop-in visitors standing up and outside one's office, if possible. This is a barrier to the visitor's discourteous intrusion.

Consider an intruder who "knows it is not regular office hours but just needs one minute for a 'quick' question." The scene might go as follows. The one-minute intrusion *minimally* involves the following, without exaggeration:

1. Thinking about what you were doing ends;
2. Your mind switches gear to contain anger at the disruption first, and then to think about what the intruder is asking;

3. Time is taken in order to respond coherently, masking flaming anger;
4. You listen to the almost sure second and third questions and/or comments of the intruder;
5. You respond again while secretly vowing not to let this situation be repeated, making a mental note to mandate that to your secretary;
6. You bid farewell and emphasize that it would be a pleasure to talk again—simply telling the intruder to make an appointment or come in during regular office hours;
7. Something is needed to calm your nerves so you get coffee or something else that is aimed to satisfy yourself; and
8. You sit down trying to recall what you were doing prior to the intrusion and where you were on the matter that was a priority.

Conclusion: This intrusion costs at least 30 minutes, ignoring the non-quantifiable, indirect cost to your nervous system.

The telephone is another interrupting piranha because it can ring anytime, and sometimes just the ring is intrusive. If possible, have a secretary screen calls on the following basis: "immediate response is required" and "delayed response is acceptable." Handle the immediate calls and arrange telephone hours to return other calls. When available, have a secretary place the calls and then transfer them to the caller. Caller identification on telephone lines also may help.

Managing Meetings

Mackenzie (1972) and Mackenzie and Nickerson (2009) stated that people tended to devote time and effort to tasks that have an inverse relationship to their importance. He called this fact Parkinson's Second Law. Mackenzie offered many rules for getting more out of meetings. Here are a choice few together along with the personal beliefs of this author:

1. Start on time—give warning only the first time;
2. End on time;
3. Develop an agenda and circulate it to the attendees prior to the meeting;
4. Only those people who are needed or involved in the meeting's purpose should attend a meeting;
5. Gather information prior to a meeting and summarize it during the meeting;
6. Stick to the agenda, avoid interruptions, and squelch side trips around or away from the agenda;

7. Limit the amount of time for a particular agenda item and be sure that the intended agenda items get accomplished;
8. Arrange for a comfortable environment but not so plush that people would rather be there than somewhere else;
9. Type and distribute items that involve one-way communication by their nature because verbal announcements plus one-way communications usually wastes time; and
10. Have a secretary take and distribute the minutes of the meeting within one week from the date of the meeting. Minutes should record the issues and the decisions. Brief reports of the points of discussion may be included. When minutes are verbatim accounts of the meetings, the secretary wastes time and so do all the readers—if in fact the minutes are read.

Managing People

Time-management books, such as those in the references at the end of this chapter, include a portion on delegating. The focus is to alert the manager that managers lead people to accomplish goals. Therefore, managers should work toward delegating work to others when followers are ready—willing, able, confident, and functioning at self-esteem and self-actualized levels in relation to an identified task.

As the reader is aware by now, managers must use a variety of styles to help followers mature in relation to accomplishing a task. Depending on the system's level of maturity or performance readiness at a certain time and place, the manager must appropriately tell to, sell to, participate with, or delegate to followers (Hersey et al., 2008). Managers must examine themselves in order to discern whether they use different leader behavior styles because the system needs them or because of their own needs.

When a system's maturity indicates, the push is always toward delegation because then the manager has freed time for other managerial and/or specialty tasks. It behooves managers to examine themselves and then to give followers the leadership they need, always pushing followers toward maturity and performance readiness. This is a responsibility of managers, and in terms of time management, it is a reward of management.

Springing the Time Trap

In *The Time Trap*, Mackenzie (1972) included an appendix on time wasters he most commonly encountered, their causes, and their possible solutions. The list is not exhaustive but certainly can help to raise one's consciousness. Table 12.2 contains his work.

TABLE 12.2   How to Spring the Time Trap

TIME WASTERS	POSSIBLE CAUSES	SOLUTIONS
Lack of planning	Failure to see the benefit	Recognize that planning takes time but saves time in the end.
	Action orientation	Emphasize results, not activity.
	Success without it	Recognize that success is often in spite of, not because of, methods.
Lack of priorities	Lack of goals and objectives	Write down goals and objectives. Discuss priorities with subordinate.
Overcommitment	Broad interests	Say "no."
	Confusion in priorities	Put first things first.
	Failure to set priorities	Develop a personal philosophy of time. Relate priorities to a schedule of events.
Management by crisis	Lack of planning	Apply the same solutions as for lack of planning.
	Unrealistic time estimates	Allow more time. Allow for interruptions.
	Problem orientation	Be opportunity-oriented.
	Reluctance of subordinates to break bad news	Encourage fast transmission of information as essential for timely corrective action.
Haste	Impatience with detail	Take time to get it right. Save the time of doing it over.
	Responding to the urgent	Distinguish between the urgent and the important.
	Lack of planning ahead	Take time to plan. It repays itself many times over.
	Attempting too much in too little time	Attempt less. Delegate more.
Paperwork and reading	Knowledge explosion	Read selectively. Learn speed reading.
	Computeritis	Manage computer data by exception.
	Failure to screen	Remember the Pareto Principle. Delegate reading to subordinates.

TABLE 12.2   How to Spring the Time Trap *(continued)*

TIME WASTERS	POSSIBLE CAUSES	SOLUTIONS
Routine and trivia	Lack of priorities	Set and concentrate on goals. Delegate nonessentials.
	Over-surveillance of subordinates	Delegate; then give subordinates their space. Look to results, not details or methods.
	Refusal to delegate; feeling of greater security dealing with operating detail	Recognize that without delegation it is impossible to get anything done through others.
Visitors	Enjoyment of socializing	Do it elsewhere; meet visitors outside. Suggest lunch if necessary. Hold stand-up conferences.
	Inability to say "no"	Screen. Say "no." Be unavailable. Modify the open-door policy.
Telephone	Lack of self-discipline	Screen and group calls. Be brief.
	Desire to be informed and involved.	Stay uninvolved with all but essentials. Manage by exception.
Meetings	Fear of responsibility for decisions	Make decisions without meetings.
	Indecision	Make decisions even when some facts are missing.
	Over-communication	Discourage unnecessary meetings. Convene only those needed.
	Poor leadership	Use an agenda. Stick to the subject. Prepare concise minutes as soon as possible.
Indecision	Lack of confidence in the facts	Improve fact-finding and validating procedures.
	Insistence on all the facts —paralysis of analysis	Accept risks as inevitable. Decide without all facts.
	Fear of the consequences of a mistake	Delegate the right to be wrong. Use mistakes as a learning process.
	Lack of a rational decision-making process	Get facts, set goals, investigate alternatives and negative consequences, make the decision, and implement it.

(continued)

TABLE 12.2   How to Spring the Time Trap (continued)

TIME WASTERS	POSSIBLE CAUSES	SOLUTIONS
Lack of del-egation	Fear of subordinates' inadequacy	Train. Allow mistakes. Replace if necessary.
	Fear of subordinates' competence	Delegate fully. Give credit. Ensure corporate growth to maintain challenge.
	Work overload in subordinates	Balance the work load. Staff up. Reorder priorities.

Note. Reprinted, by permission of the publisher, from *The time trap: Managing your way out*, by R. Alec Mackenzie, © 1972 by AMACOM, a division of American Management Association, pp. 173–176. This list is adapted from "Troubleshooting Chart for Time Wasters." In R. Alec Mackenzie (Ed.), *Managing time at the top*. New York, NY: The President's Association, 1970.

SUMMARY

The concept of time is a constant phenomenon. Each person has all the time there is, and no one ever has enough time. The intent of applying time management techniques is to get "a little more" out of the time given.

Time involves references for understanding and describing an occurrence and the sequence of events. Activities can be classified as time wasters or time consumers, which are relative terms. The Pareto Principle is a way of explaining how 20% of one's time consumed in activities that are aimed at accomplishing a goal (called *time consumers*) actually produces 80% of positive outcomes. Eighty percent of expended time in activities that are time wasters results in 20% of positive outcomes. The trick or goal is to have the least amount of effort produce the greatest number or amount of positive outcomes.

Managers have specialty time for themselves and managerial time spent interacting in some form with others. The time management process parallels the problem-solving or managerial method. It can be used to guide a manager toward goal fulfillment in professional and personal areas.

Time management techniques were discussed in the last part of the chapter. The intent of these techniques is to offer managers a potpourri of interventions against the parasites and piranhas of time. It is essential that each person recognize his or her inherent potential to waste and to save time—that is, his or her own time as well as another's time.

●●● REVIEW CONCEPTS AND QUESTIONS

1. Present and discuss the historic developments of time management principles. Explain how time is classified, the Pareto Principle, and kinds of time.
2. Compare the Time Management Process with the Managerial Method.
3. Explain 12 of your favorite time management techniques. Differentiate your personal techniques from those presented in this book.

●●● SUGGESTED ASSIGNMENTS

1. Take your notebook and hold it in the landscape design—horizontal. Divide the page(s) into three columns and from left to right, label those columns Column I, II, and III. After having an evening dinner on a normal work day, write down everything that you did that day in Column I, spacing between your accomplished tasks and numbering them consecutively. In parenthesis following each numbered task, state the approximate amount of time that you use to accomplish the task.

    In Column II, write down what you did to accomplish each numbered item in Column I, lettering each behavior from A to Z, as needed. In Column III, think about how you could have been more effective in accomplishing each task and behavior. What behaviors would you have changed, omitted, or added in order to save you time.

    Classify the tasks and activities in Column I according to the As, Bs, and Cs. Write a short narrative on what you may do differently if you had the day to repeat.
2. Take the first assignment and share it with a peer. Have him or her evaluate every step. Reverse the process and evaluate your peer's analysis of a day in his or her work life.
3. Think about a social gathering such as a holiday weekend when you are having company or a party that you are planning. Apply the appropriate time management techniques and attempt to write a planning process that should result in less time spent preparing for a wonderful function.

REFERENCES

Berwick, D. M., Godfrey, A. B., & Roessner, J. (2002). *Curing health care: New strategies for quality improvement*. San Francisco, CA: Jossey-Bass.
Bohn, R., & Jaikumar, R. (2000). Stop fighting fires. *Harvard Business Review, 78*(4), 82–91.
Brown, D. (1980). *The use of time: A looking-into-leadership monograph*. Fairfax, VA: Leadership Resources.
Drucker, P. F. (2009). *The effective executive*. New York, NY: HarperCollins. (Original work published 1967).
Ferri, R. (1987). In search of the excellent one-minute megatrend . . . or how to tolerate the five minutes burden. *American Journal of Nursing, 87*(1), 109–110.

Getting things done. (2004) *Nursing, 34*(2), 76.

Graf, P. (1979). *Ten techniques for improving time management*. Unpublished manuscript.

Hersey, P., Blanchard, K. H., & Johnson, D. E. (2008). *Management of organizational behavior: Leading human resources* (9th ed.). Upper Saddle River, NJ: Pearson Prentice Hall.

Juran, J. (1995). *Managerial breakthrough: The classic book on improving management performance* (Rev. ed.). New York, NY: McGraw-Hill.

Lakein, A. (1989). *How to get control of your time and your life*. New York, NY: New American Library. (Original work published 1973)

Mackenzie, R. A. (1970). Troubleshooting chart for time wasters. In R. Alec Mackenzie, *Managing time at the top*. New York, NY: The President's Association.

Mackenzie, R. A. (1972). *The time trap: Managing your way out*. New York, NY: AMACOM (A Division of the American Management Association).

Mackenzie, R.A. (1990). *The time trap*. New York, NY: AMACOM. (Original work published 1972).

Mackenzie. R. A. (1997). *The time trap*. New York, NY: AMACOM. (Original work published 1972)

MacKenzie, R. A. & Nickerson, P. (2009). *The time trap* (4th ed.). New York, NY: AMACOM. (Original work published 1972 by MacKenzie)

Marquis, B. L., & Huston, C. J. (2011). *Leadership roles and management functions in nursing: Theory and application* (7th ed.). Philadelphia, PA: Lippincott Williams & Wilkins.

Marriner, A. (1979). Time management. *Journal of Nursing Administration, 9*(10), 16–18.

McCay, J. (1995). *The management of time*. Englewood Cliffs, NJ: Prentice Hall. (Original work published 1959)

McConnell, C. R. (1983). Supervisor, manage yourself. *Health Care Supervisor, 1*(3), 57–68.

McConnell, C. R. (1991). Self-management: Your key to success as a supervisor. *Health Care Supervisor, 9*(3), 1–9.

Morgenstern, J. (2004). *Time management from the inside out* (2nd ed.). New York, NY: Henry Holt.

Oncken, W., & Wass, D. L. (1999). Management time: Who's got the monkey? *Harvard Business Review, 77*(6), 178–186. (Original work published 1974)

Oncken, W., & Wass, D. L. (2008). Management time: Who's got the monkey? Watertown, MA: (Original work published 1974).

Northcraft, G. B., Schmidt, A. M., & Ashford, S. J. (2011). Feedback and the rationing of time and effort among competing tasks. *Journal of Applied Psychology, 96*(5), 1076–1086.

Porter-O'Grady, T., & Malloch, K. (2007). *Quantum leadership: A resource for health care innovation* (2nd ed.). Sudbury, MA: Jones and Bartlett.

Rigolosi, E. L. (2013). *Unlock your CAGE*. North Charleston, SC: CreateSpace.

Smith, M. J. (1985). *When I say no, I feel guilty: How to cope—using the skills of systematic assertive therapy*. New York, NY: Random House. (Original work published 1975)

Swansburg, R. C. (1996). *Management and leadership for nurse managers* (2nd ed.). Boston, MA: Jones and Bartlett.

Tappen, R. M. (2000). *Nursing leadership and management: Concepts and practice* (4th ed.). Philadelphia, PA: F. A. Davis.

Volk-Tebbitt, B. (1978). Time: Who controls you? *Supervisor Nurse, 9*(4), 17–22.

Waldroop, J., & Butler, T. (2000). Managing away bad habits. *Harvard Business Review, 78*(5), 89–98.

Experiential Learning Activities:
Managerial Skills—
The "How-To" Satellites

ACTIVITY 9	COMMUNICATION: ARE YOU GOOD AT FOLLOWING DIRECTIONS?

Purposes

1. To diagnose reading comprehension.

2. To find out how well one follows directions.

Facility

A classroom large enough to accommodate participants.

Materials

Worksheet 9-A: Following Directions.

Pencil or pen.

Time Required

Thirty minutes.

Group Size

Unlimited.

Design

1. Instruct group members to proceed to Worksheet 9-A and follow directions.

2. State that members who complete the worksheet should sit quietly until the entire class is finished.

3. When the entire group is done, discuss the experience in the large group. The following questions may form the basis of discussion.

   Are members good at following directions?

   Can members scan written messages and still comprehend them? If not, why not?

   Can comprehension be learned? If yes, why and how?

WORKSHEET 9-A: FOLLOWING DIRECTIONS

The following test is designed to find out how well you read and how well you can follow directions. It has been used by a California teacher with junior high school students. It should not take longer than three minutes to complete if you concentrate.

1. Read everything before you do anything.

2. Put your name in the upper right-hand corner of this paper.

3. Circle the word *name* in Step 2.

4. Draw five small squares in the upper left-hand corner of this paper.

5. Put an X in each square.

6. Put a circle around each square.

7. Sign your name under the title.

8. After the title write *yes, yes, yes*.

9. Put an X in the lower left-hand corner of this paper.

10. Put a circle around each word in Step 7.

11. Draw a triangle around the X in Step 9.

12. On the reverse side of this paper, multiply 703 by 1,805.

13. Draw a rectangle around the word *paper* in Step 4.

14. Call out your first name when you get to this point in the test.

15. If you think you have followed directions up to this point, call out "I have."

16. On the reverse side of this paper, add 8,950 and 9,850.

17. Put a circle around your answer. Put a square around the circle.

18. Count out loud in your normal speaking voice backward from ten to one.

19. Now that you have finished reading carefully, do only Steps 1 and 2.

Note. This material was received at the School of Nursing, University of Massachusetts, 1972. Author is unknown.

ACTIVITY 10	COMMUNICATION: OBSERVATION

Purposes	1. To sharpen observational skills.
	2. To increase perception of nonverbal behavior.
Facility	A classroom large enough to accommodate participants.
Materials	None.
Time Required	Twenty minutes.
Group Size	Unlimited pairs.
Design	1. Members should form pairs.
	2. Pairs should sit facing one another silently for two minutes, each person observing everything about his or her partner. If necessary, it can be suggested that certain items be noted, such as posture, eye contact, placement of hands and feet, facial expressions, dress, jewelry, and so forth.
	3. Members of each pair should then turn back to back with the agreed-upon partner changing five things about herself or himself.
	4. When changes have been accomplished, members should once again face each other, continuing to be silent. The observing partner should verbalize the noticed changes.
	5. Roles are reversed.
	6. Discuss the experience.
Variation	The activity can be lengthened by using the same pairs and requesting members to change five more things about themselves. This occasionally poses a problem and people often do not know what to change further. During discussion, ask participants if they thought of asking for help from another close member of a different pair who was also searching for changes. If they did, how did they feel about needing help on a seemingly simple task? If they did not request assistance, why not?

Source: *The Nursing Process: A Humanistic Approach*, (p. 294), by E. L. La Monica, 1979, Upper Saddle River, NJ: Pearson Education, Inc. Copyright 1979. Reprinted with permission. The idea for this activity came from Kenneth Blanchard, School of Education, University of Massachusetts, 1973.

ACTIVITY 11	COMMUNICATION: INTERPRETING NONVERBAL BEHAVIOR

Purposes

1. To increase awareness of how emotions can be expressed nonverbally.

2. To interpret perceptions of nonverbally expressed emotions.

3. To validate perceptions of nonverbal behaviors.

Facility

Large enough room to accommodate participants sitting around a table or on the floor in a circle.

Materials

Small pieces of paper.

Two hats or baskets.

Time Required

Thirty minutes or more, depending on group size.

Group Size

Twelve to 15 is ideal; two or more groups may be formed if the group is over the ideal size.

Design

1. In a large group, ask participants to verbalize emotions or feelings. Write one each on a slip of paper, fold the paper and place it in a hat.

2. Repeat Step 1, except this time ask that participants verbalize parts of the body that can be used to express emotions or feelings.

3. A person from the group should then distribute or have participants pick a slip of paper from each hat.

4. Request each participant who has picked an emotion and body part to role play the emotion nonverbally, primarily using the designated body part.

5. Group participants should then try to guess what feeling is being expressed and the dominant body part that was used to express the emotion or feeling.

6. Discussion follows.

7. Role players should place papers back in each respective hat, and Steps 3 through 6 should be repeated. This should be done so that all members have a chance to role play.

(continued)

ACTIVITY 11

COMMUNICATION: INTERPRETING
NONVERBAL BEHAVIOR *(continued)*

Variation

If two or more groups of 12 are possible, equalize
the number of emotions and body parts for both
groups and time how long it takes for groups to
carry out the task. Then have groups work against
one another; all role plays should result in the
group accurately diagnosing the emotion and
dominant body part used in expression. Only then
may they proceed to the next role play. The group
finishing first has the sharpest observational skills,
given those people who are present.

ACTIVITY 12	COMMUNICATION: PERCEIVING

Purposes

1. To increase awareness of the variety of perceptions that can be elicited from a given situation.

2. To raise self-awareness regarding individual perceptual fields.

Facility

Room to accommodate the class size in groups of six.

Materials

Worksheet 12-A: Scenarios.

Paper and pencils.

Time Required

One hour.

Group Size

Unlimited groups of six.

Design

1. Have participants individually read Scenario 1 and write down their perceptions and reactions concerning what happened, their feelings in the situation, and what conclusions they reach.

2. Ask that participants share these notations with their small group.

3. Observe and discuss perceptual differences, possible reasons for such, and rationale for conclusions. Dichotomous differences between or among members should be studied more fully.

4. Repeat the design with Scenario 2.

Variation

Participants can develop their own scenarios based on actual or hypothetical experiences. They can then share them with their small group and follow the design for as many scenarios as time permits.

(continued)

Note. From *The Nursing Process: A Humanistic Approach*, (pp. 296–297), by E. L. La Monica, 1979, Upper Saddle River, NJ: Pearson Education, Inc. Copyright 1979. Adapted with permission.

WORKSHEET 12-A: SCENARIOS

Scenario 1

It is 11:15 a.m. Ms. Blue, a supervisor, is making rounds on a surgical unit. She observes a patient with traction of the right leg, a basin of water on the bedside table, the bed stripped, a gown placed over the patient's chest, and the patient, Ms. Green, reading a book. As the supervisor enters the room, the patient explains that the student nurse assigned to assist her with a bath had struck his head against the crossbar of the traction frame at 10:30 a.m. The nursing instructor had taken him to the emergency room. On the way to the nurse's staff room, the supervisor notices several nursing personnel including the nurse manager, drinking coffee in the utility room. As she begins calling the nursing school office to report that a nursing student and an instructor had left a patient unattended, the nurse manager comes in to tell her about the accident.

Scenario 2*

The setting is a general hospital unit in an urban city. Three people are involved: Ms. King, the new head nurse of the medical unit; Ms. James, the Director of Nursing Services; and Ms. Carmichael, the day supervisor of the building. Ms. King gives the patients' nursing care files a last-minute check to be sure that all patients' activities, treatments, medications, and so forth are taken care of or are in process of being completed. Then she checks the patients, going from room to room. "It's going pretty well," she softly comments—she is particularly satisfied with the way Ms. Garcia is responding to the care plan now. She has spent a great deal of time working with Ms. Garcia. Certainly, Ms. King thinks, Ms. James can find nothing wrong here; the patients are all receiving excellent care. Ms. King has heard a lot about these "spontaneous rounds" by Ms. James. Shortly thereafter, Ms. James and Ms. Carmichael arrive on the unit by the backstairs, so it is some time before Ms. King even knows that they are there.

During the "rounds" with Ms. James and Ms. Carmichael, Ms. King makes several attempts to comment on certain patients and their progress. Ms. James ignores the attempts and starts to jot down notes on her clipboard. Ms. James and Ms. Carmichael maintain a general conversation about the unit while they finish the rounds. No attempt is made to draw Ms. King into the conversation. After rounds are completed on the unit, Ms. King asks if there is any additional information they need. Ms. James says, "No, however there are a few small items I would like to call to your attention, Ms. King. The shelves in the medicine cupboard are rather dusty, and the utility room is extremely cluttered. Will you please see that these things are taken care of?" With that Ms. James and Ms. Carmichael leave the unit.

On the way to the next unit, Ms. James remarks to Ms. Carmichael, "On the whole, I think Ms. King is doing a good job with her unit. She should make a fine head nurse."

---

*Source: This scenario was received at the College of Nursing, University of Florida, 1966. Author is unknown.

ACTIVITY 13

COMMUNICATION: LEADER/FOLLOWER INTERACTIONS

Purposes	1. To focus on verbal and nonverbal messages that may be emitted in the interactions between a manager and a follower.
	2. To validate messages received with messages sent.
Facility	Large enough room to accommodate group members seated around tables or in circles on the floor.
Materials	None.
Time Required	One hour or more, depending on group size and number of volunteers.
Group Size	Unlimited groups of 12.
Design	1. Paired volunteers should be given a couple of minutes to develop a hypothetical leader/follower interaction. They should decide which of them is to be the leader and which is to be the follower. A hypothetical leader/follower interaction is a made-up interchange in which the leader is functioning in one of the four leader behavior styles, according to Hersey, Blanchard, and Johnson (2008)*:

        a. High task, low relationship—telling;

        b. High task, high relationship—selling;

        c. High relationship, low task—participating; or

        d. Low task, low relationship—delegating.

2. The pair should then role play the situation with direction being given to the leader that he or she should decide whether to be effective or ineffective in the role. Only the leader should be aware of what is decided. This decreases the discomfort in a player's perceived ability actually to be effective or ineffective—in essence, it is a safeguard.

(continued)

---

*The source for Situational Leadership is *Management of Organizational Behavior: Leading Human Resources* (9th ed.), by P. Hersey, K. H. Blanchard, and D. E. Johnson, 2008, Upper Saddle River, NJ: Prentice Hall.

ACTIVITY 13   COMMUNICATION: LEADER/FOLLOWER
                            INTERACTIONS *(continued)*

3. Following the roleplay, players and the group members should give feedback on their reactions and perceptions of what was nonverbally and verbally communicated. Players should reveal their intent after group members give feedback.

4. Discuss the experience.

Variations

1. The instructor can prepare the scenes to be role played prior to class.

2. Learners may be given a homework assignment to prepare a scene prior to the class in which the exercise will take place.

| ACTIVITY 14 | COMMUNICATION: VERBAL DIRECTIONS |

Purposes

1. To practice giving verbal directions.
2. To validate messages received with messages sent.

Facility

A classroom large enough to accommodate participants.

Materials

Plain paper or construction paper.

Pencils, crayons, or magic markers.

Time Required

Thirty to 45 minutes.

Group Size

Unlimited pairs.

Design

1. Members should form into pairs, back to back.
2. One member of each pair should take paper and a pencil or crayon and draw a geometric design. An example of a design is as follows:

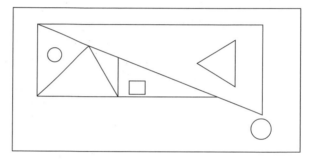

3. Provide partner with paper and pencil. Partners should not be able to see each other's work. The member who has drawn a design or used the example provided should verbally describe to the partner, step by step, what was drawn. Each step should be one clear statement. For example, "put a circle on the top corner of the triangle." Descriptions should not be expressed more than once, neither should they be revised. No questions should be asked or answered.

(continued)

Source: This exercise is adapted from "The Nurse and the Patient: Communication Skills. Introduction to Communication," by F. Hewitt, 1981, *Nursing Times*, *77*(4), Suppl. 1–4.

ACTIVITY 14   COMMUNICATION: VERBAL DIRECTIONS
                               (continued)

4. The member receiving directions should draw the geometric design as perceived.

5. Upon completion, compare the design that was verbally directed with the original. How good were the directions?

Variation   The design can be repeated with the same partners, only two-way communication is allowed— the receiver can ask the sender questions and receive answers. Discuss the differences between one-way and two-way communication at the conclusion of this experience.

ACTIVITY 15   **POWER: THE NEW-CAR DILEMMA**

Purposes	1. To further develop group decision-making abilities.
	2. To experience potential and actual power struggles.
	3. To practice the roles of supervisor, follower, or process observer.
Facility	A classroom large enough to accommodate unlimited groups of six.
Materials	Magic markers for name tags.
	For each participant—a name tag for the name of the character to be played. Process observers are called "pros."
	Worksheet 15-A: General Instructions.
	For each character player—Worksheet 15-B containing further information only on the role to be played. (These descriptions should be individually typed on separate sheets of paper and distributed after members have selected their roles.)
	Information from Worksheet 15-B should not be common knowledge to all participants.
	For each process observer—Worksheet 15-C: Processing the New-Car Dilemma.
Time Required	One hour for the activity and 30 minutes for processing.
Group Size	Unlimited groups of six.
Design	1. Pairs of teams will work together. One team of six will be players sitting in an inside circle and the other team, usually smaller in number, will be process observers sitting around the players in an outside circle.
	2. The team of players should choose the characters to be role played by each player. If the role play team only contains five players, discard the role of Eileen.

(continued)

Note. This simulation was adapted into health care from a business exercise. The original material is from "The New Truck Dilemma," *Supervisory and Executive Development: A Manual for Role Playing* (pp. 20–37), by N. R. Maier, A. R. Solem, and A. A. Maier, 1957, New York, NY: John Wiley.

ACTIVITY 15   **POWER: THE NEW-CAR DILEMMA**
                         (continued)

3. After the roles have been selected, players should fill out their name tags and then should receive only the part of Worksheet 15-B that describes their particular character. Instruct players not to discuss roles with anyone else and not to read about other roles. Players should not receive Worksheet 15-B prior to role selection because its contents should not be known by everyone.

4. Process observers should not communicate verbally with the role players. They should use Worksheet 12-C to assist them in observing the players' group dynamics.

5. When all members are ready, the instructor should signal for the role plays to begin. All groups should start role playing at the same time. The role play should last 45 minutes.

6. At the end of the role play, the process observers should report their observations to the group they observed. Group members should also join in the process observations. Were they satisfied with the decision? They should be able to provide rationale for their satisfaction and/or dissatisfaction. A general class discussion should conclude the experience—who received the new car in each group and why? Processes used by groups to make decisions may be shared.

WORKSHEET 15-A: GENERAL INSTRUCTIONS

You work for a state-supported community care service that investigates reports of child abuse. One of you will be the director, and the others will be members of the professional interdisciplinary team. Each team member has a caseload; responsibilities include making home visits, collaborating with professionals in hospitals, meeting doctors in their offices, visiting teachers in schools, and participating in various nonprofit health organizations.

The director is usually a promoted staff member, which is true in this case. She has a small caseload in comparison with others, spending a great deal of time at the main office in administrative detail and writing grant reports and proposals. She accompanies other team members on various cases as needed; on average, this amounts to two days of a five-day work week. Of course, this time is spread out over the entire week. Each team member works alone and ordinarily is involved in several cases or assignments in a day.

The team members drive to various locations in the district to do their work. The health care service is located in a large town, but cases are referred in from a 50-mile radius of the city. Members drive compact cars that are assigned to them for as long as they work for the health care service. The car is used only during working hours. Members drive their personal cars to and from the main office in the morning and in the evening. Members seem to take pride in keeping their business cars looking good; they have a possessive feeling about their cars because other people seldom if ever drive them. Maintenance is requested by the individual team members and is carried out when the members have a block of work to accomplish in the home office.

Here are some facts about the team members and their cars:

EILEEN JONES, B.S., R.N., a psychiatric nurse practitioner, has been with the agency for 17 years and has a 2-year-old Ford.

BILL SMITH, Ph.D., a state-licensed psychologist, has been with the agency for 11 years and has a 5-year-old Dodge.

JOHN ALLEN, M.S., a psychiatric social worker, has been with the agency for 10 years and has a 4-year-old Ford.

CHARLIE GOLD, M.S.N., R.N., a psychiatric and pediatric nurse specialist, has been with the agency for 5 years and has a 3-year-old Ford.

MARY HERTZ, M.D., a child psychiatrist, has been with the agency for 3 years and has a 5-year-old Chevrolet.

JANICE MARSHALL, Ph.D., the director, has been with the agency for 8 years and has no car assigned to her. She is a psychiatric nurse with a doctorate in psychology. Generally, she rides places with others.

Most of the team members do all of their driving in the town; John and Charlie cover most of the cases in the suburbs.

In role playing your part, accept the facts as given, as well as assuming the attitude supplied in your specific role. From this point on, let your feelings develop in accordance with the events that transpire in the role playing process. When facts or events arise that are not covered by the roles, make up things that are consistent with the way it might be in a real-life situation.

(continued)

WORKSHEET 15-B: CHARACTER INFORMATION

EILEEN JONES: When a new Chevrolet becomes available, you think you should get it because you have seniority, and you do not like your present car. Your own car is a Chevrolet, and you prefer a Chevrolet for business, too. You had one assigned to you before you got the Ford.

BILL SMITH: You feel you deserve a new car. Because the more senior team member has a fairly new car, you feel you should get the next one. You have taken excellent care of your present Dodge and have kept it looking like new. A man deserves to be rewarded if he treats a company car like his own.

JOHN ALLEN: You have to do more driving than most of the other team members because you work in the suburbs. You have a fairly old car and feel you should have a new one because you do so much driving.

CHARLIE GOLD: The heater in your present car is inadequate. Furthermore, since Mary backed into the door of your car, it has never been repaired to fit right. You attribute your frequent colds to the cold air that the door lets in. You want a warm car because you have a good deal of driving to do and you often work in the colder, north part of town. As long as it has good tires, brakes, and is comfortable, you do not care about its make.

MARY HERTZ: You have the poorest car in the crew. It is five years old, had been in a bad wreck before you got it, and has never been mechanically sound. You have put up with it for three years and feel the next new car should be yours. You have a good safety record. The only accident you have had was when you sprung the door of Charlie's car when he opened it as you backed out of the garage. This was certainly not your fault. You hope the new car is a Ford because you prefer to drive that make.

JANICE MARSHALL: You are the director of the team; each member of the group drives a compact car to and from various case assignments. Every so often you get a new car to exchange for an old one, and you have the problem of deciding which of the team members should receive the new car. There are often hard feelings because each member seems to feel he or she is entitled to the new car. You have a tough time being fair—as a matter of fact, most people usually disagree with whatever you decide. You now have to face the issue again because a new car has just been allocated to you for assignment. The new car is a Chevrolet.

In order to handle this problem, you have decided to put the decision up to the team members themselves. You will tell them about the car and pose the problem in terms of what would be the fairest way to assign the car. You decide not to take a position yourself because you want to do what the members think is most fair. Your leadership style will be high relationship and low task.*

---

*The source for Situational Leadership is *Management of Organizational Behavior: Leading Human Resources* (9th ed.), by P. Hersey, K. H. Blanchard, and D. E. Johnson, 2008, Upper Saddle River, NJ: Prentice Hall.

WORKSHEET 15-C: PROCESSING THE NEW-CAR DILEMMA

The following items are furnished as a guide for observing what the leader did and how the team reacted:

1. How did the director present the problem?

    A. In presenting the problem, did the director's attitude convey asking for help?

    B. Was the director's presentation of the problem brief and to the point?

    C. Did the director scrupulously avoid suggesting a solution?

2. What occurred in the discussion?

    A. Did all group members participate?

    B. Was there free exchange of feelings between or among group members?

    C. Did the group use social pressure to influence any of its members?

    D. On which member(s) of the team was social pressure used?

    E. Was the director permissive?

    F. Did the director avoid taking sides or favoring any person?

    G. What were the points of disagreement in the group?

3. What did the director do to facilitate problem solving?

    A. Did the director ask questions to help the group explore ideas?

    B. Did the leader and others accept all ideas equally?

    C. Did the director avoid hurrying the group to develop a solution?

    D. Did the director avoid favoring any solution?

    E. Who supplied the final solution?

    F. What, if anything, did the director do to get unanimous agreement on the final solution?

    G. What were the bases of the final solution (for example, was the decision reached on the basis of seniority)?

    H. How effective was the leader?

ACTIVITY 16

CONFIDENT COMMUNICATION:
THE COMPASSION TRAP

Purpose	To gauge the extent to which one is in the Compassion Trap: that is, existing to serve others and providing tenderness and compassion to all at all times.
Facility	A classroom large enough to accommodate participants.
Material	Worksheet 16-A: The Compassion Trap Quiz.
	Worksheet 16-B: Scoring Key.
	Pen or pencil.
Time Required	Thirty minutes.
Group Size	Unlimited.
Design	1. Instruct members to respond individually to the items in Worksheet 16-A, following directions on the instrument.
	2. After completing Step 1, go to Worksheet 16-B to score responses and to read interpretations.
	3. Discuss findings in small groups.
Variation	This can be a self-study assignment.

WORKSHEET 16-A: THE COMPASSION TRAP QUIZ

DIRECTIONS. Gauge the extent to which you are in the Compassion Trap by taking the quiz that follows. Answer each question honestly, choosing only one answer. If you have not personally experienced some situations, choose the response that most closely approximates the way you think you would respond. After you have finished, go to Worksheet 16-B and add up your score according to the key. The interpretation of your score will tell you how "trapped" you really are.

1. You have been seeing this man socially for several weeks, but you are beginning to feel bored and uninterested in continuing the relationship. He likes you very much and would like to see you more often. Do you:

   A. Tell him you'd prefer not to see him, feeling you've been honest with yourself?
   B. Feel a sudden attack of the Hong Kong flu coming on?
   C. Continue to be the object of his affections, because leaving would really hurt his ego?
   D. Tell him that he bores you to tears, and that even if you were both marooned on a desert island, you would camp out on the opposite shore?

2. You invited a friend of yours who lives out of the state to spend her/his two-week vacation with you at your home. It is now one month later, and your friend shows no intention of leaving, or reimbursing you for food and telephone bills. You would like your friend to leave. Do you:

   A. Not mention anything about your expenses or feelings, because you don't want to damage the friendship?
   B. Leave a note saying that you're terribly sorry, but your mother has decided to live with you, and you'll need the room?
   C. Tell your friend that you really value your friendship, but her/his extended visit is putting a strain on it and ask that your friend make plans to leave?
   D. Put all of your friend's belongings out on the doorstep with a note: "Don't call me; I'll call you"?

(continued)

Note. The source of this instrument is from *The Assertive Women* (4th ed.), by S. Phelps and N. K. Austin, © 2002, Reproduced for Springer Publishing Company, Inc., by permission of Impact Publishers, Inc., P.O. Box 6016, Atascadero, CA 93423. Further reproduction prohibited.

WORKSHEET 16-A: THE COMPASSION TRAP QUIZ *(continued)*

3. You are enjoying one of your rare visits to San Francisco, and you are staying with your brother and sister-in-law. One of your favorite things to do in San Francisco is to sample the fine restaurants. Your brother and sister-in-law are terrible cooks, but they insist on "treating" you by cooking for you themselves. You would much prefer going out to eat. Do you:

   A. Decide to have dinner at your brother and sister-in-law's home because you don't want to disappoint them by refusing their offer?
   B. Tell them that you appreciate their thoughtfulness, and explain that one of the reasons you come to San Francisco is to enjoy the restaurants and suggest that all of you go out to eat instead?
   C. Loudly tell them that you're not there for their food?
   D. Call and claim that you are unavoidably detained, tell them not to wait dinner for you, and then sneak out and eat by yourself?

4. You are working on a project that is very important to you. Some friends drop by unexpectedly. You'd really like to continue working on your project. Do you:

   A. Shelve your project, prepare hors d'oeuvres, and apologize for your cluttered living room?
   B. Loudly berate your friends for not having called first?
   C. Explain that you're in the middle of an important project and arrange to see them at a mutually convenient time?
   D. Ignore your friends and continue working on your project while they are there, hoping they'll get the message?

5. Your 10-year-old daughter customarily walks to school, but today she wants you to drive her. You have driven her on rainy days, but it is not raining today. She continues to ask you to drive her, adding, "Besides, everyone else's mother drives them." Do you:

   A. Tell your daughter she can walk to school today, as usual?
   B. Begin by telling your daughter that you won't drive her to school but after a short time you give in and drive her, feeling guilty that you hesitated?
   C. Reply "Oh, okay, I'll drive you," thinking of all the other children whose mothers faithfully drive them and you will feel like a neglectful mother if you don't drive your daughter to school?
   D. Threaten to call the truant officer and report on your daughter if she doesn't leave for school immediately?

WORKSHEET 16-B: SCORING KEY

1. A.   An assertive choice   (3)
    B.   Honesty is the best policy here.   (0)
    C.   Don't forget *your* feelings.   (0)
    D.   Don't forget *his* feelings.   (0)

2. A.   You'll feel resentful later. You're trapped.   (0)
    B.   This may get her/him out, but how *do you* feel about trapping   (1)
          yourself with *that* one?
    C.   Right. This will also get her/him out, and leave you with your   (3)
          self-respect.
    D.   This will get your friend out of your life, also.   (0)

3. A.   This Compassion Trap will result in your disappointment and   (0)
          indigestion.
    B.   The assertive thing to do.   (3)
    C.   Better look for a hotel room—your brother- and sister-in-law   (0)
          won't want to have you as a guest for some time.
    D.   You'll soon run out of excuses. Then what?   (0)

4. A.   The Compassion Trap.   (0)
    B.   Only if you *never* want to see them again.   (0)
    C.   Ain't it the truth?   (3)
    D.   You're wasting time; it may take hours for them to get the hint!   (0)

5. A.   You've got it!   (3)
    B.   A good start—but you're in the Compassion Trap here.   (1)
    C.   Are you really neglectful? The Compassion Trap again.   (0)
    D.   You avoided the Compassion Trap, but stepped into the   (0)
          Aggression Trap!

Add up your total points and gauge the extent of *your* Compassion Trap.

   Total Points: _____

(continued)

Note. The source of this instrument is from *The Assertive Women* (4th ed.), by S. Phelps and N. K. Austin, 2002, Reproduced for Springer Publishing Company, Inc., by permission of Impact Publishers, Inc., P.O. Box 6016, Atascadero, CA 93423. Further reproduction prohibited.

WORKSHEET 16-B: SCORING KEY *(continued)*

Score Interpretations

14+   We couldn't ask for more. You can choose what to do without being trapped. Be on the lookout, though, for other situations that may trap you.

9–13:   You can avoid the Compassion Trap most of the time, and you're moving in the right direction. Give some extra attention to the people/situations that continue to trap you, and attempt more assertive ways of handling them.

2–8:   Consider the price you are paying when you do things at the expense of your own happiness. With some practice, you can leave the Compassion Trap and enjoy what you choose to do. Be an assertive person and be loved for it.

ACTIVITY 17

CONFIDENT COMMUNICATION: SITUATIONS TO ROLE PLAY

Purposes	1. To role play assertiveness in common situations.
	2. To receive feedback on one's own assertiveness.
	3. To recognize assertiveness in others.
	4. To give feedback to others on their assertiveness.
Facility	A classroom large enough to accommodate the class in groups of six to eight.
Materials	Worksheet 17-A: Situations.
	Worksheet 17-B: Responses.
	Pencil or pen.
Time Required	One to one and one-half hours.
Group Size	Unlimited groups of six to eight.
Design	1. Lecture or discussion on confident communication and assertion theory should precede this exercise.
	2. Have participants individually respond to the situations in Worksheet 17-A, using the space provided following each situation.
	3. After completing Step 1, ask participants to form into groups of six to eight and practice role playing the five situations in pairs. Participants not involved in the immediate role play should give feedback to the players on their assertiveness.
	4. After group members have completed Steps 2 and 3, hand out Worksheet 17-B and have them compare their responses with the examples of responses provided. Discuss these results.
Variation	Participants can also write down personal scenarios as an assignment or in class. Their names should not be placed on the scenarios. This can be collected, put together on paper, and distributed to participants for further study. Steps 2 through 4 can be followed on the worksheets prepared for the variation.

(continued)

WORKSHEET 17-A: SITUATIONS

1. You and Jessica are associates on a patient care unit. Jessica asks you to give her a ride home every afternoon from now on. You don't want to do it. You say:

    _____

    _____

    _____

    _____

2. It is your lunch hour. You're waiting for a friend. She breezes in a half hour late and, without any reference to her lateness, asks, "How are you?" You answer:

    _____

    _____

    _____

    _____

3. Just as you're about to leave for the hospital, your cousin George calls you on the telephone. He starts to tell you about a problem he's been having with his parents. You're anxious to get off the phone. You say:

    _____

    _____

    _____

    _____

4. You're standing in line in a restaurant waiting to be seated. The hostess says, "Who's next?" It is your turn. The woman next to you says, "I am." You turn to her and:

    _____

    _____

    _____

    _____

Source. The situations and responses from Worksheets 17-A and 17-B, Activity 17, are a slight modification of those presented in *The new assertive woman*, by L. Bloom, K. Coburn, and J. Pearlman. Copyright 1975 by Delacorte Press. Reprinted with permission.

WORKSHEET 17-A: SITUATIONS *(continued)*

5. You're at an agency-wide directors' meeting. An associate speaks up and urges members not to appropriate extra funds to the nursing budget. He gives inaccurate information in his attempt to persuade people that there is no need for extra positions. You disagree with his ideas and his data. You:

_____

_____

_____

_____

(continued)

WORKSHEET 17-B: RESPONSES

Responses to Situation 1:

- "Well . . . uh . . . I guess I could. (pause) . . . Uh. O.K." (*Nonassertive:* pauses with apparent hesitancy)
- "I'd love to take you, but sometimes I have to stop at the market on the way home. And sometimes I leave late." (*Nonassertive:* excuses)
- "What's the matter? Haven't you and Norman gotten around to buying that second car yet?" (*Aggressive:* sarcastic)
- "You've got nerve! Do you think I have nothing better to do than chauffeur you around?" (*Aggressive:* attempt to make the requester feel guilty)
- "I know it's a pain to wait around for Norman to pick you up, but I'd rather not be tied down to giving you a ride every day. I'd be happy to do it once a week, though." (*Assertive:* compromise)
- "I understand that you don't like having to wait for Norman to pick you up every day, but I really don't want to be tied down to having to take you." (*Assertive:* direct refusal)

Responses to Situation 2:

- "Fine, thanks," said with a smile. (*Nonassertive:* denial of actual feelings)
- "O.K., I guess," said with a frown on your face. (*Nonassertive:* attempt to communicate the real message, but indirectly)
- "What do you mean, how am I? How do you think I am, sitting here, waiting for you and staring at the ceiling? Do you ever stop to think of anyone but yourself?" (*Aggressive:* attempt to humiliate the latecomer)
- "Well, I'd been looking forward to our lunch, but because I've been waiting so long, I've really gotten upset. Now we'll have only a half hour together." (*Assertive:* a direct statement of feelings)

Responses to Situation 3:

- You listen . . . and listen . . . and listen . . . . (*Nonassertive:* accommodation of the other's needs at the expense of your own)
- "Look, I'm too busy to talk to you now. You've always got some little problem, and I have more important things to do. Good-bye." (*Aggressive:* disregard of the other's wishes and feelings)
- "I'd like to hear more about it later. I was just on my way to work when you called. I'll call you back tonight." (*Assertive:* direct statement of wishes)

WORKSHEET 17-B: RESPONSES *(continued)*

Responses to Situation 4:

- Smile. (*Nonassertive:* accommodation of the other's needs at the expense of your own)
- Frown silently. (*Nonassertive:* attempt at indirect communication of your wishes)
- Mutter under your breath, "Some people are so pushy"—but you say nothing directly to anyone. (*Nonassertive:* repression of your own wishes)
- "No you're not. I was here first. You can't take advantage of me, lady." (*Aggressive:* hostile overreaction)
- "I believe I was here before you." (*Assertive:* direct expression of your own wishes)

Responses to Situation 5:

- Say nothing to anyone. (*Nonassertive:* refrain from expressing your own opinion)
- Stand up and say, "I don't know much about this. I'm no expert, but. . ." (*Nonassertive:* self-demeaning and self-deprecating)
- Whisper to the person sitting next to you about how stupid the speaker is. (*Nonassertive:* indirect, inhibited behavior)
- Stand up and say, "You're a liar. You don't know what you're talking about." (*Aggressive:* intent to humiliate)
- Stand up and say, "I've heard what you have to say, and I disagree with you. I would like you to listen to my point of view." (*Assertive:* stand up for legitimate rights without violating the other's rights)

| ACTIVITY 18 | CONFIDENT COMMUNICATION: THREE LEADERSHIP ROLES |

Purposes

1. To experience roles in different aspects of the communication process.

2. To learn how different aspects of a leadership role can affect communications and feelings.

Facility

A classroom large enough to accommodate groups of three, given the total class size.

Materials

Two large and unlined sheets of paper or construction paper for each group of three.

Pencils, pens, crayons, or magic markers for each group of three.

Time Required

Forty-five minutes to one hour.

Group Size

Unlimited groups of three.

Design

1. One person is designated as the "artist"; the second person is designated as the instructor; the third person is the observer and is the only person who is allowed to take notes.

2. The artist closes his or her eyes and the instructor guides the artist by telling the artist what marks to make on the page. The instructor gives guidelines based on whatever is created in that person's head at that time. Ten minutes are given to complete the drawing. No discussion follows this step until reaching Step 5.

3. At the end of the 10 minutes, the artist becomes the observer, the observer becomes the instructor, and the instructor becomes the artist. Step 2 should be repeated.

4. At the end of another 10 minutes, the observer becomes the instructor, the instructor becomes the artist, and the artist becomes the observer. Step 2 should be repeated.

Note. The concepts in this activity were presented by Patricia M. Raskin, Ph.D. She is an Associate Professor Emerita of Psychology and Education in the Department of Organization and Leadership, Teachers College, Columbia University, New York. The original source of the activity is unknown. The exercise, as presented, was formatted and arranged by Elaine La Monica Rigolosi, author of this book.

ACTIVITY 18   **CONFIDENT COMMUNICATION: THREE LEADERSHIP ROLES** *(continued)*

5. At the end of Step 4, the dynamics of the activity are processed and discussed in the group as a whole. Each participant should describe their feelings and thoughts about each role that was experienced.

How easy was it to give or follow instructions?

To what extent was each person willing to take control as an instructor, or to give up control as an artist?

As an observer, what was noticed?

Everyone in the group should have an opportunity to discuss all aspects of the experience.

| ACTIVITY 19 | CONFIDENT COMMUNICATION: LISTENING |

Purposes	1. To practice the art of listening.
	2. To understand the individual differences that people perceive when listening to the same story.
Facility	A classroom large enough to accommodate teams of two people, given the total class size.
Materials	None.
Time Required	Thirty to 45 minutes.
Group Size	Pairs of two and participants totaling 15 to 20.
Design	1. The team is divided into either a talker or a listener.
	2. The talker begins by telling a story for five minutes. It can be a story about anything, created during the moment. The listener is not permitted to take notes but should simply sit and listen. All pairs follow Step 2 at the same time.
	3. At the conclusion of Steps 1 and 2, the total group is assembled. The listeners then tell the stories heard to the entire group, while the talkers sit and listen.
	4. After all of the stories have been heard, process how accurate the listeners were in sharing the stories heard.

Were the facts accurate?
Were the feelings accurately reflected?
What was left out?
How did talkers feel about how listeners
    reflected their stories?
In what ways were the listeners distracted?

Note. The concepts in this activity were presented by Patricia M. Raskin, Ph.D. She is an Associate Professor Emerita of Psychology and Education in the Department of Organization and Leadership, Teachers College, Columbia University, New York. The original source of the activity is unknown. The activity, as presented, was formatted and arranged by Elaine La Monica Rigolosi, author of this book.

ACTIVITY 19   CONFIDENT COMMUNICATION:
                                     LISTENING *(continued)*

5. When Steps 3 and 4 are completed, pairs should sit with each other again and talk about the experience in terms of what was shared and heard. Focus on both content and process—verbal and nonverbal communications. The talker and the listener should discuss the accuracy of what was communicated and what was perceived. Experiences of other pairs may be discussed.

6. Roles can be reversed in Step 1 and the entire design repeated.

| ACTIVITY 20 | CONFLICT RESOLUTION: SATURN'S FIRST HOSPITAL STATION |

Purposes

1. To develop group collaboration and planning.
2. To experience conflict resolution.
3. To foster group team building.
4. To facilitate setting group goals.

Facility

A classroom large enough to accommodate participants.

Materials

Paper and pencil or pen.

Blackboard and chalk.

Time Required

One and one-half to two hours.

Group Size

No more than five groups of six to eight participants.

Design

1. Explain the following to the group:

   The entire class has been carefully selected to set up the first space hospital station on the planet Saturn. The class will be transported tomorrow on the Columbia Star Cruiser. Members will spend the rest of their lives on Saturn. The shuttle that routinely transports people and equipment will visit Uranus and Mars after stopping at Saturn and then return to Earth.

   The next visit to Saturn for transporting equipment and personnel is unknown, but it will not be before 10 Earth years have passed. The class must decide what is needed to survive and what is needed to equip the hospital. Due to constraints of space on the Columbia Star Cruiser, each person can bring only five specific items on board. These items include personal and hospital needs. Air concentration that is needed to sustain human life is guaranteed, as are dried food packets and water. Nothing else is promised. Duplicates of items are not permitted.

2. Have members individually write down the five items that they wish to bring. (5 minutes)

ACTIVITY 20	**CONFLICT RESOLUTION: SATURN'S FIRST HOSPITAL STATION** *(continued)*

3.   After completing Step 2, notify the class that word has been received that extra fuel is required on board as a result of a meteor storm that is expected between Saturn and Uranus. The space allocated to the hospital crew has been cut. Class members should therefore form into pairs (have triads if there is an odd number in the group) and select five things out of their combined list of ten items to bring to Saturn. (10 minutes)

4.   After Step 3 has been completed, a spacegram is received with the following message: "President orders that the interstellar missile tracking station be housed on Saturn." The effect of this message on the hospital crew is elation. However, all materials for the missile tracking station must now be transported in tomorrow's voyage. Space is again decreased and each group of six to eight can only bring five items on board the shuttle to Saturn.

5.   After grouping into six to eight members, each group must decide what five items to bring. Pairs (triads) formed in Step 3 should be in the same group. (15 minutes)

6.   When groups have selected their five items, announce the following: There is a massive surplus in the country's budget—enough for a sister hospital station in Uranus. The President has selected the crew for Uranus; both crews will be transported together. *Each crew* will bring only five items due to the shortage of space on the ship.

(continued)

ACTIVITY 20   **CONFLICT RESOLUTION: SATURN'S FIRST**
                                   HOSPITAL STATION *(continued)*

7. Each group should be instructed to choose
    a negotiator and plan a strategy for selling
    other groups on the importance of taking
    their items. (15 minutes) Negotiators from
    each group will then meet around a table at
    the head of the class to select the five items
    that will be brought to Saturn.

    Negotiations will take place in three rounds
    within the following time limits:
    Round 1—meeting of negotiators (15 minutes)
    Round 2—negotiators consult with their
    groups (15 minutes)
    Round 3—meeting of negotiators (15 minutes)
    The decision on the five items must be made
    by the end of Round 3. Only the negotiators
    can talk during Rounds 1 and 3; groups must
    be quiet.

8. After the five items have been selected,
    list them on a blackboard and discuss
    the experience with the class as a whole.
    Questions that can be asked and areas that
    usually engender discussion are:

    A. What did the items chosen by individuals
        represent in comparison with those
        chosen by groups?
    B. Was there movement from counting
        on self to counting on others and the
        interactions between and among others?
    C. Were the resources of the group studied?
        Could people build things, grow things,
        and so forth?
    D. Did the final items represent any
        particular area of Maslow's hierarchy?
        Explain.
    E. How were the negotiators chosen? Were
        needed attributes of the negotiators
        specified?
    F. Was creative problem solving evident as
        the experience developed?
    G. What was learned from the experience
        that applies in the present?

ACTIVITY 21	TIME MANAGEMENT: TIME ANALYSIS SHEETS

Purposes	1. To facilitate identification of time wasters.
	2. To analyze time wasters.
	3. To use time more effectively.
Facility	None—this exercise is a self-study homework assignment.
Materials	Worksheet 21-A: Time Analysis Worksheet.
	Worksheet 21-B: Biggest Time Wasters.
	Worksheet 21-C: Time Analysis Worksheet.
	Pen or pencil.
Time Required	Variable.
Group Size	Unlimited—homework assignment.
Design	Three worksheets are provided for use in individual analysis for professional and/or personal aspects of one's life. It is suggested that they be used in order for the first time—Worksheet 21-A, Worksheet 21-B, and then Worksheet 21-C. Then they can be reused over and over as one wishes to be more aware of and in control of time.
	Worksheets 21-A and 21-B require simply filling in the blanks. Worksheet 21-C requires specifying daily goals and keeping a log of activities for the day. The log can then be analyzed using Worksheets 21-A and/or 21-B, with new goals set for the next day. Progress can be traced by reviewing these sheets. Group members can be encouraged to share analyses with peers. Class time can be allotted for small and large group discussions.

(continued)

WORKSHEET 21-A: TIME ANALYSIS WORKSHEET

What items do I spend too much time on?	What am I doing that does not need to be done at all?
What items do I spend too little time on?	What am I doing that could be done better (more economically or more effectively) by others?
Items in which I can make my most important savings.	Ways by which I can avoid overusing the time of others.
Other ways in which I can make effective savings.	Other suggestions.

Note. The source is *The Use of Time: A Looking-Into-Leadership Monograph* (p. 9), by
D. Brown, Copyright 1980, Fairfax, VA: Leadership Resources. Reproduced with permission.

WORKSHEET 21-B: BIGGEST TIME WASTERS

Specifically, my biggest time wasters are

1. _____

2. _____

3. _____

4. _____

5. _____

6. _____

7. _____

8. _____

Imposed By	Cause	Solution
1. _____	_____	_____
2. _____	_____	_____
3. _____	_____	_____
4. _____	_____	_____
5. _____	_____	_____
6. _____	_____	_____
7. _____	_____	_____
8. _____	_____	_____

(continued)

_____

Note. The source is *Time Management* by P. Graf, 1979. Unpublished material.

WORKSHEET 21-C: TIME LOG

Date _____ Day of the Week _____

Goals: 1. _____   4. _____

2. _____   5. _____

3. _____   6. _____

Time	Activity	Priority Rating A, B, or C	Comments
8:00 8:30			
9:00 9:30			
10:00 10:30			
11:00 11:30			
12:00 12:30			
1:00 1:30			

Note. The source is Time Management by P. Graf, 1979. Unpublished material.

WORKSHEET 21-C: TIME LOG (continued)

Time	Activity	Priority Rating A, B, or C	Comments
2:00 2:30			
3:00 3:30			
4:00 4:30			
5:00 5:30			
6:00 6:30			
7:00 7:30			
8:00 8:30			
Evening			

Managerial Roles:
The "Action" Satellites

The purposes of Part IV of this book are to discuss the roles that a manager must assume while in a management and leadership position. The "action" satellites involve content for managerial behaviors in various roles that encompass what a manager does in day-to-day activities. Parts II and III have presented how managers should work in every role. Part IV focuses on the actual roles that managers must embrace.

The five roles that are covered in this book—change facilitator, teacher, team builder, interviewer, and performance appraiser—were selected because they are the most basic roles in leadership. The chapter topics are not meant to include all of the possible roles that form a manager's position. However, they are the predominant roles.

Consistent with the preceding chapters, a conceptual framework is provided in each of the five satellite areas in Part IV. Each chapter focuses on the basic concepts and theories, recognizing that education in this area should be ongoing and continuous through the lifespan. The Experiential Learning Activities at the conclusion of Part IV are aimed at putting life into the presented words.

Change Facilitator

EXPECTED LEARNING OUTCOMES

- To describe the levels of change and the implications for their applications in practice
- To understand the change process

- To learn how to apply force field analysis to action plans
- To conceptualize how people develop during periods of change
- To become aware of the various strategies available for change facilitators
- To understand the reactions to change in organizations and ways that may assist managers to effectively lead in a journey through change

Everyone exerts influence on another—changes another—implicitly, explicitly, covertly, and overtly. This fact is especially important in management and leadership. At an informal level, each time a person interacts with another by sending a message, the receiver's response to the sender is shaped by the message received. In a sense, the receiver has formed a response to fit a message sent by another. The sender, therefore, has influenced the receiver.

To influence another means that a person elicits something from another or engenders something in another. This is change, and recalling from previous chapters, change is learning, and learning is change. Human beings do not interact in a vacuum; people are part of a system that exerts constant influence over individual behavior. This is a sociological perspective, of course, and contemporary management practice embraces this approach.

At a more formal level, managers are constantly attempting to change a system—to move the system from where it is in a given area (the actual) to where the manager wishes it to be in a particular area (the optimal). The processes for accomplishing this change were discussed earlier in Parts I, II, and III of this book. At this point, a major assumption (a given) is that managers change people and people change managers.

Changing a system is not simply one aspect of a manager's responsibilities—if one is managing and leading, one is changing people. Change is a wide ribbon with its unique threads that are spread throughout all of the colorful patterns of management. Change is synonymous with growth. Growth should be occurring in every aspect of management practice—within and between people and the environment. As underscored by Burke, Lake, and Paine (2009), change is constant. It lives every moment; it is evidenced and viewable in past behavior and is predictable in the future.

According to Kotter (1999), to cope with environmental forces such as technology, competition, and demographics, leaders must be involved in changing how their organizations function. Tushman and O'Reilly (2004) discussed the reality that success precedes failure for leaders unless leaders elicit change on an ongoing basis. Why? Because leaders work to align effectively all of the facets in an organizational system—strategy, structure, and culture, and these alignments lead them to success. This type of success is referred to as *evolutionary change*. When evolutionary changes occur, nevertheless, there continue to be changes in the extrinsic and intrinsic forces in an environment that require monitoring on a continuous basis. At a strategic point in time, these new changes require that leaders incorporate new influences that change what has previously made a company successful. This is called *revolutionary change*.

To put the preceding types of changes—evolutionary and revolutionary— into the perspective of this author, if a person or company does not continue to grow (change) in a positive direction, a person or a company will change in a negative direction. Philosophically, people either look at themselves as living or dying. A company either grows or fails. Changes are not permanent; rather they must be considered as a dynamic and ongoing journey. They are continuous even though at any given point in time and at the identified benchmarks, a manager and follower should consider that success was reached.

In the pursuit of knowledge and in order to understand more thoroughly leader behavior and, therefore, to be able to exert greater productive control over oneself and others, the following theories and concepts on change are presented and discussed in this chapter. These concepts and theories are force field analysis (field theory), levels of change, the change process, strategies of change, resistance to change, and combatting this resistance.

FORCE FIELD ANALYSIS

Lewin's (1947) force field analysis is a useful theory for understanding what is happening when a manager wishes to move a system from actual to optimal in a particular area. A problem or goal was defined in Chapter 1 as the difference between actual and optimal (see Figure 1.2., Chapter 1). This "difference" can be further explained using force field analysis. An example might help in explaining this concept. Suppose that the problem or goal definition is as follows:

Actual	Staff members on the East Wing are continuously late to the day shift;
Optimal	Staff arrive on time for the day shift so that report can be given and the night staff released;
Problem	Lateness on the morning shift;
Goal	To have day staff arrive on time; and
Opportunity	To educate staff so that behavior moves toward *optimal*.

FIGURE 13.1   Movement for Goal Accomplishment

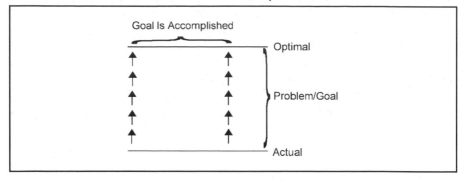

A manager wants to move actual to optimal, thereby eradicating the problem and accomplishing the goal. Figure 13.1 portrays this movement. Imagine the line symbolizing actual as a state that is suspended between forces that are working toward moving actual to optimal (driving forces) and forces that are working against the move from actual to optimal (restraining forces). Weights can be added to these forces to portray the relative importance of each force. Figure 13.2 contains such a force field.

If an equal amount of restraining and driving forces were operative in the field, there could be no movement in the actual line, which would be in a state of equilibrium. If driving forces outweigh restraining forces, then actual would shift toward optimal. Conversely, if restraining forces were greater in weight than driving forces, the movement would be toward escalating the problem. A manager can accomplish change, therefore, by either increasing and amplifying the driving forces and/or by eradicating and suppressing the restraining forces. In either case, the actual line would move toward the optimal line. This type of discriminating analysis can

FIGURE 13.2   Force Field

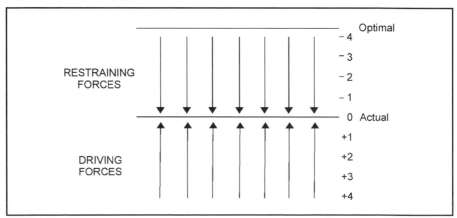

FIGURE 13.3   Driving and Restraining Forces in a Case Example

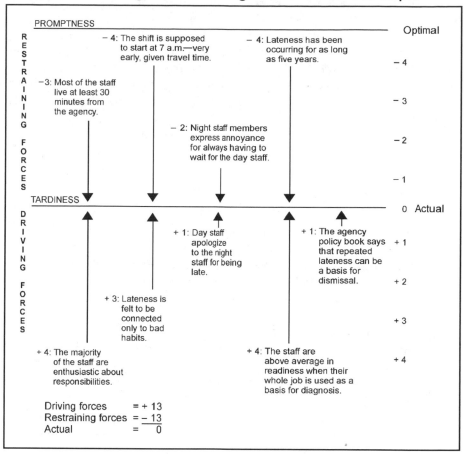

provide the manager with items of concentration for the solution phase of the managerial method.

Going back to the example, a force field analysis of the problem or goal might look like that shown in Figure 13.3. The manager must assign a weight to each force—it is a relative figure that reflects one's best judgment on the importance of the identified forces. In the example provided, the driving forces equal the restraining forces. The manager can focus on either set of forces or both sets of forces to engender change. It is the belief of this author, however, that the positive should always be amplified. When this is done, the negative looks less formidable because positive behavioral emphases consume the greater portion of time used in accomplishing a given goal. Force field analysis is a way to document this belief quantitatively.

A problem or goal must still be analyzed to diagnose self, the system, and the task, and then to arrive at a leader behavior style that has the highest

probability for accomplishing the identified goal. The manager can then select forces that become the content in developing the solutions or actions. The
forces relate to *what* is focused on in the strategy; *how* a manager focuses is the
leader behavior style and the manager's behavior on the educative journey.

Any leader behavior style can be applied to any force; *what* and *how* coexist as separate entities and are united by a manager in the unique action
plan. Any single force or a combination of forces, even driving and restraining ones, can be the content of a problem solution. A manager is advised,
however, to focus on the forces with the highest weights because they have
the greatest impact on producing change. This is the effort–payoff ratio that
was discussed in Chapter 12.

LEVELS OF CHANGE

Once a problem has been analyzed, including a delineation of the force
field, understanding the levels of change and change cycles can be useful. Hersey and Blanchard (1988) and Hersey, Blanchard, and Johnson
(2001) cited and discussed four levels of change: knowledge, attitudes,
individual behavior, and group behavior. Figure 13.4 shows the four
change levels.

Changes in knowledge tend to be easiest to make because they can result
from reading a book or listening to a respected lecturer. Attitude structures
are emotionally charged in a positive and/or negative way. They are, therefore, more difficult to change than knowledge. Moving to greater difficulty,

FIGURE 13.4   Change Levels

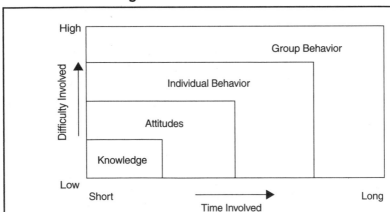

Note. From *Management of organizational behavior: Utilizing human resources* (5th ed.,
p. 4), Hersey, P., & Blanchard, K. H., 1988, Upper Saddle River, NJ: Prentice Hall, Inc.
Copyright 1988. Reprinted with permission.

individual behavior comes next. A manager may know about and understand primary care nursing, for example, like it, and still not behaviorally apply it into practice for a variety of reasons, like feeling uncomfortable with the perceived 24-hour responsibility. Group behavior is the hardest to change because of the numbers of people involved. Trying to change customs, mores, and traditions is also difficult (Hersey, Blanchard, & Johnson, 2001). Hersey, Blanchard, and Johnson (2008) emphasized the importance of performance readiness in obtaining behavioral changes with followers.

Two conceptual change cycles are identified from the four levels of change. These are participative change and directive or coercive change (Hersey et al., 2001).

Participative Change

A *participative change cycle* occurs when change proceeds from knowledge to group behavior, as shown in Figure 13.5. Followers are first provided with knowledge, with the intent that they will develop positive attitudes on a subject. Because research suggests that people behave on the basis of their attitudes, a manager's desire is that this holds to be true. Once individuals behave in a certain way, these people become teachers and therefore influence others to behave accordingly—group behavior then tends to change also.

Participative change cycles can be used by managers with personal and/ or positive power; personal power, however, is the dominant force. Change

FIGURE 13.5 Participative Change Cycle

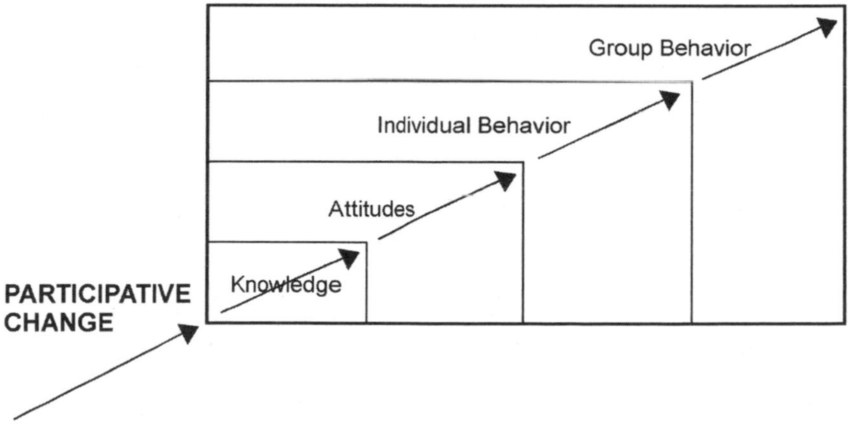

Note. From *Management of organizational behavior: Leading human resources* (8th ed., p. 391), by Hersey, P., Blanchard, K. H., & Johnson, D. E., 2001, Upper Saddle River, NJ: Prentice-Hall, Inc. Copyright 2001. Reprinted with permission.

is somewhat slow and evolutionary, but it tends to last because followers generally believe in what they are doing—the change is intrinsically imposed rather than extrinsically demanded (Hersey et al., 2001). This strategy is viewed as the most appropriate in nursing practices (Hagerman & Tiffany, 1994) unless financial exigencies are in focus.

Directive (Coercive) Change

Figure 13.6 shows that *directive change* occurs in the opposite direction from participative change. Using position power, higher management gives directions about the mode of behavior that will be used in the system; actually, an entire organization may be the focus. The dicta are set into place and followers are expected to attend to and abide by them. The hope of managers is that once followers see the plan in operation, they will develop positive attitudes about it and then gain further knowledge. This type of change is volatile; it tends to disappear when managers are not present to enforce it (Hersey et al., 2001). Position power is essential in the directive change cycle.

Implications for Change Cycles

There is informal agreement among managers that participative change is the best, especially when followers move in the participative change cycle

FIGURE 13.6   Directive (Coercive) Change Cycle

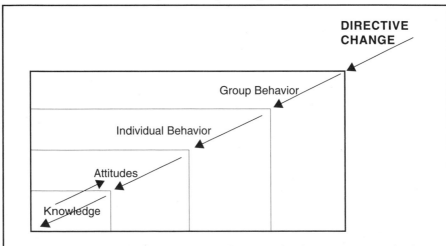

Note. From *Management of organizational behavior: Leading human resources* (8th ed., p. 391), by Hersey, P., Blanchard, K. H., & Johnson, D. E., 2001, Upper Saddle River, NJ: Prentice-Hall, Inc. Copyright 2001. Reprinted with permission.

in harmony with their performance readiness. There are, however, specific instances when a leader must use a directive style. These instances relate to the implications for different leader behavior styles (Haffer, 1986).

A directive style is necessary when an organization is in crisis and when people must behave in a certain way or in particular ways immediately in order for the organization to continue viably. The participative cycle is usually appropriate for followers who are average to above average in maturity or performance readiness, whereas those followers who are below average to average in maturity or performance readiness may need and prefer a directive cycle as efforts are begun or continued to facilitate group members becoming willing and able.

The participative and the directive change cycles can be used by a manager regardless of the readiness or maturity of the system. A participative cycle, for example, can be used with followers who require high structure and low consideration leader behavior, using the Ohio State Model of Leadership as an example (Bass, 2008; Bass & Stogdill, 1990; Fleishman, 1973). The solution or strategy for accomplishing a goal simply starts with knowledge—the manager can require followers to attend lectures, to read, and so forth.

A directive cycle can be used with mature followers, even though such an intervention is risky. The need and benefits of this intervention must outweigh the probable consequences. As another example using the leadership theory stated previously, if a manager used a participative change cycle with followers who required high consideration and low structure leader behavior, the group might sit together and plan how they would like to gain the knowledge. Maybe they could suggest guest speakers and so forth.

THE CHANGE PROCESS

The change process, as early defined and discussed by Lewin (1947) and Kelman (1958), lends further understanding to the experience of changing. The process can guide the manager in developing problem solutions that have a high probability for being effective because they are based on what is known about human behavior. Lewin (1947) identified three phases in the change process: unfreezing, changing, and refreezing.

Unfreezing

Unfreezing involves breaking down the normal way people do things—interrupting patterns, customs, and routines—so that a person is ready to accept new alternatives (Hersey et al., 2001). Participants in the change process may communicate the need for change (Maxwell, 2005). Forces that act on and within an individual are "melted down" or "thawed." This phase involves externally motivating someone to take the journey toward goal accomplishment. (If necessary, refer back to Chapter 2 for a discussion of motivation.)

Changing

Once people are motivated to change, they are primed to accept new patterns of behavior. Taking on these new behaviors involves changing attitudes. Kelman (1958) suggested three ways this happens: compliance, identification, and internalization, as discussed in the following paragraph.

Compliance occurs when change is forced by someone with position power who manipulates rewards and punishments. *Identification* means that role models for the new behavior are available and individuals learn by identifying with them and trying to be like them. *Internalization* occurs when individuals are left to change on their own power. The need and desire to change is present, and people must learn the new patterns of behavior by employing intrinsic resources. Self-learning and self-discovery fall into this last category (Kelman, 1958).

Refreezing

Refreezing occurs when new behaviors become part of one's personality. The behavior occurs because one has knowledge, positive attitudes, and experience with these new behaviors. Refreezing has occurred in followers when a leader has accomplished long-term goals whereby followers function effectively in a task when the leader is in Leader Behavior Style 4—low structure and low consideration, using the Ohio State Model of Leadership (Bass, 2008; Bass & Stogdill, 1990; Fleishman, 1973). New behaviors should be positively reinforced by leaders to ensure that refreezing occurs within followers (Ferster & Skinner, 1957; Ferster et al., 1997).

STRATEGIES OF CHANGE

Problems of change can be approached by individuals and groups in a variety of ways, and each strategy by each manager is unique—one's strategy did not, cannot, and will not exist again in an exact form. Strategies are usually a melding of a variety of methods, modes, and sub-strategies that are employed by the leader. Themes in change strategies, however, are evident.

Olmosk (1972) identified and discussed the following seven pure strategies of change: fellowship, political, economic, academic, engineering, military, and confrontation. Some of these may sound familiar. In reality, a manager's strategy combines two or more of these pure strategies; however, one may stand out over the others. The concepts provided by Olmosk provide the basis for the discussion and application of each strategy.

Fellowship Strategy

Everyone is treated equally and emphasis is placed on team building in a group, getting to know group members, and building social bonds among members. This strategy is ideal for followers who have high social and esteem needs. Hence, it is ideal when Leader Behavior Style 3 is required by a system—high consideration and low structure, using the Ohio State Model of Leadership (Bass, 2008; Bass & Stogdill, 1990; Fleishman, 1973).

Engaging the key players in planning (Spiro, 2011), such as getting people together at an informal dinner party to discuss new directions for a unit, is an example of this strategy. Other examples of the fellowship strategy include creative learning (Marshall, 2003), creating open exchanges in a conference or dialog (Murphy et al., 2004), mentoring (Brown, 1999; Klein & Dickenson-Hazard, 2000; Mundt, 2001; Records & Emerson, 2003; Vance, 2000), and encouraging groups to write and publish (Baldwin & Chandler, 2002; Daly, 2000).

Political Strategy

A *political strategy* means identifying the formal and informal power structures. Once these structures are identified, efforts are made to influence those in power. The assumption of this strategy is that something will get accomplished if the influential people in a system wish it to be carried out. Directors who want to change from having nurses write separate notes to having them record on the progress notes might identify the key people in hospital policymaking and discuss the goal with them individually prior to bringing the recommendation to a formal gathering.

Economic Strategy

Money talks! Emphasis is on acquiring or controlling material goods. With material resources, anything and anybody can be influenced—that is, bought and sold. Inclusion in a group is often based on possession or control of marketable resources. Fundraisers often employ this strategy.

Academic Strategy

In academia, knowledge or the pursuit of knowledge is the primary influencer. The belief is that people are logical, rational, and objective and that decisions will be based on what research suggests is the best path to follow. Emotions are not usually acknowledged in an academic strategy, even though it is intrinsically known that people can never be entirely objective about anything. A bias that can range from narrow to wide always exists. In suggesting ways that result in more effective outcomes of patient care, a manager might cite research studies that support the identified goal for a unit.

Engineering Strategy

The engineering method for facilitating change in people tends to ignore the subjects by attending to the surrounding environment. It is, therefore, a sociological approach with the belief that if the surroundings change, the people in those surroundings will also change. Health care planners have used this strategy when designing patient units so that beds are in close proximity to the nurse's station. The logic is that if nurses are close to patients, they will spend more time "at the bedside," and the quality of care will increase.

Military Strategy

Physical force and real threats are the names of this game. "Ruling with an iron hand" and "running a tight ship" describe the climate in this environment. Position power is used in the form of threats and punishment if the leader's wishes are not obeyed. This is a high-structure strategy. The iron hand may be disguised in a warm, sweet velvet glove; however, all concerned are fully aware that the iron fist exists and will be used if necessary. An example in this area is hardly needed. Be cognizant, however, that a physical force of control may be used in hospitals by health care personnel on patients. Posey restraints are one such example. A manager must assess the need for such a strategy—it should be the last possible approach with careful and knowledgeable attention to legal guidelines.

Confrontation Strategy

This approach induces nonviolent and nonphysical conflict among people. By doing this, a manager forces people to hear and to see what is happening in a situation. The intent is that once people are aware of what is occurring, cognitive logic will prevail and change will follow. This may or may not be a result. People are often polarized into groups or cults as a result of this strategy. When groups feel that they will not or cannot be heard in any other way, this strategy is often employed. A union strike is one example.

RESISTANCE TO CHANGE

The literature on change is riddled with articles on the manager's responsibility for changing the health care system and on the role of the "change agent" (Barnum & Kerfoot, 1995; Ironside, 2003a, 2003b). Just the term *change agent* can arouse defensiveness in the subjects of change and can threaten the agent. No one really wants to change because people like the comfort of behaviors that have worked in the past. Who wants to trade in their security blankets, and who wants to be the one to say that old security blankets must be burned in favor of new ones?

To say that people will change or that someone is a change agent engenders resistance. Change is often perceived as a "bad word." Newstrom (2011) explained this resistance as one of three types: resistance based on (a) rational opposition to the nature of the proposed change; (b) the method used to change; and (c) personal factors such as emotional and selfish desires. In the first type of resistance, followers may believe and provide evidence substantiating their belief that the costs of the change exceed the benefits. The term "costs" is used literally and figuratively. In the second reason for resistance, people may resent not being informed or included in the early process that generated the need to change, for example. In the third type of resistance, followers may ignore the benefits of the outcomes of change because of their own personal needs and fears.

COMBATTING RESISTANCE TO CHANGE—CHANGING THE LANGUAGE

One of the best ways to combat resistance to change is by believing that change is a natural process that occurs continuously in everyone's life at every minute. The overriding concept is to build support for change if time is not critical. Make the journey an opportunistic happening. The label of change can be an insidious wart. The process of changing is simply cell regeneration—it happens without cognitive awareness, and no one really feels it.

Managers should do their job, lead people, and forget labels. Instead of using the word *change* in conversations, use different words such as coach (Hughes, 2003; Nelson, Apenhorst, Carter, Mahlum, & Schneider, 2004), influence, grow, teach, empower, and so forth. Change will happen. In a sense, managers and teachers provide experiences and challenges through which followers and students are able to learn (Barker, 2003; Kegan & Lahey, 2009). The next chapter focuses on the role of teaching with more detail. Just remember, being a change facilitator is being a teacher too.

Moving away from a philosophical but most important approach that should underlie the more concrete ways to combat resistance, various authors offer suggestions. Silber (1993) suggested that an individual's ability to cope with change depends on his or her flexibility. Barnum and Kerfoot (1995) suggested providing answers to the following questions that are commonly felt by those being changed. Will the change cause my position to be different? Will my status, power, job content, freedom, and so forth be affected? Will my financial status be improved?

Schweiger (1980) stated that the manager should make the tangible benefits of change clear. Furthermore, the change should reflect the followers' existing values and ideas. Newstrom (2011), Bass (2008), and Bass and Stogdill (1990) believed that follower participation is the best way to gain support for change. This principle is also evident in the theory for diagnosing the task that was discussed in Chapter 6 (Vroom & Yetton, 1973). If followers must accept a decision, that is, if followers must do something to solve the problem, then they must be involved in the actual problem-solving process. Followers often need to feel included in the creation of a solution. Newstrom also suggested that employees must see gains for themselves to support change.

Using imagery, the new thread (the change) must be introduced in a way that it fits in with an existing pattern. The wearer and holder of the pattern must see the creative benefit of the new fabric and either like it or be coached into at least understanding its important statement.

SUMMARY

Change occurs constantly. Change is learning, and learning is change. Managers are constantly trying to move a system from one point to another—to solve a problem. Managers, therefore, are constantly developing strategies to change people and to solve problems. This is leadership.

The force field analysis theory was used to explain the forces that operate within the discrepancy between where a system is on an issue (the actual) and where a manager wishes it to be on that same issue (the optimal). Driving and restraining forces were identified, and change can occur by amplifying the driving forces and/or suppressing the restraining forces.

The four levels of change identified were knowledge, attitudes, individual behavior, and group behavior. A participative change cycle moves from knowledge to group behavior, and a directive cycle moves in the opposite direction. The change process involves unfreezing old patterns of behavior, introducing a change, and refreezing the new mode of behavior.

Strategies for change in a given situation are all unique and usually involve several approaches, with one or two dominant approaches. Seven pure strategies were identified and discussed: fellowship, political, economic, academic, engineering, military, and confrontation. Resistance to change can be expected. Philosophical and concrete approaches to combatting this resistance were offered in conclusion of this chapter.

● ● ● REVIEW CONCEPTS AND QUESTIONS

1. Describe Lewin's Force Field Analysis. Provide an example of how it can be used pointing out driving and restraining forces.
2. State the levels of change and the implications for use of the Change Cycles.
3. Discuss the steps of The Change Process.
4. Name six strategies of change and discuss how each may be used by a manager.
5. Analyze why change incurs resistance and describe what can be done to combat such resistance.

● ● ● **SUGGESTED ASSIGNMENTS**

1. Describe a goal that is desired in the home or social environment. Compare the actual state with the optimal state. Use Lewin's Force Field Analysis to identify the driving forces and restraining forces in the situation. Design and defend an Action Plan to move the actual state toward the optimal state.
2. Repeat the suggested assignment stated previously using an example from the professional environment.
3. Repeat the suggested assignment stated previously using an example from your own behavior and plan a strategy using self-empowerment and self-analysis to develop a plan of action for self. A new approach for looking at a process for self-empowerment can be found in another book by this author, Elaine La Monica Rigolosi (2013) entitled *Unlock Your CAGE*.

REFERENCES

Baldwin, C., & Chandler, G. E. (2002). Improving faculty publication output: The role of a writing coach. *Journal of Professional Nursing, 18*(1), 8–15.

Barker, A. (2003). Faculty development for teaching online: Educational and technological issues. *Journal of Continuing Education in Nursing, 34*(6), 273–278.

Barnum, B. S., & Kerfoot, K. M. (1995). *The nurse as executive* (4th ed.). Gaithersburg, MD: Aspen.

Bass, B. M. (2008). *The Bass handbook of leadership: Theory, research & managerial applications* (4th ed.). New York, NY: Free Press.

Bass, B. M., & Stogdill, R. M. (1990). *Bass & Stogdill's handbook of leadership: Theory, research, and managerial applications* (3rd ed.). New York, NY: Free Press.

Brown, H. N. (1999). Mentoring new faculty. *Nurse Educator, 24*(1), 48–51.

Burke, W. W., Lake, D. G., & Paine, J. W. (Eds.). (2009). *Organization change: A comprehensive reader.* San Francisco, CA: Jossey-Bass.

Daly, J. M. (2000). *Writer's guide to nursing periodicals.* Thousand Oaks, CA: Sage.

Ferster, C. B., & Skinner, B. F. (1957). *Schedules of reinforcement.* New York, NY: Appleton-Century-Crofts.

Ferster, C. B., Skinner, B. F., Cheney, C. D., Morse, W. H., & Dews, P. B. (1997). *Schedules of reinforcement.* Acton, MA: Copley Publishing Group.

Fleishman, E. (1973). Twenty years of consideration and structure. In E. Fleishman & J. G. Hunt (Eds.), *Current developments in the study of leadership: A centennial event symposium held at Southern Illinois University at carbondale.* Carbondale, IL: Southern Illinois University Press.

Haffer, A. (1986). Facilitating change. Choosing the appropriate strategy. *Journal of Nursing Administration, 16*(4), 18–22.

Hagerman, Z. J., & Tiffany, C. R. (1994). Evaluation of two planned change theories. *Nursing Management, 25*(4), 57–60, 62.

Hersey, P., & Blanchard, K. H. (1988). *Management of organizational behavior: Utilizing human resources* (5th ed.). Englewood Cliffs, NJ: Prentice-Hall.

Hersey, P., Blanchard, K. H., & Johnson, D. E. (2001). *Management of organizational behavior: Leading human resources* (8th ed.). Upper Saddle River, NJ: Prentice-Hall.

Hersey, P., Blanchard, K. H., & Johnson, D. E. (2008). *Management of organizational behavior: Leading human resources* (9th ed.). Upper Saddle River, NJ: Pearson Prentice Hall.

Hughes, S. (2003). Promoting independence: The nurse as coach. *Nursing Standard, 18*(10), 42–44.

Ironside, P. M. (2003a). New pedagogies for teaching thinking: The lived experiences of students and teachers enacting narrative pedagogy. *Journal of Nursing Education, 42*(11), 509–516.

Ironside, P. M. (2003b). Trying something new: Implementing and evaluating narrative pedagogy using a multimethod approach. *Nursing Education Perspectives, 24*(3), 122–128.

Kegan, R., & Lahey, L. L. (2009). *Immunity to change: How to overcome it and unlock the potential in yourself and your organization.* Boston, MA: Harvard Business Press.

Kelman, H. C. (1958). Compliance, identification and internalization: Three processes of attitude change. *Journal of Conflict Resolution, 2*(1), 51–60.

Klein, E., & Dickenson-Hazard, N. (2000). The spirit of mentoring. *Reflections on Nursing Leadership, 26*(3), 18–22.

Kotter, J. (1999). Making change happen. In F. Hesselbein & P. M. Cohen (Eds.), *Leader to leader: Enduring insights on leadership from the Drucker Foundation's award-winning Journal.* San Francisco, CA: Jossey-Bass.

Lewin, K. (1947). Frontiers in group dynamics: Concept, method, and reality in social science: Social equilibria and social change. *Human Relations, 1*(1), 5–41.

Marshall, M. C. (2003). Creative learning: The mandala as teaching exercise. *The Journal of Nursing Education, 42*(11), 517–519.

Maxwell, P. D. (2005). Resistance to change and change management. In N. Borkowski (Ed.), *Organizational behavior in health care.* Sudbury, MA: Jones and Bartlett.

Mundt, M. H. (2001). An external mentor program: Stimulus for faculty research development. *Journal of Professional Nursing, 17*(1), 40–45.

Murphy, M. M., De Back, V., Bunkers, S., Koerner, J., McBeth, A., Papenhausen, J., Burgess, C., Michaels, K., & Ethridge, P. (2004). Open exchange as a model for continuing education. *Nursing Administration Quarterly, 28*(1), 6–10.

Nelson, J. L., Apenhorst, D. K., Carter, L. C., Mahlum, E. K., & Schneider, J. V. (2004). Coaching for competence. *MedSurg Nursing, 13*(1), 32–35.

Newstrom, J. W. (2011). *Organizational behavior: Human behavior at work* (13th ed.). New York, NY: McGraw-Hill.

Olmosk, K. (1972). Seven pure strategies of change. In J. Pfeiffer & J. Jones (Eds.), *The 1972 annual handbook for group facilitators* (pp. 163–172). San Diego, CA: University Associates.

Records, K., & Emerson, R. J. (2003). Mentoring for research skill development. *Journal of Nursing Education, 42*(12), 553–557.

Rigolosi, E. L. (2013). *Unlock your CAGE.* North Charleston, SC: CreateSpace.

Schweiger, J. (1980). *The nurse as manager.* New York, NY: Wiley.

Silber, M. B. (1993). The "C's" in excellence: Choice and change. *Nursing Management, 24*(9), 60–62.

Spiro, J. (2011). *Leading change step-by-step: Tactics, tools, and tales.* San Francisco, CA: Jossey-Bass.

Tushman, M. L., & O'Reilly, C. A. (2004). In B. M. Staw (Ed.), *Psychological dimensions of organizational behavior* (3rd ed.). Upper Saddle River, NJ: Pearson Prentice-Hall.

Vance, C. (2000). Discovering the riches in mentor connections. *Reflections on Nursing Leadership, 26*(3), 24–25.

Vroom, V., & Yetton, P. (1973). *Leadership and decision-making.* Pittsburgh, PA: University of Pittsburgh Press.

Teacher

EXPECTED LEARNING OUTCOMES

- To differentiate between formal and informal teaching methods and the applications for each
- To apply the problem-solving process for educational purposes
- To understand and experience effective teaching strategies
- To apply teaching strategies to development and enhancement techniques for team members
- To review the similarities between teaching and leading

All managers and leaders are teachers. The purpose of teaching is to facilitate learning in another person. Learning is intrinsic, occurring within the receiver. It denotes an integration of knowledge, attitudes, and experiences in a person's past and present (La Monica, 1985). When someone learns, change occurs in that individual. The manager's primary goal is motivating others to accomplish goals.

Managers should constantly be developing strategies to influence people to do what is needed in order to accomplish the goals of an organization on the continuous journey of growth. To effect this change, followers must *learn* what the task requires; managers must facilitate this learning by *teaching*. Teaching should motivate followers to join their collective aspirations with future goals of the organization (Fuda & Badham, 2011). Donaldson (2008) referred to this process as mobilizing ideas and energy with taking initiatives.

Being a teacher is a satellite role of a manager's position. The intent of a teacher is to facilitate learning. The focus of this chapter is to discuss the most common teaching methods and processes that are available to managers.

FORMAL AND INFORMAL TEACHING

Teaching can be formal or informal. Formal processes occur when teaching programs are explicit—planned, organized, and evaluated. Staff development, continuing education, or inservice education are common labels for teaching units in health care organizations. Such departments predominantly run formal programs in the following areas: orientation, ongoing education, executive development, and patient education. Teaching formal programs becomes the responsibility of managers when teaching units and their staff are not separate components in an agency or the content taught in teaching departments is not planned or has not been presented.

Incidental teaching (informal) is also done through teaching units but on a much smaller scale. This type of teaching is often called coaching (Fournies, 2000; Hersey, Blanchard, & Johnson, 2008; Hughes, 2003; Nelson, Apenhorst, Carter, Mahlum, & Schneider, 2004; Whitmore, 2002). Coaching involves the daily or almost daily reinforcement and development carried out by a manager as an employee is guided through the learning process. This is also known as the process of change.

Both formal and informal teaching takes place through role modeling and leading by example (Yaffe & Kark, 2011). This results in a constant state of teaching and is an important player in how leaders influence others. It is particularly noted as a major facet of transformational and visionary leadership (Bass, 1985; Conger & Kanungo, 1987).

Managers often participate in formal educational programs, which may draw learners from an array of units within hospitals or other health

TABLE 14.1   The Teaching Method and the Managerial Method

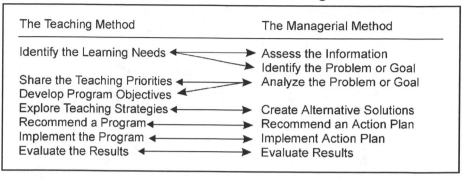

The Teaching Method	The Managerial Method
Identify the Learning Needs ⟷	Assess the Information
	Identify the Problem or Goal
Share the Teaching Priorities ⟷	Analyze the Problem or Goal
Develop Program Objectives ⟵	
Explore Teaching Strategies ⟷	Create Alternative Solutions
Recommend a Program ⟷	Recommend an Action Plan
Implement the Program ⟷	Implement Action Plan
Evaluate the Results ⟷	Evaluate Results

care agencies, or which may be targeted to one specific group. Usually, however, managers have greater responsibility for on-the-spot teaching of their immediate system. In this sense, more informal teaching is involved. This type of teaching can be impromptu or can be planned, organized, and evaluated. The target system usually is composed of those people who are led by the manager; it may be only a portion of the total group.

THE TEACHING METHOD

Teachers can use the problem-solving method to increase their probability for effectiveness in the outcome goals of teaching. This process can be either thought about quickly, as in impromptu teaching situations, or it can be applied over a period of months. Teachers involved in formal and/or informal teaching would use the same process—the detail to which each would become involved as well as the amount of time devoted to the teaching project would differ.

The problem-solving method in teaching is analogous to The Managerial Method that was presented in Chapter 1. Table 14.1 shows a comparison between these two methods. The first five steps of The Teaching Method shown in Table 14.1 are discussed separately in this chapter. Evaluation of achievement of Program Objectives follows Implementation of the Plan.

IDENTIFY LEARNING NEEDS

Identifying learning needs is the first step in the problem-solving method. The process of diagnosis is appropriate for diagnosing learning needs of others and of self. Brookfield (1995) discussed the critically reflective process of teachers and presented four lenses for discovering and examining assumptions in order to identify learning needs. These lenses involve the following:

1. Self-reflection and personal study;
2. Looking through the eyes of students and learners;
3. Conversing with colleagues regarding their perceptions and experiences; and
4. Reading literature on the topic in focus.

After thoughtful analysis as presented previously, a learning need for the team is identified by the difference between what a system actually knows (actual) and what one should know in order to accomplish a goal (optimal). Figure 14.1 illustrates this point.

Suppose a nursing supervisor observed during the past six months that an increasing number of patients on chemotherapy protocols were received on the unit. The supervisor would first need to identify the system responsible for the care of these patients. Then information would have to be gathered, examined, and interpreted from primary and secondary sources on whether the system had the knowledge and experience to provide quality individualized nursing care to patients on chemotherapy protocols. A comparison of the outside standard for quality care—what should be known and experienced according to experts—with what is known by the system would result in the specification of a difference that is the learning need. If a difference exists, then a learning need also exists. For example:

Actual   A new chemotherapeutic agent is being used in treatment protocols. Nurses are used to working with clients who receive chemotherapy, but the nurses are unfamiliar with the new drug, the different protocol, and the record-keeping system required for research purposes.

Optimal   All nurses caring for patients on the new chemotherapy protocols must have knowledge and understanding of the drug actions and side effects, administration regimen, special

FIGURE 14.1 Identifying a Learning Need

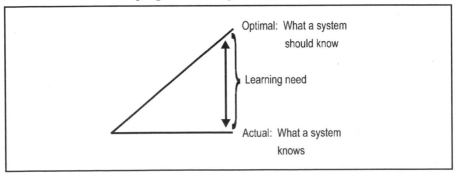

orders, nursing implications, and record-keeping systems as recommended by agency and expert protocols.

Learning Need   Knowledge and understanding in all areas of nursing care for patients on the new chemotherapeutic agent.

STATE THE TEACHING PRIORITIES

Systems of human resources most often have many learning needs. How does a manager decide what to teach first? Obviously, all learning needs cannot be priorities. Maslow's (1954/1970, 1954/1987) hierarchy of needs (refer to Figure 2.2 in Chapter 2) can be used to answer this question.

A health care manager should attempt to identify all of the learning needs for all followers, given a specific context and time. The number of people who have the learning need in focus should be specified; this is the size of the system. Learning needs can then be placed into one of Maslow's (1954/1970, 1954/1987) five levels: physiological, safety/security, social/ affiliative, esteem/recognition, and self-actualization. Table 14.2 provides a format for accomplishing this process; the procedure for stating teaching priorities is discussed more fully in the following paragraphs.

Learning needs usually involve two areas: (a) those needs essential to quality and individualized nursing care (areas of nursing's clinical responsibility), and (b) those that must be met for the development of the staff (teamwork). Recalling the description in Chapter 4 of the needs in Maslow's (1954/1970, 1954/1987) hierarchy, Table 14.3 presents guidelines

TABLE 14.2   Format for Stating Teaching Priorities

LEARNING NEEDS	NUMBER OF LEARNERS (SIZE OF THE SYSTEM)	MASLOW'S NEED LEVEL
1. _____	_____	_____
2. _____	_____	_____
3. _____	_____	_____
4. _____	_____	_____
5. _____	_____	_____

(Table can be increased to whatever size necessary)

Note. The source for Maslow's needs is Maslow, A. (1954/1970). *Motivation and personality* (2nd ed.). New York, NY: Harper & Row. The needs in order of priority are physiological, safety/security, social/affiliation, esteem/recognition, and self-actualization.

TABLE 14.3   Maslow's Hierarchy of Needs Paralleled With Areas of Clinical Responsibility and Teamwork Needs

AREAS OF CLINICAL RESPONSIBILITY[a]	MASLOW[b]	TEAMWORK NEEDS
Nutrition Sleep, rest patterns Elimination Prevention of complications Assurance of physiological status—health maintenance	Physiological	Ongoing clinical education regarding physiological client needs Salary
Comfort Exercise Personal hygiene Safety Environmental considerations Spiritual comfort and assistance Emotional support, counseling Teaching	Safety/Security	Orientation Ongoing clinical education regarding safety/social client needs Working conditions Job security Company and administrative policy
Diversional activities Socializing and privacy	Social/Affiliative	Ongoing clinical education regarding social/affiliative client needs Interpersonal relations with superiors, associates, and followers
An amplification of what has emerged before, but considering the client's need for achievement	Esteem/Recognition	Ongoing clinical education regarding esteem/recognition client needs Executive development Advancement Status Job enrichment
The client can take care of self—allow it!	Self-actualization	The system can take care of itself—let it!

[a]The source for areas of responsibility is the author of this book, Elaine La Monica Rigolosi, published in a previous publication: La Monica, E. L. (1985). *The humanistic nursing process*. Boston, MA: Jones and Bartlett.
[b]The source for Maslow's needs is Maslow, A. H. (1954/1970). *Motivation and personality* (2nd ed.). New York, NY: Harper & Row.

for classifying areas of nursing responsibility and teamwork needs using Maslow's five levels.

Once the format for stating teaching priorities has been completed, then those learning needs that are first priority—physiological needs— are immediate concerns. Second, third, and fourth priorities—safety/security, social/ affiliative, and esteem/recognition—should be handled in that order. This is not to say that all physiological needs must be filled before a manager thinks of or plans for safety needs, for example. The size of the system becomes important. Small systems containing only a few people or maybe only one person with a specific learning need can be taught much more quickly and more informally than can larger groups or systems. Also, a manager can address the needs in priority and then proceed to look at the higher order needs and the developments that may become necessary.

A learning change at one level of priority has an effect on all other identified learning needs. Therefore, continuous assessment of needs becomes essential in the ongoing process of diagnosing what needs to be taught and its priority in the teaching journey at any given point of time.

When a large number of people require teaching in a certain area, then a more formal program should be developed and priorities for the large program also should follow Maslow's (1954/1970, 1954/1987) theory. Managers, however, can meet a smaller system's needs concurrently. Also, do not forget to use other teaching resources: national, state, and local continuing education programs; in-house programs for people with similar needs; an associate "buddy" system (whereby two managers with the same staff needs split teaching responsibilities, and so forth). Creative use of resources is limitless. The only obstruction to creative thinking is oppression or managers who are unable to allow themselves and/or others to use their minds and think outside of the rituals of past behaviors.

DEVELOP PROGRAM OBJECTIVES

After a manager decides what is to be taught, several activities are necessary. The more formal the teaching program, the more explicit these activities should be. Mager (1962/1997), in his well-known and ever-living book, said that the goal of a program must first be stated, followed by instructional objectives. The method to evaluate the program's effectiveness should be directly related to the instructional objectives.

The example statement of a learning need that was presented earlier in the chapter is the goal. A description of the course content and procedures may also be given (Mager, 1962/1997). An objective describes the desired outcome of the course, and an evaluation must elicit information on whether the desired outcome has been achieved. An objective should be observable and measurable.

The Experiential Learning Activities at the ends of Parts I, II, III, and IV of this book contain purposes for the exercises. At the beginning of each chapter in this book are also Expected Learning Outcomes. These purposes and outcomes are general by design; other examples of terminal objectives can be specific and precisely measureable (Mager, 1962/1997). Purposes and a discussion of terminal objectives are presented so that the reader can make an informed decision on the exact type of objective that should be used in a program. The degree of program formality must be considered in making this choice. Applications for continuing education units require explicit terminal objectives and a means for evaluation. Implicit objectives and evaluation criteria may only be required, for example, when reviewing colostomy care procedures for a new graduate on the unit.

Mager's (1962/1997) steps for developing an instructional objective are as follows:

1.   Identify the terminal behavior or expected outcome by content name and specify the acceptable behavior indicating that learning has occurred;
2.   Define the behavior by stating the conditions under which the behavior should occur; and
3.   Specify acceptable performance.

An example of the previous process follows.

Orientation Goal

To review pharmacology, dosages, and solutions.

Terminal Objectives

1.   To be able to pass a written 30-item objective pharmacology test at the conclusion of the orientation program with 90% accuracy.
2.   To be able to pass a written 25-item objective test on dosages and solutions at the conclusion of the orientation program with 100% accuracy.

Explanation

The content names of the terminal behaviors or expected outcomes are pharmacology in the first objective and dosages and solutions in the second objective. The condition under which the behavior should occur is a written test at the conclusion of the orientation program for both objectives. Acceptable performance is the accuracy level required. The evaluative test is the evaluative mechanism.

Evaluating a program is a control process. Newman (1975) specified three types of controls—steering, yes–no, and post-action—as discussed in Chapter 7. The most frequently used method of evaluation is the post-action type, in which the evaluation occurs at the end of a program. Leaders who run programs over a long span of time, however, should employ a yes–no control such as a midpoint evaluation. An experienced teacher uses steering controls when evaluating a teaching approach by eliciting discussion when people ask questions and by responding to learners' needs during a presentation.

There are many ready-made program evaluation forms that can be applied, adapted, or used as a reference by teachers. The Experiential Learning Activities at the conclusion of Part IV contain three such forms.

In short, when developing program objectives, Jay (2011) advised setting SMART goals. SMART is an acronym for the following guidelines: (a) be **S**pecific; (b) develop goals that are **M**easurable; (c) make goals **A**ction-oriented; (d) be sure goals are **R**ealistic; and (e) make goals **T**ime-bound.

EXPLORE TEACHING STRATEGIES

With objectives specified, the content and method(s) for achieving the objectives must be delineated—what will be taught and how it will be taught. This area refers to the ever-familiar concepts of content and process.

Content

It is essential to delineate a detailed outline (at least) of the content that must be taught in order to fulfill program objectives. This is the knowledge base. In the pharmacology example discussed in an earlier section of this chapter, the content would generally include common drug classifications and actions with details on the most commonly used drugs in each category. Specific actions, dosages, administration principles, and side effects would be discussed for the specific drugs. General principles of dosages and solutions would also be taught along with intravenous therapy procedures. The agency's medication procedure would also be content. Moving developmentally and given these content areas, what is the best way to teach?

Learning Principles

Learning principles must be considered when deciding how to teach. The literature is replete with discussions of learning theory; a basic overview is provided in this section.

1. A learner must perceive (Bruner, 1960/1977; Dewey, 1938/1998, 1916/2011).
2. Individual differences such as past experience, intellectual variations, and developmental maturation affect what is learned (Ginsburg & Opper, 1988; Wadsworth, 1996). Experience is positively related to memory (Carnevali & Thomas, 1993).
3. The environment influences learning (von Bertalanffy, 1968/2003; Watson, 1928/1976).
4. The learner's degree of motivation affects what is learned (Marquis & Huston, 2011; Maslow, 1954/1970, 1954/1987).
5. Behavioral reinforcement increases the probability that the desired behavior will recur in another context (Bruner, 1960/1977). Coaching is an important means for reinforcing desired behaviors and empowering followers (Orth, Wilkinson, & Benfari, 1990).
6. Repetition facilitates learning (Bower, 1994; Thorndike [cited in Bower & Hilgard, 1948/1981]).
7. People learn by imitating others (Pohl, 1981).

Rogers (1969) and Rogers and Freiberg (1969/1994) believed that learning has a quality of personal involvement—it is self-initiated and self-reliant. The following learning principles that reflect these beliefs were offered.

1. Human beings have a natural potential to learn.
2. Learning is greatly enhanced when learners perceive relevance in the content being taught.
3. Learning that threatens one's self-image tends to be resisted; reduction of external threats eases this effect and facilitates experience.
4. Learning is facilitated when the learner is involved in the process.
5. Self-initiated learning is most powerful—it is lasting and pervasive.
6. Learning the process of learning is most important because it allows one to be continually open to experience.

Within the framework of learning principles, a variety of instructional modes and media—teaching strategies—can be used to fulfill learning objectives. Each will be discussed individually, even though one or more are usually used in a particular program.

Instructional Modes and Media

Conley (1973) distinguished modes from media by defining *modes* as types of conversations between the teacher and learner(s) and *media* as devices or vehicles to amplify and/or augment various modes of teaching. Various modes and media are presented and explained (Conley, 1973), with additional sources cited when pertinent and appropriate.

Modes

1. *Lecture*—The lecture mode is widely used in formal educational systems and involves one-way communication from teacher to learners. It is useful when a large group has a particular learning need and is best when followed by small-group discussion to reinforce learning. Content that is in the cognitive domain is often taught by the lecture mode.

2. *Group Discussion*—This mode involves two-way communication between teacher and learners and between learner and learners. It is one of the best ways to teach content in the affective domain. Moreover, problems can be shared and support groups or teams can be facilitated. Keenan (1982) referred to this method as a "cooperative goal structure" (p. 487).

3. *Panel Discussion*—Expert panel members discuss a topic or an issue among themselves, and/or an interchange among learners and panel members may occur.

4. *Seminar*—One or more members present an issue or a problem, and the entire group participates in the discussion. A patient conference is one example of this method. The seminar is useful in self-learning peer groups.

5. *Demonstration*—Role modeling in an actual or hypothetical case is one example of demonstration. Any media can be used by the teacher to personify intended learning. Demonstration and laboratory instruction are especially useful when learning involves the psychomotor domain.

6. *Laboratory Instruction*—This mode involves learner self-discovery in a safe, low-risk environment. Simulations such as the Experiential Learning Activities in this book may be involved. The learner actually "tries on" what is being taught.

7. *Team Teaching*—Two or more professionals have responsibility for teaching a particular program; this mode requires coordination and integration of efforts. Learners have the opportunity to hear different points of view on the same issue.

Media

1. *Television*—Closed-circuit and public television are becoming increasingly popular. Television specials on topics such as rape and life after death are also media that can be used by a teacher.

2. *Programmed Instruction and Computer-Assisted Instruction*—The learner is carried step-by-step through content, using teaching machines or books (Barker, 2002, 2003). The learner receives immediate feedback. Even though this feedback can be thought of

as two-way communication, learning occurs better when group or individual discussion follows use of these media.

3. *Motion Pictures and Videotapes*—Films and videotapes on specific content areas can amplify and demonstrate content. Particularly, videotapes are helping in assessing competencies (Minardi & Ritter, 1999; Winters, Hauck, Riggs, Clawson, & Collins, 2003).

4. *Simulations*—Laboratory learning and role modeling are involved in simulations. The preface of this book provided discussion of a rationale for this medium of instruction.

5. *Pictorial Presentations, PowerPoint Presentations, and the Printed Language*—Pictures, figures, graphs, slides, overhead transparencies, and computer generated programs are examples of this category. In *Communication Briefings* (2011), as adapted from Dan Roam's book entitled *Blah Blah Blah: What To Do When Words Don't Work*, the following possibilities in this mode are also suggested: portraits, charts, maps, timelines, flowcharts, and multivariable plots.

6. *Tape and Disc Recordings*—These are most useful in seminars and group discussions. They also often augment slides, films, and other similar media.

7. *Models*—These are representations of objects needed in demonstration, such as those used in teaching life support systems.

Different media can be used in the teaching modes. Selection should be guided by what would be most suitable given the objectives, what would be most well-received, and what is most enjoyable for the teacher. Do not overlook the latter statement—people are best at what they like to do, and there is no substitute for a teacher who enjoys what is being done. Learners catch the excitement. This could be called "transformational teaching," a parallel with transformational leadership.

RECOMMEND A PROGRAM

This section is the next step in the problem-solving teaching method. It involves writing out the following in formal teaching situations and rehearsing the following to oneself in informal situations.

- Title of the program (stemming from the learning need)
- Description of the program
- Objectives
- Outline of content
- Teaching methods—modes and media

- Faculty/teachers and the required education and experience needed to conduct the program
- Evaluation methods
- Required textbooks and/or reading
- Bibliography
- Handouts (optional)

SUMMARY

Teaching is ubiquitous in management, and all managers and leaders are teachers. Because teachers facilitate learning in people, they change people.

The process of teaching can be informal or formal. Both types should follow the problem-solving method for teaching: identify learning needs, state the teaching priorities, develop program objectives, explore teaching strategies, and recommend a program. Details in each of these areas formed the basis of this chapter. All teaching must reflect knowledge and application of learning principles—what research has suggested to have a high probability for facilitating learning as a result of teaching.

REVIEW CONCEPTS AND QUESTIONS

1. Differentiate between informal and formal teaching methods. Cite examples for use of each.
2. Discuss The Teaching Method and compare it with The Management Method.
3. Describe the process for identifying learning needs of individuals and groups. Name and explain how theory can be applied in identifying the priorities of learning needs.
4. Explain how program objectives may be developed.
5. Compare content strategies and process strategies for teaching. Provide several modes and media in the latter.

SUGGESTED ASSIGNMENTS

1. Assess a work or clinical environment. Using each step of The Teaching Method up to Implementation, write a paper identifying the learning needs and how they may be prioritized. Select three priorities and write a teaching program for each. Develop Program Objectives, select Teaching Strategies, and recommend a Program Plan. This can be done with any number of priorities.
2. Assess your home environment. Follow the same procedure as in the first suggested assignment.

3. Conduct a self-diagnosis of yourself and your own learning needs. Choose as many needs as desired or assigned, and follow the same procedure delineated in the first assignment. During the time span of the course in which leadership content is taught, implement your plan and evaluate your own achievements at the conclusion of the course.

REFERENCES

Barker, A. M. (2002). A case study in instructional design for web-based courses. *Nursing Education Perspectives, 23*(4), 183–186.

Barker, A. M. (2003). Faculty development for teaching online: Educational and technological issues. *The Journal of Continuing Education in Nursing, 34*(6), 273–278.

Bass, B. M. (1985). *Leadership and performance beyond expectation.* New York, NY: Free Press.

Bower, G. H. (1994). In appreciation of E. R. Hilgard's writings on learning theories. *Psychological Science, 5*(4), 181–183.

Bower, G. H., & Hilgard, E. R. (1981). *Theories of learning* (5th ed.). Englewood Cliffs, NJ: Prentice Hall. (Original work published 1948)

Brookfield, S. D. (1995). *Becoming a critically reflective teacher.* San Francisco, CA: Jossey-Bass.

Bruner, J. (1977). *The process of education.* Cambridge, MA: Harvard University Press. (Original work published 1960)

Carnevali, D. L., & Thomas, M. D. (1993). *Diagnostic reasoning and treatment decision making in nursing.* Philadelphia, PA: Lippincott.

Communication Briefings. (2011). Presenting with power: Turn your ideas into pictures. *Communication Briefings, 31*(2), 5.

Conger, J. A., & Kanungo, R. N. (1987). Toward a behavioral theory of charismatic leadership in organizational settings. *Academy of Management Review, 12*(4), 637–647.

Conley, V. (1973). *Curriculum and instruction in nursing.* Boston, MA: Little, Brown.

Dewey, J. (1998). *Experience and education. Sixtieth anniversary edition.* West Lafayette, IN: Kappa Delta Pi. (Original work published 1938)

Dewey, J. (2011). *Democracy and education: An introduction to the philosophy of education.* New York, NY: Free Press. (Original work published 1916)

Donaldson, G. A., Jr. (2008). *How leaders learn: Cultivating capacities for school improvement.* New York, NY: Teachers College Press.

Fournies, F. F. (2000). *Coaching for improved work performance* (Rev. ed.). New York, NY: McGraw Hill.

Fuda, P., & Badham, R. (2011). Fire, snowball, mask, movie: How leaders spark and sustain change. *Harvard Business Review, 89*(11), 145–148.

Ginsburg, H. P., & Opper, S. (1988). *Piaget's theory of intellectual development* (3rd ed.). Englewood Cliffs, NJ: Prentice Hall.

Hersey, P., Blanchard, K. H., & Johnson, D. E. (2008). *Management of organizational behavior: Leading human resources* (9th ed.). Upper Saddle River, NJ: Pearson Prentice Hall.

Hughes, S. (2003). Promoting independence: The nurse as coach. *Nursing Standard, 18*(10), 42–44.

Jay, J. (2011). Make your SMART goals WISE goals. *Communication Briefings, 31*(2), 1.

Keenan, M. J. (1982). Collaboration in students: How can we improve it? *Nursing & Health Care, 3*(9), 486–488.

La Monica, E. L. (1985). *The humanistic nursing process.* Boston: Jones and Bartlett.

Mager, R. F. (1997). *Preparing instructional objectives: A critical tool in the development of effective instruction* (3rd ed.). Atlanta, GA: Center for Effective Performance. (Original work published 1962)

Marquis, B. L., & Huston, C. J. (2011). *Leadership roles and management functions in nursing: Theory and application* (7th ed.). Philadelphia, PA: Lippincott Williams & Wilkins.

Maslow, A. H. (1970). *Motivation and personality* (2nd ed.). New York, NY: Harper & Row. (Original work published 1954)

Maslow, A. H. (1987). *Motivation and personality* (3rd ed.). New York, NY: Harper & Row. (Original work published 1954 and later published 1970)

Minardi, H. A., & Ritter, S. (1999). Recording skills practice on videotape can enhance learning: A comparative study between nurse lecturers and nursing students. *Journal of Advanced Nursing, 29*(6), 1318–1325.

Nelson, J. L., Apenhorst, D. K., Carter, L. C., Mahlum, E. K., & Schneider, J. V. (2004). Coaching for competence. *MedSurg Nursing, 13*(1), 32–35.

Newman, W. H. (1975). *Constructive control: Design and use of control systems.* Englewood Cliffs, NJ: Prentice Hall.

Orth, C. D., Wilkinson, H. E., & Benfari, R. C. (1990). The manager's role as coach and mentor. *Journal of Nursing Administration, 20*(9), 11–15.

Pohl, M. L. (1981). *The teaching function of the nursing practitioner* (4th ed.). Dubuque, IA: W. C. Brown.

Rogers, C. R. (1969). *Freedom to learn: A view of what education might become.* Columbus, OH: Merrill.

Rogers, C. R., & Freiberg, H. J. (1994). *Freedom to learn* (3rd ed.). Upper Saddle River, NJ: Prentice Hall. (Original work published 1969 by Carl Rogers)

von Bertalanffy, L. (2003). *General system theory: Foundations, development, applications.* New York, NY: Braziller. (Original work published 1968)

Wadsworth, B. J. (1996). *Piaget's theory of cognitive and affective development: Foundations of constructivism* (5th ed.). White Plains, NY: Longman.

Watson, J. B. (1976). *Psychological care of infant and child.* New York, NY: Arno Press. (Original work published 1928)

Whitmore, J. (2002). *Coaching for performance: Growing people, performance and purpose* (3rd ed.). London, England: Nicholas Brealy.

Winters, J., Hauck, B., Riggs, C.J., Clawson, J., & Collins, J. (2003). Use of videotaping to assess competencies and course outcomes. *Journal of Nursing Education, 42*(10), 472–476.

Yaffe, T., & Kark, R. (2011). Leading by example: The case of leader OCB (organizational citizenship behavior). *Journal of Applied Psychology, 96*(4), 806–826.

Team Builder

EXPECTED LEARNING OUTCOMES

- To understand that groups and teams most often are synonymous concepts in organizations
- To recognize that effective groups and teams generate effective goal accomplishments

- To explore strategies for effectively functioning in goal-directed health care groups
- To have knowledge of the complexity of group dynamics

Building and developing teams of people who work together to accomplish organizational goals involves the study and analysis of how people interact and communicate with each other in face-to-face small groups. The study of group dynamics, therefore, provides a vehicle to analyze group communications with the intent of rendering the groups more effective as they work together as teams (La Monica, 1985; Newstrom, 2011).

For the purpose of this chapter, work groups are teams. A manager is a team builder who must accomplish team development through application of effective group dynamics. Therefore, this chapter involves the study of group dynamics—knowledge and skills that a health care or nurse manager must apply in developing effective groups of people who are a team.

This chapter begins with a discussion of the purposes for studying group dynamics, followed by details of what can be observed in groups. One area for observation, group roles, is presented in a separate section. Processing group behaviors is then discussed at the conclusion of the chapter.

PURPOSES FOR STUDYING GROUP DYNAMICS

According to general system theory (von Bertalanffy, 1968/2003), a system is more than the sum of its parts. It involves pooling the energy of a group of human and material resources toward goal accomplishment (refer to Chapter 2 for a thorough discussion of general system theory). Contemporary management practices apply this theory. Leadership must be conceptualized as community development (Barker, 1998). It follows, therefore, that a manager's best bet is to motivate the group (or team) to work together toward goal accomplishment.

The more effectively a group works as a team, the higher the probability for cost-effective services. A team spirit must be fostered and nurtured (Porter-O'Grady & Malloch, 2007) because information sharing and social exchange play an important part in effective team performance (Mesmer-Magnus & DeChurch, 2009; van Ginkel & van Knippenberg, 2008; Zhang & Peterson, 2011).

Because fostering teamwork is one of the purposes of a manager's communications, studying group dynamics is an important facet of organizational work (Buzaglo & Wheelan, 1999; Risser et al., 1999; Wheelan, Burchill,

& Tilin, 2003). What a system (group or team) accomplishes has as much to do with the goal as it does with how well the group works together as a team. Establishing a group identity and trust among group members are essential as a foundation for all that occurs within and as a result of group processes (Druskat & Wolff, 2001).

Effective teamwork expands the flexibility of people and is essential in modern work environments (Hersey, Blanchard, & Johnson, 2008). Psychological and team empowerment have a major effect on the motivation and accomplishments of followers in organizations (Seibert, Wang, & Courtright, 2011).

Lippitt and Seashore (1980) delineated more specific purposes for studying group dynamics. The manager's goal is to develop an effective team by facilitating the following:

1.   A clear understanding of purposes and goals;
2.   Flexibility in how a group accomplishes goals;
3.   Effective communication and understanding among members— on personal feelings and attitudes as well as on task-related ideas and issues;
4.   Effective decision-making strategies that secure commitment of members to important decisions;
5.   An appropriate balance between group productivity and individual satisfaction;
6.   Group maturation so that leader responsibilities can be shared according to the group's ability and willingness;
7.   Group cohesiveness while maintaining the needed measure of individual freedom;
8.   Use of members' different abilities;
9.   Group processing on how its problems are solved; and
10.   Developing a balance between emotional and rational behavior and steering emotions into productive teamwork.
11.   Weick and Sutcliffe (2000) expanded into resilience as the capacity for improvisation.
12.   Zhang and Peterson (2011) referred to communication among followers and group members as advice and social networks.

WHAT TO OBSERVE IN GROUPS

There are many aspects of group behavior that can be studied. The labels attached to these aspects differ. Dimensions of group behavior that are discussed in this chapter are goals, background, participation, communication patterns, cohesion and membership, climate, norms, and decision-making procedures. Group roles will be discussed in the section that follows the present one.

Group Goals

It has been stated repeatedly in this book that groups must have a goal. Sometimes the goal is formal, and sometimes it is informal, such as celebrating an achievement or having a complaint session to let off steam. These goals represent the tasks of the group. How the group as a team accomplishes these tasks is group behavior.

Group Background

The history and traditions of the group bear directly on the life of the group as it seeks to accomplish its immediate task (Lippitt & Seashore, 1980). Traditions, norms, procedures, and activities should be studied in terms of how they affect the present. Positive aspects of past group behavior (aspects that a manager considers as having the probability to facilitate task accomplishment) should be fostered. Strategies to counteract previous negative dimensions must be specified and implemented.

Group Participation

A manager's goal should be to facilitate the fullest possible participation of the system's human resources. Recalling von Bertalanffy's (1968/2003) assumption of an open system—a group is more than the sum of its parts (discussed in Chapter 2)—the more energy that members put into teamwork, the more output will result from the group. The manager has to apply motivation theory to accomplish this most important aspect of group behavior.

Communication Patterns

This area involves the social organization of the group. The primary reasons for studying communication patterns are to draw out member issues and focus on task issues more effectively. Areas that should be discussed are who is talking with whom, what is said, how it is said, nonverbal behavior, and who is listening to whom (La Monica, 1985; Lippitt & Seashore, 1980).

Communication Networks

Various communication networks have positive and negative effects on variables such as speed of performance, accuracy, job satisfaction, flexibility, and so forth. Figure 15.1 shows three classic communication networks. Obviously many other patterns can exist, but the figure portrays the primary ones.

Leavitt (1951) was early in suggesting that the circle network resulted in slow group speed, poor accuracy, no informal leader, good job satisfaction,

FIGURE 15.1   Classic Communication Networks

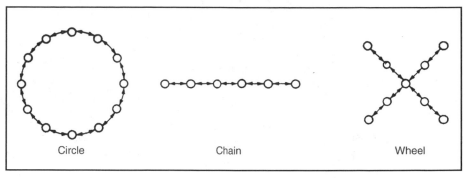

Circle   Chain   Wheel

and fast flexibility to change. The chain resulted in speedy performance, good accuracy, increased likelihood that a leader would emerge, poor job satisfaction, and slow flexibility to change. The wheel, called such because all communications are channeled through the center person, obviously has a pronounced and dominant leader. Performance is speedy and accuracy is good with this network; however, job satisfaction tends to be poor and flexibility to change is slow. Later, it was underscored by Newstrom (2011) that groups naturally solve their assigned problem as efficiently as possible using networks that are necessary or staged. One network, therefore, is as good as another, depending on the system.

Transactional Analysis

Transactional analysis (TA) is another method that can be used to study communication behaviors between and among people. It was developed by Berne (1972/1986, 1964/1996) and led into further popularity by Harris (1969/2004), among others.

According to TA (Berne, 1972/1986, 1964/1996), people have three ego states—parent, child, and adult. The parent state is the evaluative part of us all. It is our conscience, which provides the home for values, rules, standards, and so forth. The two kinds of parent states are nurturing parent and critical parent (Berne). The child ego state is emotion-laden and contains the "natural" impulses and attitudes that are usually identified in children. The child ego state can be categorized as happy and destructive (Berne).

The adult is the rational, reality-oriented ego state. The adult solves problems and makes decisions by balancing the child ego state and the parent ego state against the realities of the environment at a specific time and place (Berne, 1972/1986, 1964/1996). Figure 15.2 shows the three ego states with subcategories.

Berne (1972/1986, 1964/1996) further discussed TA by saying that all three ego states exist in people at different times. A problem occurs when one or two of the ego states dominate. Parent-dominated people tend to believe that

FIGURE 15.2   Transactional Analysis: Ego States

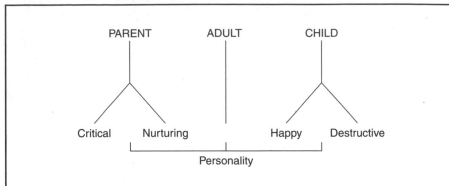

Note. The original sources for transactional analysis are as follows:

Berne, E. (1986). What do you say after you say hello?: The psychology of human destiny. London, England: Corgi Book. (Original work published 1972)

Berne, E. (1996). Games people play: The handbook of transactional analysis. New York, NY: Ballantine Books. (Original work published 1964)

their answers are right; they know exactly what is right and wrong. Adult-dominated people are always diligently working and attempting to be objective and fair. Child-dominated individuals are often selfish in a group and not inclined to be rational and to think outside of self.

Transactions can be complementary or crossed, as seen in Figure 15.3. A principle in complementary styles is that responses can be expected. Crossed transactions result in communication breakdowns because responses are usually inappropriate and confusing. Figure 15.4 portrays various transactions with examples of each.

FIGURE 15.3   Types of Transactions

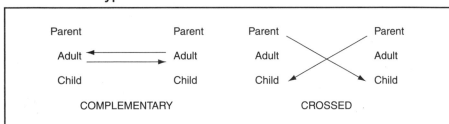

Note. The original sources for transactional analysis are as follows:

Berne, E. (1986). What do you say after you say hello?: The psychology of human destiny. London, England: Corgi Book. (Original work published 1972)

Berne, E. (1996). Games people play: The handbook of transactional analysis. New York, NY: Ballantine Books. (Original work published 1964)

FIGURE 15.4   Examples of Crossed and Complementary Transactions

PARENT-TO-PARENT COMPLEMENTARY

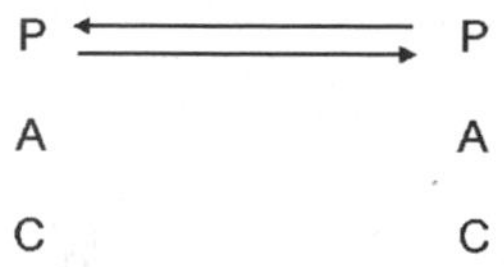

Coordinator to supervisor:
"Primary nursing is the best
model of nursing care delivery."
Response: "I certainly agree."

CHILD-TO-CHILD COMPLEMENTARY

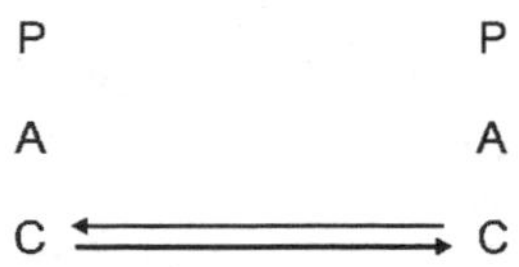

Associate to associate: "I'm tired
of always being interrupted by you!"
Response: "Well, next time
don't talk so much."

PARENT-TO-CHILD COMPLEMENTARY

Supervisor to staff nurse: "Come
to my office at 9 a.m. tomorrow."
Response: "Yes. [Silence] Did
I do something worng?"

CROSSED-TRANSACTION

Supervisor to nurse's aide:
"You should not be doing this
procedure by yourself."
Response: "I have been
doing this for five years, and
I am in a hurry at the moment.
I have work to do."

ADULT-TO-ADULT COMPLEMENTARY

Head nurse to orderly: "Would you
please turn Mr. Robinson in Room 246?"
Response: "Yes, as soon as I get
Mr. Jones back in bed."

Note. The original sources for transactional analysis are listed below. The examples were
developed by Elaine La Monica Rigolosi, the author of this book.

Berne, E. (1986). *What do you say after you say hello?: The psychology of human destiny.*
London, England: Corgi Book. (Original work published 1972)

Berne, E. (1996). *Games people play: The handbook of transactional analysis.* New York,
NY: Ballantine Books. (Original work published 1964.)

Group Cohesion and Membership

Lippitt and Seashore (1980) saw group cohesion as the "attractiveness of the group to its members" (p. 4). Cohesion involves the willingness of members to accept group decisions and whether group activities are grounded on commitment to a common goal or on likes and dislikes of persons for each other.

Subgroups may form in groups (often called "cliques"). They are usually based on friendships or common needs. It must be noted that cliques who are in harmony with a manager's goal will be extremely effective team players and accomplishers. In contrast, cliques who are opposed to a manager's goals can be powerful and obstructive—that is when they need to be divided by a manager. If group desires are split among members, two or more factions within a group may develop. Ideally, a group should work together—unified—while members maintain their individuality (Lippit & Seashore, 1980).

Group Climate

The climate of the group refers to the tone and atmosphere that is created by the group. Are members competitive, tense, polite, friendly, flat, energetic, and/or enthusiastic, for example? Creating a positive group climate is important because enthusiasm and energy are catching and tend to snowball in growth. Unfortunately, the converse—a negative climate—also is catching and grows (La Monica, 1985).

Group Norms

Group norms involve standards or ground rules. The beliefs of the group's majority usually set the norms—"what behavior should or should not take place in the group" (Pfeiffer & Jones, 1972, p. 24). Norms may be explicit, implicit, or operating outside of the member's awareness. A manager should seek to facilitate awareness and frequent examination of group norms.

Group Decision-Making Procedures

The procedures used by a group to make decisions should be studied. Schein (1969/1988, 1998) discussed six ways in which groups make decisions; they remain the basics in group decision-making procedures.

1.   *Decision by lack of response (the "plop").* This occurs when members suggest decisions without due discussion of issues and

alternatives; the group simply bypasses the ideas. Then one idea is suggested, and the group immediately decides that it is the best. There are usually hidden attitudes operating, which are often a lack of commitment to the goal and/or feelings of powerlessness on the part of some members. Results of this type of group decision-making procedure often are negative feelings about self and other group members.

2. *Decision by authority rule.* Authority is delegated to someone in a position of power—the leader. This type of group decision making is acceptable if the leader communicates that he or she will make the decision but needs advice. If the leader, however, communicates that the group can decide on a course of action and then concludes the session by ignoring the group's suggestions, then the group may feel duped—rightfully so. Such action usually results in many negative feelings toward the leader, with potentially harmful long-range effects and at least, a negative resolution aftermath.

3. *Decision by majority rule.* One or more people use pressure tactics to railroad a decision in this decision-making style. The remaining members are left feeling impotent, helpless, and "out-of-breath." They may wonder what happened.

4. *Decision by majority rule: voting and/or polling.* This is the most common style of group decision making. The position of each group member on the issue is requested either formally (by voting) or informally (by polling). A member can be for or against an issue or resolution or can abstain from making a decision.

The best group procedure is to state the issue and then facilitate group discussion on all sides of the issue; decision by voting and/or polling follows. If the group must implement the decision—that is, they must individually do something in order for the goal to be attained—then group decision by the majority rule is not best. Decision by consensus would be better than a majority ruling because it is more probable that group members will be committed to the decision and less probable that the decision or task will be undermined during implementation.

5. *Decision by consensus.* This is a psychological state in which group members see rationale in the decision and agree to support it. This operates even though some members may be more or less committed than others; there even may be a minority vote.

6. *Decision by unanimous vote.* This method, although desirable, is rarely attained in organizations. It is demanded in jury trials, but consensus is usually sufficient in management situations. This decision involves the most time, and the effort–payoff ratio must be considered in its use.

The roles that the leader and members play in a group also deserve observation. They are discussed in the following section.

GROUP ROLES

Understanding the roles that members play in a group can increase the effectiveness of outcomes in group projects. Equally important is members' awareness of how they perceive their roles, juxtaposed or consonant with how others perceive their roles. The role of the formal leader is discussed first, followed by a list of common roles that all group members (including the formal and informal leader[s]) can play. It should be noted that members may be observed in one or more roles during a particular group session.

Role of the Formal Leader

It is the formal leader's responsibility to begin with a clear vision or a goal. The formal leader's further development of the goal and strategy for goal completion in a group can range from almost complete control to delegation, or almost complete control by the group. It follows that the functions required to propel a group toward its goal can be assumed by the leader or can become the responsibility of the members.

The precise dimensions of the formal leader's role are decided after the system is diagnosed (see Chapter 4), and an appropriate leader behavior style (LBS) is selected based on the system's diagnosis (see Chapter 5). Recalling that a leader can behave in any of four leader behavior styles, the roles that a leader plays in group decision making fit into the four leadership styles noted below, using the Ohio State Model of Leader Behavior (Bass, 2008; Bass & Stogdill, 1990; Fleishman, 1973). It should be noted that Hersey, Blanchard, and Johnson's (2008) Situation Leadership Theory is parallel with the Ohio State Model. The two theories can be applied almost interchangeably even though Hersey, Blanchard, and Johnson are current in their published theoretical explanations, an adaptation of which follows. The four Ohio State Leadership Styles are as follows:

High structure and low consideration   (LBS1)

High structure and high consideration   (LBS2)

High consideration and low structure   (LBS3)

Low structure and low consideration   (LBS4)

Group decision making should only be a leader's option in LBS2, LBS3, and LBS4. In other words, a system that is immature or not willing and able (requiring LBS1) should not be involved in group problem solving because the group requires knowledge and experience first in order to be effective in group problem solving activities. More discussion about the issue should be introduced by the manager later. Group problem solving is an intervention in the leadership aspect of consideration because it involves two-way communication—leader to followers and followers to leader (adapted from material learned from Hersey et al., 2008).

When LBS2 is required, given the system's diagnosis, consideration and structure should be high. When LBS2 is required, however, the system is only beginning to move toward maturity or performance readiness. The leader should not, therefore, relinquish too much control to the group. In LBS3, greater control in problem solving should be shifted from the leader to the group. Last, in LBS4, when the group is mature and ready (willing, able, and confident) in relation to carrying out the task, the leader can delegate to the group and leave the group alone to solve problems and make decisions (adapted from material learned from Hersey et al., 2008).

The types of management decision styles discussed in Chapter 6 (Vroom, 1973) can be applied to make more precise how a leader should behave in a group. The reader can refer back to Table 6.1 and Figure 6.1 for a refresher on these styles.

Remember, it is the role of the leader or manager to cultivate and foster engagement in followers (Vlachoutsicos, 2011). Even though leaders should start off with a clear vision or goal (The Motivational Manager, 2011), that is considered to be only the beginning, according to Vlachoutsicos (2011). Managers should then perceive themselves as catalysts for problem solving rather than simply as those responsible for making the decisions. Vlachoutsicos went on to list six lessons that managers and leaders must learn:

1. To be modest;
2. To listen intently so that it clearly is perceived by followers;
3. To allow disagreeing exchanges among group members;
4. To have an agenda and to follow it;
5. To not to answer or have answers for everything; and
6. To allow decisions to be made at another time.

Schaubroeck, Lam, and Peng (2011) added an emphasis on the importance of building trust with and among followers.

In short, Vlachoutsicos (2011) underscored that managers should see group interaction as a way to tap into and expand the expertise of followers. This process is important for the group itself as well as for succession planning from within the group.

Roles of Group Members

In order for group goals to be accomplished, two categories of functions must be performed in the group: task functions and maintenance functions. Task functions relate to what the group must accomplish, whereas maintenance functions are concerned with how the group carries out its task. These activities can be controlled variously by the leader in accordance with the requirements of the group for leader behavior. Given the selected leader behavior, members can assume different roles. Figure 15.5 portrays the relationship between leader behavior styles and group roles.

FIGURE 15.5   Relationship Between Leader Behavior Styles and Group Roles

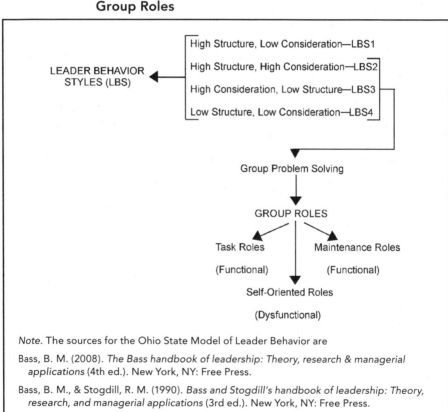

Note. The sources for the Ohio State Model of Leader Behavior are

Bass, B. M. (2008). *The Bass handbook of leadership: Theory, research & managerial applications* (4th ed.). New York, NY: Free Press.

Bass, B. M., & Stogdill, R. M. (1990). *Bass and Stogdill's handbook of leadership: Theory, research, and managerial applications* (3rd ed.). New York, NY: Free Press.

Fleishman, E. (1973). Twenty years of consideration and structure. In E. Fleishman & J. G. Hunt (Eds.), *Current developments in the study of leadership: A centennial event symposium held at Southern Illinois University at Carbondale.* Carbondale, IL: Southern Illinois University Press.

The source for the group roles is

Benne, K., & Sheats, P. (1948). Functional roles of group members. *Journal of Social Issues, 4*(2), 41–49.

Benne and Sheats (1948) identified three major categories of group roles. Although different labels may be used in the literature, the basics remain the same. A partial list of the roles is provided (La Monica, 1979, pp. 280–281*), and a complete list can be obtained from the original source.

Task Roles
These relate to the task with which the group is involved.

1. *Initiator*—Introduces new ideas or procedures and tries to establish movement toward the goal.
2. *Information Seeker*—Tries to obtain needed information or opinions, points out gaps in information, asks for opinions, and responds to suggestions.
3. *Evaluator*—Tries to determine where the group stands on an issue, tests for consensus, and evaluates progress.
4. *Coordinator*—Points out relationships among ideas or procedures, pulls ideas together and builds on the contributions of others, and takes things one step further.
5. *Procedural Technician*—Expedites group work by performing routine tasks, distributing material, and so forth.
6. *Recorder*—Writes down ideas, decisions, and recommendations and keeps minutes.

Maintenance Roles
These are oriented toward the functioning of the group as a whole unit, building group-centered attitudes, and strengthening productivity.

1. *Encourager*—Offers warmth and support to another's contribution and accepts what each member says.
2. *Harmonizer*—Mediates the differences between and among members and attempts to reconcile disagreements.
3. *Compromiser*—Seeks a middle position between opposing viewpoints.
4. *Standard Setter*—Tries to bring to awareness of the norms and standards of the group.
5. *Gatekeeper*—Keeps communication channels open, facilitates participation of all members, and keeps track of time.

---

*Reprinted by permission from La Monica, Elaine L., *The nursing process: A humanistic approach*, pp. 280–281. Copyright ©1979. Reprinted by permission of Pearson Education, Inc., Upper Saddle River, NJ.

Self-Oriented Roles

These roles involve attempts by members to satisfy their own needs through the group and are usually not directed toward effective group work. Self-oriented roles are often seen as dysfunctional.

1. *Aggressor*—Deflates the status of others, attacks the group, its individual members, or the task, and displays envy toward the contributions by taking credit for them.
2. *Blocker*—Negative, stubborn opposition who reintroduces issues that have been previously decided upon.
3. *Recognition Seeker*—Works in myriad ways to call attention to self, boastful, and self-centered.
4. *Playboy or Playgirl*—Displays lack of interest by being cynical or humorous on important issues.
5. *Dominator* —Asserts authority or superiority over others by manipulating the group; flatters, interrupts, or gives authoritative directions.
6. *Help Seeker*—Calls attention to self and seeks a sympathetic response from the group.

PROCESSING GROUP BEHAVIOR

Processing group behavior involves giving feedback to the group on how it functioned. The intent is to increase shared understanding about the behavior, feelings, and motivations of individuals; to facilitate development of a growth relationship by building trust and fostering openness among members; and to increase awareness of how people affect others. Criteria for feedback are found in Chapter 8. The criteria should be applied both to one-to-one and group interactions.

When team building, time should be allotted at the conclusion of meetings to process how the group worked on its task. Group process observation sheets are provided for this purpose in the Experiential Learning Activities at the conclusion of Part IV. These forms are arranged from simple to complex, and they should be used for learning in that order as group members mature (gain knowledge and experience) in processing group behavior.

SUMMARY

Group dynamics involves the study of how people interact with each other in small groups. The goal of study is to render the groups more effective. The more effectively a group works as a team, the higher is the probability for cost-effectiveness of the services. Studying group dynamics is, therefore, an essential aspect of the manager's responsibilities; that is, fostering team maturity is a manager's responsibility.

Areas of group behavior that require observation and study include the following: goals, background, participation, communication patterns, cohesion and membership, climate, norms, and decision-making procedures. Group roles are other important areas in group dynamics. The formal leader's behavior can range from almost complete control to delegation or almost complete control by the group. How a manager behaves specifically is governed by the maturity or performance readiness level of the system in relation to the system's ability to carry out the task.

Task functions and maintenance functions are performed in group problem-solving activities. Group members can assume various functional and dysfunctional roles in each of these categories. Processing group behavior involves giving the group feedback on how it functioned.

Health care professionals must facilitate group problem solving in a variety of informal and formal situations. This is building teamwork, and group dynamics must be studied whenever groups are working toward an identified goal. There is no end to the rainbow—group dynamics can constantly be in focus with the goal of building more effective teams who accomplish more effective goals in a short amount of time. There is a strong and positive relationship between effective teamwork and effective goal accomplishment.

● ● ● REVIEW CONCEPTS AND QUESTIONS

1. What subject areas should be observed in groups?
2. Name and describe the three predominant types of communication networks.
3. What is Transactional Analysis and when should it be applied?
4. Describe the group roles of a leader and when they should be applied to followers.
5. Differentiate among task roles, maintenance roles, and self-oriented roles as they pertain to group members. Provide examples of each role.

● ● ● SUGGESTED ASSIGNMENTS

1. Write a two-page essay on why it is important to study group dynamics when working within health care organizations. Provide personal experiences with your rationale.
2. Define, analyze, and critique Transactional Analysis. Provide personal experiences for your positions.

3. Describe the group role for an ideal leader. What would they do in a group situation and how would they act. Provide a rationale for everything presented.
4. Have a group of six to eight members develop a hypothetical interdisciplinary situation and act out designated group roles in front of classmates who are unaware of the roles being played. At the conclusion of the role play, classmates should discern the roles that were played and provide feedback. These can be repeated with different players and observers.

REFERENCES

Barker, R. A. (1998). The future of leadership research. *Futures Research Quarterly, 14*(1), 5–16.

Bass, B. M. (2008). *The Bass handbook of leadership: Theory, research & managerial applications* (4th ed.). New York, NY: Free Press.

Bass, B. M., & Stogdill, R. M. (1990). *Bass and Stogdill's handbook of leadership: Theory, research, and managerial applications* (3rd ed.). New York, NY: Free Press.

Benne, K., & Sheats, P. (1948). Functional roles of group members. *Journal of Social Issues, 4*(2), 41–49.

Berne, E. (1986). *What do you say after you say hello?: The psychology of human destiny.* London, England: Corgi Books. (Original work published 1972)

Berne, E. (1996). *Games people play: The basic handbook of transactional analysis.* New York, NY: Ballantine Books. (Original work published 1964)

Buzaglo, G., & Wheelan, S. (1999). Facilitating work team effectiveness: Case studies from Central America. *Small Group Research, 30*(1), 108–129.

Druskat, V. U., & Wolff, S. B. (2001). Building the emotional intelligence of groups. *Harvard Business Review, 79*(3), 81–90.

Fleishman, E. (1973). Twenty years of consideration and structure. In E. Fleishman & J. G. Hunt (Eds.), *Current developments in the study of leadership: A centennial event symposium held at Southern Illinois University at Carbondale.* Carbondale, IL: Southern Illinois University Press.

Harris, T. A. (2004). *I'm OK—You're OK.* New York, NY: Harper Collins. (Original work published 1969)

Hersey, P., Blanchard, K. H., & Johnson, D. E. (2008). *Management of organizational behavior leading human resources* (9th ed.). Upper Saddle River, NJ: Pearson Prentice Hall.

La Monica, E. L. (1979). *The nursing process: A humanistic approach.* Menlo Park, CA: Addison-Wesley.

La Monica, E. L. (1985). *The humanistic nursing process.* Boston, MA: Jones and Bartlett.

Leavitt, H. J. (1951). Some effects of certain communication patterns on group performance. *Journal of Abnormal and Social Psychology, 46*(1), 38–50.

Lippitt, G. L., & Seashore, E. W. (1980). *Group effectiveness: A looking-into-leadership monograph.* Fairfax, VA: Leadership Resources.

Mesmer-Magnus, J. R., & DeChurch, L. A. (2009). Information sharing and team performance: A meta-analysis. *Journal of Applied Psychology, 94*(2), 535–546.

Newstrom, J. W. (2011). *Organizational behavior: Human behavior at work* (13th ed.). New York, NY: McGraw-Hill.

Pfeiffer, J. W., & Jones, J. E. (Eds.). (1972). *The 1972 annual handbook for group facilitators.* San Diego, CA: University Associates.

Porter-O'Grady, T., & Malloch, K. (2007). *Quantum leadership: A resource for health care innovation* (2nd ed.). Sudbury, MA: Jones and Bartlett.

Risser, D. T., Rice, M. M., Salisbury, M. L., Simon, R., Jay, J. D., & Berns, S. D. (1999). The potential for improved teamwork to reduce medical errors in the emergency department. *Annals of Emergency Medicine, 34*(3), 373–383.

Schaubroeck, J., Lam, S. K., & Peng, A. C. (2011). Cognition-based and affect-based trust as mediators of leader behavior influences on team performance. *Journal of Applied Psychology, 96*(4), 863–871.

Schein, E. H. (1988). *Process consultation: Its role in organization development.* Reading, MA: Addison–Wesley. (Original work published 1969)

Schein, E. H. (1998). *Process consultation revisited: Building the helping relationship.* Reading, MA: Addison-Wesley Longman.

Seibert, S. E., Wang, G., & Courtright, S. H. (2011). Antecedents and consequences of psychological and team empowerment in organizations: A meta-analytic review. *Journal of Applied Psychology, 96*(5), 981–1003.

The Motivational Manager. (2011). Take the lead in energizing your team—and yourself. *The Motivational Manager.* Chicago, IL: Ragan Management Resources.

van Ginkel, W. P., & van Knippenberg, D. (2008). Group information elaboration and group decision making: The role of shared task representations. *Organizational Behavior and Human Decision Processes, 105*(1), 82–97.

Vlachoutsicos, C. A. (2011). How to cultivate engaged employees. *Harvard Business Review, 89*(9), 123–126.

von Bertalanffy, L. (2003). *General system theory: Foundations, development, applications.* New York, NY: Braziller. (Original work published 1968)

Vroom, V. (1973). A new look at managerial decision-making. *Organizational Dynamics, 1*(4), 66–80.

Weick, K., & Sutcliffe, K. (2000). High reliability: The power of mindfulness. *Leader to Leader, 21*, 33–38.

Wheelan, S. A., Burchill, C. N., & Tilin, F. (2003). The link between teamwork and patients' outcomes in intensive care units. *American Journal of Critical Care, 12*(6), 527–534.

Zhang, A., & Peterson, S, J. (2011). Advice networks in teams: The role of transformational leadership and members' core self-evaluations. *Journal of Applied Psychology, 96*(5), 1004–1017.

●●●● 16

Interviewer

EXPECTED LEARNING OUTCOMES

- To begin understanding the dynamics of interviewing for various purposes
- To study different interview techniques
- To gain knowledge about the principles of interviewing
- To view interviewing as both an art and a science

Note. This chapter is an adaptation and expansion of the chapter on interviewing that was written by this author: La Monica, E. (1985). *The humanistic nursing process.* Boston, MA: Jones and Bartlett. Reproduced with permission.

The interview is the primary procedure used in data collection—this can be for various purposes, such as gathering information on a client for the health care plan, gathering information from potential and hired employees, or gathering information during a performance appraisal. On a smaller scale, a manager can interview an employee informally regarding a situational event.

The process of interviewing is a human interaction during which information is needed and/or is shared. It usually involves face-to-face contact or telephone interactions (Kreitner & Kinicki, 2010; Roussel, 2009). The people interacting determine the exact process; the interview has a highly interpersonal component and also is seen as a developmental procedure. Gathering data through an interview is a skill that is built on other skills. Observation, listening, and communication are particularly essential.

WHAT IS AN INTERVIEW?

In many areas of the literature, the interview is recognized as a strategy. Marquis and Huston (2011) conceived the interview as purposeful conversation. Hein (1980) stated simply that interviewing is a human interaction during which information is requested and/or shared. Brune (2003) described an interview as a conversation that contains both questions and answers. Borkowski (2009) referred to interviewing as a time to identify knowledge, abilities, skills, and other aspects that employee candidates must have in order to meet the requirements in a position.

In discussion of health care and nursing care planning, Bermosk (1966) defined the interview as a special time when caregivers focus particular attention on the client and/or the client's system or family. Interpreting this definition in management, the manager's client essentially is the employee, potential employee, or follower. The principles of interviewing apply in whatever situation is in focus. The eventual purpose of the interviewing process, according to Keltner (1975), is determined by the people involved in the unique process. Bermosk and Mordan (1973) believed that the interview involved sequenced, directed, and progressive changes in all participants of the interview process.

PURPOSES OF AN INTERVIEW

Perhaps the primary purpose of an interview has been explicated by Hein (1980) in discussion of health and nursing care planning. This author interprets Hein's original description for health care management. In the practice of management, verbal communication is used to interrelate with a potential or an actual employee with the intent of facilitating, educating, and/or restoring the person to his or her fullest potential. It is therefore a strategy for data collection to help the manager discern another's world, recognize areas requiring assistance or education, and plan an individualized program that is aimed toward accomplishing the stated goals.

Marriner-Tomey (2008) termed the interview as goal-directed communication. The following specific purposes for an interview are described. Hiring, promotion, and retention refer to employee interviewing; planning individualized care refers to client interviewing; and describing an event or collecting data refers to both.

Hiring

The interview that occurs prior to employment generally is aimed at collecting and sharing information: (a) to discern whether the person being interviewed has the behaviors necessary for success in the position (Monson, 2001); (b) to describe the position to the applicant; (c) to sell the job to the applicant; (d) to answer questions from the applicant; and (e) to ascertain the applicant's career commitment (Brydon & Myli, 1984; Cullen, 2002; Finders, Keepers, 2002; Maiocco, 2003). Platt, Tripp, Fraser, Warnock, and Curtis (2008) added that interviewers also seek to learn about an interviewee's capacity to collaborate and his or her enthusiasm for the position. Executive Leadership (2011) pointed out that interviewers should ask difficult questions to cultivate whether potential hires can problem solve and think on their feet.

The interviewer should be keenly aware of the laws governing discriminatory questions because legal actions against health care institutions for unlawful pre-employment interviews are possible (Poteet, 1984). Also, be aware that laws are changed constantly. Managers who must conduct interviews should check with the personnel departments in their organizations personally and consistently to be sure that they remain up-to-date on the legal aspects of interviewing. Administrative personnel offices usually should have guidelines and procedures readily available. Although agencies should have a list of acceptable and unacceptable inquiries on a variety of subjects, be aware that inquiries cannot legally be made regarding age, marital status, children, race, sexual preference, financial or credit status, national origin, or religion (Marquis & Huston, 2011).

Promotion

Employees are often interviewed prior to the selection of a person who will potentially be promoted. In this instance, the pre-promotion interview is similar to the interview for hiring. Basically, one wishes to collect information from a candidate that could lead to the best decision regarding success in a designated position. Beware of the "similar to me" phenomenon

(Sears & Rowe, 2003), also known as the halo-horn effect. Fairness and objectivity, to the degree that is humanly possible, is sought by the interviewer.

On the other hand, employees are interviewed upon promotion to collect information on their feelings, goals, and so forth. This type of interview can occur immediately following promotion, and/or can occur as a delayed interview one to two months following promotion to discover how the person feels in the new position and what, if any, particular assistance is required as a result of being in the position for a short time.

Retention

The interview that is conducted for the purposes of retention is most often called the performance evaluation. This topic will be discussed in Chapter 17.

Planning Individualized Care

This care planning interview is often called the therapeutic interview (Bermosk, 1966). Bermosk (p. 205) described this as:

> . . . A specific kind of communication which is in operation when the professional person focuses attention on the patient and attends to the business of helping this person to better understand what is happening or what has happened . . . at a particular moment in a particular situation. . . . [The health caregiver] encourages . . . [the client] to describe . . . actions and to express . . . thoughts and feelings so as to identify needs and to establish goals which will help . . . to regain, maintain, or improve his [or her] health status.

Categories of information that may be obtained during the process of interviewing refer to those areas of the PELLEM Pentagram (La Monica, 1985) (see Figure 17.1, Chapter 17, in La Monica's 1985 book for a complete discussion of the PELLEM Pentagram, a Model of Self, developed by Eunice M. Parisi and Elaine L. La Monica and originally published in La Monica, 1979). Chapter 3, Figure 3.1, in this book also has an explanation and diagram of the PELLEM Pentagram. These categories of information are the following:

1. Description of the happening;
2. Perceptions of the client regarding the event;
3. Behaviors of the client;
4. Attitudes and beliefs of the client;

5. Client feelings—physically and emotionally; and
6. Client values.

Questions and statements by the health care interviewers should have the purpose of generating information on the categorical guidelines as stated above. They should describe and elaborate, clarify, validate, substantiate, interpret, and compare. In a sense, the interviewer's comments should be levers by which the interviewee can find further self-expression.

Because the manager conducting the health care interviews from clients is often the primary nurse, it is important to see the gathering of client information and developing the subsequent care plans as essential functions in one's position. If there is a shortage of nursing personnel, for example, the nurse manager may be found to be the only professional nurse who is guiding nursing care. Actual nursing care may be provided by technical nurses and other personnel. Although the previous situation is definitely not the wish of this author, increasingly it often can be observed as reality. As any good manager knows, contingency planning is the best way to meet demands in any situation.

Describing an Event or Collecting Data

Occasionally, situations occur in which a description is required for records or just discussion. The purpose of this type of interview is to gather data on the attitudes, feelings, values, and perceptions of interviewees—or those involved in the situation. In a sense, the manager is collecting information so that decisions and actions can be based on a complete record of data that are considered to be valid. This type of interview is usually open-ended with the interviewer stating the situation and asking the interviewee to share what was thought to have occurred. An exit interview is another example of this type of interview. In must be noted that listening is important in any interview, but it is critical and dominant in this kind of interview.

TYPES OF INTERVIEWS

The interview can be structured, semi-structured (Donnelly, Gibson, & Ivancevich, 1998), or unstructured.

> *Structure* implies that specific questions related to topic areas are posed by the interviewer and are asked of all people being interviewed for a specific purpose.

Semi-structure is less rigid than the structured interview, allowing the interviewer more flexibility; only some questions are prepared in advance (Donnelly, Gibson, & Ivancevich, 1989).

Unstructured relates to the fact that the interviewer's wording of questions is not specified prior to the interview. General content is identified; however, questions flow spontaneously from the interview context. Different interviewees may be asked different questions, depending on the flow of conversation and responses.

The purposes of a specified interview may remain constant in all types of interviews. Also, the rule of thumb is that the more experienced the interviewer, the less structure is required to obtain the needed information.

Formal and *informal* are words used to further classify interviewing. Formality broadly represents the fact that time, place, and content are arranged prior to the interaction. It generally involves a longer period for interviewing than does the informal interview. Informal interviewing can be anything from a lengthy, unplanned talk over lunch to a five-minute, spontaneous interaction in a hallway.

CONTINGENCIES OF THE INTERVIEW

Schatzman and Strauss (1973) stated various contingencies that shape the interview's form and content. These contingencies are presented as follows:

1. *Expected duration:* How long is it expected to last? Will it be interrupted? Can it be extended or shortened as guided by the interaction?
2. *Single interview versus a series:* Is this the only one? Is there a series? Where in the series does this one fall?
3. *Setting:* Is this a public or a private place? What does the environment feel like? Is this feeling conducive to the interview's purpose? Is a specific conversational style more appropriate than others in this setting?
4. *Identities:* Is the interviewer an outsider or insider to the system? Can the interviewer and the interviewee be seen as part of the same group?
5. *Style of the respondent:* Is the interviewee comfortable enough to provide responses that are not overshadowed and skewed by anxiety?

In addition to those noted above, this author, Elaine L. Rigolosi, includes the following two contingencies:

6. *Style of the interviewer:* Is the interviewer warm and thoughtful during the interview process? Does the real personality of the interviewer show?
7. *Harmony between the respondent's style and that of the interviewer:* Do both the interviewer and the interviewee seem comfortable during the interview? Does either person involved seem overly stressed?

Steps in the Interview Process

Even though the interview involves a dynamic interaction that may be viewed as circular rather than vertical, the following guidelines are provided as a framework for conducting an interview.

1. The interviewer should do the necessary homework prior to the interview. Background information should be available for discussion. Notes on the content of the interview should be delineated. If the interview is formal, the meeting's time and place should be stated. The interviewee should be instructed on what to study, bring, think about, and/or prepare.
2. The applicant/interviewee should be greeted. The aim is to quickly establish rapport and put the interviewee at ease. If introductions are necessary, they should occur during this step.
3. The purpose(s) of the interview should be stated briefly.
4. Ground rules should be established—boundaries regarding the purpose, time limits, people who will be involved, and so forth.
5. The next step is the exploration phase where data are collected and/or shared. Structured interview questions may be asked during this portion of the interview.
6. The interviewer should review notes to be sure that all information has been covered.
7. The interviewee should be asked if he or she has any questions. These should be answered as is feasible and within the responsibility and authority of the interviewer. The interviewer may refer to other sources on questions not within his or her scope of practices, if necessary.
8. The interview should be closed. Follow-up, if indicated, should be specified regarding time and place—or a new interview procedure should be described if necessary.

9. Following the interview, the process and content of the interview should be evaluated to determine if it was successful in accomplishing its purpose(s) or unsuccessful in that the stated goals were not met.

PRINCIPLES OF INTERVIEWING

Kahn and Cannell (1957/1983) viewed the interview as a lengthy conversation in which there are three conditions for success: accessibility, cognition, and motivation. The first, accessibility, requires that the information received by the interviewer be in a conscious, clear, and relevant form. It must relate to the purposes of the interview for each unique interviewee. Cognition requires that the person interviewed understand his or her role and the reasons for data collection. Finally, motivation, or willingness to interact, is the major requirement for a successful interview.

Because client motivation has been observed as a paramount and necessary condition, much research by social scientists has been devoted to the area. In one example, Kahn and Cannell (1957/1983) postulated both instrumental and intrinsic factors in their motivational framework. They regarded the interview as a complex social phenomenon. *Instrumental factors* of motivation focused heavily on the interviewee's belief that the results of the interview will have some positive effect on what happens to him or her. The second type of motivational factors, *intrinsic* (Kahn & Cannell, 1957/1983), reflected the qualities of the interviewer. Receptiveness, warmth, understanding, and interest were all important. It is also pertinent to note that the principles of communication that were presented in Chapter 8 are necessary for a productive and effective interview.

Certain principles for an effective interview must be integrated into interview techniques. Hein (1980, p. 26*) explicated the following essentials; they are hereby adapted for the health care and/or nurse manager.

1. An interview is effective to the degree that the manager creates an atmosphere that encourages and supports the employee's or potential employee's freedom of expression.
2. An interview is effective to the degree that the manager clearly establishes and understands the goals of the interview.
3. An interview is effective to the degree that the manager can relate to the follower without using value judgments.
4. An interview is effective to the degree that the manager examines, encourages, and clarifies mutual thoughts and feelings that may affect the issue and outcome.

---

*The source is Hein, E. (1980). *Communication in nursing practice* (2nd ed.). Copyright © 1980 by Little, Brown and Co., Inc. Reprinted with permission.

5. An interview is effective to the degree that the manager consistently evaluates needs, goals, and the behavioral responses of the interviewee.
6. An interview is effective to the degree that the manager is able to evaluate his or her communication behavior objectively in relation to the needs and behavioral responses evidenced by the interviewee.
7. An interview is effective to the degree that the manager employs and encourages the use of feedback in conveying, implementing, and evaluating goals.

In addition, Bermosk (1966, pp. 207–210*) stated other requisites.

8. The climate the manager creates within the interaction influences the substance of the interview.
9. Professional attitudes of warmth, acceptance, objectivity, and compassion are essential for effective interviewing.
10. The identification and clarification of conflicting thoughts and feelings of the participants lead toward a harmony of goals in the interview.

THE ART OF INTERVIEWING

Brune (2003) presented 15 tips that were developed by three experts who were from the professions of business and finance, particularly auditing—Amy Schillings, Jim Waddell, and Joe Buckley. These experts and Brune labeled these tips "The Art of Interviewing." The tips are presented as follows:

1. Be prepared;
2. Outline expectations;
3. Select an appropriate environment;
4. Consider the number of people present since the greater the number, the higher the stress level of the interviewee;
5. Avoid taping;
6. Be time conscious;
7. Consider the appropriateness of small talk;
8. Gain the interviewee's trust;
9. Choose questions carefully;
10. Listen;

*The source is Bermosk, L. (1966). Interviewing: A key to therapeutic communication in nursing practice. *Nursing Clinics of North America, 1*(2), 205–214. Reprinted with permission.

11.   Be patient;
12.   Look for nonverbal behaviors;
13.   Be aware of your own body language;
14.   Confirm information; and
15.   Keep lines of communication open.

Even though these tips seem easy to understand and covertly evident to the interviewer, they are important aspects of communication that must be reviewed periodically. As a manager gains experience, these tips may seem more complex than simple. Remember, it is important to establish an environment during the interview that has the greatest probability for generating all of the information required—to the degree possible (Hill, 2004; Rosen, 2002a, 2002b).

PERCEPTIONS OF INTERVIEWS

It should be evident that interviewing is both an art and a science. It takes knowledge and experience and gets better with experience— successful and positive experience.

Be aware, however, that interviews are subjective in nature. This has both positive and negative views. Dorio (1994) suggested that the popularity of an interview results from its subjectivity and the ability of the interviewer to exercise personal judgment. On one hand is the question: Is what the interviewer perceives close to reality? Generally, however, measurement specialists suggest that the greater the number of people who say or perceive the same thing, or the greater the number of times a person perceives the same thing, the more likely it is that what is perceived is closer to the truth. Perhaps this is the main reason that most positions require more than one or two interviews, conducted by different people at different levels in the organization. So, when in doubt about perceptions, repeat the interview yourself or have others interview the person in focus.

On the other hand, subjectivity means that a manager has freedom to exercise personal judgment (Lauer, 2004; Marquis & Huston, 2011). This trust in self and ability to create new avenues to gather information from the person being interviewed, however, comes with previous and positive experiences in the interviewing process.

SUMMARY

It becomes clear that interviewing is a complex social process involving the principal people interacting, purposes guided by principles of interviewing, and many extraneous variables that also must be considered. This chapter contained a discussion about the primary purposes of an interview along with the types of interviews that can occur, depending on the preference and experience of the interviewer and the reasons for the interview. The section on interview contingencies included the generic steps of the interview process. The chapter concluded with principles of interviewing—the art and the science—and a discussion of the various perceptions that interviewers may have of their interviewees.

● ● ● REVIEW CONCEPTS AND QUESTIONS

1. Describe an interview and discuss the various purposes for which it is conducted.
2. Explain the types of interviews and give examples for which each type can be used.
3. Narrate sequentially the steps in the interview process.
4. Convey the basic principles of an interview that stand out as most important from learning and experience.
5. Differentiate between the art and science of an interview.

● ● ● SUGGESTED ASSIGNMENTS

1. Participants should role play interviewing each other for the following purposes: promoting a colleague to a higher position in an organization, hiring a new co-worker, obtaining data for a patient care history, and/ or collecting information on a critical incident that occurred during a patient's hospitalization.
   Participants can create their own hypothetical situations or they can write situations from experiences. Faculty can also participate in the creation of the role plays used in this assignment.
2. The role plays in Suggested Assignment No. 1 can be observed by the class and then feedback can be provided to the players. Refer to the section on "Giving and Receiving Feedback" in Chapter 8 entitled "Communication" in this book for guidance in providing feedback.
3. Role plays can be practiced in home, social, and study group environments applying different interview techniques such as a structured interview, an unstructured interview, or a mixed method.

REFERENCES

Bermosk, L. S. (1966). Interviewing: A key to therapeutic communication in nursing practice. *Nursing Clinics of North America, 1*(2), 205–214.
Bermosk, L. S., & Mordan, M. J. (1973). *Interviewing in nursing.* New York, NY: Macmillan.

Borkowski, N. (2009). *Organizational behavior in health care* (2nd ed.). Sudbury, MA: Jones and Bartlett.

Brune, C. (2003). The artful interviewer: Three experts offer a refresher course on the basics of conducting an interview. *Internal Auditor, 60*(11), 25–27.

Brydon, P. C., & Myli, A. R. (1984). After the interview: Who gets the job? *American Journal of Nursing, 84*(6), 736–738.

Cullen, K. V. (2002). Sift with savvy. *Nursing Management, 33*(2), 19–21.

Donnelly, J. H., Jr., Gibson, J. L., & Ivancevich, J. M. (1998). *Fundamentals of management* (10th ed.). New York, NY: Irwin/McGraw-Hill.

Dorio, M. (1994). *Staffing problem solver: For human resource professionals and managers.* New York, NY: Wiley.

Executive Leadership. (2011). Can potential hires think on their feet? *Executive Leadership, 26,* 7.

Finders, Keepers. (2002). *Nursing Management, 33*(4), 20.

Hein, E. C. (1980). *Communication in nursing practice* (2nd ed.). Boston, MA: Little, Brown.

Hill, K. S. (2004). Defy the decades with multigenerational teams. *Nursing Management, 35*(1), 32–35.

Kahn, R. L., & Cannell, C. F. (1983). *The dynamics of interviewing: Theory, techniques, and cases.* Malabar, FL: Krieger. (Original work published 1957)

Keltner, J. (1975). *Interpersonal speech-communication: Elements and structures.* Belmont, CA: Wadsworth.

Kreitner, R., & Kinicki, A. (2010). *Organizational behavior* (9th ed.). New York, NY: McGraw-Hill/Irwin.

La Monica, E. L. (1979). *The nursing process: A humanistic approach.* Menlo Park, CA: Addison-Wesley.

La Monica, E. L. (1985). *The humanistic nursing process.* Boston, MA: Jones and Bartlett.

Lauer, C. S. (2004). How to land the best. *Modern Healthcare, 34*(3), 26.

Maiocco, G. (2003). Critical care: From classroom to CCU. *Nursing Management, 34*(3), 54, 56–57.

Marquis, B. L., & Huston, C. J. (2011). *Leadership roles and management functions in nursing: Theory & applications* (7th ed.). Philadelphia, PA: Lippincott.

Marriner-Tomey, A. (2008). *Guide to nursing management* (8th ed.). St. Louis, MO: Mosby.

Monson, M. S. (2001). Should you hire that nurse? *Nursing Management, 32*(10), 21.

Platt, A. D., Tripp, C. E., Fraser, R. G., Warnock, J. R., & Curtis, R. E. (2008). *The skillful leader II: Confronting conditions that undermine learning.* Acton, MA: Ready About Press.

Poteet, G. W. (1984). The employment interview: Avoiding discriminatory questioning. *Journal of Nursing Administration, 14*(4), 38–42.

Rosen, L. S. (2002a). Background screening and safe hiring: An introduction. *Occupational Health & Safety, 71*(4), 16–18.

Rosen, L. S. (2002b). Ten safe hiring tools. *Occupational Health & Safety, 71*(7), 30.

Roussel, L. (with Swansburg, R.). (2009). *Management and leadership for nurse administrators* (5th ed.). Sudbury, MA: Jones and Bartlett.

Schatzman, L., & Strauss, A. L. (1973). *Field research: Strategies for a natural society.* Englewood Cliffs, NJ: Prentice Hall.

Sears, G. J., & Rowe, P. M. (2003). A personality-based similar-to-me effect in the employment interview: Conscientiousness, affect versus competence-mediated interpretations, and the role of job relevance. *Canadian Journal of Behavioural Science, 35*(1), 13–24.

●●● **17**

Performance Appraiser

EXPECTED LEARNING OUTCOMES

- To understand the need and process for developing job descriptions
- To gain knowledge in developing fair rating processes
- To study interview techniques as they pertain specifically to appraising performance

- To apply the performance appraisal process to various processes
- To articulate performance skills necessary for effectively accomplishing a role

Performance appraisal is one method for a manager to control what is occurring in the organization. It is a way to compare the outcomes of individual and group behaviors toward goal accomplishment with the initiatives and expectations that were planned. Further, it is the way most managers formally and informally guide employees in their professional development within an organization.

The literature is replete with articles on the topic of performance appraisal. There are authors who have developed objective performance appraisal systems (Crane & Crane, 2000; Harwood et al., 2003; Malloch, 1999; Speroff, James, Nelson, Headrick, & Brommels, 2004; Zimmerman, 2003); others have studied the process for conducting the performance appraisal (Arnold & Pulich, 2003; Pendergast & Buchda, 2003; Syptak, Marsland, & Ulmer, 1999). Investigators also have studied the effects of feedback and other processes on employee development (Clark, 2003; Donaldson, 2008; Kreitner & Kinicki, 2010; Roberts, 2003; Smith, 2003). There is literature on the factors that should be included in various criterion-referenced performance appraisals (Johnson & Luciano, 1988; Lampe, 1986; Neal, 2009), and then there is discussion about whether performance appraisals really work in producing the desired outcomes (Heneman, 2003; Momeyer, 1986; Salladay, 2002; Zemke, 1985).

Even though discussions about performance appraisals from both managers and followers always involve some degree of hesitation, anxiety, and unfortunately, even discomfort or pain, the performance appraisal seems here to stay—in one form or another. The purpose of this chapter, therefore, is to discuss the general reasons for the performance appraisal, the principles of appraisal, tactics for appraising, and classic methods used in conducting the performance appraisal.

PURPOSES OF THE PERFORMANCE APPRAISAL

There are two general purposes for the performance evaluation: judgmental purposes and developmental purposes (Donnelly, Gibson, & Ivancevich, 1998). Each will be separately discussed.

Judgmental Purposes

When performance appraisals are accomplished for the purposes of determining salary standards and salary increases and/or awarding merit increases, then they are being carried out for judgmental purposes. Other reasons in this area include selecting qualified individuals for promotions and/or transfers and demoting or terminating employment because of unsatisfactory performance (Roussel, 2009; Rowland & Rowland, 1997). Performance appraisals that are done for judgmental purposes carry the highest stakes and often result in both the rater and the person being rated having anxiety.

Developmental Purposes

Developmental purposes are predominantly educative and involve coaching the employee to gain professionally by working within organizational goals. Self-learning and personal growth are both involved (Donnelly et al., 1998; Hersey, Blanchard, & Johnson, 2008). Rowland and Rowland (1997) described specific examples such as the following: identifying talent in the organization, determining training and development needs of individuals or groups, improving interpersonal relationships among group members, establishing standards of performance and gaining acceptance of those standards, providing employee recognition, discovering employee aspirations and reconciling them with the goals of the organization, team building, and giving employees feedback. This list is not meant to be all inclusive.

A developmental performance appraisal is appropriate in any learning situation when one wants to compare an actual state with a planned and optimal state that has been reached or is in the journey toward task accomplishment. This educative method can be used with individuals or with groups, both informally and formally. The goal of a performance appraisal is to energize an individual or a group to achieve. This is also known as motivation (Roussel, 2009).

Perhaps the importance of an ongoing and developmental performance appraisal process in health care was best concluded by a research report presented by Gabriel, Diefendorff, and Erickson (2011). Their findings suggested that nurse's well-being would be enhanced by creating and restructuring work environments so that their achievements could be perceived in practice. According to research, this would have the effect of lowering the stress that can result from perceptions of low task accomplishment.

PRINCIPLES OF PERFORMANCE APPRAISAL

There are certain principles of performance appraisal that must be met in order for an appraisal to be useful in any purpose. These principles will be presented in this section.

First, the appraisal must contain content that is *relevant* to the individual being appraised in a particular setting (Donnelly et al., 1998). This answers the question, "What is to be appraised?" In other words, the content of the appraisal must encompass a valid sample of the behaviors or traits that are seen as important in a specified position. The affective, the cognitive, and the psychomotor areas involved in carrying out specified responsibilities in a position must be represented. Therefore, the appraisal should be based on a position analysis and a resultant position description for a given level of expertise. In typical clinical career ladders, for example, there are different position descriptions for the role of staff nurse with two years of experience in contrast with a nurse with two to five years of experience, and so forth. At each level of experience, an employee should be able to achieve excellence.

Second, the *criteria* that will be used to appraise performance should be stated and *standards* should be specified whenever possible. The criteria may be stated in a paper-and-pencil rating scale by a follower or maybe a paper-and-pencil self-report or a test, for example. The standard is the minimally acceptable level of performance, such as a 90% passing rate on a test or writing care plans on all patients within 24 hours of their admission, for example. It is important that the criterion method be reliable, that is, that it be stable over time and between/among raters. If two raters rated the same person and had the same information, would their ratings be very similar? If a criterion method is said to be reliable, both raters would have similar scores. This same principle applies when the same rater is rating at two different intervals. If no change has occurred, then the score should be similar. In contrast, if the employee is expected to have grown or learned in the area being evaluated, then the score on the criterion should show improvement.

Third, a performance appraisal should be able to *discriminate* between excellent, good, and poor performance (Donnelly et al., 1998). Any purpose for which an appraisal is done should involve identification of areas requiring further development and areas that just need to continue in the effective vein with possibly some enrichment.

Fourth and last, any performance appraisal must be *practical* (Donnelly et al., 1998) or in measurement terminology, it must have *utility*. There are many organizations and people in those organizations that spend tremendous amounts of time developing, testing, and implementing extremely lengthy performance appraisals. In contemporary health care and nursing practice, one must evaluate the effort/payoff ratio in such an endeavor. Sometimes people develop a criterion-referenced appraisal over such a long time that the content is no longer valid given the requirements of the position, which seem to change quickly in current health care environments and systems. Further, the longer the appraisal forms, the less likely managers are going to find time to complete them. In short, performance appraisal forms should be efficient, precise, and condensed.

TACTICS OF PERFORMANCE APPRAISAL

The process of the performance appraisal can be paralleled with the managerial method that was presented, discussed, and applied in Part I of this book. Table 17.1 contains a comparison of these two processes. The performance appraisal process noted is a blend by this author of information contained from many sources. Operationally, it identifies the steps for planning, conducting, and following up on the evaluation.

TABLE 17.1   Comparison of the Management Method and the Performance Appraisal Process

THE MANAGERIAL METHOD	THE PERFORMANCE APPRAISAL PROCESS
1. Assess the information	Define the job requirements— expectations
2. Identify the problem/goal	Define the standards (benchmarks of performance for a particular role

3. Analyze the problem/goal
   Select the system
   Diagnose the system (self and others)
	Specify the employee qualifications
	Review the objectives set by manager and employee
	Review the performance records
	Tentatively complete the appraisal form

4. Choose leader behavior	Conduct the appraisal
5. Create alternative solutions	Co-develop a perfomance improvement plan using goal setting principles
6. Recommend an action plan	Agree on a plan of action
7. Implement action plan	Provide on-the-job coaching or daily reinforcement and development activities
8. Evaluate results	Provide ongoing feedback on performance

Who Should Appraise?

Donnelly et al. (1998) identified five possible parties who could appraise or rate another person: a supervisor, peers, the ratee, subordinates of the ratee, and/or raters outside of the organizational environment. In most cases, employees should be rated by their immediate supervisor at the minimum because this person has the greatest opportunity to observe the individual's behavior with organizational objectives and the expectations of the particular role. The supervisor's appraisal is best when coupled and compared with a self-rating by the follower being appraised. Expectations of performance of each person can be learned and matched.

Who Should Be Appraised?

Most organizations appraise employees at all levels of the organization—from the bottom of the organizational chart right to the top managerial levels. Education and development can occur anywhere and everywhere; people require feedback as a stimulus to develop further in specified directions.

When Should Appraisals Occur?

There is no rule on when appraisals should occur; however, most organizations appraise older or tenured employees about once or twice a year. New employees are appraised about six weeks to two months after being hired. Employees at various stages of development may be appraised more or less often than twice a year, depending on the objectives set during the previous appraisal and needs that have been identified that require follow-up. Progressive discipline procedures are examples of appraisals that may occur as often as every two weeks. An appraisal should contain a progress note at the bottom that is written by the appraiser; it should designate when the next appraisal will occur and the objectives for the period of time until that date.

The Appraisal Interview

The appraisal interview is a way of providing formal feedback to the employee (Newtrom, 2011). As previously mentioned and worthy of underscoring, the author of this book recommends that both the rater and the ratee complete the appraisal form or make notes relative to each criterion. Following discussion in the interview, a record can be made by the appraiser that reflects information from all involved.

TABLE 17.2   Guidelines for Preparing and Conducting an Appraisal interview

---

PREPARING FOR THE INTERVIEW

1. Hold a group discussion with employees to be appraised and describe the broad standard for their appraisals.

2. Discuss your employees with your own manager and several of your peers.

3. Clarify any differences in language between the formal written appraisal and the interview.

4. If you are angry with an employee, talk about it before the interview, not during the interview.

5. Be aware of your own biases in judging people.

6. Review the employee's compensation plan and be knowledgeable about his or her salary history.

7. If you already have given the employee a number of negative appraisals, be prepared to take action.

CONDUCTING THE INTERVIEW

1. Focus on positive work performance.

2. Remember that strengths and weaknesses usually spring from the same general characteristics.

3. Admit that your judgment of performance contains some subjectivity.

4. Make it clear that responsibility for development lies with the employee, not with you (the rater).

5. Be specific when citing examples.

Note. The source is Ivancevich, J., Donnelly, J. H. Jr., & Gibson, J. L. (1989). *Management: Principles and functions* (4th ed., p. 534). Homewood, IL: BPI/Irwin.

In addition to the principles and discussion in Chapter 16 on interviewing, Ivancevich, Donnelly, and Gibson (1989) provided guidelines for preparing and conducting an appraisal interview. Their thoughts can found in Table 17.2.

Research Findings on Performance Appraisal

The following insights regarding performance appraisal seem important for the appraiser and the appraisee to keep in mind. With the exception of the first finding presented, Kreitner and Kinicki (2001, 2010) synthesized these results from several sources, including Hedge and Kavanagh (1988) and Landy and Farr (1980).

- Kraiger and Ford (1985) found that appraisers typically rate same-race appraisees higher. In a meta-analysis involving 74 studies and 17,159 individuals, White supervisors favored White subordinates. Similarly in a meta-analysis of 14 studies and 2,248 people, Black supervisors favored Black subordinates. These findings support the findings of Hornstein (1976) in his classic research on prosocial and antisocial behavior with similar and dissimilar groups.
- No consistent gender bias was found.
- The more experienced rater and the higher performance manager tended to result in higher-quality appraisals. Training and development had positive effects on appraisal quality.
- Peer ratings and self-evaluations tended toward leniency when compared with ratings from a supervisor.

PERFORMANCE APPRAISAL METHODS

There are many methods that can be used to appraise a person. The ones used predominantly in health care systems will be presented and discussed.

Graphic Rating Scales

This is the most widely used method of appraising performance and involves having behavior statements or traits each rated on a continuum that may be quantitative or qualitative. The Likert-type scale that moves from 1 (*poor*) to 5 (*excellent*), for example, is a quantitative scale. Occasionally, qualitative adjectives such as poor, average, and excellent may be used to describe numbers. This author recommends the following: *Outstanding, Acceptable, Unacceptable,* and *Not Applicable.*

Graphic rating scales can be used by superiors in rating subordinates, or they may be used in self-reports or ratings by peers. When the quantitative scale is used, an overall appraisal score can be derived by adding all the individual scores and dividing it by the number of items. Items not rated, such as those not observed or not applicable, should not be included in the total numbers of items.

In graphic rating scales, it is important to understand that the greater the number of quantitative intervals, the greater the chance that the intervals will not be stable across raters. In other words, if two raters are observing the same person in the same context and have been given the same information, their ratings will be more similar as the number of rating possibilities decreases. Ratings should therefore be assigned that signal critical areas of strength and weakness in the person being rated (Platt, Tripp, Fraser, Warnock, & Curtis, 2008).

Applying this author's preference, noted previously, objectives for any unacceptable behaviors can be notated and evaluated during the next appraisal process. Also, positive and effective behaviors can be enriched. Both can be written at the end of the behavioral portion of the appraisal form.

Critical Incidents

These are examples of good and bad performances that are written down soon after occurring. In a sense, they are a diary of significant events in the work performance of an employee. Critical incidents should focus on work-related behaviors and not on personality traits (Kreitner & Kinicki, 2001).

Written Essays

This is a narrative description of one's perception of another's work-related performance or it may actually be written as a self-report. This is the most subjective of the appraisal techniques because something liked (the halo effect) or something disliked (the horn effect) often runs through and flavors the entire essay. Furthermore, they often are usually written long after the actual behavior has been observed; hence, they are subject to the distortion caused by time.

Goal Setting

This method employs Drucker's (1985/2002; 1967/2009) Management by Objectives or modifications of the method. In Management by Objectives, results are emphasized rather than activities. Objectives are mutually set between supervisor and follower, and a time period during which the goals are to be met is specified. When the date is reached, another discussion takes place in which actual results are compared with expected outcomes and a new set of objectives is formulated.

In practice, a manager can also designate activities into the plan so that the follower will have a map of how to attain the stated goals. This author recommends that goal setting be included in any type of performance appraisal. In a sense, there should be a portion of an appraisal report that is open for writing objectives that are expected to be met in the future within a specified time. All unsatisfactory performances should have at least one objective that is intended for alleviating the unsatisfactory performance. Enrichment activities and areas of talent should be amplified in this section also.

Rankings

This technique involves ranking employees on a particular dimension of work performance (Kreitner & Kinicki, 2001). If there are several dimensions on which employees are to be ranked, then their rankings can be summed to provide an overall ranking for each employee. In health care systems, this type of appraisal is usually not evident formally. However, many supervisors have this rating system readily available in their own thought processes.

Behaviorally Anchored Rating Scales

This type of rating scale is similar to the graphic scale, only at each point there are behavioral statements that define what each rating represents. For example, there are specific behaviors that represent excellent, good, average, and poor performance (Roussel, 2009). This method usually results in greater inter-rater reliability of the appraisal even though it is time-consuming to develop.

A PERSONAL NOTE ON APPRAISALS

Performance appraisals must be in complete harmony with position descriptions. A person must be hired with full knowledge of expectations that are held for the position. These expectations in the position description are then rated or quantified and a performance appraisal results. In actuality, a position description should be developed prior to a performance appraisal.

It is possible to spend a lifetime developing a rating scale that is both reliable and valid. That is, the scale ratings are consistent across raters and among items (reliability), and the scale is used to measure a sample of behaviors that adequately represents the responsibilities in a given position (validity). Both of these concepts must be evaluated—a judgment is made that the reliability and validity of an appraisal form are adequate given the purposes for which the appraisal is used.

The amount of time that a manager has in a health care organization for the purposes of conducting performance appraisals varies greatly. However, it is safe to say that the process of appraisal is among many equally important responsibilities. It therefore should not be a totally time-consuming activity, expending a great amount of effort for an important but moderate payoff.

The time spent in developing the performance appraisal form and establishing reliability and validity of the instrument should be a careful and planned consideration. It has been observed that such a great amount of time can be spent on developing reliability and validity tests that by the time the developer or researcher concludes that it should be implemented, the behaviors of practice have changed—which renders the instrument not valid.

Make both position descriptions and performance appraisals short and specific, but not all inclusive. Items should be in the performance appraisal that open up the possibilities for other examples or expected responsibilities. Develop the part of the appraisal that points people in directions for growth. The end of the appraisal should have room for the appraiser's notes—goals for the next appraisal time period with specific ways that the goals will be attained. Then comments could be made in a continuous record, thereby documenting growth.

Be clear in a performance appraisal of what is acceptable and unacceptable behavior—and then, what is exceptional or distinguished. So often, managers use a rating scale that moves from 1 (*poor*) to 5 (*excellent*). It is difficult to know the differentiation between a rating of 2 or 3 and 3 or 4. Furthermore, is such a fine discrimination really important in charting the growth of an individual over the next six months or a year? Keep the appraisal short, simple, educative, and positive—for both the appraiser and the employee being appraised.

SUMMARY

Performance appraisal was presented as a process that may have both judgmental and developmental or educative purposes. Principles of performance appraisal were presented followed by specific tactics that the appraiser should understand. The performance appraisal process was compared with the managerial method. The chapter concluded with various methods that are used in performance appraisal programs, especially in health care environments.

● ● ○ REVIEW CONCEPTS AND QUESTIONS

1. Describe the two main purposes for applying the performance appraisal process in the work environment. Provide examples for each and the rationale for their usage.
2. Present and discuss the four principles that must be met in order for the performance appraisal to be useful.
3. Compare the performance appraisal process with the managerial method. Explain similarities and differences.
4. Discuss various performance appraisal methods that can be used. Critique the positive and negative factors for each.

● ● ● SUGGESTED ASSIGNMENTS

1. Recall from experience the most positive performance appraisal that you have encountered. Narratively, describe the purpose of the appraisal, the principles used, the tactics, and the method. According to your belief, what made this the most positive experience using the appraisal process? In order for it to have been even more positive and rewarding, would you have suggested anything be done differently?
2. Follow the assignment in Suggested Assignment No. 1, using the most negative performance appraisal that you have encountered.
3. Imagine that you are writing the script for your next performance appraisal either in the environment in which you work or your educational environment. Describe the situation and purpose for the appraisal. List the principles, tactics, and methods that you suggest should be applied and discuss your rationale.

REFERENCES

Arnold, E., & Pulich, M. (2003). Personality conflicts and objectivity in appraising performance. *The Health Care Manager, 22*(3), 227–232.

Clark, K. (2003, January 13). Judgment day; It's survival of the fittest as companies tighten the screws on employee performance reviews. *U.S. News & World Report, 134*(2), 31–32.

Crane, J. S., & Crane, N. K. (2000). A multi-level performance appraisal tool: Transition from the traditional to a CQI approach. *Health Care Management Review, 25*(2), 64–73.

Donaldson, G. A., Jr. (2008). *How leaders learn.* New York, NY: Teachers College Press.

Donnelly, J. H., Jr., Gibson, J. L., & Ivancevich, J. M. (1998). *Fundamentals of management* (10th ed.). New York, NY: Irwin/McGraw-Hill.

Drucker, P. F. (2002). The discipline of innovation. *Harvard Business Review, 80*(8), 95–100, 102, 148. (Original work published 1985)

Drucker, P. F. (2009). *The effective executive.* New York, NY: HarperCollins. (Original work published 1967)

Gabriel, A. S., Diefendorff, J. M., & Erickson, R. J. (2011). The relations of daily task accomplishment satisfaction with changes in affect: A multilevel study in nurses. *Journal of Applied Psychology, 96*(5), 1095–1104.

Harwood, L., Lawrence-Murphy, J. A., Ridley, J., Malek, P., Boyle, L., & White, S. (2003). Implementation challenges of a renal nursing professional practice. *Nephrology Nursing, 30*(5), 503–510, 515.

Hedge, J. W., & Kavanagh, M. J. (1988). Improving the accuracy of performance evaluations: Comparisons of three methods of performance appraiser training. *Journal of Applied Psychology, 73*(1), 68–73.

Heneman, R. L. (2003). Job and work evaluation: A literature review. *Public Personnel Management, 32*(1), 47–72.

Hersey, P., Blanchard, K. H., & Johnson, D. E. (2008). *Management of organizational behavior: Leading human resources* (9th ed.). Upper Saddle River, NJ: Pearson Prentice Hall.

Hornstein, H. (1976). *Cruelty and kindness: A new look at aggression and altruism.* Englewood Cliffs, NJ: Prentice Hall.

Ivancevich, J. M., Donnelly, J. H., Jr., & Gibson, J. L. (1989). *Management: Principles and functions* (4th ed.). Homewood, IL: BPI/Irwin.

Johnson, J., & Luciano, K. (1988). Managing by behavior and results—Linking supervisory accountability to effective organizational control. *Readings from JONA: Readings in nursing administration.* Philadelphia, PA: Lippincott.

Kraiger, K., & Ford, J. K. (1985). A meta-analysis of ratee race effects in performance ratings. *Journal of Applied Psychology, 70*(1), 56–65.

Kreitner, R., & Kinicki, A. (2001). *Organizational behavior* (5th ed.). New York, NY: McGraw-Hill/Irwin.

Kreitner, R., & Kinicki, A. (2010). *Organizational behavior* (9th ed.). New York, NY: McGraw-Hill/Irwin.

Lampe, S. (1986). Getting the most out of needs assessments. *Training, 23*(10), 101–104.

Landy, F. J., & Farr, J. L. (1980). Performance rating. *Psychological Bulletin, 87*(1), 72–107.

Malloch, K. (1999). The performance measurement matrix: A framework to optimize decision making. *Journal of Nursing Care Quality, 13*(3), 1–12.

Momeyer, A. G. (1986). Why no one likes your performance appraisal system. *Training, 23*(10), 95–98.

Neal, J. E. (2009). *Effective phrases for performance appraisals* (11th ed.). Perrysburg, OH: Neal.

Newtrom, J. W. (2011). *Organizational behavior: Human behavior at work* (13th ed.). New York, NY: McGraw-Hill/Irwin.

Pendergast, D. K., & Buchda, V. L. (2003). Charting the course: A quality journey. *Nursing Administration Quarterly, 27*(4), 330–335.

Platt, A. D., Tripp, C. E., Fraser, R. G., Warnock, J. R., & Curtis, R. E. (2008). *The skillful leader II: Confronting conditions that undermine learning.* Acton, MA: Ready About Press.

Roberts, G. E. (2003). Employee performance appraisal system participation: A technique that works. *Public Personnel Management, 32*(1), 89–98.

Roussel, L. (with Swansburg, R.). (2009). *Management and leadership for nurse administrators* (5th ed.). Sudbury, MA: Jones and Bartlett.

Rowland, H., & Rowland, B. (1997). *Nursing administration handbook* (4th ed.). Gaithersburg, MD: Aspen.

Salladay, S. A. (2002). Fair appraisal, or hatchet job? *Nursing, 32*(12), 65.

Smith, M. H. (2003). Empower staff with praiseworthy appraisals. *Nursing Management, 34*(1), 16–17, 52.

Speroff, T., James, B. C., Nelson, E. C., Headrick, L. A., & Brommels, M. (2004). Guidelines for appraisal and publication of PDSA [Plan, Do, Study, Act] quality improvement. *Quality Management in Health Care, 13*(1), 33–39.

Syptak, J. M., Marsland, D. W., & Ulmer, D. (1999). Job satisfaction: Putting theory into practice. *Family Practice Management, 6*(9), 26–30.

Zemke, R. (1985). Is performance appraisal a paper tiger? *Training, 22*(12), 24–32.

Zimmermann, P. G. (2003). Tips for getting a good evaluation. *Nursing, 33*(7), 73.

Experiential Learning Activities: Managerial Roles— The "Action" Satellites

ACTIVITY 22   CHANGE FACILITATOR: FORCE-FIELD
                               ANALYSIS FOR SELF-DIRECTED GROWTH*

Purposes	1. To learn the process of force-field analysis.
	2. To develop an awareness of one's needs.
	3. To analyze the need area using a force-field approach.
	4. To develop a strategy for meeting one's need.
Facility	None—this exercise is a self-study homework assignment.
Materials	Worksheet 22-A: Problem Areas.
	Worksheet 22-B: Force Field.
	Worksheet 22-C: The Strategy.
	Pen or pencil.
Time Required	One hour.
Group Size	Unlimited—it is a homework assignment.
Design	Explain to participants the purpose of the activity and then the design of the activity. Participants can be instructed to do the exercise individually as a home assignment.

1. Using Worksheet 22-A, have participants jot down 10 problems in personal and/or professional aspects of self. Then rank order them from 1 (*low priority*) to 10 (*top priority*).

2. Choose the top-priority problem and identify the actual and the optimal situation. Write the resulting problem area statement, including the actual and optimal situations in the space provided on the top of Worksheet 22-B. Continue to use Worksheet 22-B for Steps 3 through 6.

3. List the forces that are pushing or driving to solve, eliminate, or overcome the problem.

4. List the forces that are blocking, impeding, or restraining the change.

---

*Every aspect of this book is directed toward changing people. When a manager leads, it is for the purpose of changing others—moving them from actual to optimal.

ACTIVITY 22	**CHANGE FACILITATOR: FORCE-FIELD ANALYSIS FOR SELF-DIRECTED GROWTH** *(continued)*

5. Weigh each of the driving and restraining forces from 1 (*low-energy force*) to 10 (*high-energy force*). How does the situation look? Are driving and restraining forces equal?

6. Examine both sets of forces. Can any restraining forces be reduced or eliminated? Can any driving forces be amplified or increased?

7. Focus on the three driving and the three restraining forces that have the highest energy. Develop a step-by-step strategy for increasing each driving force and decreasing each restraining force. Use Worksheet 22-C.

Variation

This Experiential Learning Activity can be done in class and shared in small groups at the end of Steps 4, 6, and/or 7. The amount of time to do the activities, of course, increases with group involvement.

(continued)

WORKSHEET 22-A: PROBLEM AREAS

Problems	Rank Order
_____	_____
_____	_____
_____	_____
_____	_____
_____	_____
_____	_____
_____	_____
_____	_____
_____	_____
_____	_____

Top-Priority Problem _____

_____

_____

Actual Situation _____

_____

_____

Optimal Situation _____

_____

_____

WORKSHEET 22-B: FORCE FIELD

Problem _____

Actual Situation _____

Optimal Situation _____

Driving Forces (+)	Weight	Restraining Forces (−)	Weight
_____	_____	_____	_____
_____	_____	_____	_____
_____	_____	_____	_____
_____	_____	_____	_____
_____	_____	_____	_____
_____	_____	_____	_____
_____	_____	_____	_____
_____	_____	_____	_____
_____	_____	_____	_____
_____	_____	_____	_____
_____	_____	_____	_____
_____	_____	_____	_____

(continued)

WORKSHEET 22-C: THE STRATEGY

Force (+ or −)	Action
1.	A.
	B.
	C.
	D.
	E.
2.	A.
	B.
	C.
	D.
	E.
3.	A.
	B.
	C.
	D.
	E.

WORKSHEET 22-C: THE STRATEGY *(continued)*

4.

    A.

    B.

    C.

    D.

    E.

5.

    A.

    B.

    C.

    D.

    E.

6.

    A.

    B.

    C.

    D.

    E.

ACTIVITY 23	TEACHER: A BEGINNING

Purposes	1. To begin the experience of teaching.
	2. To gain experience in using different instructional modes and media to teach a content area.
	3. To experience a variety of teaching strategies.
Facility	Large room to accommodate class.
Materials	Specified by the students in their teaching module.
Time Required	Ten minutes per member.
Group Size	Under 25.
Design	1. As a homework assignment, ask learners to think of anything (skill, philosophy, belief, and so on) that they know or do well.
	2. Then have them prepare a five minute to seven minute teaching module on the area chosen. The module should include objectives and teaching modes and media.
	3. Request that preparation be made for a class presentation.
	4. At a subsequent class, have students teach the module to small groups of peers.
	5. Encourage group discussion of the experience, focusing on the teacher's experience as well as that of the learner.
Variation	Management, health care, or nursing clinical practice skills or competencies as well as theory can be substituted for the content in the original design.

Note. This Experiential Learning Activity is adapted by permission from *The nursing process: A humanistic approach* (p. 302), by La Monica, Elaine L., 1979. Upper Saddle River, NJ: Pearson Education. Copyright 1979. Reprinted by permission of Pearson Education, Inc.

ACTIVITY 24	TEACHER: APPLYING THE TEACHING PROCESS

Purposes	1. To apply the teaching process.
	2. To broaden experience in diagnosing the teaching needs of clients and colleagues in a health environment.
	3. To increase awareness of the teaching diagnoses that others perceive in the same situation.
	4. To identify appropriate objectives and the most effective teaching strategies to accomplish them.
	5. To evaluate a teaching intervention.
Facility	Large room to accommodate participants seated in groups of six.
Materials	Worksheet 24-A: Scenarios.
	Worksheet 24-B: Instructional Analysis.
	Paper and pencils.
Time Required	One to two hours.
Group Size	Unlimited groups of six.
Design	1. Participants should consider themselves as nurse managers. Using all or any combination of the scenarios from Worksheet 24-A, ask participants to individually respond to the following in each situation:
	A. Is there a teaching need? If the answer is *yes*, use Worksheet 24-B to complete Step 1. (Worksheet 24-B may have to be duplicated.)
	B. If there is a teaching need, what needs to be taught and to whom? Give rationale for response.
	C. Identify objective(s) for teaching.
	D. Specify teaching strategy: mode(s) and medium (media).
	E. Delineate how the accomplishment of objectives would be evaluated.
	2. In groups of six, participants should share and discuss their responses. Different perceptions between/among learners should receive particular attention.

(continued)

Note. This Experiential Learning Activity is adapted by permission from *The nursing process: A humanistic approach* (p. 303), by La Monica, Elaine L., 1979. Upper Saddle River, NJ: Pearson Education. Copyright 1979. Reprinted by permission of Pearson Education, Inc.

ACTIVITY 24

TEACHER: APPLYING THE TEACHING PROCESS (continued)

Variation

1. Step 1 may be done as a homework assignment.

2. Individuals or small groups can develop and actually carry out the teaching strategy with their peers, as in Activity 23.

3. The students' actual clinical placement can be the scene for identifying a learning need and carrying out the process, even to the point of teaching the staff and having them evaluate the program.

WORKSHEET 24-A: SCENARIOS

1. Three times in the past two days you've found that elderly patients who have been gotten out of bed rather early in the morning have stayed up sitting in chairs for the rest of the morning. In each case when you noted this, the patient's respiration was either labored or rapid. The pulse was rapid, and the patient appeared tired and said that he or she was tired.

2. A patient on your unit has been on a Stryker frame for two weeks. You have been told that tomorrow, a newly employed graduate nurse and two senior nursing students will be with you for the first time.

3. A patient on your unit has been on a Stryker frame for two weeks. Today when you go in to help turn her, two medical students ask if they may come with you to see what you are doing.

4. During afternoon conference, a patient was mentioned who had just returned from the operating room following "repair of a fractured hip." A nurse's aide said, "We'll have to be careful of his back since he'll have to stay on it for some time."

5. When making rounds on your unit after lunch, you notice that although many patients are in their beds, most of the beds are elevated, and in many cases the linen is rumpled. A television set is audible through most of the area, and three of your staff members are talking rather loudly in the corridor.

6. On Monday, Mr. Smith tells you that his doctor told him he might be going home in a couple of days. Mr. Smith has congestive heart failure, has been on digitalis and a diuretic, still has some peripheral edema, and is on a low-sodium diet. He lives alone.

7. Ms. Jones has asked for and received a prescribed narcotic for pain for several days prior to and following her surgery. The nurse assigned to give medications and the one assigned to care for her yesterday both questioned "if she really needed it." The doctor was told of this and gave permission for a PRN placebo. Today it is discussed by others on the team. Ms. Jones responded well the first time the placebo was given but then seemed to "want the other medicine" (she seemed to recognize that a different injection had been given). The physical therapist today said he felt Ms. Jones had no real need for the narcotic, but another nurse said he thought Ms. Jones acted as if she really had pain.

8. When an aide attempting to change a patient's position was experiencing evident difficulty, a physician came over to the aide, assisted, and then explained the procedure both to the aide and the patient.

(continued)

Note: Scenarios were received by this author at the College of Nursing, University of Florida, 1966. Author is unknown. Scenarios have been adapted by this author.

WORKSHEET 24-A: SCENARIOS *(continued)*

9. You observe a patient walking down the corridor in a coat and hat, carrying a suitcase—an aide is walking beside the patient. A graduate nurse leaves the nurse's station, greets the patient, takes the suitcase, and hands it to the aide. The nurse discusses the patient's plans for discharge as they walk down the hall toward a wheelchair. The situation was discussed with the aide after the aide returned from taking the patient to the hospital lobby in a wheelchair.

10. A team leader asked an aide to do a sugar and acetone test for a patient and reminded the aide not to obtain the urine for testing from the patient's tube (indwelling Foley catheter). The aide took a sample from the drainage bottle and reported the test to the team leader, who then recorded the results.

11. A patient is shaking the side rails and is stating in a loud voice that he wants to go to the bathroom. The aide and practical nurse remove the side rails, explaining to the patient why side rails are necessary. (He had slipped getting out of bed yesterday.) The practical nurse escorts the patient to the bathroom and waits to escort him back to bed.

12. A graduate nurse wheels a patient into the solarium, places the wheelchair close to another patient, and introduces them to each other. The nurse then asks each patient to demonstrate active and passive exercises of their arms. As the nurse leaves the room, the patients continue the exercises and discuss each other's progress.

WORKSHEET 24-B: INSTRUCTIONAL ANALYSIS

Scenario No. _____

What needs to be taught and to whom?

Program objective(s):

Teaching strategy—mode(s) and medium (media):

Evaluation procedure:

ACTIVITY 25   TEACHER: COURSE EVALUATIONS

Purpose	To provide feedback to the course planner/instructor.
Facility	Regular classroom setting.
Material	Evaluations 25-A, 25-B, and/or 25-C.
Time Required	Approximately 10 to 15 minutes for each evaluation.
Group Size	Unlimited.
Design	The course evaluations may be used when the instructor desires feedback from the learners. Each can be administered in class or taken home for completion. All evaluations can be either anonymous or identified with the students. They can be openly discussed with relevant participants or the entire group.

1. Evaluation 25-A is usable at any point during the semester in which the class is given. It provides a means for evaluating the needs of students midway through the semester in order for adjustments to be made as indicated by the responses. Instructors must list in the left-hand column the broad content areas covered to the date of the evaluation.

2. Evaluation 25-B is a short, end-of-course evaluation.

3. Evaluation 25-C is a more descriptive end-of-course report.

Note. The procedure and Evaluations 25-A and 25-C are reprinted by permission and Evaluation 25-B is adapted by permission from: La Monica, Elaine L. (1979). *The nursing process: A humanistic approach* (pp. 342–347). Copyright © 1979. Reprinted by permission of Pearson Education, Inc., Upper Saddle River, NJ.

EVALUATION 25-A: COURSE CONTENT EVALUATION

Circle the number that best describes each content area.

Course Content Areas	Too Little	Just Right	Too Much
	1	2	3
	1	2	3
	1	2	3
	1	2	3
	1	2	3
	1	2	3
	1	2	3
	1	2	3
	1	2	3
	1	2	3
	1	2	3
	1	2	3
	1	2	3
	1	2	3

(continued)

EVALUATION 25-B: END-OF-COURSE EVALUATION

For each item, circle the number that best represents your evaluation.

	Poor			Average			Excellent		
A. Subject Content									
Interesting in terms of new knowledge	1	2	3	4	5	6	7	8	9
Valuable in terms of daily activities	1	2	3	4	5	6	7	8	9
Up to date in terms of current trends, issues, and problems	1	2	3	4	5	6	7	8	9
B. Program Leader									
Attitude toward participants	1	2	3	4	5	6	7	8	9
Command of subject matter	1	2	3	4	5	6	7	8	9
Ability to hold participants' interest	1	2	3	4	5	6	7	8	9
Organized presentation of material	1	2	3	4	5	6	7	8	9
Coverage of material	1	2	3	4	5	6	7	8	9
Use of handouts	1	2	3	4	5	6	7	8	9
C. Overall Evaluation of Program	1	2	3	4	5	6	7	8	9

EVALUATION 25-B: END-OF-COURSE EVALUATION *(continued)*

D. **Program Comments**

1. What was of most value to you in the course/program?

_____

_____

_____

_____

_____

2. What was of least value?

_____

_____

_____

_____

_____

3. Do you have any specific suggestions to improve the course/program?

_____

_____

_____

_____

_____

(continued)

EVALUATION 25-C: END-OF-COURSE EVALUATION

Course number and title:

Professor:

Date:

Using the scale provided, rate each item as an overall course evaluation of the subject requested. Rate your responses according to the following scale descriptions:

1   Strongly disagree

2   Moderately disagree

3   Slightly disagree

4   Slightly agree

5   Moderately agree

6   Strongly agree

Content

1.	The objectives are appropriate for the course content.	1	2	3	4	5	6
2.	The objectives were met through class seminars, clinical practicum, and course design.	1	2	3	4	5	6
3.	The course has provided me with extensive knowledge in the content area and is applicable in my professional practice.	1	2	3	4	5	6
4.	Course requirements cover essential aspects of the course and have learning value.	1	2	3	4	5	6

Note. This was adapted from a faculty evaluation form used by this author at the University of Massachusetts School of Nursing, 1975. Author is unknown.

EVALUATION 25-C: END-OF-COURSE EVALUATION *(continued)*

5. This course has increased my learning, given me new viewpoints and appreciation, and increased my capacity to think and to formulate questions.

    1   2   3   4   5   6

6. Contrasting viewpoints, current developments, and related theory were integrated into class topics.

    1   2   3   4   5   6

Process

7. The instructor is clear, states objectives, summarizes major points, presents material in an organized manner, and has extensive knowledge of the subject.

    1   2   3   4   5   6

8. The instructor is sensitive to the responses of the class, encourages student participation, and facilitates questions and discussion.

    1   2   3   4   5   6

9. The instructor is available to students, conveys a genuine interest in students, and recognizes their individuality in learning.

    1   2   3   4   5   6

10. The instructor enjoys teaching, is enthusiastic, and makes the course content stimulating and alive.

    1   2   3   4   5   6

11. The instructor has provided a class environment that increases my motivation to do my best and to acquire knowledge independently.

    1   2   3   4   5   6

(continued)

EVALUATION 25-C: END-OF-COURSE EVALUATION *(continued)*

12. This course, as taught by this instructor, is one that I would recommend. On the whole, the course was excellent.

    1   2   3   4   5   6

What was of most value in the course?

What was of least value in the course?

Other suggestions or comments?

ACTIVITY 26	TEAM BUILDER: GROUP PROCESS OBSERVATION SHEETS

Purposes	1. To gain experience in studying small-group processes. 2. To gain experience in communicating with group members on process observations (giving and receiving feedback). 3. To provide feedback on group functioning in relation to task accomplishment. 4. To foster team building.
Facility	Room large enough to accommodate group members seated around tables or in circles on the floor.
Material	Worksheets 26-A and 26-B: Evaluation of Group Effectiveness.
Time Required	Ten to 30 minutes for each Worksheet.
Group Size	Unlimited small groups of six to eight members.
Design	Worksheets 26-A and 26-B are to be used following any of the Experiential Learning Activities in this book when the members of the group wish to study their group process in relation to accomplishment of their group task (how they functioned as a group). 1. At the conclusion of group work, reserve 10 minutes or more for group processing. Request members to individually respond to the items in Worksheet 26-A or Worksheet 26-B. 2. Instruct the total group to share their responses with one another, amplifying their rationale for choices. Differences in point allocations should be discussed because they point out various group members' perceptions. Worksheet 26-A is a less complicated instrument than is Worksheet 26-B. The Worksheets should be used progressively from A to B as groups move toward above-average maturity or performance readiness in group processing activities.

(continued)

Note. Adapted by permission from La Monica, Elaine L. (1979). *The nursing process: A humanistic approach* (pp. 307–310. Copyright © 1979. Reprinted by permission of Pearson Education, Upper Saddle River, NJ.

WORKSHEET 26-A: EVALUATION OF GROUP EFFECTIVENESS

Rate the group on each statement below, with 4 representing your greatest agreement and 1 representing your least agreement with the statement.   Circle the number that best approximates your rating of the behavior exhibited by the group.

	Disagree		*Agree*	
1. Group members understood the problem under discussion.	1	2	3	4
2. Group members stayed on the topic.	1	2	3	4
3. Group members avoided premature closure on the discussion.	1	2	3	4
4. Group members contributed equally to the discussion.	1	2	3	4
5. Group members agreed with group consensus and/or discussions.	1	2	3	4
6. Group members discussed their opinions openly without hiding personal feelings.	1	2	3	4
7. Group members were able to resolve conflict or discontent.	1	2	3	4
8. Group members displayed commitment to the group tasks.	1	2	3	4
9. Group members indicated satisfaction with the group process.	1	2	3	4
10. Group members indicated satisfaction with the group outcomes.	1	2	3	4

Note. This instrument was obtained by this author at the University of Massachusetts, School of Education, 1974. Author is unknown.

WORKSHEET 26-B: EVALUATION OF GROUP EFFECTIVENESS

The following five content areas will be used to critique workgroup activity: climate, conflict, communications, decision making, and commitment to objectives.

- *Individual evaluation.* Each person will evaluate the activity of the work group, distributing 100 points among the four alternatives for each content area. The greater the number of points distributed in each of the four content items, the more that item described the rater's perception of the group's process following the workgroup activity. Each content area should have 100 points allocated. It is not necessary to give all items points. For example, one item may receive all 100 points if that is the perception of the rater.

- *Workgroup evaluation.* The group will discuss the point allocations for every item in order to hear every member's perception of how workgroup activity took place. Any approach that assures that the thinking of each member on each item is heard and is considered may be used. Averaging of individual answers to get a single workgroup rating is to be avoided. The purpose is to probe for differences in points of view and discuss them.

Climate:

1. _____ One or more people tried to take over and control the decisions; it was a competitive, tense, win-lose conflict.

2. _____ The discussion was penetrating and challenging—a very rewarding session to which we all were committed.

3. _____ The discussion was polite, easygoing, and pleasant—a very friendly session.

4. _____ The discussion was rather flat and lifeless; comments slid from point to point with little evidence of commitment.

(continued)

Note. This instrument was obtained by this author at the University of Massachusetts, School of Nursing, 1974. Author is unknown.

WORKSHEET 26-B:
EVALUATION OF GROUP EFFECTIVENESS *(continued)*

Conflict:

1. _____ There was considerable unnecessary and unprofitable disagreement; competitiveness resulted in win-lose conflict.

2. _____ Disagreements were explored to help the group produce the best possible decisions; conflict was confronted and resolved.

3. _____ We were quite polite and pleasant; we took care to avoid conflict.

4. _____ There was very little open disagreement or conflict.

Communication:

1. _____ Ideas and opinions were expressed to "win one's own point"; few members listened to conflicting points of view.

2. _____ Ideas and opinions were expressed openly and with candor; close attention was paid to both majority and minority opinions so that we could fully understand all points of view.

3. _____ Ideas and opinions were expressed politely; we listened to all contributions attentively; no feelings were hurt.

4. _____ Ideas and opinions were expressed with little conviction, and people listened with little evidence of concern.

Decision Making:

1. _____ To complete the task, decisions were "railroaded" by one or a few.

2. _____ Once each member understood all points of view, the work group reached a decision to which all were committed.

3. _____ Decisions were made in a way that gave maximum consideration to all people; we did not want to "rock the boat."

4. _____ Compromise was the key to decision making; the traditional decisions resulted from majority rule.

WORKSHEET 26-B:
EVALUATION OF GROUP EFFECTIVENESS (continued)

Commitment to Objectives:

1. _____ We attempted to stay directly with the problem, and we solved it as quickly and efficiently as possible.

2. _____ There was an attempt to look at the problem as broadly and deeply as possible. Involvement and creativity characterized the discussion.

3. _____ We often seemed to be more interested in harmony than in getting the job done.

4. _____ There was little consistent focus on the problem; we solved the problem as rapidly as possible based on precedents.

ACTIVITY 27	TEAM BUILDER: GROUP PROCESS SELF-DIAGNOSIS

Purposes	1. To raise consciousness of one's own behavior in groups.
	2. To self-diagnose learning needs regarding small-group functioning.
Facility	None—homework assignment.
Material	Worksheet 27-A: Self-Diagnosis of Small Group Behavior.
Time Required	Fifteen to 30 minutes.
Group Size	Unlimited—individual homework assignment.
Design	1. Using Worksheet 27-A, have class members respond to the items in terms of the categories represented.
	2. Ask that they consider the following:
	A. Why do they take certain functions most often?
	B. Why are certain functions never or rarely carried out?
	C. How can they experience functions they would like to practice? What assistance, if any, is needed?
Variation	Self-diagnosis can be discussed within small groups; familiar members can offer feedback on their perceptions.

Note. This is adapted by permission from La Monica, Elaine L. (1979). *The nursing process: A humanistic approach* (pp. 311–313). Copyright © 1979. Reprinted by permission of Pearson Education, Inc., Upper Saddle River, NJ.

WORKSHEET 27-A: SELF-DIAGNOSIS OF SMALL-GROUP BEHAVIOR

Listed below are functions that are performed by members of discussion groups. Considering each category, check the columns that apply to you.

Frequency of Behaviors

	I perceive myself to use most often	I seldom use	I never use	I would like to practice
Task roles:				
1. Initiator				
2. Information Seeker				
3. Evaluator				
4. Coordinator				
5. Procedural Technician				
6. Recorder				
Maintenance Roles:				
1. Encourager				
2. Harmonizer				
3. Compromiser				
4. Standard Setter				
5. Gatekeeper				

(continued)

WORKSHEET 27-A:
SELF-DIAGNOSIS OF SMALL-GROUP BEHAVIOR (*continued*)

Frequency of Behaviors

Self-Oriented Roles:	I perceive myself to use most often	I seldom use	I never use	I would like to practice
1. Aggressor				
2. Blocker				
3. Recognition Seeker				
4. Playboy/ Playgirl				
5. Dominator				
6. Help Seeker				

Respond to each question explicitly. Use extra paper if necessary.

A.   Why do I use certain roles most often?

B.   Why are certain roles never or rarely carried out?

C.   How can I experience roles that I would like to practice? What assistance, if any, do I need?

| ACTIVITY 28 | INTERVIEWER: ROLE PLAYS |

Purposes

1. To develop personal interview formats based on one's individual philosophy of practice.

2. To experience using these formats in role plays with peers.

Facility

A large room where participants can form dyads and interview one another.

Materials

Paper and other writing materials.

Time Required

One hour or more.

Group Size

Unlimited dyads.

Design

1. As a homework assignment, have participants read Chapters 16 and 17 and other related articles and written materials on the topic.

2. Request each learner to bring to class a structured script for one of the following interview purposes:

   Hiring;

   Promotion;

   Planning individualized nursing care; or

   Describing an event.

3. Request that members form into dyads and use their scripts on each other. The student being interviewed should then provide feedback on the process, if requested by the interviewer. Roles should reverse.

4. Personal reactions of the interviewer and interviewee may be shared.

5. Interview formats can then be re-evaluated and changed by the interviewer, based on the results of this experience.

6. Reform into a total group and discuss the experience.

Variations

1. This activity may be done completely as a homework assignment.

2. Participants may repeat the experience using different purposes for the interview and/or different types of interviews such as the semi-structured and unstructured interview.

ACTIVITY 29

PERFORMANCE APPRAISER: RATING SCALE FOR CLINICAL STAFF NURSING PRACTICE

Purpose	1. To appraise the clinical performance of a staff nurse.
	2. To practice using a Likert-type rating scale for appraising performance.
	3. To develop strategies for meeting the clinical learning needs of a staff nurse.
Facility	None. This is a clinical assignment.
Material	Worksheet 29-A: Clinical Nurse Performance Appraisal Form.
	Pen or pencil.
Time Required	One hour or more.
Group Size	Unlimited dyads.
Design	1. As a homework assignment, have participants read Chapter 17, plus other related articles and written materials on the topic.
	2. Ask that participants form into comfortable pairs—teaming with a peer who is seen as nonthreatening and/or is a friend. Using Worksheet 29-A, ask that each pair member observe the other's clinical practice for a period of one to two shifts, trying particularly to assess the areas noted in the performance appraisal form.
	3. Using Worksheet 29-A, each pair member should appraise their partner's performance in writing. Following the written appraisal, the pair should meet and role play with discussions of the performance appraisals. Each pair member should have the opportunity to be the appraiser and the person being appraised. Together, they should develop an action plan for the next month.

ACTIVITY 29

PERFORMANCE APPRAISER: RATING
SCALE FOR CLINICAL STAFF NURSING
PRACTICE *(continued)*

Variations

The pair member being appraised may complete
Worksheet 29-A as a self-report prior to the role
play discussion. Then both appraisals can be
discussed—the self-report and the appraisal by
a peer. Also, the period being appraised can be
longer than one to two shifts, depending on the
available time. Worksheet A can be adapted to fit
any health care professional role.

(continued)

WORKSHEET 29-A: CLINICAL NURSE PERFORMANCE APPPRAISAL FORM

Name of Appraisee _____

Name of Appraiser _____

Date of Appraisal _____

Rate each area according to the following abbreviations:

U	=	Unacceptable
A	=	Acceptable
D	=	Distinguished
N/O	=	Not Observed
N/A	=	Not Applicable

Clinical Skills	U	A	D	N/O	N/A
Data Collection					
Taking nursing histories					
Interviewing					
Interpreting clinical data					
Consulting with colleagues					
Talking with families					
Conducting physical assessments					
Nursing Diagnosis					
Processing data					
Determining diagnoses					
Setting priorities					
Nursing Orders					
Writing nursing orders					
Maintaining individualized care					

WORKSHEET 29-A: CLINICAL NURSE PERFORMANCE APPPRAISAL FORM *(continued)*

Clinical Skills	U	A	D	N/O	N/A
Providing Care Giving direct care					
Effectively using interpersonal processes					
Quality of technical skills					
Quality of teaching methods					
Advocating for the client/family					
Making appropriate referrals					
Coordinating care					
Delegating care appropriately					
Supervising other nursing personnel					
Evaluating outcome					

(continued)

WORKSHEET 29-A: CLINICAL NURSE PERFORMANCE
APPPRAISAL FORM *(continued)*

Goals for Next Appraisal Period _____

Date for the Next Appraisal _____

1. _____

2. _____

3. _____

4. _____

5. _____

• • • V

The Managerial Mind

Part V of this book concerns the managerial mind. It is philosophic and is intended to be thought-provoking. Previous parts of this book presented a framework for leadership and management followed by the following parts: "Managerial Responsibilities: The Core"; "Managerial Skills: The 'How-To' Satellites"; and "Managerial Roles: The 'Action' Satellites." The last part of this book entitled "The Managerial Mind" contains brush strokes through the ideal minds of leaders and managers in health care environments.

"The Managerial Mind" is written differently from the previous four parts of this book. Essays are written by the author, Elaine La Monica Rigolosi, on personal, philosophic thoughts that began early in her career and were developed throughout the years that followed. They are intended to provide the reader with her beliefs—thoughts and feelings—on the kind of minds that are best when embracing the world of leadership and management in an arena of clients and caregivers who need help and guidance.

The areas presented, creativity, diversity, and ethics, include what the author believes must be within the awareness framework of every leader and manager's mind and behavior, as each helper paints on their own canvas. Again, similar to Part II, Managerial Responsibilities: The Core, Part V contains only the essentials and is not meant to be all inclusive and theoretical. Rather, the author's thoughts are given to the reader. Occasionally, they are underscored with theory or material from the literature.

Part V is intended to be a section of the book that provides a foundation for continued thinking as leaders and managers develop in their careers. Actually, it is the end . . . and then it is the beginning. It is written to stimulate continuous self-education. Therefore, three short essays are presented without Selected Assignments and Experiential Learning Activities. A managerial mind is a self-thinker and analyzer in constant motion. Continuous learning energy should be the driver as one paints a picture on one's unique canvas.

Creativity

The health care environment in the current and future world is evolving rapidly. It is known that a framework in health care will always exist. That is, people will need care so that they stay well, and people will get sick and need care to heal best. Caregivers will provide whatever help and assistance is needed. Further, in various health care venues, caregivers will have leaders and managers. What has just been stated will occur—it is known and definitively predictable.

What is unknown is how health care will be accomplished in the future. Various cultures, technological advances, rapidly changing health care venues, economics, potential legalities, new foci for professional caregivers, and global emphases, to name a few impacting avenues on and into health care, remain unpredictable but on the horizon.

EXPANDING THE MOLD

The question shouts: What can managers and leaders do to prepare themselves to guide the basics of human care, to lead and educate others during the journey of change and opportunity, and to keep pace with innovation? On May 10, 2011, *Daily Word's* message was entitled "Creativity." The booklet shared a legend that Michelangelo insisted that his part in creating his sculpture involved only chipping away at a piece of marble to uncover the masterpiece that lay within. This masterpiece is the world-renowned sculpture called *David*, housed in Florence, Italy.

Think about Michelangelo for a minute. Did David really lie within the marble? Or, was the world-famous creation chipped away from within the artist's mind through his behavior? Ponder that thought. . . .

This author believes that creativity lies within, waiting to be let out. It is within all people who live. In children, one can see the easy spirit of creativity. Children are always seeking to put pieces together and painting their views of a world or happenings as they see them. Whatever they express most often is viewed with praise, and it is evident that grown-ups love to foster the creativity in children. New and different expressions from children are generally seen as good.

Children then grow up and are encouraged to "fit" into the world. Nurses are taught in nursing schools to act like other nurses, physicians are encouraged to be like other physicians, and so on. Role modeling at any age is the loudest and most influential educator in life; role modeling is the human way to perpetuate the status quo—the expected. Change, therefore, is slow, and it becomes easy for creativity to be either oppressed or suppressed. Existing outside of "the box" in which one is supposed to fit becomes difficult.

What is not evident in the aforementioned "box" is that if a person is not creatively seeking to make "the box" bigger or into a new shape, "the box" will most definitely get or appear smaller . . . and smaller . . . and smaller. . . . Why? A simple explanation is that as human beings continue to repeat the same behaviors, the shorter road for achieving one's goal—the step saver—is usually sought. That is why it is more difficult to change as people age. It is not one's age that is of issue, but the number of times that a person has repeated the same behavior. An older person can think: Why change when what I do is so easy . . . I do not even have to think in order to behave—my behavior is in my left pocket!

Today, it is known and believed that innovation and creativity are critically important because a health care provider shapes and lives in tomorrow's health care world. The literature is replete with this message and philosophic push (Drucker, 1985; Herzlinger, 2006; Liu, Chen, & Yao, 2011; Madjar, Greenberg, & Chen, 2011; Mueller & Kamdar, 2010; Smith, 2011; Tierney & Farmer, 2011). Danker (2011) reported that Eric Lesser, from the IBM Institute for Business Value, saw creativity as trumping other leadership qualities.

THE CREATIVE PROCESS: BRAINSTORMING

So, how does a health care leader begin to foster innovative opportunities that will shape and change health care delivery in the future? The typical scientific method and parallel management method has been previously presented throughout this book. (Refer to Table 1.1 in Chapter 1 for more detailed information) For the current explanation, The Management Method is presented in the following text, simply:

1. *Assess* the problem and study the point of view;
2. *Identify* the problem, goal, or opportunity;

3. *Analyze* the problem, goal, or opportunity and choose a leader behavior;
4. *Create* alternative solutions;
5. *Recommend* an action plan;
6. *Implement* the action plan; and
7. *Evaluate* the results.

The Creative Process comes to life in Steps 3 and 4 mentioned previously: analyzing the problem, goal, or opportunity and creating alternative solutions. It involves what is referred to as *brainstorming*. Simply, brainstorming involves stepping outside of the usual box when attempting to develop a pathway for reaching a goal or solving a problem. It means putting aside old formulas, traditions, routines, and current practices, and saying:

If I could solve this problem or accomplish this goal in any way possible, what would I do?

There is no evaluation during the brainstorming step. It is important to be daring and to think of all possibilities. . . . Like Michelangelo, chip away from within.

When there is a list of possibilities or if working with a group, everything everyone shared has been expressed and written down, these possibilities are referred to as the *alternative solutions*. Only when the brainstorming step has been completed are the alternative solutions evaluated for possible positive and negative outcomes if they were to be implemented. This step has been referred to as *mapping your strategies* (Anthony, Eyring, & Gibson, 2006).

Recommend an action plan by selecting one or two creatively designed ways to accomplish the specified goal or bring life to an opportunity. Experiment with a slightly new approach. Change the shape of "the box" little by little. Evaluate if what is done works to everyone's satisfaction.

Remember, change is realized best by looking backwards and noting where you were against the backdrop of the here and now. It is not necessary to shock others to feel or see that change occurred or that "the box" has been redesigned. Add or delete the created, new methods and former methods for behaving in bite-size chunks. Then look backwards over time and add up the accumulated chunks. Think about the fact that the Great Wall of China was built with hand carried bricks—brick by brick. Now there is a wall that is referred to as one of the Seven Wonders of the World.

THE CREATIVE ENVIRONMENT

This author would be remiss if she did not emphasize the environment necessary for creativity to flourish. To think outside of "the box," it is best to "be" outside of "the box." "The box" reinforces old practices by just the sights and feelings that are contained within it. Go to a different conference room, present different food, rearrange the tables and chairs, and use different paper, pens, and media for creative thinking. Use colors too and meet in a different venue. This author could go on but only one dominant message is reflected in the words: do something different than what is the "usual."

Also, remember that creativity does not occur best (if at all) in an oppressive, directive, or evaluative environment. Freedom to chip away within one's own mind to create something new mandates that one does not have to protect against someone chipping away his or her skin.

SUMMARY

This essay formed the beginning of three chapters in the last part of this book; it began with thinking about the managerial mind. The need to expand the mold in health care was emphasized, followed by guidance on how this can be accomplished. The creative process of brainstorming was introduced. This essay concluded with guidance on providing a new or different environment that is seen as necessary to elicit creativity from within. Michelangelo's expression of self was the frame on which the essay developed.

REFERENCES

Anthony, S. D., Eyring, M., & Gibson, L. (2006). Mapping your innovation strategy. *Harvard Business Review, 84*(5), 104–113.

Daily Word. (May 10, 2011). Creativity. *Daily Word, 149,* 22.

Danker, S. (October 10, 2011). Singapore sessions: Building talent capital. *The New Yorker*, pp. 53–57.

Drucker, P. F. (1985). The discipline of innovation. *Harvard Business Review, 63*(3), 67–72.

Herzlinger, R. E. (2006). Why innovation in health care is so hard. *Harvard Business Review, 84*(5), 58–66.

Liu, D., Chen, X. P., & Yao, X. (2011). From autonomy to creativity: A multilevel investigation of the mediating role of harmonious passion. *The Journal of Applied Psychology, 96*(2), 294–309.

Madjar, N., Greenberg, E., & Chen, Z. (2011). Factors for radical creativity, incremental creativity, and routine, noncreative performance. *The Journal of Applied Psychology, 96*(4), 730–743.

Mueller, J. S., & Kamdar, D. (2011). Why seeking help from teammates is a blessing and a curse: A theory of help seeking and individual creativity in team contexts. *Journal of Applied Psychology, 96*(2), 263–276.

Smith, M. A. (2011). Are you a transformational leader? *Nursing Management, 42*(9), 44–50.

Tierney, P., & Farmer, S. M. (2011). Creative self-efficacy development and creative performance over time. *The Journal of Applied Psychology, 96*(2), 277–293.

Diversity

Diversity is one little nine-letter word that shouts throughout the world and can be referred to as a "universal bell" that should ring for everyone. In a sense, it is a trump card that every hand should hold.

This essay focuses on diversity from a health care perspective, particularly for caregivers who work in national and international environments where peers, colleagues, and clients are growing more ethnically and racially diverse. Couple this increasing diversity with the emphases that all people strive to be treated with pure equality as they increasingly take greater responsibility for their own health care agenda. The bottom line then becomes:

> *Everyone must or must learn to understand each other.*
> *Further, everyone must do their best*
> *to express care and compassion*
> *on all of the channels*
> *through which others listen, hear, and speak.*

CULTURAL COMPETENCE IN THE MAZE OF DIVERSITY

Let us continue by looking at diversity as a simple expression that reflects the environmental maze of ethnicity, cultures, and races among the unique spaces in which caregivers live and work on a daily basis. All that you should do is look around yourself and notice the world in which you live. Diversity is an evident fact of life. It clearly is observable. It is bright and it is loud—if you choose to see and to hear it.

There are noticeable differences among colleagues, peers, and clients. Schools have courses and programs in various languages. Ethnic groups tend to cluster in different communities. Everyone living works with everyone around them. There is no way to live today without touching another ingredient of ethnic and racial tastes.

Health care personnel have a particular form of responsibility because when diverse people need help and assistance, it is the health care provider's responsibility to be sure that what they listen to is perceived accurately and that what they share in response is heard with clarity and is understood. This whole process should be wrapped in compassionate and caring behaviors.

It should be clear that diversity is only the frame on a picture of life. The behaviors that must be learned to carry out the professional responsibilities of caregivers, leaders, and managers, all of whom should carry the banner of excellence in health care, can be referred to as cultural competence.

THE CHALLENGE OF FINDING THE RIGHT CHANNELS: LISTENING, HEARING, AND SPEAKING

Diversity can be referred to conceptually. Cultural competency, however, has been referred to in the literature as critically important in improving health care practices, as well as eliminating differences in health care among various groups of people (Cabral & Smith, 2011; InforMed, 2008; Rodgers, 2011; Salahuddin & O'Brian, 2011).

Cultural competence is involved in finding the matching channels between or among those people communicating. Remember, if you are the leader, manager, or caregiver, the responsibility for finding this match is yours! So, if you even slightly surmise that the person or family with whom you are speaking may not understand, then you must do everything within your powers and knowledge to check, validate, and ensure a match.

Let me help with some possibilities that I hope will assist you in making the previous idea be a match in your experiences.

1.   Count on yourself and trust your intuitions. Validate what you hear and ask others to validate in their own words what they hear and perceive that you said. Analyze the match.

2. If others have different language channels, get an interpreter. If you are a leader or manager in charge of hiring, look for different language skills in potential employees. Cover the pool of languages that you see as probably being needed in the future. Encourage children and adults to learn different languages of their choice.

3. Try to pair peer caregivers and clients with those that match in ethnicity. It is a well-researched and believed fact that people who are similar or who see themselves as similar act more pro-socially toward each other when compared with ethnically different people (Cabral & Smith, 2011; Hornstein, 1976). This also applies when people have shared the same experience in life, the same recoveries such as addictions, the same diseases, and so forth.

4. Create environments that reflect and attend to the cultures of people who live in that environment. Be flexible in changing the scenery so that it is seen as in harmony with all.

5. Philosophically, if verbal interpretations do not match most nearly perfectly, then focus predominantly on nonverbal behaviors. Nonverbal behavior is a universal language. Why? Because every person is human and every human contains the same ingredients. This fact makes diversity almost philosophically nonexistent. Carrying on, focus intently on what you observe—in the message sent to you as well as the response to your message by the receiver. Look at facial expressions, particularly the expressions and messages in one's eyes and mouth.

If your options to find matching channels are not what you expect or need, however, and you are in a situation that has no liberty of time, then I offer the following guidance on what you give to others (La Monica, 1979, p. 494; La Monica, 1985, p. 376).

The Golden Helping Rule

Whenever you feel unable to respond to another;
Whenever you do not know what to say;
Whenever you want to help but do not know
what would be helpful. . . .

Place yourself in the other's world;
Be in that time and space;
Ask yourself the questions asked you;
Feel what you think the other person feels . . .

Then say what you would like to hear; and
Do what you would like to have done.

The "Golden Helping Rule" was developed and written by this author, Elaine La Monica Rigolosi, and was first published in 1979. Originally, it was written to refer to clients; it was adapted in this book to refer to any other person. To this author, at this time, it says it all. . . .

EXPLORING THE DIVERSITY AND CULTURAL COMPETENCE WITHIN MYSELF

As has been evident in this book, self is the first primary focus, and self-study is essential. The magnitude in which we are culturally competent to analyze the differences within ourselves is directly and positively, strongly related to the magnitude in which we can analyze and perceive in others. Therefore, it is essential and is critical that you know yourself. Self-awareness and self-education is the beginning. Be honest with and within yourself. Diverse environments abound today, so diversity and cultural competence may seem normal and known to you. Nevertheless, who you are today is made up of from whence you came as well as all of the role models in your entire life who have influenced you overtly and covertly.

Self-education and consciousness-raising are important and are considered to be a continuous beginning. More formal educational steps, nevertheless, are effective as well as conscious changes within ourselves, our workplace environments, our families, and the care that is given to others. As leaders and managers, we can pave the future by being role models of diverse, culturally competent matchmakers in communications and broadly speaking, all behaviors. This is the way that we can chart a future in which "diverse" is viewed as all we are and all there is. . . .

IMAGINING TOMORROW'S WORLD OF HEALTH CARE

Imagine tomorrow's world of health care as "being"
the culturally competent people that we strive to become today. . . .
Tomorrow's world of health care may be as easy, natural, and normal
as we are when we currently change television channels. . . .

SUMMARY

The essay entitled "Diversity" begins with a description of diversity; it is a universal bell that should be heard, held, and embraced by everyone. Cultural competence is the behavioral canvas that has its home within the frame of diversity. The maze on a health care canvas comprises oneself, peers, colleagues, and clients, to name the dominant groups.

Cultural competence involves the challenge of finding matching channels of communication between and among people. Assistance in finding these matches was presented. The essay concluded with a dream, imagining tomorrow's health care world.

REFERENCES

Cabral, R. R., & Smith, T. B. (2011). Racial/ethnic matching of clients and therapists in mental health services: A meta-analytic review of preferences, perceptions, and outcomes. *Journal of Counseling Psychology, 58*(4), 537–554.

Hornstein, H. (1976). *Cruelty and kindness: A new look at aggression and altruism.* Englewood Cliffs, NJ: Prentice Hall.

InforMed (2008). *Physician update: Cultural competency.* Trenton, NJ: Author.

La Monica, E. L. (1979). *The nursing process: A humanistic approach.* Menlo Park, CA: Addison-Wesley.

La Monica, E. L. (1985). *The humanistic nursing process.* Belmont, CA: Wadsworth.

Rodgers, J. O. (2011). Deliberate Diversity™: Time to go on offense. *Insight Into Diversity, 77–78*(6,1), 16–17.

Salahuddin, N. M., & O'Brien, K. M. (2011). Challenges and resilience in the lives of urban, multiracial adults: An instrument development study. *Journal of Counseling Psychology, 58*(4), 494–507.

Ethics

It is by distinct and planned design that the focus on ethics is the concluding chapter in this book. Ethics is a concluding concept . . . it is also the beginning step in the circle of life. Ethics must embrace all that one knows and one should know in the law, in medicine, in nursing and health care, and in the humanities, to name a few. This knowledge, experience, and awareness dances within, around, and between one's inner self and one's surrounding, outer world. Nevertheless, the heart and soul of ethics lies within the caregiver. It is in one's heart and mind that a human being makes ethical decisions—this is where ethical choosing takes place. Always remember, an ethical choice comes from within yourself.

ETHICAL LEADERSHIP

Before this chapter paints a philosophic picture of ethics, it is necessary to point out the growing literary focus on the ethics of leadership and management (Cady, 2011, Etzioni, 1996; Filipova, 2011; Johnson, 2012; Kanungo & Conger, 1993; Kreitner & Kinicki, 2010). This involves the moral aspects of a manager's behavior—it involves moral issues and choices. Increasingly, ethics and moral reasoning also are receiving attention in leadership literature, in nursing, and in health care (Burkhardt, Nathaniel, & Walton, 2009; Edge & Groves, 2005; Johnson, 2002; Offermann & Malamut, 2002; Staal & King, 2000; Turner, Barling, Epitropaki, Butcher, & Milner, 2002). Maloney (1990) pointed out that although concern with ethics is not new, the content in the professions and business worlds has changed, refocused, and evolved. Nevertheless, "the individual struggle with justice—right and wrong—remains essentially the same" (p. 119). These principles involve being human, and age does not change the struggles that humans have within themselves.

As adults, leaders, and particularly managers have the opportunity to influence another person's life more than any other living individual. Consider the fact that if one works full time as an adult, one spends at least 40 hours per week out of a possible 168 hours per week in a life at one's job. This is almost one quarter of a person's life. What other adult individual besides a manager has a greater amount of time to directly affect another's behavior?

Think about another important point. Leaders and managers have the ability to create worker satisfaction or dissatisfaction. If leaders are having emotionally bad days, the probability is high that those feelings will be spread to followers. If leaders set goals that are consistently unattainable, followers may never feel successful, getting caught in a downward emotional spiral. In positive contrast, no matter on what beginning place (actual) followers start the journey toward goal accomplishment, they should be coached in "bite-sized chunks" to reach an optimal place. Then they should be encouraged to celebrate success in their achievements. This reinforces their abilities and becomes the stimulus for journey to the next optimal goal.

Hodgson (1992) developed general moral principles for managers, calling them *"The Magnificent Seven."* These general moral principles for managers follow.

1. There is a dignity to human life that must be respected completely. Every life should be respected, treated as sacred, and preserved.
2. Autonomy exists within each person. A manager should act in ways that show a respect for the worth and dignity of each person, as well as their right to self-determination.
3. Honesty, integrity, truth telling, and honor should encompass the manager's communication. People who have the right to know the truth, in fact, should be so told.
4. Remain loyal with promises, contracts, and commitments. Be reliable in transactions between and among people.
5. People should be treated fairly, impartially, and justly. Accept differences and diversity among people in determining equal and unbiased approaches to issues, problems, and goals.
6. Managers should be human focused and accept the ethical responsibilities of accomplishing good and avoiding evil.

7. It is important to possess an umbrella goal that looks toward a common good in all behaviors. Further, at times, a manager should make decisions based on the best for the greatest number of people.

A leader's choices must be decided carefully, and moral principles must be studied and contemplated with thoughtful study. It is suggested that ethics be consistently and developmentally studied so that thinking about self—where one's culture; one's organizational attachments; and one's political, legal, and economic influences melt into one's being and behavior (Kreitner & Kinicki, 2010)—develops with one's role as manager and leader. Remember, as a manager and leader, you have the power to be a positive role model for others and to impact the lives of your followers either negatively or positively. You have the power to make them feel successful or inadequate. What you do will develop a part of their lives. In a sense, your role as an adult leader is similar to that of the role parents have with children.

ETHICAL CHOICES

A health care provider's ethical choices can be paralleled with the concept of diversity, which has been discussed in the previous chapter of this book . . . and, I must add, by conscious choice. Leaders should always move others from the known and familiar to new goals and pathways. This is a message that has run throughout this book, and this writer would be remiss if she did not practice what she shared. So, the question should be asked: "Why does ethics follow diversity?"

Diversity can involve many channels—differences among people, within and between social and environmental contexts, and among languages, naming only a few. As shared in the previous chapter, cultural competency in the maze of diversity means that health care and nurse leaders must perceive, listen, respond, and meet the unique needs of all who walk under their guidance and care. Everyone in the circle or team is involved, all are diverse and unique individuals, and each person must be respected and heard. It is the leader's responsibility to give everyone a presence and a voice, including himself or herself. Diversity is a common interactive factor within and between all team players, including clients.

Ethics is seen as an extension of diversity. An ethical dilemma occurs within an individual when two or more diverse choices are on the screen at the same time. A choice must be made. A conflict within an individual becomes an active dance inside of one's mind and body. Festinger (1957) called this dance "cognitive dissonance." This is an uncomfortable state in one's mind—within one's self—that involves at least two relevant perceptions that are not in harmony with one another.

How do people cope with cognitive dissonance—an argument that lies within? The discussion, analysis, and critique of all sides and facets of the issues or choices require self-examination. Knowledge and experience should come from all possible sources and avenues—that is, self, others, the law, previous similar issues, the literature, ethics committees, and many others. Use every resource available and take the time that is deemed necessary to feel comfortable with the ethical choice that should result.

ETHICAL EYEGLASSES

What should become evident is that ethics and ethical choices involve a variety of lenses and a magnitude of frames—rarely can any be found to be exactly the same. There are different eyeglasses for different channels:

1.   There are eyeglasses that are put on when caring for others;
2.   There are eyeglasses that are worn when one is studying one's own personal thoughts and beliefs; and
3.   There are eyeglasses through which one sees and feels the world of another and imagines a walk in another's shoes.

Only after careful deliberation using every pair of eyeglasses and lenses that are pertinently available . . . does one make an ethical choice.

WHAT HAPPENS AFTER . . . OR, THE UNCERTAINTIES OF CHOICE

The answer to what happens after making an ethical choice is best explained by this author's colleague, Dr. Maxine Greene* (1985, pp. 272–273, 285–286).

It is seldom easy, and we must begin with a recognition of the uncertainties, the tensions, associated with ethical choosing. We must begin with some awareness that the ability to act morally demands what Kierkegaard (1843/1947) described as a particular kind of courage—the courage to be (pp. 106–107). That means a capacity to recognize when one stands at a crossroads in life, a place where— usually without guarantees—one is bound to move one way or

---

*At the time the work was written, Dr. Maxine Green, A.B., Ph.D., L.H.D., was a professor of Philosophy and Education and the William F. Russell Professor in the Foundations of Education, Teachers College, Columbia University, New York, New York. Dr. Green continues to teach at Teachers College on a part-time basis, has written extensively, has founded the Maxine Greene Foundation for Social Imagination, and is the recipient of 10 Honorary Degrees in the Humanities.

another. Robert Frost's (1972) poem, *"The Road Not Taken"* comes to mind. It begins, the reader may recall:

Two roads diverged in a yellow wood,
And sorry I could not travel both
And be one traveler, long I stood
And looked down one as far as I could
To where it bent in the undergrowth (p. 171).

Both roads were equally fair, both were covered with leaves [on which few previous steps were taken], and the poet knows that, even if he saved one for another day, it was doubtful he would ever come back. He had, nevertheless, to choose one; never sure that it was the right one or the best one. "I took the one less traveled by, / and that has made all the difference" (Frost, 1972). Looking back later, unable to retrace his steps, he could say nothing else. The alternative, of course, was to turn his back and avoid the problem of diverging roads. If he had done that, he would have been like Levin [in Tolstoy's (1875–1877/1946) *Anna Karenina*], thinking of excuses. He would have been like the people in Camus's novel [1948, *The Plague*] who resigned themselves to the plague and stayed at the bars or the card tables, bowing down (as the doctor would have put it) to pestilence. There are always those who do not choose to choose, but here we are concerned with the ones willing to acknowledge "the road not taken," the risk, the uncertainty, the problem of choice. How *does* one decide what choice to make, what (in particular situations) one ought to do?

Now, it must be clear that questions like this cannot be answered with statements of fact. Values, unlike facts, cannot be empirically verified; statements of value cannot be demonstrated to be true or false. We are in the domain of values once we begin talking about moral choice. Values may be thought of as conceptions of the desirable, of what appears worthy of appreciation or cherishing, of that which is believed to be good or right. Not all values, of course, have to do with morality; we may value certain objects, works of art, modes of recreation, and ways of proceeding in solving problems or affirming truths. When value words are applied to human conduct, we make what might be called moral judgments about others or ourselves. To describe a person or a course of action as decent, humane, honest, courageous, fair, or compassionate is ordinarily to make such a judgment. It is to express approval or to recognize that some standard or norm is being complied with, that a person (given what is valued in the culture) can be described as a good person or that the course of action can be described as right. . . .

The nurse [physician, leader, or manager] may look to the future, trying to anticipate what will result from what is done; he or she can reflect on what still works within because of the forgotten past; he or she can turn to fellow participants in dialogue.

But then there is the leap, the risk. There is the recognition of the road not taken. There is the choice—and all we can ask is that it would be a decent one, reflected on, authentic, concerned. It is finally a choice of the self, not as victim but as agent, a choice of the self in its freedom, a way of being in the world.

SUMMARY

Chapter 20 covered the concept of ethics, which was presented as an extension of diversity, previously discussed in Chapter 19. Ethical leadership was presented first, followed by ethical choices that must be made by health caregivers. A view through ethical eyeglasses followed. The chapter moved into a more philosophic canvas and looked at what happens after an ethical choice is made. This section focused on the uncertainties of choice and was written and previously published by Dr. Maxine Greene in an earlier book written by this author, Elaine La Monica Rigolosi entitled *The Humanistic Nursing Process.*

It is with Dr. Maxine Greene's words that this book concludes . . . and begins. . . .

REFERENCES

Burkhardt, M. A., Nathaniel, A. K., & Walton, N. A. (2009). *Ethics & issues in contemporary nursing* (3rd ed.). Canada: Nelson Education Limited.

Cady, R. F. (2011). Accountable care organizations: What the nurse executive needs to know. *JONA's Healthcare Law, Ethics, and Regulation, 13*(2), 55–60.

Camus, A. (1948). *The plague.* New York, NY: Knopf. (Original work published 1947)

Edge, R. S., & Groves, J. R. (2005). *Ethics of health care: A guide for clinical practice* (3rd ed.). Albany, NY: Thomson Delmar Learning.

Etzioni, A. (1996). *The new golden rule: Community and morality in a democratic society.* New York, NY: Basic Books.

Festinger, L. (1957). *A theory of cognitive dissonance.* Stanford, CA: Stanford University Press.

Filipova, A. A. (2011). Ethical climates in for-profit, nonprofit, and government skilled nursing facilities: Managerial implications for partnerships. *JONA's Healthcare Law, Ethics, and Regulation, 13*(4), 125–133.

Frost, R. (1972). The road not taken. In O. Williams, (Ed.), *The new pocket anthology of American verse: From colonial days to the present.* New York, NY: Washington Square Press.

Greene, M. (1985). Ethical choosing. In E. L. La Monica, *The humanistic nursing process.* Monterey, CA: Wadsworth.

Hodgson, K. (1992). *A rock and a hard place: How to make ethical business decisions when choices are tough.* New York, NY: AMACOM.

Johnson, C. E. (2012). *Meeting the ethical challenges of leadership: Casting light or shadow* (4th ed.). Thousand Oaks, CA: Sage.

Johnson, W. B. (2002). The intentional mentor: Strategies and guidelines for the practice of mentoring. *Professional Psychology: Research and Practice, 33*(1), 88–96.

Kanungo, R. N., & Conger, J. A. (1993). Promoting altruism as a corporate goal. *The Academy of Management Executive, 7*(3), 37–49.

Kierkegaard, S. (1947). Either/or. In R. Bretall, (Ed.), *Kierkegaard.* Princeton, NJ: Princeton University Press. (Original work published 1843)

Kreitner, R., & Kinicki, A. (2010). *Organizational behavior* (9th ed.). New York, NY: McGraw-Hill/Irwin.

Maloney, E. (1990). Managerial ethics. In E. La Monica, *Management in health care: A theoretical and experiential approach.* New York, NY: Springer Publishing.

Offermann, L. R., & Malamut, A. B. (2002). When leaders harass: The impact of target perceptions of organizational leadership and climate on harassment reporting and outcomes. *Journal of Applied Psychology, 87*(5), 885–893.

Staal, M. A., & King, R. E. (2000). Managing a multiple relationship environment: The ethics of military psychology. *Professional Psychology: Research & Practice, 31*(6), 698–705.

Tolstoy, L. (1946). *Anna Karenina.* Cleveland: World Publishing. (Original work published 1875–1877)

Turner, N., Barling, J., Epitropaki, O., Butcher, V., & Milner, C. (2002). Transformational leadership and moral reasoning. *Journal of Applied Psychology, 87*(2), 304–311.

Epilogue

For Learners . . .

What you give to yourself as you walk and create

your unique journey. . . .

No matter what you do, make it your best.
Leave nothing undone.

Be sensitive to your own way of growing
And

Have clear goals for yourself.
Be strict in your journey
Toward their fulfillment.

Learn to know and to feel with yourself.
Only then will you be free to know and
To feel with others.

Set high goals and then
Put your mind on reaching them.

In all, only hold on to the positive and
Illuminate it.
Life can then be full of light.
Life can then be successful
At every moment. . . .

Elaine Lynne La Monica Rigolosi

Note. The above Epilogue was developed and written by the author of this book. It was first published in 1983 and most recently published in 2005 in Dr. Rigolosi's book entitled *Management and Leadership in Nursing and Health Care: An Experiential Apprach* (2nd ed.), Springer Publishing Company, New York, NY.

Author Index

Subject Index

The notations *b*, *e*, *f*, and *t* located in some entries denote: *b*ox, *e*xhibit, *f*igure, and *t*able respectively.